FOAL

# Walt before Mickey

# Disney's Early Years, 1919–1928

Timothy S. Susanin

University Press of Mississippi / Jackson

www.upress.state.ms.us

The University Press of Mississippi is a member of
the Association of American University Presses.

This book makes reference to various Disney copy-
righted characters, trademarks, marks, and registered
marks owned by The Walt Disney Company and
Disney Enterprises, Inc.

Photographs courtesy of The Walt Disney Company.

First printing 2011
∞
Library of Congress Cataloging-in-Publication Data

Susanin, Timothy S.
 Walt before Mickey : Disney's early years, 1919–1928 /
Timothy S. Susanin.
     p. cm.
 Includes bibliographical references and index.
 ISBN 978-1-60473-960-2 (cloth : alk. paper) — ISBN
978-1-60473-961-9 (ebook)  1. Disney, Walt, 1901–1966.
2. Animators—United States—Biography. I. Title.

 NC1766.U52S5658 2011
 791.43092—dc22
 [B]
                          2010045040

British Library Cataloging-in-Publication Data available

*To Michael Barrier, Didier Ghez, Howard Green,*
*Diane Disney Miller, and Dave Smith, with thanks*

*For Barb, Jack, Annabel, and Boo, with love*

# Contents

# Preface

—DIANE DISNEY MILLER

I have always loved to hear my dad talk about his life, especially the early part
. . . his childhood, family, the Kansas City days, and especially how he met and
courted my mother. Tim has done an amazing job of chronicling the lives of
the people in that period who affected dad's life. His research brought out the
fact that some of dad's early benefactors were his neighbors on Bellefontaine,
people who had seen him grow up and were aware of his industrious nature.
Dad, it appears, was never shy about asking for a loan. But he was diligent about
repaying it.

Tim follows dad to Hollywood, along with most of his Kansas City col-
laborators. The partnership with his older brother Roy begins, and my mother
comes down from Idaho to visit her closest sister. Despite their decisions not to
marry until each had a certain amount of money in the bank, they tire of their
shared bachelor existence. Edna Francis has been waiting patiently for Roy to
return to his job with the bank in Kansas City, and dad has been seriously
courting mother, who worked for them as a sometime secretary ("I was a lousy
secretary," she admitted) and an inker of cels.

Roy sent for Edna, and they were married in April 1925. My parents married in July that same year, one week after the brothers had made a down payment on a lot at 2719 Hyperion Avenue, the site of the first Walt Disney Studio.
That studio building is long gone, but the homes the brothers built nearby on
Lyric Avenue are still there, with caring owners. They were Pacific Ready-Cut
Homes, identical, and the first homes any of them had owned. It was exciting
for the entire family.

Tim continues on for several more years, all exciting for the brothers and
their wives, though not without periods of anxiety. He ends with the loss of
Oswald the Rabbit and the creation of Mickey Mouse. Dad's telegram to Roy
as he, with my mother, were about to depart New York for home was "Leaving tonight stopping over KC arrive home Sunday morning seven thirty don't
worry everything OK will give details when arrive—Walt." He didn't mention
the fact that they had lost Oswald. They would need a new plan, a new character. Roy, who had been caring for my parents' chow dog Sunnee, recalls that

nothing was said until Roy inquired, "Tell me about it, kid . . . What kind of deal did you make?" "We haven't got a deal," dad cheerfully replied. "We're going to start a new series."

I have always been curious about why dad, with his bride of a few years, chose to stop over in Kansas City for a few days rather than return immediately home to give Roy the bad news. My theory is that he wanted to touch base with his long-time friend and benefactor, Dr. Cowles, knowing that he might need his support again. Another possibility is that he wanted mother to meet Frank "Dad" Land, the founder of DeMolay. Dad was a charter member of DeMolay, and was very fond of Dad Land. I heard them both express affection for him when I was very young. Whatever the reason, it was on that long train ride that dad conceived of a new cartoon subject, a mouse who was then refined and further developed by Ubbe Iwwerks (who later changed the spelling to "Ub Iwerks"), and given his name by my mother.

# Introduction: Thanksgiving, 1966

During Thanksgiving week, 1966, Walt Disney, two weeks shy of his sixty-fifth birthday, returned to his studio in Burbank, California. He had been out for a while, and was looking forward to getting back to work. He had tried to run the studio even though he had not been there. One of his executives visited him to discuss upcoming projects, and one of his writers prepared a memorandum for him about the studio's script selection process. He even had a secretary bring him his mail each day.

On Monday, November 21, when he finally got back to the studio, and for the next two days, Walt immersed himself in his company's upcoming projects. He stopped by the animation building. He discussed a new script with one of his writer-directors. On one of those three days, Walt was driven to nearby Glendale, where he checked up on theme park projects in development. That afternoon, after he was driven back to the Burbank backlot, Walt screened a rough cut of one of the studio's future releases, a musical comedy he hoped would match the phenomenal success of the Oscar-winning box office smash of 1964, *Mary Poppins*.

One wonders if the new film, *The Happiest Millionaire*, a World War I-era musical comedy, caused this forward-looking man to, for a few moments, cast his gaze in the opposite direction. World War I separated Walt's youth from his adulthood, and the war's end coincided with the start of his career. He drove a Red Cross ambulance in France for a year after the war ended, and within a few months of returning to the United States, was introduced to the field of animation.

*Millionaire* must have left Walt contemplating that period of his life. The movie opens in 1916 and features a montage of newspaper headlines trumpeting the events that preceded America's entry into the war, such as "President Wilson Re-elected," "British Transport Sunk," and "Germany Announces Unrestricted Submarine Warfare." The lead character, a middle-aged father, tries to enlist but is rejected as too old. He winds up on a Marine Corps recruiting tour and, in the movie's last scene, is visited by Marines who bring him the good news he has orders to report to Parris Island as a provisional captain. At the very least, the artwork in the film's opening titles (if they were completed by the time of Walt's screening) would have left Walt thinking of the similar-looking illustrations that graced the pages of the *Kansas City Star* and other newspapers and magazines he read almost a half century earlier.

Walt had another reason to be contemplative of the past that week: he was ill and did not have long to live. He had been admitted to St. Joseph's Hospital, across the street from his studio in Burbank, on Wednesday, November 2, after an X-ray (administered prior to an operation to relieve neck pain caused by an old polo injury) revealed a tumor on his left lung. Surgeons removed part of the lung the following week, but informed Walt's family that the tumor was cancerous and that Walt—who had smoked since his teens—would probably not live longer than six months to two years.

If Walt reflected on his postwar years upon his return to the studio that Thanksgiving week, he thought about a little-known story. While most followers of the Disney canon know Walt served with the Red Cross in France from 1918 to 1919, and that he had some experience animating silent cartoons before his career took off with Mickey Mouse in the 1920s, most do not know the details of the decade between Walt's service overseas and *Steamboat Willie*. This is the untold story of that period of Walt's career, and of the four studios that brought Walt, who was seventeen years old when his art career started after the end of the war, to the brink of international renown when Mickey Mouse was created nearly ten years later.

The prologue to Walt's journey begins in Kansas City, Missouri, where he worked in commercial art and advertising before discovering animation at a film advertisement company. He later experimented with this relatively new art form in his father's garage at night. The story unfolds across Walt's two Kansas City studios, Kaycee Studios and Laugh-O-gram Films, Inc., and, after his train ride west to Hollywood in 1923, two Los Angeles studios, Disney Brothers Studio and the Walt Disney Studio. (The Walt Disney Company does not consider Disney Brothers Studio and the Walt Disney Studio to be separate companies, but given that these two studios operated under different names and at different locations, they will be discussed separately herein.)

This part of Walt's incredible journey establishes numerous facets of the man. He was both a frustrated actor and a talented animator. He was a likable kid who some thought had a prickly, self-centered side. He was an astute businessman and innovator with a relentless work ethic. His initial successes appeared as dependent on family, friends, and his local community contacts as they were on his own formidable artistic and producing abilities. And he was resourceful and optimistic enough to persevere in the face of loss and failure—indeed, early on, he suffered a series of bad breaks that seems a reverse mirror image of the dazzling successes that followed.

This is the picture, then, of Walt Disney, drawn by the reflections of Walt himself and others who were there in the 1920s. It is a portrait fleshed out by an examination of the Kaycee, Laugh-O-gram, Disney Brothers, and Walt Disney studios—the physical plants, the several dozen colleagues who worked there, and the films they produced. It is the story about which Walt was perhaps thinking if, near the end of his life, he reflected on his career, before Mickey.

*Book One*

# Kansas City

# Prologue—The Road to the First Studios

## COMMERCIAL ART, FILM ADS, AND
## "HOME EXPERIMENTING," 1919–1921

"I was 18 years old when I actually started out on my career," recalled Walt Disney. His "first job was with the Gray Advertising [C]ompany in Kansas City. I worked as an art apprentic[e]." Walt "started working with Gray's the latter part of October, 1919[.]" Walt (who, despite his recollection, was still seventeen years old at the time) had returned to the United States on Friday, October 10, 1919, after working as a driver for the Red Cross Ambulance Corps in France after the end of World War I. After spending nearly a year overseas, Walt—described by his daughter as "truly a Missourian"—settled in Kansas City, Missouri. Upon arriving back in the city where he lived from the ages of nine to fifteen, Walt wondered about his future, asking himself, with regard to two lifelong interests, "[W]as I going to be an actor or an artist?"

Walt "decided on art because it was easier to get a job." After being turned down for a position at the *Kansas City Star*, Walt learned from his older brother about an art apprenticeship. Roy Disney, twenty-six, a Navy veteran of the war, was a clerk at the First National Bank in downtown Kansas City. The bank, a large, imposing, high-ceilinged marble building with columns inside and out, was located towards the north part of downtown, just south of the Missouri River. Roy heard about the apprenticeship at work. A bank colleague told Roy: "I have two friends named Pessman [*sic*] and Rubin. They run an art shop for the Gray Advertising Company. The other night they mentioned that they need an apprentice."

Louis A. Pesmen, twenty-seven, was born in Russia and came to the United States when he was about eight years old. His family settled in Kansas City, where he returned after serving in the Army in World War I. Like his father, Pesmen was an artist, and he worked elsewhere in Kansas City before working with Rubin at Gray Advertising. Pesmen had light brown hair and light blue eyes, and one relative remembers him as "a man of medium height, slender, serious demeanor, and somewhat imperious in nature." Another recalls that Pesmen was "meticulously groomed . . . . [and] always wore beautiful silk bowties, and had a carefully-trimmed mustache."

By the fall of 1919, Pesmen had been married for several months and was a partner in what he later called the "Pesmen-Rubin Commercial Art Studio," although he seems to have been the only source for that name. Pesmen-Rubin appears to have been a captive studio within the Gray Advertising Company, which was located in the two-story Gray Building at 14th and Oak Streets in Kansas City. Pesmen also taught evening classes at the Kansas City Fine Arts Institute.

Pesmen's partner was twenty-four-year-old Bill Rubin, who, with his wife, Edith, lived two blocks from Lou and Reba Pesmen on East 28th Street. Rubin was of medium height and build with black hair and blue eyes. The son of a Russian-born insurance solicitor, Rubin was a self-employed commercial artist and worked in the Gray Building prior to going into business with Pesmen.

Pesmen and Rubin produced artwork for such Gray clients as farm supply and machine companies and local theaters. When Walt heard of the opening at Gray Advertising, he went to the Gray Building and spoke with Pesmen and Rubin. Walt struck Pesmen as a "quiet, polite young man" and stood out in Pesmen's memory because he'd neglected to bring his portfolio with him and, according to Pesmen, "[w]henever an artist goes job hunting, he carries a portfolio of samples[.]" Both Pesmen and Rubin liked the seventeen-year-old's manner and asked to see samples. Walt later returned with "all these corny [cartoons] I'd done in France about the fellows finding cooties," which Pesmen thought were "good quality" drawings. He and Rubin decided to give Walt a job but determine his salary after a one-week trial period.

During that week, Walt "worked at this drawing board and during the day I never left it." If he "had to go to the toilet I just held it until noon." Pesmen and Rubin assessed Walt's work and concluded, "He's good."

Walt, however, was less confident in his future at Gray Advertising. By the end of the week, Walt "thought I was going to get fired." To his surprise, Pesmen and Rubin offered him a job at a salary of $50 a month. Pesmen recalled Walt responded to the offer with "'That'll do fine,' . . . in his pleasant, soft-spoken manner, without looking up from his work." But despite his cool outward demeanor, Walt—who had hoped for even half that salary—thought the pay was "magnificent" and was so thrilled with Rubin's offer that he "could have kissed him!"

Since "[m]ost of the work done by this advertising concern was for farm journals[,]" Walt's job

> consisted of pencilling drawings for ads of egg-laying mash, salt blocks for cattle, farm equipment and so on. . . . I drew hens sitting on nests with baskets overflowing with eggs, hens hatching out dollars and various

things of this order to show the results of feeding hens the egg-laying mash. I also sketched cattle enjoying the salt blocks, and happy farmers showing pride in their up-to-date equipment.

Walt also created the stencils used by artists for work made with an airbrush.

Walt got more than art experience at Gray's. "About that time," Walt later recalled, "I made the acquaintance of Ubbe Iwwerks, a young apprentice artist" who also worked for Pesmen and Rubin and became Walt's friend and future partner. Ubbe Eert Iwwerks, eighteen, started at Gray's the month before Walt did. Prior to that, Ubbe had left high school and spent a year or two working on a farm in Scotland, Arizona. Ubbe returned to Kansas City in September 1919.

According to Ubbe's granddaughter, Ubbe's job at Gray's did not please his mother, the former Laura May Wagner, forty-four, who was not optimistic about an art career for her son. Laura Iwwerks was the third wife of Iwwerks' father, sixty-three-year-old Eert Ubben Iwwerks, a German-born barber whom the family believed left Laura for another woman when Ubbe was in the ninth grade. A short time after Ubbe worked for Pesmen and Rubin, however, he appeared to be living in a house on Landis Court with both his mother and his father (who by then had stopped cutting hair and was trying his hand as a studio photographer).

Lou Pesmen recalled that he and Bill Rubin hired Ubbe because he was "a fantastic lettering man[.]" They paid Ubbe $60 a month, $10 a month more than they paid Walt. While Ubbe and Walt had many things in common, they were polar opposites in personality; Walt was an outgoing salesman, and Ubbe was shy.

An anecdote from this period, though, has the two playing against type: Ubbe recalled that, soon after meeting Walt, Ubbe played poker with other studio artists while Walt worked diligently at his desk, practicing variations of his name and signature. Whether or not this vignette occurred, it certainly is plausible; Walt experimented with variations of his name as early as the ninth grade, when he was a member of the art staff of *The Voice*, the monthly magazine of Chicago's McKinley High School, alternating between signing his cartoons as Walter Disney, W. E. Disney, and Walt Disney.

At Gray's, Walt's "rough pencil sketches were completely redrawn by my bosses," but this did not seem to bother him. Even though "[f]ew of my drawings actually were used" by Pesmen and Rubin, Walt "felt I was making a great success." Pesmen assigned Walt to do layout work for an ad for the Carey Salt Company, a Gray client that made salt blocks for farm animals. Pesmen made changes to the layout and wondered if Walt would be offended since Pesmen knew that young artists were "sensitive to constructive criticis[m]." Pesmen was surprised to find that Walt did not fit this mold; Pesmen's revisions were "all right with [Walt]" who "in fact, encouraged" such criticism.

Walt's apprenticeship at Gray Advertising was important to his career not only because it introduced him to Ubbe, but also because it exposed him to a client who would later screen the first Disney cartoon. Among Lou Pesmen's accounts was Frank L. Newman, twenty-nine, the owner of several Kansas City theaters, including its downtown flagship, the Newman Theatre, located in the 1100 block of Main Street. The Newman Theatre—marketed in the *Kansas City Star* as "The Dominant Theater"—opened in June, 1919. Frank Newman spared no expense in making the Newman his most lavish theater; it cost $400,000 and featured hand-painted murals, Grecian figures, and Italian tapestries. Pesmen designed the cover of the weekly *Newman Theatres Magazine*, and assigned Walt to work on the Newman account.

For one issue, Walt worked on a cover illustration that shows a stage proscenium and curtain with the magazine's title at center stage. Above the title is an insert illustration of the front façade of the theater. For another issue, Pesmen created a cover that incorporated the elephant that was seen in an electric sign hanging over a Newman theater marquee. After Pesmen completed the layout, he asked Walt to "go ahead with the finished art." Walt asked if he should also work on the back cover, which featured a donut ad. Pesmen replied, "No, just one [cover] at a time." Later that day, Walt's "familiar grin . . . like the 'cat that swallowed the canary'" told Pesmen that Walt was up to something. Walt not only altered Pesmen's front cover by giving the elephant a smile, he completed the back cover and donut ad as well. Pesmen, though, felt that "[n]o apologies were necessary. The job was OK."

Walt also worked on a Newman ad for a Gloria Swanson movie that premiered in Kansas City on November 23, 1919, and ran for over two weeks. "I was asked to do some layouts on an important new account," he recalled, "a motion picture produced by Cecil B. DeMille titled 'Male and Female.'" But, "all I had to work with was a standing photo of the stars, Gloria Swanson and Thomas Meighan. Well, I thought it would make a better ad if they were lying down, and that's how I drew them."

Walt spent approximately six weeks at Gray's, working on drawings and stencils for farm equipment and theater clients "until early in December [1919,] when I was fired." By some accounts, Walt's apprenticeship was always envisioned as a short-term position, one that was designed to help Pesmen and Rubin produce the large amount of artwork needed for their clients' holiday season catalogues. The Pesmen family, however, recalls that it was the loss of a large tractor account that required the studio to let Walt go.

If Walt was upset about being let go by Pesmen and Rubin, that reaction has not been recorded, and Walt's comments about his experience working at Gray's were positive. "When you go to art school you work for perfection," Walt said. "But in a commercial art shop you cut things out, and paste things over, and scratch around with a razor blade. I'd never done any of those things in art school. Those are time-saving tricks." At Gray Advertising, Walt met Ubbe Iwwerks and worked on projects for Frank Newman, but he also learned the "tricks of the commercial trade[.]" "That's what I learned in [those] six weeks," he said.

Ubbe remained on the staff at Gray's in December of 1919 while Walt looked for new employment. "To tide me over the holidays," Walt said later, "I got a job carrying mail during the Christmas rush. New Year's Day 1920 found me out of a job again." Walt contemplated opening his own ad agency, and was "feeling well qualified after my brief experience with the Gray Advertising Company."

At the same time, he still thought about being a cartoonist, and was impressed by cartoonists' income. He thought that "fate was against letting me be a successful cartoonist [. . . . but g]osh, how I used to envy the guys who were knocking out what looked like big jack in those days and I wondered if I could ever reach the top." With his dual interests, it was not surprising that, when a federal census enumerator visited the Disney home at 3028 Bellefontaine Avenue, southeast of downtown Kansas City, on Wednesday, January 7, 1920, Walt said he was both a commercial artist and a cartoonist.

Within weeks of the census, Ubbe was let go by Pesmen and Rubin and complained to Walt that he too was "out of a job." Walt replied, "I've got an idea. Let's go into business together." Ubbe's reaction told Walt that Ubbe "couldn't quite fathom that," but he agreed, and Iwwerks-Disney—what Walt called "a little commercial art shop"—was born.

To finance Iwwerks-Disney, so named because the pair, now both eighteen, thought Disney-Iwwerks "sounded like an optical firm or something," Walt used a portion of the savings he brought home from France. Walt wrote to his mother in Chicago (Walt's parents lived in Chicago at the time, but still owned the family home in Kansas City), "Please send me the $500 I left with you," and she wrote back, "Your father and I want to know what you want to do with it." He responded, "[I]t's my money. I'm going into business." His parents forwarded about half of his savings. Walt promptly spent the money on the supplies needed to launch Iwwerks-Disney, including drawing boards, an airbrush, and a tank of compressed air.

Walt and Ubbe could not afford to rent office space for their agency, but one of the company's first jobs led to what might be called Walt's very first studio—an unused bathroom in the headquarters of the National Restaurant Association. The secretary of the National Restaurant Association was thirty-year-old Alvin Buell Carder, who published, through the Carder Martin Publishing Company, an Association publication called the *Restaurant News*. Both the National Restaurant Association and the *Restaurant News* had offices in Suite 207 of the Mutual Building, located at the southeast corner of 13th and Oak Streets, one block from the Gray offices.

Carder's parents, Joseph and Grace Carder, lived at 3026 Bellefontaine Avenue and were next-door neighbors of the Disney family, which had lived at 3028 Bellefontaine since 1914. Joe Carder had been a produce merchant when he moved his wife and six children from St. Joseph, Missouri, to Kansas City in 1907. The Carders moved to Bellefontaine sometime after 1910, but by then Alvin Carder no longer lived with his parents. By mid-1917, Alvin, now a tall, medium-built twenty-seven-year-old with blue eyes and light brown hair, had his own printing business—Carder Menu Services—in Suite 201 of the Graphic Arts Building. Alvin was married and lived with his wife and two young children on East 37th Street.

Walt's initial overture to Alvin Carder was not for office space but to hire Iwwerks-Disney to create artwork for the *Restaurant News*. The publication had no need for outside artists; however, when Walt offered art services in exchange for desk space, Carder agreed to hire Walt and Ubbe to do *Restaurant News* artwork in exchange for $10 a week and office space. Walt and Ubbe were assigned desks located in a bathroom, complete with toilet and sink.

In addition to *Restaurant News* artwork, Iwwerks-Disney "managed to pick up a few odd jobs which enabled me to keep a little spending money in my pocket," recalled Walt. Walt did the marketing and cartooning while Ubbe did lettering and drawing. They called on local printers to expand their client base, offering to design such things as letterheads and theater ads.

One printer hired Iwwerks-Disney to draw an ad for the sale of oil wells. "The firm that was selling the oil wells told us to draw them the way they would look when the oil came in," Walt recalled. "You should have seen the amount of oil we got into those drawings." Ubbe's granddaughter, perhaps referring to the same project, wrote that one of Iwwerks-Disney's "early project[s] was creating the cover for an oil company's promotional prospectus," resulting in Ubbe's illustration of "an oil well that gushed $20 bills."

Another Bellefontaine neighbor led to additional work for Iwwerks-Disney. After his family moved to the Bellefontaine house six years earlier, Walt Disney befriended "school chum" Walter Pfeiffer, whose family lived three houses away at 3022 Bellefontaine. Like Disney's parents, Walter's had moved to Kansas City from Chicago, where John Pfeiffer was a harness maker. In Kansas City, John became the General Secretary and Treasurer of the United Leather Workers International Union. He and his German-born wife Clara also had two daughters who were older than their son, and Disney often spent his free time at the Pfeiffer house.

Walt Pfeiffer recounted that Walt Disney "was always welcome at our house and he was one of the family and we always looked on him as that." Pfeiffer felt that Clara was like a "second mother" to Disney. Disney's daughter later recalled that Walt "felt so happy" in the Pfeiffer home, saying, "He loved being with them. They had a warmth that I think his family lacked."

The Pfeiffers also supported the two Walters' interest in show business. "I had started out to be an actor," recalled Disney, and Pfeiffer "had stage ambitions, too." Together, Disney and Pfeiffer "got up a vaudeville skit" that "wowed the kids, so [we] thought we were great stuff."

"[Pfeiffer's] father," said Disney, "coached us and his sister played the piano while we sang." Disney and Pfeiffer billed themselves as "The Two Walts," and the act, which appeared at local amateur theater nights and featured Disney's impersonation of Charlie Chaplin, "won several prizes," according to Disney (although he also claimed they "got the hook the first night!").

By the time Disney and Iwwerks were trying to get their studio off the ground in 1920, the Pfeiffers had moved from Bellefontaine Avenue, but John Pfeiffer, then forty-nine, was still the General Secretary of the leather workers' union, and he used his union ties to get Iwwerks-Disney a project. Walt and Ubbe drafted the letterhead for the *Leather Workers Journal* and created the cover for its February 1920 issue, which featured the journal's title inside a hanging animal hide surrounded by saddles, suitcases, and other leather goods. The work Iwwerks-Disney obtained from Walt's Bellefontaine connections, among others, allowed the pair to earn more in their first month in business than their combined monthly salaries at Gray. "The first month [of Iwwerks-Disney,] we made a total of $125, which we thought wasn't bad," said Walt.

The two eighteen-year-olds were encouraged enough by Iwwerks-Disney's initial success that they decided to move out of the *Restaurant News* office and into their own space at the Railway Exchange Building nine blocks away. The Exchange was on the southeast corner of 7th and Walnut Avenues and its eight floors housed various insurance and railway companies. How long Walt and Ubbe would have flourished there as commercial artists is unknown, as the pair came across a *Kansas City Star* "help wanted" ad soon after they opened Iwwerks-Disney. Though that advertisement led to Iwwerks-Disney's quick demise, it also introduced Walt Disney to a form of filmmaking called animation.

◂ ◂ ◂

Throughout his career, Walt associated his start in animation with the two years he spent at the Kansas City Film Ad Service, a company that made slide and film advertisements for movie theaters. "I started, actually, to make my first animated cartoons in 1920," Walt recalled. "It was with the slide company that I got my start in the animated-cartoon game." Walt joined the firm, then called the Kansas City Slide Company, after he and Ubbe saw a Slide Company "help wanted" ad in the *Kansas City Star* "Help Wanted—Male" section of the classifieds: "Artist, Cartoon and Wash Drawings; First Class Man Wanted; Steady. K. C. Slide Co., 1015 Central." The ad ran from Thursday, January 29, 1920, through Saturday, January 31.

Walt and Ubbe hoped the Slide Company's need for a cartoonist might be an opening for Iwwerks-Disney. In the "second month [of Iwwerks-Disney, when business] was not so good," Walt called on the Slide Company's president, Arthur Vern Cauger, and suggested his cartooning needs could be met by Iwwerks-Disney. Cauger had no interest in outsourcing the work, but he liked Walt and offered him the cartoonist position instead. Walt recognized that, "[i]n some manner I impressed the boss, A. V. Cauger, that I had possibilities as a cartoonist and he offered to hire me at $35 a week," or almost triple his Gray Advertising salary, and over double his monthly take at Iwwerks-Disney. Walt said the offer "nearly floored me."

Walt told a reporter almost twenty years later, "I knew I wasn't worth [the salary offered by Cauger], but I decided to try it." Walt accepted the position after Ubbe encouraged him to do so. Ubbe's granddaughter wrote that Ubbe and Walt decided that Walt would work for Cauger while Ubbe would run Iwwerks-Disney. That Ubbe followed Walt to the Slide Company within weeks raises the possibility that Walt accepted Cauger's offer to get a foot in the Slide Company door for both of them. Regardless, in February 1920, Walt "turned what there was of the commercial art business over to Iwwerks and went to work for the slide company."

The Kansas City Slide Company made "Slides and Animated Cartoon Films for Moving Picture Theatre Advertising," and was located at 1015–1017 Central Street, about a half-mile southeast of Iwwerks-Disney's Railway Exchange office. The forty-one-year-old Cauger oversaw twenty employees and a million dollars in sales. He had previously been a theater exhibitor in Illinois and Missouri. According to his son, as an exhibitor Cauger "would get the local merchants, such as the local milk or bread company, to buy advertising on the theater screen." Cauger "got so much response that he began to think that this was the business he ought to be in."

In 1910, Cauger moved to Independence, Missouri, and opened the Slide Company on Grand Avenue in nearby downtown Kansas City. A few years later, he moved the company to the Central Avenue location where Walt was hired. By that time, he also bought a house on Bellefontaine Avenue approximately four blocks from the Disney home, presumably to avoid having to make the fifteen-mile commute to his home in Independence each day.

The Slide Company artists drew theater advertisements on glass plates or cards that were photographed. They also made filmed ads, both live and animated, which were becoming commonplace in the industry. Walt was assigned to work on animated ads.

"Of course," said Walt, "they were very crude things then and I used . . . oh sort of little puppet things. . . . I used to make little cut-away things and joints were pinned and we'd put them under the camera and we'd maneuver them and we'd make him do things." The cut-out figures had tacked joints applied by a rivet gun. They were pinned to sheets of paper and photographed—then the joints were moved, and the figure was photographed again.

For other animated film ads, Walt explained, the Slide Company photographed the action in reverse:

> I'd start with a big card covered with neatly lettered advertising copy.
> I'd hold it before a camera for the length of time it would be seen on
> the screen at the end of the ad. After that, using the stop-camera process,
> I began to cut those letters out and move them around until, in the fin-
> ished film, they seemed to come flying in to gather in orderly sequence
> on the screen. . . . If I wanted to emphasize a telephone number, I'd have
> that number march on the screen on little legs, one numeral at a time.
> Then one number would land in the wrong place and it would have to
> scurry around until it found its rightful position in relation to the other
> numbers.

While Walt learned how to create animated ads, Ubbe struggled to keep Iwwerks-Disney afloat. Walt thought the problem was that Ubbe was a recalcitrant salesman. Walt, perhaps referring to Al Carder or John Pfeiffer, recalled that, "the few customers I had would call [Ubbe]—he would just sit there [because] he couldn't give the old sales pitch." Once Walt had been at the Slide Company for a few weeks, Ubbe asked to join him. Walt's memory that "[t]wo months [after starting at the Slide Company,] I was able to obtain a job for Iwwerks at the place" suggests Ubbe started at the Slide Company in April 1920. Ubbe, however, recalled joining the company in March. Ubbe was no doubt relieved to move on from Iwwerks-Disney, but Walt noted that Ubbe was frustrated to learn he would be paid less at the Slide Company than Walt was.

Not long after Walt started at the Slide Company, its office moved to 2449–2451 Charlotte Street in the city's hospital district southeast of downtown. Walt took to his responsibilities at the company, writing to a Red Cross friend in May 1920: "I got a fine job here in K.C. and I'm going to stick with it. I draw cartoons for the moving pictures—advertiser films—. . . and the work is interesting."

Walt and his colleagues created the art and copy work for such advertisers as a clothier, a furniture company, an automobile canvas roof dealer, and several banks. Slide Company ads from this timeframe included one for a bed company with the tag line, "Our salesman stands beside every bed we sell!" and a laundromat ad that joked, "Don't kill your wife. Let us do the dirty work." Walt found the advertising copy "a little stiff" and frequently suggested improvements.

He explained that, "[Y]ou had to think up little gags, little catch things, you know. So I had this spanking, shining car drive in and I had a character on the street. He hailed the driver and he says, 'Hi, old top, new car?' and the guy in the car says, 'No[,] old car, new top.'"

He was asked to work on a hat company ad, and skirted his inability as a portrait artist by making cartoon faces under the hats. Cauger liked the result. For a thrift company ad, Walt wrote, "You'll never get anywhere until you get on the right savings track," and drew a cow being chased down railroad tracks by a train. His other bank ads showed a man running hard on a treadmill with the caption, "You'll never get anywhere if you don't SAVE!" and a man on a raft navigating a river with the caption, "You can't drift through your life."

While they honed their cartooning and copy writing skills, Walt and Ubbe befriended several other young Slide Company employees. One was George E. "Jimmy" Lowerre, a twenty-six-year-old Kansas native who lived with his widowed mother, older brother, and sister-in-law and described himself as a film salesman and photographer. As one of the Slide Company cameramen, Jimmy let Walt and Ubbe run the camera and showed them how stop-motion photography worked.

Another colleague was William McAtee Lyon, known as "Red" (although he signed his letters to his mother, "Mac"), also twenty-six and born and raised in Illinois. Red's father was a schoolteacher and farmer in Ashton, Illinois, before moving his family to Chicago, where he worked as a publishing house proofreader. By 1920, just before he started at the Slide Company, Red lived with his now-widowed mother in Moline Ward, Illinois, and worked out of the home as a photographer. Within a year, Red moved to Kansas City and worked at the Slide Company, where he supposedly impressed Walt with the claim he had once been a cameraman in Hollywood.

Around 1921 Cauger changed the name of the company to the Kansas City Film Ad Service. That same year, nineteen-year-old cartoonist Fred C. Harman, Jr. joined the Film Ad team of Show Card and Title Men—the cartoon animators and cameramen—of which Walt and Ubbe were a part. Harman had previously been a clerk at a Kansas City title company, but he spent his formative years in the "busty frontier town" of Pagosa Springs, Colorado.

Fred's father, Fred, Sr., was born in Missouri (Fred, Jr. called him a "Missouri farm boy turned lawyer"), but he spent a number of years homesteading in Colorado when his children were young. Fred, Jr.'s love of drawing came from a "heap of self learning . . . stimulated by hand-drawn ads in mail order catalogs whose voluminous pages I would copy through to the saddle and harness section." In Pagosa, said Fred, Jr., "Long winter nights found me and my two little brothers [Hugh and Walker] at the round dining table forever trying to draw pictures." Hugh Harman confirmed that "All of us started drawing; we'd copy drawings, we'd copy covers of magazines. So we developed a capacity for draftsmanship." Finally, said Fred, "Someone sent a drawing of mine to the St. Joseph, Missouri, News-Press for a Saturday edition contest for young hopefuls. Mine was printed. Six years old and I was on my way."

The Harmans moved to Kansas City when Fred, Jr. was fourteen years old. City directories and census records from this period indicate that Fred's father, at various times, managed a collections department and was an adjustor with a law office. After serving in the Missouri Home Guard in World War I, Fred, Jr. spent summers working at the family ranch in Colorado and winters in Kansas City. One year, Fred worked as a pressman's helper at the Kansas City Star, where between runs he would "go up to the art department where for the first time I saw artists drawing for money." He was "mighty impressed" with their hand-drawn pen and ink artwork, and "swore that someday I would get that easy money[.]"

One winter, Fred returned to Kansas City determined to "find that warm seat at a drawing board. Luck was with me as I soon hired out to the Kansas City Film[ Ad] Company at thirty dollars per week! Man, but I had hit the jackpot. I was in the money." A photograph from 1921 or 1922 shows what the Film Ad Service was like when Walt, Ubbe, and Fred worked there.

One studio room consisted of glass windows on one side, and three rows of tables. Nine people, including James Edward MacLachlan—the "Art Boss," as Fred called him—are seen in the photograph sitting at the tables. Walt (wearing a visor) and Fred, each with pipes, sit in the back row and work at their drawing boards. Ubbe sits in the middle row, alongside MacLachlan and two female employees. The woman to Ubbe's left is MacLachlan's daughter, Marjorie, who was seventeen or eighteen and was an artist and card writer at Film Ad for several years.

MacLachlan, a forty-one-year-old father of five when Walt started at the company, described himself as an "artist" in the "moving pictures" business. A tall Canada native with a medium-sized frame, brown hair, and gray eyes, MacLachlan had lost his right leg below the knee. MacLachlan had worked for Cauger since at least 1917, and Walt felt that MacLachlan "was kind of sore" at him because Walt was "a little too inquisitive and maybe a little too curious[.]" Walt also thought MacLachlan "felt the boss paid me too much."

After working for Film Ad for a year, Fred got a raise to $40 a week, and he recalled that Walt did, too. The young artists earned enough to buy nice clothes and eat in good restaurants. Walt was supposedly well-liked by the women who worked at Film Ad, and dated a few of them. During this period, he attended the Kansas City Artists Ball dressed as a cowboy.

A picture of Walt, Ubbe, and Fred, believed to be taken in 1921, shows that Fred was most dapper of this well-dressed threesome. Fred, at nineteen two months younger than Walt, is seen in this photograph with his hands in his pocket, wearing a hat with a brim, a three-piece suit with a pocket watch chain attached to his vest, leather shoes, and a trench coat. Ubbe, who is probably twenty in the photo, has his hair slicked back and wears a tie and a vest. His hands are in the pockets of his knicker-like pants, which are tucked inside his tall leather boots. The nineteen-year-old Walt wears a cap, a dark three-piece suit, and leather shoes.

Over time, Walt, explaining that he "doubled in brass," began appearing in some Film Ad's filmed advertisements, playing a mechanic or salesman. Once, when an automobile crashed in front of the Film Ad building, a cameraman grabbed Walt and took him to the scene. Walt played a dazed accident victim in footage that became an ad for an insurance company.

Walt eventually wrote and filmed his own ads. He remembered being frustrated that he "would plan things with my drawings and I couldn't get those guys [at Film Ad] to do it. . . . The cameramen weren't doing half of what you prepared."

Like Walt, Ubbe did some acting at Film Ad. According to his granddaughter, Ubbe also modified the stop-motion process that Jimmy Lowerre showed them so that it no longer required both a cameraman, who turned the camera crank, and a second person, who replaced the drawings under the camera. "Tinkering with the camera during his off-hours," Iwwerks' granddaughter wrote:

Ubbe came up with a solution to the problems of the manual-cranking process. He devised a motor drive with a telegraph-key switch that would automatically turn the crank on the camera, creating a consistent exposure. This allowed one person to perform the entire task while seated in front of the animation table. Ubbe had just streamlined a key part of A. Vern Cauger's production line.

Walt's and Ubbe's love of animation took root during their time at Film Ad, and as they became more and more intrigued by it, they looked outside of work to increase their knowledge and hone their animation skills. They spent their free time going to the movies and devoured a seminal book on animation from the Kansas City Public Library, E. G. Lutz's 1920 book, *Animated Cartoons: How They Are Made, Their Origin and Development.*

Said Walt about Lutz's book, "Now, it was not very profound; it was just something the guy had put together to make a buck. But, still, there are ideas in there" and, Walt claimed, "I gained my first information on animation" from it. Referring to Lutz's book, Walt recalled that "there was only this one book in the library," but he checked out other art books as well, joking that "any book that offered information on drawing was likely to be found listed on my card, and over-due books were the chief reason for my usually depleted bank account."

In addition, Ubbe showed Walt *Animals in Locomotion* by Eadweard Muybridge, which the Kansas City Public Library had obtained in 1917. The book consists of frame-by-frame photograph sequences of humans and animals engaged in various activities such as walking, running, jumping, and swinging a baseball bat. Walt had photostats of the Muybridge sequences made, and they helped him "get the phases of action" necessary to animate motion. Walt was fascinated by "the mechanics of the whole thing," and said, "The trick of making things move on film is what got me." He and Ubbe frequented the Kansas City Art Institute, and Walt pressed a former Film Ad employee for information about animation when that employee visited Kansas City.

The result of Walt's and Ubbe's preoccupation with animation and their outside study of it was that, as Walt recalled, "[W]e started doing it a different way." While experimenting with cut-outs, Walt "would bend an elbow so that the viewer couldn't see where it was being bent and he'd make joints that looked like natural creases in cut-out bodies." Walt eventually adopted Lutz's ideas about using drawings rather than cut-outs with joints to show movement. Thus, he focused on what he called "[n]ew tricks and phases of action" that "[Film Ad staffers] hadn't done," although he stated that, "I didn't invent [the new technique]. . . . I got it out of [the Lutz] book at the library." Walt's brother

Roy recalled that Walt's and Ubbe' innovations led to their continued success at Film Ad:

> Walt and Ubbe made a great team together [at Film Ad] because Ubbe was not only a good artist but a kind of a mechanical genius, too. They just worked it out together, and . . . they upgraded [Cauger's] business with new methods, better methods and came up with better stuff. That's why the old man liked them very much.

Nevertheless, Cauger rejected Walt's efforts to refine Film Ad's animation process. "We made a few things for him[ the new way], but he never went for it too much," Walt said. "He just didn't want to do it." But Cauger did not prevent Walt from continuing to experiment, going so far as to allow Walt to take home a mahogany box camera with a hand crank that Walt noticed at Film Ad. At first, Cauger resisted. "He kept saying, 'What are you going to do with it?'" according to Walt, although Cauger must have known the answer, since he repeatedly told his own children that "Walt wanted to experiment on his own."

"[M]y boss," summed up Walt, "let me take home an old camera. I set it up in an unused garage and began experimenting in my spare time." Thus, Cauger's loaned camera enabled Walt to, for the first time, animate his own cartoons.

◂ ◂ ◂

In early 1921, after a year at Film Ad, nineteen-year-old Walt Disney began what he called "[m]y home experimenting," using the garage of his family home at 3028 Bellefontaine to create his own cartoons. Roy Disney said that their father, Elias, built the garage "for income. . . . So he gets the garage started and was talking about renting it and Walt said, 'You've got a customer. It's rented.'" Walt told an interviewer he rented the small cement-block structure for $5 a month.

With Roy's help, Walt built a stand for Cauger's camera and mounted incandescent lights on boxes, testing them until Walt was satisfied with the exposure. Roy recalled that Walt "set up a cartoon shop in there. He'd come home long after everyone else was in bed and be out there still puttering away, working, experimenting, trying this and that. That's when he'd borrow Cauger's equipment, bring it out, use it at night." Walt's younger sister Ruth explained that "He'd be out there till way late at night with the light on and we didn't exactly pay too much attention to what he was doing[.]" "[T]hat was Walt all the time," said Roy, "driving himself frantic, day and night."

Referring to the advancements made beyond the cut-out models employed at Film Ad, Walt said he "wanted to experiment with this other method, which is the method that was then being employed by the theatrical cartoonists." He created his own logo, which was a cartoon self-portrait. It showed a young man in a vest, bow tie, polka-dotted pants, and spats, with a pencil tucked behind an ear sitting at a drawing board as discarded papers float to the ground. Tying together his commercial art, film ad, and cartooning experience, Walt's caption stated: "Walt. Disney, Cartoonist, Comic Cartoons, Advertising Cartoons, Animated Motion Picture Cartoons, 3028 Bellefontaine, Kansas City, Missouri."

While toiling in the garage, Walt's focus was on animated cartoons. "I had some ideas," he said. "One was to do a sort of animated cartoon commentary on local topics for the Kansas City screen." One issue that caught his attention was a reorganization of the Kansas City police department to eliminate political patronage from the ranks.

By February 1921, the *Kansas City Star* was reporting on "the first shake-up in reorganization of the police department." Six officers, including the chief of police and the head of detectives, were transferred to different positions. "It's for the good of the service," explained the chief. "We want new blood in some important places." According to the *Star*, these reassignments were the "forerunners of a general constructive shake-up to be made by the new commissioners" who determined that a few dozen "politically created" "'chair warming'" jobs would be eliminated, especially where, as in the Nineteenth District, "many politically protected 'joints' and resorts" were harbored.

Walt decided to lampoon the police shake-up and made a twenty-three-second cartoon showing several policemen entering the Kansas City police department. After the building shakes and vibrates, defrocked policemen are thrown out onto the street as the words "Your [sic] fired" appear. Finally, a man follows them out of the building and hangs up a sign reading "Cops Wanted."

Walt animated other current events cartoons in his father's garage, but used a different style of animation to do so. Unlike the "police shake-up" cartoon, these other cartoons were created in the "lightning sketch" style, in which a hand holding a pen on screen draws the cartoon in a sped-up manner. Walt explained, "It wasn't really my hand[ on screen]. . . . I couldn't get my hand under the camera. But I had a photograph made of my hand holding a pen, and I rephotographed that photograph so that on the screen there was an illusion of my hand doing the sketching."

One of Walt's lightning sketch cartoons dealt with Kansas City's slow streetcar service. Walt's former boss Lou Pesmen explained, "There was a street-car problem in Kansas City at that time—the cars were not running often enough[.]" Walt animated a daisy growing on a woman's leg during her long wait for the streetcar. "[B]y the time the street-car arrived," wrote Pesmen, "she was surrounded with flowers." Walt also showed a young man waiting, and "growing into an old man with a long, white beard before the street-car arrived."

Walt also made at least three other lightning sketch cartoons during this period, and they addressed such topics as crime in Kansas City, the latest ladies' fashions, and the state of disrepair of Kansas City streets. The crime cartoon is thirty seconds in length and bears the caption, "Cleaning Up!!?" It shows a masked burglar named "Crime" being kicked out of Kansas City. The tag line reads, "Get Out + Stay Out!"

The fashion cartoon is fifty-one seconds long and its title card reads:

Kansas City Girls are rolling their own now—
Ladies stockings come so high now
they have to roll them down at the top————
(As seen on Petticoat Lane).

The lightning sketch shows a dry goods storefront window featuring leg and feet mannequins with dark hose and shoes, and head and chest mannequins with camisoles. Signs in the window read, "Waist Special," "Hose Special," and "Waists Special To-Day."

The last of these cartoons is twenty-five seconds long and its caption asks, "Did You Ever Take A Ride Over Kansas City Streets 'In A Fliver[?]'" The lightning sketch illustrates a car and its two occupants bouncing around a Kansas City street filled with potholes.

At some point Walt also filmed a live-action introduction to one or more of the animated segments. In the scene Walt plays an artist at his drawing board contemplating what to draw. This sequence is ten seconds and shows Walt in a tie, vest, and visor, and behind him on the wall are his cartoonist logo and other illustrations. Walt reaches into his vest pocket for a match, lights his pipe, and scratches his head before beginning to draw. The idea, apparently, was to provide a transition to the first lightning sketch; the viewer would see Walt pick up his pen, and then—once the lightning sketch cartoon began—see what Walt drew.

It took Walt about a month to finish some of these projects, which he may have initially called *Local Happenings*. Walt's "home experimenting" had "led to the making of my first animated cartoon," he recalled, and he described a "200-foot film concerning various local incidents in Kansas City." These films are significant, not only because they were the first Disney cartoons, but also because they were animated solely by Walt.

One of the friends Walt showed *Local Happenings* to was Lou Pesmen, who said he "laughed long and hard" at the film and suggested Walt take it to

Pesmen's client, Frank Newman, to see if Newman would run it in one of his theaters. Walt's father told a reporter that Walt "named [his film] Newman's [*sic*] 'Laugh-O-Grams,' without ever talking to [Newman]"—thus it appears that Walt renamed *Local Happenings*, made new titles for it, and edited it in order to try to sell it to Newman.

A surviving collection of these films (which may have been edited together years later) begins with a title card featuring Walt's cartoonist logo beneath the words, "Newman Laugh-O-Grams" and above the words, "Produced Especially for Newman Theatre." The live-action introduction featuring Walt preparing to draw is the film's first scene, followed by the lightning sketch cartoons about crime, ladies fashion, and street disrepair (the cartoon about waiting for street-cars does not appear in the surviving film). After the lightning sketch cartoons, a title announces "Kansas City's spring clean-up, Newman Laugh-O-Grams," which introduces the last segment, the fully animated (i.e., non-lightning sketch) cartoon about the police shake-up. The entire film runs two minutes and twenty-five seconds.

Walt's father remembered that, after putting the Newman name on his film, Walt "went down to [Newman to] sell it. With shaking knees he talked to the big theater man. Newman admired Walter's nerve, liked his picture, and bought it for $150. He also ordered some more." Walt himself told differing versions of how he sold his film to Newman. Years later, in a letter to Frank Newman, Walt noted that he dealt not with Newman but with Milton Feld, the manager of Newman's Royal Theatre at 10th and Main (who had also managed the Newman Theatre, two blocks away at 12th and Main). "Of course," wrote Walt, "all of my contacts at that time were through Milton Feld and I did not see much of you."

Similarly, Walt told an interviewer that he took the film to Milton Feld, recalling that, "The fellow who was running the theater, Milton Feld . . . was very interested in it and he said, 'Send that kid up to see me.' So I was scared to death." According to this version, Feld told Walt, "I like it, kid. . . . I can use one every week." Yet in other interviews, Walt claimed that he "sold the film to Frank Newman, operator of the Newman Theatre, for $60 . . . . and I made a deal with Mr. Newman to make one film a week, cartooning local happenings[:]"

> I was sitting behind [Newman] in the theater, just the two of us. I was nervous as a cat, wondering what he would think of it, when he whirled around and snapped, "I like it. Is it expensive?" I blurted out quickly, "No, sir; I can make it for thirty cents a foot." He said, "It's a deal; I'll buy all you can make." I went out walking on air, and it must have been an hour before I realized I had forgotten one small detail—the profit. Thirty cents a foot was exactly what it cost me to make it.

Thus, by this account, "Frank Newman, who owned three theaters in Kansas City, was the first—in a long line of showmen—who gave me a helping hand. He bought those early efforts of mine at 30 cents a foot."

At the time Walt sold his cartoon to Newman, Newman's theater program included a semi-regular newsreel feature called *Newman News and Views*, which the theater described as "[a] digest of the most important world events edited by the management from the leading film weeklies [and l]ocal subjects taken by the Newman Staff Cameramen[.]" Walt's topical, satirical cartoons were a natural fit with *News and Views*. His *Newman Laugh-O-Grams* premiered as part of *News and Views* at the Newman Theatre on Sunday, March 20, 1921. Walt was nineteen years old at the time of his first movie premiere, and would not turn twenty for another nine months.

On the day of the *Laugh-O-Grams* debut, the Newman Theatre was showing a Constance Talmadge movie that it promoted as the "most delightful entertainment of her entire career." According to Newman's newspaper ad, *Mamma's Affair* was "a Peppy Play of Fits and Starts[:]" "Eve got the apple—Mamma got pity—but when Connie learns woman's pet trick—She shows them all up with a display of 'nerves' that rids her of a ready made romance and wins her a handsome husband[.]"

*Mamma's Affair* ran seven times between 11:00 a.m. and 9:30 p.m. that day. A "Special Added Feature" consisting of a "Short Symphony Concert of Music By Kansas City Composers" would run before three of the showings, and the Newman Concert Orchestra, under Conductor Leo F. Forbstein and featuring local soprano Helen Taylor and "Pianiste" Richard R. Canterbury, was scheduled to play before four of the showings.

The first print reference to a Disney production appears at the very bottom of the *Kansas City Star* ad placed by the Newman Theatre on March 20. In small print the ad lists the five segments included in that day's *News and Views* feature, including news of world events, local happenings such as a banquet, a ball, and a tournament—and (albeit misspelled) Disney's cartoon:

> In the News and Views This Week, Cub winners in basket ball tournament—$25.00 Irish Stew Banquet—Y.M.H.A. ball—Newman Laugh-a-Grams [*sic*]—World Events.

There appears to be no firsthand account of the *Newman Laugh-O-Grams* premiere, but Walt said, "The film created quite a little interest" and he was asked to provide weekly *Laugh-O-Grams*, which he did for several months.

Feld gave Walt various other assignments as well. For the Newman Theatres' Anniversary Week, Feld asked him to animate the movie stars of upcoming films popping out of an anniversary cake. He also had Walt make cartoons concurrent with political campaigns and holidays. When Feld wanted a film to address the problem of audience members who read title cards out loud during showings, Walt animated his first named cartoon character, Professor Whosis, who dispensed of noisy movie patrons by whacking them with a mallet or pulling a lever that dropped down a chute out to the street.

Because Walt sold his cartoons to Newman at cost, the *Newman Laugh-O-Grams* and other Newman projects were not money-making ventures, and even then Walt had to work to "catch [Newman treasurer Gus Eyssell] to collect my 30 cents a foot." "But," said Walt, "I didn't care" about the lack of profitability. "[Newman] was paying for my experiment." While the Newman cartoons did not earn Walt a profit, they did earn him some local renown, and he basked in it. "I got to be a little celebrity in the thing," he said, and he enjoyed being recognized and complimented by his friends, neighbors, former schoolmates, and even his current boss. Cauger's son recalled that Cauger "was pleased with Walt's success," and borrowed the *Newman Laugh-O-Grams* to show Film Ad employees as well as potential clients.

By the middle of 1921, nineteen-year-old Walt, the "little celebrity," had worked at Film Ad for almost eighteen months. He made $40 per week, and worked alongside friends like Ubbe Iwwerks, Fred Harman, and Red Lyon, who shared his passion for filmmaking and animation. He had a boss who not only approved of his work, but supported his outside animation pursuits as well. Those efforts resulted in a degree of early success and fame, earning Walt a standing arrangement with the theater owner whom Walt's father called "[t]he big showman in Kansas City at that time[.]"

Considering the positive developments that had transpired since his return from France nearly two years earlier, Walt decided it was time to open his first film studio. Perhaps remembering how quickly his opportunity at Gray Advertising evaporated and how briefly Iwwerks-Disney flourished, Walt opted to hedge his bet and keep his day job. While he launched his very first movie studio, he would continue to work for Cauger at Film Ad, just as he had while creating cartoons for the Newman Theatre. Walt was ready to go out on his own, but not without a safety net—at least not yet.

# Kaycee Studios
## *1921–1922*

By the fall of 1921, Walt and his Film Ad friend and colleague Fred Harman decided to open a studio. They rented "this little shop" above a streetcar barn at 30th and Holmes Streets, and established what might have initially been called the Harman-Disney Studio. Walt and Fred continued working at Film Ad by day and spent their evenings at the studio. Their boss at Film Ad, Vern Cauger, claimed to have let Walt rent space in a vacant house a few steps up a hill from Film Ad, but the streetcar barn was not a few steps away; it was six blocks south and one block west of Film Ad's address at 24th and Charlotte.

Fred remembered that he and Walt rented the office space "secretly," but since Cauger loaned Walt a camera to use after hours—and enjoyed the success of *Newman Laugh-O-Grams*—it is likely Cauger had some idea of Walt and Fred's enterprise. As for the office, Fred's younger brother Hugh explained that the "little studio" above the car barn "shook as if there were an earthquake, all day long and all night long. It never stopped. . . . But it was a great place. Dinky little rooms; you could put two or three of them in this room. But it was nice, and so clean; their little desks, and animating desks, too. Everything about their place was shipshape, always."

With savings from Film Ad, Walt and Fred purchased a Universal movie camera and tripod for $300. Fred later wrote he and Walt had their sights set "for long-range money and fame," and their plan was to make a film and then attract business based on the strength of that first film. Hugh Harman confirmed that Walt and Fred "were moonlighting [from Film Ad], they had their own studio on the side, and they were determined they were going to quit as [Film Ad] employees and become their own Paul Terrys[, a noted animator at that time]."

Walt and Fred's first cartoon was titled *The Little Artist*, in which an artist's easel comes to life. Hugh recalled that Walt and Fred "would come [to Kaycee] after their day's employment [at Film Ad] was over, after having a quick bite, they'd go to work at their studio." They would "work all night" and it took them "months and months" to complete *The Little Artist*. Hugh did not "know when [Walt and Fred] slept" (although when they did sleep, it was at the Elsmere Hotel, six blocks away, where Fred, Hugh, their younger brother, Walker, and a fourth roommate lived; Walt frequently slept in the Harmans' room). In *The Little Artist*, said Hugh, "an artist, a cute little fellow, [was] standing at his easel, and he was making a picture, and as I recall it came to life on his easel, and they had a little play back and forth."

Walt and Fred also tried to sell the *Kansas City Journal*, the morning version of a local daily newspaper, on a companion newsreel segment called the *Kansas City Journal Screen Review*, but were unsuccessful. They experimented with live-action film, shooting a girl wading in water, and a woman and a girl with a doll and buggy.

Walt and Fred soon renamed their venture Kaycee Studios, derived from the local nickname for Kansas City, "K.C.," although it is unclear who came up with the name. At Kaycee, Walt and Fred experimented with special effects, namely reversing film, and one such effort appears to show Walt (perhaps in the same dark suit, tie, and cap in the 1921 photograph in which he, Fred and Ubbe are dressed up) jumping from the ground to the roof of his family's Bellefontaine house. In the clip, Walt faces the camera, with the rear of his home behind him. His mother and someone else are seen inside the back door. A young man with light hair, perhaps Fred, is seen in the lower left of the frame. Walt stands on the ground and suddenly jumps up and, still facing the camera, moves slightly backwards over the roof, lands on the roof, and waves.

The same trick was used in a film involving Walt's niece, Dorothy, the young daughter of Walt's older brother, Herbert. Dorothy later recalled, "Walt was experimenting . . . . [and] took movies of me walking down the sidewalk and dropping a milk bottle. Then he reversed the film and the pieces of the bottle came back together again." This film shows Dorothy walking on a sidewalk in front of a house. She wears a winter coat, a hat, tights, and leather shoes, and holds a full milk bottle in front of her. She steps into view from the right, drops the bottle, watches it shatter, then steps backwards and looks at the camera. Another film shows similar action, but in reverse: Dorothy walks in from the right, a broken bottle and spilled milk on the sidewalk come together and the reformed bottle, full of milk, leaps off the sidewalk up into Dorothy's outstretched hands.

Other versions of this effect filmed behind the Disney home feature Flora Disney, Walt's mother, and a newspaper (Walt's parents had returned to Kansas City in mid-1920). In one scene, Flora stands with the back of the house behind her. She puts out her right hand and a newspaper comes flying in from the right. Flora catches the newspaper, unfolds it, and reads it. In another scene, a newspaper leaps off the ground; Flora catches it and opens and reads it as she walks off.

Other footage using trick photography shows Walt playing three characters, each on the screen at the same time. In the scene, three Walts stand in front of a black curtain. Walt wears different coats, hats, and ties as each of the three characters, and sports make-up eyebrows and moustaches. All three characters smoke a cigarette and appear to be conversing with each other.

Walt and Fred also filmed a ten-second skit in which they appear outside of their studio door. By the time of this skit, the studio had moved four blocks east and two and one-half blocks south to 3241 Troost Avenue, to a second-floor office above a record store called the Standard Phonograph Company (Kaycee may have been located at another address after moving from Holmes Street and before moving to Troost Avenue). The Troost Avenue studio, according to Hugh Harman, "was just bare floor—just a couple of cubicles partitioned off for [Walt's and Fred's] desks."

In the clip made outside this location, the name "Kaycee Studios" is seen on the office door's glass window. Walt, on the left, wears a top coat, tie, and a hat, and smokes a cigarette. Fred, wearing a suit, tie, and hat, enters from the right. Walt and Fred shake hands and talk. Walt points to the door and opens it for Fred. They both enter.

A paper sign stating, "Cartoonist Wanted" appears on the office door. A third young man, whose face is not seen, walks up, reads the sign, and looks through the window. In a variation of this scene, one reminiscent of his "police shake-up" cartoon, Walt enters the storefront with the "Cartoonist Wanted" sign on the door. Several others follow, then run back out, after which a man exits, removes the sign, and tosses it away.

Walt and Fred also tried to compete with Vern Cauger and the five or so other local film ad companies by trying to get ad work from local theaters. They went so far as to spend Film Ad savings on a used Model T and, according to Fred, worked "very hard, traveling all around the neighboring towns in Missouri and Kansas [in the hope of] signing up movie theaters for filmads [sic] we hoped to make, but we just couldn't swing it." Roy Disney explained that Cauger "had a lot of theaters lined up for his slide films and Walt figured, 'Well, they're not selling to this theater over here so I can sell 'em over here[.]'" Roy felt that Cauger came to see Walt and Fred as competitors, and Cauger's son confirms that this is the case.

Walt and Fred failed to sell any theater owners on Kaycee, however, and they gave up. Fred explained, "Our rent was due and finally the Ford was repossessed." Before they lost the car, however, Walt and Fred might have driven it to Atherton, Missouri, approximately twenty miles northeast of Kansas City, to make a sepia-toned film called *The Old Mill*. In *Mill*, drawings of a mill and an old man dissolved into live action. The man Walt filmed claimed to be a descendant of Jesse James.

In late October, probably not more than a couple of weeks or months after Kaycee Studios was formed, the American Legion Convention was held in Kansas City. Pathé News, the French newsreel production company, commissioned Kaycee Studios to film the convention from the air. Pathé agreed to pay Kaycee one dollar per foot of usable film, which meant a profit for Walt and Fred of 95 cents per foot, since each foot of raw film cost just a nickel. "We could clean up[,]" Fred thought. The convention began on Sunday, October 30, 1921, with arrival ceremonies at Union Station for Vice-President Calvin Coolidge and Italian and Belgian military heroes. The *Kansas City Star* predicted that "[t]housands of persons will be at the station to meet . . . thousands of . . . heroes of this country's former army."

Walt and Fred had never been in an airplane before, and had no idea how to film in flight. A cameraman friend advised them to "stop [the camera] down all you can—limit the exposure to the barest minimum." A flying circus that Walt and Fred were to film was scheduled to debut on Sunday afternoon. The *Star* reported that over "fifty contesting and visiting airplanes are due here today from various parts of the country," and their antics were to include wing walking, stunt flying, and parachute landings at Legion Field. The night before, according to Fred, he and Walt went to Film Ad, "crawled through the basement window and 'borrowed' one of [Cauger's] cameras" (perhaps Cauger stopped lending his camera to Walt and Fred once they became would-be competitors by trying to break into the film ad market).

On Sunday they met one of the pilots at Nickells Field. Walt and Fred were to fly separately in two World War I Flying Jennies. Fred later wrote that, as he and Walt stood dressed "with puttees and bill caps turned backwards," the pilot told Fred to get in for a test flight without the camera. When Fred landed, he "convinced Walt that the assignment was just too risky. It was downright dangerous. If one of the planes fell, we might bust the boss' camera!"

As a result, Walt and Fred decided to fly together and use their own Universal camera. Fred recalled that he and Walt "took several hundred feet of film" from the Jenny. Walt's daughter wrote that "Fred sat in the cockpit and held the tripod while [Walt] stood up and cranked the camera. . . . [Walt] aimed his camera at planes doing wing-overs and loop-the-loops and he had high hopes that he'd shot some spectacular stuff." Fred wrote that Cauger's camera was "safely back in his plant come Monday morning with no one the wiser." The flying circus continued on Monday, amidst Legion sessions at Convention Hall and other convention events.

On November 1, tens of thousands gathered on Memorial Hill to hear General John J. Pershing and others speak at the dedication of the Kansas City Liberty Memorial "to those who died and who fought in the world war." A few hours later, the largest crowd ever seen in Kansas City watched 60,000 American Legion members march along a three-mile parade route. The father of a schoolmate of Walt's owned a building across the street from the parade reviewing stand, and Walt and Fred carried their camera to the roof of the building to film the parade and the dignitaries in the reviewing stand.

After the convention ended, Walt and Fred shipped their film off for processing, probably to Chicago. To their great disappointment, the film shot from the Jenny was worthless. Fred said that the film "turned out to be underexposed," and, as Walt explained to a writer, the film showed only a "whirling brightness which turned out to be the halation of Jenny's single prop. After that the screen went dark and stayed that way. [Walt] had stopped his lens down too far." Fred lamented, "Our hopes for fast riches were wiped out."

The convention ended on Wednesday and the next few weeks—Walt's last as a teenager; he turned twenty on December 5—marked a transitional period within Kaycee Studios. First, it seems that Fred, Walt's first movie studio partner, gave up on his dream of "money and fame" and left Kaycee in November or December of 1921. Hugh Harman suggested that Fred departed out of frustration that Walt brought their Film Ad colleague, Red Lyon, into Kaycee as a partner and decreased Fred's ownership interest in the process. Hugh recalled that "Walt had great respect for [Red], because Red Lyon had been in Hollywood; he was a Hollywood professional, and Walt thought that was quite an attachment." Hugh remembered that "Fred told [Walt] goodbye like that; they just split[,]" although Fred "had no malice toward Walt about this[.]" Fred, however, stated that he left Walt because Kaycee was not making money. Fred then focused on his job at Film Ad.

Second, even though he from time to time continued to film live-action footage for Pathé and other news outlets, Walt made the decision to return to his cartoon roots, albeit in a genre new to him but one with which his name would become synonymous worldwide: the fairy tale. Walt's idea was to animate a one-reel fairy tale, but one set in modern times, allowing him to utilize the satirical style that made the *Newman Laugh-O-Grams* so well received.

For his first one-reeler, Walt chose to make a modern version of *Little Red Riding Hood*, and the project consumed him for the next several months. Other than Walt's comment that, "[f]or six months I spent my nights and spare time working on 'Little Red Riding Hood,'" however, little is known about the period from late 1921 until early 1922, when the cartoon was completed.

During this time, Walt, with Red Lyon, apparently continued to represent "Pathé News, for news events around Kansas City." When a studio like Pathé telegrammed Walt it wanted a particular event covered, Walt would remove his Universal camera from its stand, grab a tripod, and take a streetcar to the event. He was asked to film one hundred feet of film, for which he was paid one dollar per foot. If Pathé did not purchase the footage Walt sent, it would replace the film.

Meanwhile, Walt concluded that he needed help animating *Red Riding Hood*. On Sunday, February 5, 1922, by which time *Red Riding Hood* was probably about halfway finished, Walt placed an advertisement on behalf of Kaycee Studios in the *Kansas City Star*. Walt was looking for help, but had to somehow attract aspiring artists to assist him even though he could not offer a salary. Walt's solution was to offer to teach interested applicants rather than pay them; Walt would instruct artists in "motion picture cartooning[,]" since he could not afford to hire them outright. For this reason, he placed his ad in the "Education" section of the classifieds, rather than in the "help wanted" section. The ad stated:

CARTOONISTS. Art Students—Study motion picture cartooning. Call Sunday afternoon. Kaycee Studios. 3241 Troost [A]ve.

On Wednesday, March 8, Walt placed a more traditional ad in the "Help Wanted—Male" classifieds in the *Kansas City Times*, the morning edition of the *Star*:

CARTOONIST wanted for motion picture work, see Mr. Dirney [*sic*] after 7 p.m., K.C. [*sic*] Studios, 3241 Troost.

An aspiring artist who saw either Walt's February 5 or March 8 advertisement was eighteen-year-old Rudolph Carl Ising, a Kansas City native and one of many children raised by his widowed father, a German-born street laborer who came to the United States in 1890. "I came from a big family," Rudy explained, "[of] nine children." Rudy's father, Henry Ising, had been a farmer in Germany, and attempted to start farms in the Oklahoma Territory and Kansas. After trying ranching in Oklahoma, Henry moved to Kansas City, drove a beer truck, and later got a job at a sash and door mill company.

By the time he finished grade school at the age of thirteen, Rudy got a job at E. H. Roberts Portrait Company, the so-called "Largest Exclusive Wholesale Portrait House in the World." Company president E. H. Roberts liked to hire "live men that have some pep and ambition[,]" since he felt that the "portrait business does not require any men to sit around and talk. . . . [but] requires work and long hours." In 1919 Rudy was a printer for Roberts and by 1920 he was promoted to photographer, following in the footsteps of one of his older brothers.

After about four years at E. H. Roberts, Rudy resigned: "I had signed up for the Landon course in cartooning, and my father was very mad because I'd quit . . . . They wanted to fire some older man [at E. H. Roberts] and let me take over my job as well as his job. By this time I was more interested in cartooning[ than photography]. I had started the Landon course, and that was when I saw Kaycee Studio's ad, 'Cartoonist Wanted.'"

Rudy "read an ad [placed by Walt], and I thought I was a cartoonist. The ad said they wanted to pay a cartoonist to work at this studio and they would teach them to animate. So I answered it and [Walt] gave me the job." The fact that, in actuality, there was "no pay, for a while," did not bother Rudy, who explained, "I was intrigued with the idea of animation and wanted to learn more about it." Rudy accepted the terms because he "wanted to learn right along with Walt."

At some point in late 1921 or early 1922, and probably by the time Rudy started working at Kaycee Studios, the Standard Phonograph Company left the ground floor storefront at 3239 Troost, and was replaced by Peiser's Restaurant, a café owned by Rudolph Peiser and described by Hugh as "a very nice restaurant." Peiser, forty-three, was the son of German immigrants and hailed from Independence, Missouri, where he owned a restaurant prior to moving to Kansas City in 1914. By 1922, Peiser had a delicatessen, the Old Dutch Inn Delicatessen, also on Troost, three buildings away from his new Peiser's Restaurant. Peiser lived at the Elsmere Hotel at Linwood and Troost (Linwood took the place of 32nd Street, thus the hotel was on Troost, one-half block north of Peiser's restaurant), where Fred Harman also had a room, making it possible that Peiser knew Fred, and knew that the space beneath Kaycee was becoming available.

Rudy did not know whether anyone else responded to Walt's ad, although he said that when he started working with Walt, other than Red Lyon, "[t]he only guys in the studio were Walt and myself." Walt seems to have recalled that others besides Rudy worked at Kaycee in early 1922. For example, Walt told a reporter about a decade after hiring Rudy that young artists helped him, in their spare time make *Little Red Riding Hood*. He also said elsewhere that three artists responded to the ad, and told another interviewer that, "I put an ad in the paper, any boys wanting to learn the cartoon business and things, so they came up and they worked with me at night." Walt said that he told the two or three young artists who worked for him at this time, "I can't pay you, but I can teach you. If we get anything profitable going, you'll have part of it."

Rudy presumably started at Kaycee Studios in February or March of 1922, shortly after reading one of Walt's two newspaper ads. By the time Rudy joined Kaycee, the studio consisted of "two partitioned offices" at "the head of the stairs." The partitions, Rudy said, "weren't even plywood, they were cardboard." Rudy also remembered that, at Peiser's, "you went up the stairs, and there was a little railing, and a desk, and then the office was right out in the open," in an area that "was about 50 x 200[.]"

While Walt worked at Film Ad, Rudy, who began as an inker and painter, "would go to the studio during the day." There he found Red, who apparently quit his job at Film Ad. Rudy recalled that Red left Kaycee at some point, but "was there long enough to build the camera stand, and I'd help him on that during the day[.]" Rudy spent "three or four months" tinkering with studio equipment or helping Red during the day, and "mostly it was at night" that Rudy worked with Walt. After Red left, Rudy "had to do all the camerawork . . . . It was just [Walt and me] there for quite a long time."

While Rudy handled the camera, Walt did the drawing, which Rudy said, "kind of was Walt's territory." According to Rudy, Ubbe Iwwerks, though not a part of Kaycee, came by occasionally and did lettering work for Walt. "If there were any titles in there," said Rudy, "Ub[be] would have been the one to do them," probably referring to the titles in *Little Red Riding Hood* or other Kaycee projects. Another frequent visitor to Kaycee was Hugh Harman who, before Fred left, started coming to Kaycee on evenings and weekends to watch his brother and Walt animate.

"I was in high school at the time [I started visiting the studio]," said Hugh, "about my junior year, and I neglected my studies to come in to their studio after school. I got off about 1 o'clock, and I got there about 1:30 or 2, and I had the whole place to myself. . . . Then I would animate. . . . I'd spend a whole afternoon there, way up into the evening, sometimes late." His time at Kaycee left Hugh "imbued with the idea of animation." Hugh described the studio as "quite a large area . . . because [Peiser's] restaurant was big, below, and this was the whole top floor." The space was filled with five or six "tiny, really tiny" work spaces, separated by partitions so flimsy, said Hugh, that "[y]ou could nearly have poked your hand through it."

Even though it had almost been a year since Walt fully animated, by himself, the first of the *Newman Laugh-O-Grams*, it was Rudy's impression that "Walt didn't know that much about animation. They just had the old Lutz book on animation at Film Ad. It was very basic—at that time cartoons were pretty simple and basic." Rudy explained:

That was before celluloids and background paintings. You'd have a high skyline painting, and all the animation had to be below that skyline or whatever, where you had the pure white. The drawings were made on paper, and those were already inked and blacked in, [and] painted[ by the time Rudy photographed them].

In addition to animating *Little Red Riding Hood*, Walt and Rudy also worked on a series called *Lafflets*, three-hundred-foot shorts that combined cartoons and jokes. Rudy described *Lafflets* as a "joke reel about timely topics of the day" that sometimes used jokes from *Judge* and *Life* magazines. "They were more like a thing that went into [a] newsreel," said Rudy. He and Walt made about three *Lafflets* between February and May 1922. One *Lafflet*, as Rudy recalled, lampooned the Kansas City Police Department's decision "to have horse police, and we called it 'horsing around time.' This was a sight gag, naturally funny, I guess, around that time." He also recalled "that when the Shriners came to town we would do a camel deal." A third was made "when the short stockings came in, and the short skirts. There was a little mosquito or a fly, holding a telescope."

Some of the *Lafflets* were done in the same lightning sketch manner Walt used for *Newman Laugh-O-Grams*. Rudy recalled that the hand seen in these shorts

> was a photograph. . . . A hand would be completely out of focus at that range. . . . It also made it a little easier to move around. The drawing was made in blue pencil, because blue would not photograph. We always used positive film for the negative, then, because you got a better contrast. . . . Not just orthochromatic [film was used], but it was what they called printing stock. The thing was made in a real light pencil. So you'd do a little bit of the thing and then you'd move the hand to that point, and then you'd move the thing and as you moved it, you had to ink in that line, until you'd inked it all the way through.

*Little Red Riding Hood* was likely completed in the early spring of 1922. It is a six-minute, seventeen-second cartoon with a title card stating: "Little Red Riding Hood, Cartooned by Walt. Disney." Of the six characters seen in the film (Red Riding Hood, her mother, the villain, a heroic boy, a cat, and a dog), four of them (the boy, girl, cat, and dog) would appear again in future fairy tales made by Kaycee or its successor studio. In the Kaycee version of this tale, Red Riding Hood's mother makes donuts for the girl to take to her grandmother. A man follows Red Riding Hood to her grandmother's house and chases her until a boy flying an airplane rescues Red and utilizes a cable suspended from the plane to dispose of the villain in a lake.

Walt worked plenty of gags into the story: as Red Riding Hood's mother flings balls of dough to the stove, a cat shoots holes in them to turn them into donuts; an old man in a framed portrait hanging on the kitchen wall laughs as he watches the mother and cat make the donuts, and his beard has grown beyond the portrait's frame; in a frequently used Disney gag, when the cat is injured, nine spirits—the cat's nine lives—ascend upwards from the cat; Red Riding Hood uses an inflated donut as a spare when her dog-powered car gets a flat tire; flowers walk away from Red when she tries to pick them; and the villain's top hat flips when he sees the grandmother's note to Red stating that she has "gone to town to see the movies."

Once *Little Red Riding Hood* was completed, Walt promoted Rudy from camera work to animating. Ultimately, Rudy "did the lab work and the camera work and the animation," and felt he was a part-time animator. The first scene Rudy "ever animated on" was "in *The Four Musicians of Bremen*[,]" the follow-up to *Little Red*. Recalled Rudy, "There was a trunk, and in this trunk were the four musicians, and the trunk was out on the water . . . . It fell overboard or something. The dog character lassoed it and pulled it in. I animated the whole thing, the lasso, and him going out and pulling it in." (Although Rudy said that he "remember[ed] that scene, very definitely," the scene does not appear in the surviving version of *The Four Musicians of Bremen*.) The sense of excitement that led Rudy to want to animate survived his first few months at Kaycee. When he saw his own scene on the screen, he "got a feeling that you'd gotten some of your life into it. That's the feeling you got out of it."

*The Four Musicians of Bremen* was probably completed by May 1922. At seven minutes and nineteen seconds, it is one minute longer than *Little Red Riding Hood*. The cat and dog from *Riding Hood* appear as two of the four musicians in *Bremen*, which also co-starred a donkey and a chicken. *Bremen's* title card proclaims that the film is a "modernized version of th[e] old fairy tale," and was made "by Cartoonist Walt. Disney." Walt included a prologue for his second fairy tale:

One bright day, four musicians
Set out to search for fame.
When anybody's nerves went wrong,
These four got the blame.

They went in state to every town.
In haste did they disperse.
All tho' they did their very best,
They couldn't have done worse.

The plot centers around four animal musicians who, after being chased from town by brick-throwing villagers, try to ward off starvation by catching fish. They are unsuccessful and are in fact chased from the lakeshore to a tree by a large swordfish. They fall into a cottage, displacing masked men who shoot cannonballs at them. The musicians, however, eventually win the battle. *The Four Musicians of Bremen* also contains several gags Walt would reuse in future productions, including the cat's removal of his tail to bat away incoming cannonballs, the swordfish's removal of his "sword" to use as a saw, a pair of pants that runs away on its own, and a fish that successfully dodges his hunter. *Bremen* reuses the "cat's nine lives" gag seen in *Little Red Riding Hood* and also includes a devil with pitchfork prodding a hungry cat as a manifestation of "Pangs Of Hunger."

Perhaps because his Film Ad salary could not support both him and Kaycee, Walt started struggling financially around this time and, Rudy explained, "wrote a couple of bad checks[.]" Walt's parents had moved to Portland, Oregon, on November 6, 1921, and Walt lived in a rooming house. He had fallen behind in his rent and was asked to leave. He also had unpaid cleaning and restaurant bills. One of Walt's creditors must have gone to court against Walt or Kaycee, and Rudy told an often-repeated anecdote about Walt's efforts to dodge the process server.

When the process server climbed the stairs at Peiser's, he asked for "Mr. Dinsey" instead of "Mr. Disney." When the man asked if Dinsey was in the office, Walt answered, "No, I don't think so." The man said, "Well, I'll be back." After the man left, Walt told Rudy that the man was a process server. The process server came back over the next few weeks, asking for Walt Dinsey. Walt or Rudy would tell him, "No, he hasn't shown up today." The process server returned one day when Walt Pfeiffer, who Rudy explained was there "just as a friend, not part of the company or anything," was present:

> Walt Pfeiffer and Walt Disney were just talking away, looking at some drawings or visiting or something. And the guy came up, and before he had a chance to say anything, Walt Pfeiffer says, 'Now listen, Walt,' and so on and so on. The guy looked at him, and Walt [Disney] said, 'Yeah—I'm Walt Disney. But my name is Disney, not Dinsey!'. . . . and he handed him the process and left.

Rudy helped Walt out of his scrape. From his job at E. H. Roberts, Rudy "saved up about a thousand dollars. I don't know how I did it . . . . So Walt wanted to know if I could loan him some money, and it ended up I loaned him five hundred dollars to bail him out on a couple of these things[.]"

Despite such financial difficulties, Walt concluded that he was ready to quit his job at Film Ad (now also known as United Film Ad Service) and make a go of it as a producer of animated cartoons. His shared experiences with

Ubbe Iwwerks in commercial art and the film ad business, and his own success with "home experimenting" and the *Newman Laugh-O-Grams,* led to his first attempt at a movie studio. In the short year Kaycee Studios was in existence, Walt's focus alternated from animation to live action and back again, and his allegiance apparently shifted from Fred Harman to Red Lyon to Rudy Ising. Since the previous November, he produced two fairy tales, *Little Red Riding Hood* and *The Four Musicians of Bremen*, and several *Lafflets*. But by May 1922, the whirl of various jobs, partners, and efforts at movie-making that comprised his first few years back in Kansas City coalesced into a vision: twenty-year-old Walt Disney would quit his job and obtain financing for a legitimate studio that would produce animated cartoon fairy tales.

# Laugh-O-gram Films, Inc.
## *1922–1923*

In spring 1922, about six or seven months after beginning his first animated fairy tales at Kaycee Studios, Walt Disney decided to leave Film Ad, and, he explained, "[d]uring the next few years, I expended several of my ideas trying to crack the animated cartoon field[.]" The forum through which he "expended" his ideas was another studio that he named Laugh-O-gram Films, Inc., presumably after his successful *Newman Laugh-O-Grams* of the previous year.

Walt's father gave an interview in which he suggested that the new studio came about due to local demand. "Some time after [the *Newman Laugh-O-Grams*]," said Elias Disney, "the neighbors urged Walter to form an independent company, which he did." But while Walt surely continued to receive the same kind of neighborly support he had for past ventures, it seems clear that Laugh-O-gram Films was the natural extension of Walt's many months of experimenting with animation, first in his father's Bellefontaine garage and then at Kaycee Studios.

Thus, "When I finished [*Little Red Riding Hood*]," recalled Walt, "I quit my job [at Film Ad] and formed a company, [and] capitalized for $15,000 to make a series of these modernized fairy tales." Walt explained the capitalization in general terms: "[w]e managed to interest some investors who financed the [venture]," he said about a decade after Laugh-O-gram Films was formed. Hugh Harman described the investors as "local merchants" whom "Walt organized . . . into a plan to start a corporation[.]" The corporate documents executed upon the company's formation, however, provide more detail about the birth of Laugh-O-gram Films in May 1922.

Walt pooled $7,752 to start the company. Most of that amount, $5,052, was in the form of assets, and the $2,700 balance was cash raised from investors. Walt's biggest assets were the films he had completed at Kaycee Studios, the two fairy tales, *Little Red Riding Hood* and *The Four Musicians of Bremen*, and the *Lafflet* shorts. For reasons never understood, Walt chose to exclude *Little Red*

*Riding Hood* from the film assets he listed in the Laugh-O-gram incorporation documents.

He valued the remaining films, *The Four Musicians of Bremen* (which he listed in the incorporation papers as simply *The Four Musicians*) and the *Lafflets*, at $3,000, collectively. The additional $2,052 in assets consisted of the Kaycee office equipment and furniture, including the inkers, animating booths, and a Motor Drive Automatic Camera Stand with camera, Cooper-Hewitt Lights, Automatic Dissolve, and Vignette. As to the investors, Rudy recalled that Walt "got these people interested[.]" Other than Walt himself who, with seventy shares of Laugh-O-gram stock, was the principal shareholder, the four primary investors in the company were Red Lyon, William and Fletcher Hammond, and Edmund J. Wolf.

By the time he started Laugh-O-gram Films, Walt had known Red Lyon, who turned twenty-nine the month Laugh-O-gram was incorporated, for about a year. Walt and Red worked together for Cauger at Film Ad since 1921. Red followed Walt and Fred Harman to Kaycee later that year, although Red appears to have left that venture not long after Rudy Ising started at Kaycee in early 1922. Building on his experience as an out-of-the-home photographer in Moline, Illinois, and a cameraman at Film Ad (and, if his boast to Walt was true, prior experience in Hollywood), Red joined Laugh-O-gram Films as its "cinematographer," although his business card stated he was the company's "Technical Engineer." Red held thirty shares of Laugh-O-gram stock.

Walt's connection with the father and son Hammonds is unclear (perhaps Walt knew them through a future Laugh-O-gram benefactor, Dr. John V. Cowles, who lived two blocks from the Hammond family business from 1910 to 1920). William Fletcher Hammond, fifty, was a widowed druggist from Kansas who had two grown children, Esther and Fletcher. William's wife died a few years before 1910, when she would have been thirty-five. Initially, William remained in Flora, Kansas, raising Esther and Fletcher and continuing to work in "retail drugs." By 1916, however, Esther, then twenty-four, had relocated to Kansas City and was married there. William and Fletcher also moved to Kansas City, if not by 1916, a few years later.

By 1921, the year before William became an investor in Laugh-O-gram, he was working as a bookkeeper for his two younger brothers, John and Lycurgus Hammond. Between them, the younger Hammond brothers owned two Kansas City companies, both of which were located at 1732 Grand Avenue. One, eventually called Hammond Brothers Fuel and Ice Handling Contractors, was run by John and Lycurgus. The other, Hammond Brothers Ice & Cold Storage Co., was operated by John and two other individuals. At various times, the

Hammond Brothers handled or stored coal, iron, and ice. John and Lycurgus listed themselves as railroad contractors in the 1920 federal census, suggesting that railroad companies might have been a main client of the Hammond Brothers businesses. William was still working for his brothers as a bookkeeper when he invested in forty shares of Laugh-O-gram in May 1922.

William's son Fletcher was about twenty or twenty-one when Walt formed Laugh-O-gram, and thus, may have been, like Walt, a minor. Walt did not turn twenty-one until seven months after Laugh-O-gram's incorporation, a fact that did not prevent him from assuming the leadership of a company, but which gave him an escape hatch in the event the company failed. "I suppose it was probably illegal," Walt said, "for me to be president of a corporation at age twenty. . . . If we ever wanted to get out of anything, I suppose we could have gone to court and claimed I was a minor." Fletcher Hammond, like his father, with whom he lived at 2816 Bales Avenue, was a clerk at Hammond Brothers. By the time he invested in ten shares of Laugh-O-gram stock in May 1922, Fletcher had worked for his uncles for two years.

The last of the main Laugh-O-gram investors was Edmund J. Wolf, a fifty-year-old bank teller employed by the Linwood State Bank. Wolf and his wife, both natives of Pennsylvania, had a fifteen-year-old son. Wolf had recently been an auditor at the Troost Avenue Bank, which may explain how he knew Walt. Upon Laugh-O-gram's incorporation, Wolf held four shares of Laugh-O-gram stock.

Walt capitalized Laugh-O-gram Films at $15,000, although, with cash and assets totaling just over $7,700, only slightly more than half of the stock was subscribed. Three hundred shares of stock were issued, at $50 per share, and other investors included Walt's parents and sister. Despite the presence of other investors, Walt named himself and his four main investors—Red Lyon, William and Fletcher Hammond, and Edmund Wolf—as the Laugh-O-gram Board of Directors.

With assets, investors, and a creative vision in place, Laugh-O-gram Films, Inc. was incorporated on Thursday, May 18, 1922, when its Articles of Association were signed by Walt, Red, the Hammonds, and Edmund Wolf. The articles were recorded by the Jackson County recorder of deeds the following day. The recorder's certificate was issued on May 20, and the State of Missouri issued to Laugh-O-gram a Certificate of Incorporation on May 23.

Laugh-O-gram Films' first location was Suite 218 of the McConahy Building, 1127 East 31st Street, and the staff was in that location by Sunday, May 28. The McConahy Building was at the southwest corner of 31st Street and Forest Avenue (one block east of Troost Avenue and about two and one-half blocks northeast of Peiser's Restaurant) in one of Kansas City's main shopping districts, the South Central Business District. This commercial area was south of the city's hospital district and west of the 10th Ward residential neighborhood where the Disney family had lived. The McConahy Building also housed, in Suite 206, a photography firm called the LeMorris Studio and, elsewhere in the building, a laundry service and a pharmacy. On the first floor was the Forest Inn Café, run by Jerry Raggos and Louis Katsis.

The "Exclusive Agents" through whom Walt rented the office space were the realtors working for Lawrence Baer, thirty-seven, a Kansas City native and son of a German immigrant. Baer operated L. J. Baer & Company, "Real Estate Managers of Income Property and Agents," with an office in the Grand Avenue Temple Building at 200 Grand Avenue. Baer had advertised available space in the McConahy Building as early as six weeks before Disney moved in, in a newspaper ad that touted the new "modern 2-story building['s]" "[s]torerooms and offices[.]" The second-floor offices, the ad suggested, were "[s]uitable [for] doctors, dentists, chiropractors, osteopaths, beauty parlors, [and] ladies' shops," and the building offered "[h]eat, light, hot and cold water [in] each room [and] janitor service[.]"

Baer ran another ad in the *Kansas City Star* soon after, and then another, suggesting other uses for the McConahy office spaces; the managers now "want[ed] druggist, restaurant, bakery, millinery, hardware, dry goods, art shop, barber shop or any up-to-date line of merchandise." It added that "[s]everal fine offices" were still available on the second floor, and urged prospective tenants to "look these [offices] over."

In early May, Baer tried to nudge prospective clients by advertising that only "3 storerooms [were] left" for rent. He would now also consider renting to "gents' furnishings, . . . rug shop, . . . cleaner, tailor or any other business" in a "lease long or short time" at a "low rental" rate. Baer dropped the "3 storerooms left" language from the May 7 ad, and on May 11 touted store rooms of 21 by 50 feet (a corner room), 15 by 50 feet, and 17 by 50 feet, respectively. He also pointed out that, "Each room has toilet, lavatory, [and] steel ceiling;" that "light fixtures [would be] furnished;" and that McConahy had a "rear entrance[.]"

In his May 16 *Star* ad, Baer offered to negotiate the rent, saying he "will make low rent for right business." By Sunday, May 21, a "few fine offices [were] left" on the second floor, and one week later, May 28, Baer's ad claimed that "Four fine light offices [were] left," including the corner storeroom previously advertised in addition to two inside storerooms, 18 by 50 feet and 15 by 150 feet, respectively.

Baer's ad in the *Star* on May 28 did not mention the rooms designated as Suite 218, because by then Walt had signed a lease for that office space. Indeed, the May 28 and 29 editions of the *Star* included a Laugh-O-gram help-wanted ad that established that Walt, Red, and Kaycee holdover Rudy (whose title was "artist") had by then moved into the new studio:

> CARTOONISTS—Animators wanted for moving picture cartooning; experienced or inexperienced. Apply in person. Laugh-o-Gram Films, Inc. [sic], 1127 E. 31st st. [sic].

The new Laugh-O-gram offices were comprised of several rooms (Hugh and Rudy recalled five), including three rooms located in the northwest corner of the building, with four windows facing north onto 31st Street, and two rooms across the hall, on the south side of the building. The rooms on the south side of the hall were assigned to the animators and cameramen; Hugh said these rooms consisted of a "laboratory and camera room" and "the animating room[.]" The rooms on the north side of the hall were "a lobby and office" subdivided with a partition into offices for Walt's drawing board, a secretary, and the office manager. A bathroom was about twenty feet down the hallway.

Walt hired Leslie Bryan Mace, a twenty-four-year-old salesman, to be Laugh-O-gram's general sales manager. Mace, a Missouri native previously a salesman with the Vitagraph Company film studio, signed a contract with Laugh-O-gram on Monday, May 29, for a salary of $84 per month. Walt might have met Leslie through the Hammonds, or them through Leslie, since Leslie had been married to Esther Hammond, William Hammond's daughter and Fletcher Hammond's older sister. Mace and Esther Ida Hammond were married in Kansas City on Tuesday, July 18, 1916, when Esther was twenty-four and Mace was eighteen (although their marriage license application states that she was twenty and he was twenty-two). Within a few years of being married, the Maces had moved to Sweetwater, Texas, where they lived on Sam Houston Drive and Leslie worked as a portrait salesman.

By 1921, the marriage appears to have failed, and Esther Mace returned to Kansas City, where her father and brother lived. Even though Leslie was still alive, Esther apparently declared herself a widow (her alleged late husband was listed in the city directory as "William H." Mace, perhaps a nod to her father, William Hammond), as other separated women did at the time. Leslie Mace was back in Kansas City by at least 1922, the year Walt hired him at Laugh-O-gram Films.

Not long after advertising in the *Star* for animators, Walt hired five new artists. He also hired a scenario editor and a business manager. One of the new animators was Hugh Harman, Fred Harman's younger brother, who used to visit Kaycee Studios and who Rudy recalled "came in right about [at] the start" of Laugh-O-gram. Hugh was eighteen months younger than Fred and twenty months younger than Walt, which made him almost nineteen (and the same age as Rudy) when he joined Laugh-O-gram.

Like Fred, Hugh was born and raised in Pagosa Springs, Colorado, and had an interest in art. Hugh was eleven years old when his family returned from Colorado to Kansas City. A short time later, he entered and won an art contest sponsored by Woman's Christian Temperance Union. While in high school, Hugh did some of the artwork for the Westport High School yearbooks as well as drawings for a local department store.

By the end of high school, however, Hugh's thoughts were elsewhere. Hugh's nephew (Fred's son) recalls that, "Hugh thought about trying out for West Point. As a kid, he had the large collection of lead soldiers. They were in a large wooden box at my granddad[']s homestead during the late 20's and 30's where I lived as a kid." Hugh joined the National Guard at fifteen and remained in it through his four years of high school. "I'd hoped to go to war," he explained. By May 1922, Hugh was "just out of high school[,]" was in officer's training, and "had just come back from one Army installation, and was going to Fort Riley [approximately 130 miles west of Kansas City] to the cavalry school[.]" With World War I over, Hugh "despaired of a military career, because I thought all wars were ended."

Upon his return from officer's training, Hugh learned about Walt's new Laugh-O-gram Films studio from Fred. Hugh remembered that "Fred wasn't with Walt then, but Fred and Walt were still friendly." "With that," Hugh said, "I went to see Walt[.]" The Laugh-O-gram office "looked rather glamorous" to Hugh; he thought it was "quite a little setup, a lot of studio space[.]" As a result, "it wasn't hard for Walt to talk me into going to work for his new company[.]"

Rudy confirmed that, after graduation, Hugh "had an appointment to take an examination for West Point," but "Walt talked him into [joining Laugh-O-gram].... Otherwise he would have gone to West Point; he was really interested in that at the time." Walt hired Hugh at the salary of $25 per week.

Rudy recalled that animator Lorey L. Tague was hired at about the same time as Hugh. Lorey, twenty-five, was born in Rhode Island and a World War I veteran. When he saw Walt's ad in the *Star*, Lorey was a trolley motorman and had been married for almost eighteen months. He and his eighteen-year-old wife, Frances, and their infant, Pearl, lived with Harry Tague, a carpenter, who perhaps was Lorey's father or brother.

The third new animator hired by Walt was Carman "Max" Maxwell, nineteen, an Arkansan who saw the company's name painted on a second story window of the McConahy Building "and thought to myself that that's what I want to do." Max was raised in Hico, Arkansas, where he lived with his parents and five younger siblings. In high school Max "had done the cartoons for the school's annual." Sometime after 1920, he moved to Kansas City to continue his education (at, according to Rudy, "Kansas City State College, or something like that"). Max recalled that

> I was going to junior college in Kansas City and looking for some part-time work. . . . I saw this sign on the second story window of a little place out at 31st and Troost in Kansas City. It said, "Laugh-O-gram Films, Inc." I was interested in cartooning—I'd been doing a little of it during my high school and college career, for the annuals and things like that—so I went up there to investigate, and got a job.

Max was paid $10 per week.

Twenty-one-year-old commercial artist Alexander Wilson Kurfiss, from Kansas City, was also hired by Walt as one of the studio's new artists. Alex was the son of an architect, and he attended the Kansas City Art Institute (which may be where he met Walt). He worked as a draftsman, commercial artist, and meter reader for Kansas City Power and Light Company before working for Walt. According to Rudy, Alex was "a successful commercial artist, but [at Laugh-O-gram] did mostly the posters; we used to make a poster for each one[ of the shorts]."

A baker named Otto Louis Walliman was the fifth new animator hired by Walt at this time. Otto was born in Switzerland and remained a Swiss citizen after coming to the United States. He settled in Kansas City at the turn of the century, and at one time worked for the Schulze Baking Company there. He was still a baker when Walt hired him in 1922. At forty-six, he was by far (by approximately two decades) the oldest of the Laugh-O-gram staff members. While Lorey Tague has been referred to as the only married animator at Laugh-O-gram, Otto was married to a woman named Dorothy, although it cannot be determined whether they got married before or after Otto started working for Walt.

Rounding out the Laugh-O-gram creative team was Walt's childhood friend Walter Pfeiffer, whom Disney hired as the studio's "Scenario Editor." Like Hugh Harman, Walt Pfeiffer had attended Westport High School, where he displayed a talent for cartooning. The school's 1921 yearbook includes a detailed drawing intended to look like a piece of film that's captioned: "Animated Cartoon by W. Pfeiffer," purportedly of the IO Studios. The drawing pays tribute to—and teases—Walt Pfeiffer's fellow seniors, such as "Heinie Zimmer, Mathematical Genius," "Chas Lyons, The 'St. Louis Chappie,'" "Exley Fisher, The Human Bean-pole," and "Printz, The Boy Who 'Otto' Know."

Adolph "Jack" Kloepper, twenty-five, was hired as Laugh-O-gram's business manager. He was from Lancaster, Kansas, and attended Midland College in Atchison. By 1918, Jack was an Army veteran of World War I and had taken a job as a clerk at Ridenour-Baker Grocery Company in Kansas City. He first lived at the YMCA before becoming a "lodger" at a house in Kansas City, and became a traveling salesman of wholesale groceries. The year before Walt hired Jack, he was the sales manager of Duplex Printing Machine Company, and lived at 3112 Troost Avenue, a block west of the McConahy Building. He married twenty-two-year-old Martha Hudson in Kansas City in June 1922, probably not long after joining Laugh-O-gram. His salary was $50 per week.

On Saturday, June 13 Laugh-O-gram made a purchase from Schroer Brothers Machine Works, which was engaged in "General Machine Works, Models, [and] Manufacturing." The purchase was the first of five purchases made at Schroer's by June 30, suggesting that Walt and his staff spent the second half of June setting up the studio and offices.

Meanwhile, Walt moved to get the word out that Laugh-O-gram was open for business. On June 17 he placed an ad in the *Motion Picture News*, playing up not only how long he produced cartoons for Frank Newman, but also—probably threefold—how many fairy tales he had completed:

Laugh-O-Gram Cartoons Announced.

Laugh-O-Gram Films, Inc., is the name of a new Kansas City, Missouri concern that has just entered the production field. They will produce Laugh-O-Gram animated cartoon comedies which will be cartooned by Walter E. Disney, of Kansas City. Disney has been making these comedies exclusively for the Newman Theatre, Kansas City, for the past two years.

Six productions have already been completed in single reels, the titles of which will be announced in the near future. They will be released one every two weeks. Announcement of the plan of distribution will be made shortly.

Leslie B. Mace, of Kansas City, is the general sales manager.

The following week, Rudy became a shareholder in the company, when Walt gave him eight shares of Laugh-O-gram stock, valued at $400. The transaction came about when Walt decided to use company stock, rather than cash, to repay the loan Rudy had made to Walt at Kaycee Studios earlier in the year.

Rudy explained: "Walt decided that rather than pay me back [the Kaycee loan], he'd give me stock in the [new Laugh-O-gram] corporation. And he talked me into it. He was quite a salesman. But he was having a pretty hard time."

On Wednesday, June 28, the day after Jack's wedding, Red and Jack signed an invoice for the purchase of a "Used Tripod, 2 cranks + leg for tripod," from Chas. M. Stebbins Picture Supply Company, which specialized in "Moving Picture Machines, Stereopticons, Slides and Accessories." Rudy also recalled that "After we incorporated, we bought a developing outfit [so film no longer had to be sent to Chicago to be developed], and I did all that, too. . . . Somewhere along the line we got a projector, an electric one. . . . So that's the way we would cut our film and see our dailies."

Through July the staff continued to remodel the studio and publicize its opening. Laugh-O-gram made two more purchases from Schroer Brothers that month (and a final purchase in August) and five purchases, starting on July 10, from the Schutte Lumber Company, which claimed to have the "Largest and Most Modern Yards in the Southwest."

The first four of the five lumberyard purchases were delivered to the McConahy Building. Together these orders comprised two pieces of compo board, two pieces of clear fir, forty-eight feet of quarter round, twelve pieces of white pine, and forty-two feet of doorstops. Laugh-O-gram's fifth July order was delivered not to McConahy but to the Film Exchange Building at the corner of 17th and Main Streets—three pieces of compo board, twenty-four pieces of clear white pine, and one roll of one-ply roofing. It is unclear why Laugh-O-gram had these supplies delivered to the Film Exchange. Perhaps Walt, whose staff was allowed to review old cartoons from the Exchange, agreed, in lieu of payment, to provide the Exchange with supplies or repair work.

On July 15 Walt bought a half-page ad in *Motion Picture News* that announced "a Series of Twelve Laugh-O-grams," and featured, inside the "O," Walt's cartoonist logo from his "home experimenting" days. The ad also included the slogan, "All That The Name Implies" and a notice that "Full particulars regarding plans for distribution and release dates will be announced soon."

While the staff renovated the office and marketed *Laugh-O-gram* cartoons in the first months after its incorporation, the artists worked on the series of fairy tales Walt had advertised as completed the previous month. Rudy recalled, "We had made one or two pictures, I believe, at the time. I remember that *The Four Musicians* and *Jack and the Beanstalk*, I think, were the first couple."

Rudy may have forgotten when *The Four Musicians of Bremen* was made, since the Laugh-O-gram incorporation papers suggests that *Bremen* was finished before the company was incorporated. Rudy's recollection, however, suggests that, after *Little Red Riding Hood* and *The Four Musicians of Bremen*, the next fairy tale Walt and company tackled—and therefore the first one animated in the new McConahy offices in June and July of 1922—was *Jack and the Beanstalk*.

In the Laugh-O-gram version of *Beanstalk*, young Jack is motivated to act by his mother's tears (which require Jack to raise an umbrella) at their lack of money. Jack sells the cow for beans, and his mother and white dog and black cat watch in astonishment as the beans sprout a growing beanstalk that pushes Jack upward to the clouds. A fairy godmother on a cloud gives Jack wings, and he lands outside a giant's castle. The giant, surrounded by money bags, listens to a magic harp while a chicken looks on. Jack sees a can of paint, paints a hole in a cloud, and dares the giant to come out of his castle. The giant falls through the hole, crashes into the earth, and comes out the other side, to the surprise of three boys playing near a sign that reads "10 MILES TO HONG KONG." Jack uses a wheelbarrow to cart the harp, chicken, and bags of money home, where his mother and pets join him in a feast.

According to Rudy, *Beanstalk* marked Walt's first use, at least partially, of cels; prior to that, Walt had animated exclusively on paper:

> The first time we ever got the idea [to use cels], and I think it was my idea, was in *Jack and the Beanstalk*. Walt had animated, I think it was an eight-drawing cycle of the beanstalk growing. Because I don't even think we had vertical pans then, they were all horizontal, the only way our camera would work it. So that had to be an animated thing. And for some reason the beanstalk pictures all had to be cutouts, so the character showed behind the drawings. And they were all cut—I remember because I did it, and then glued those onto a sheet of celluloid. In effect, it became the background. And when I was cutting those, I talked to Walt about it and said, "Look, I don't know why we can't paint that on the cel instead of cutting that whole thing out," because, you know, that was a lot of work, cutting around all those leaves. And after that we began using cels a little bit more and more, for animation, for cycles, especially. But we never had the complete thing back there [in Kansas City], . . . we were still doing it on paper.

Hugh believed that the use of cels came about, in part, because of the high caliber background paintings made by Otto Walliman. "We had a very fine background man there [at Laugh-O-gram]," said Hugh. "Otto . . . . could paint, he could render, and as we worked along, his painting became . . . so obviously good that we came more and more to the use of cels, [so that characters] wouldn't interfere with the painted backgrounds."

Walt probably had three completed fairy tales (*Little Red Riding Hood*, *The Four Musicians of Bremen*, and *Jack and the Beanstalk*) before the summer was over. By mid-August, with half of his proposed slate of six cartoons likely finished, Walt decided to send his sales manager, Leslie Mace, on a month-long trip to New York to look for a distributor. Either prior to Leslie's departure, or within a few weeks of his return, Laugh-O-gram Films participated in a South Central Business Association parade.

Walt, Leslie, and Rudy represented the studio at this event. They rode in a car affixed with a Laugh-O-gram movie camera in the back seat, where Walt sat, alongside a sign that read, "These pictures will be shown at the Isis Theatre Tomorrow Night." The Isis Theatre, also one block west of McConahy, was located at Troost Avenue at 31st Street. The parade film made by Walt and his staff may have run as part of a *Topics-News* feature shown at the Isis on July 25, a *Screen Snapshots* segment that ran the following night, or *Home Made Movies* screened on October 9.

When Leslie left for New York in mid-August, he was not alone. Accompanying him was Dr. John Vance Cowles, Sr., a well-known Kansas City physician and businessman who had become Laugh-O-gram Films' Treasurer. Dr. Cowles, who was in his late forties or early fifties, was a Kansas native, a veteran of the Spanish-American war, and a Kansas City Homeopathic College graduate. He had an office over the Main Street Bank and lived at 300 East 34th Street with his wife of sixteen years, Minnie Lee, who appears to have been in her early to mid-thirties (and who may have been his second wife), and their three young children.

While the coming months would see Dr. Cowles become Laugh-O-gram's chief financial benefactor, it is unclear to what extent, if any, he invested in the company by the time he traveled with Leslie to New York. An ad about the trip placed by Walt in the *Motion Picture News*, however, establishes that Dr. Cowles was by then the Treasurer of the company:

Plan Distribution of Laugh-O-Grams.

Leslie B. Mace, Sales Manager, and Dr. J. V. Cowles, Treasurer of Laugh-O-Gram Films of Kansas City, are in New York this week. Dr. Cowles is a well-known figure in the oil business in Kansas City as well as being connected with Laugh-O-Grams, and is here in the interest of his oil business.

Mr. Mace is arranging for the distribution of a series of twelve Laugh-O-Grams to be released every other week. Laugh-O-Grams are single reel subjects, consisting of stories of modernized fairy tales in Animated

Cartoons by Walt Disney. Some of the first releases are "Little Red Riding Hood," "Jack and the Beanstalk," "Four Musicians," "Goldie Locks," "Cinderella," "Jack, the Giant Killer," etc.

Not only did this ad confirm Dr. Cowles had become a part of Walt's Kansas City universe, it also reiterated the July 15th ad's claim that twelve *Laugh-O-grams* would be offered to distributors (although Walt later changed the number back to six). In addition, the ad makes clear that Walt changed his mind about including as one of the *Laugh-O-grams* his first animated fairy tale, *Little Red Riding Hood*, which a few months earlier he had intended to exclude from the package.

Perhaps it was at the time of this decision Walt asked Alex Kurfiss to create a poster for *Riding Hood*. Alex's printed signature can be seen in the lower right corner of the poster, which shows a wolf, not seen in the reel, in black tie and tails, leering at a glamorous Red Riding Hood, and the text states, "Laugh-O-gram Films Inc. presents Laugh-O-grams, Little Red Riding Hood, cartooned by Walt Disney." Alex may have focused on the posters because he was not a natural animator. Hugh recalled that one of the Laugh-O-gram animators, likely Alex, "could <u>never</u> get the idea of a cycle. He got the idea of moving characters, but he couldn't get the idea of repetition."

While Leslie and Dr. Cowles were away, the animators probably continued to work on their fourth fairy tale, *Goldie Locks and the Three Bears*; plans for the fifth, *Puss in Boots*, were also underway. In *Goldie Locks*, a white dog and a black cat cook a pancake breakfast for a family of bears, two parents and their son. The pancakes are too hot, so the bear family, with the cat and dog, go for a bike ride. Meanwhile, Goldie Locks, a tall blonde, enters the bear home and finds the pancakes. The bears return and ask, in unison with the cat and dog, "Who has been monkeying with our pancakes?" The young bear finds Goldie in his bed, and a chase ensues. Goldie jumps from a cliff, then wakes from a dream, attended to by her mother as the white dog and black cat bring her a tray of pancakes.

As more *Laugh-O-grams* were completed, the studio created a *Laugh-O-gram* logo featuring the four recurring characters (a girl, boy, black cat, and white dog). Regarding the use of recurring characters, Rudy said that "there was never a plan to do that, it just happened that way." The logo showed the four characters sitting on a tree limb and reading a book titled "Fairy Tales." "Laugh-O-gram" appeared above the characters, and "Present" appeared below them, so the logo read, "Laugh-O-gram Fairy Tales Present."

A photograph from this period shows, from behind, three young men Walt's age in white dress shirts with sleeves rolled up, drafting at large wooden desks, and sitting in wooden chairs on rollers. A younger artist is seen to the right in profile. A boy in knickers hands one of the artists some papers, but the artist is so engrossed in his work, he does not look up. The artists in this picture could be Rudy, Hugh, Lorey, Max, or Alex (or Walt if he had walked across the hall from his own office).

On a shelf are framed *Laugh-O-gram* posters. The *Jack and the Beanstalk* poster shows a well-dressed boy with an ax, surrounded by his cat and dog, looking up a beanstalk. The poster copy reads, "Laugh-O-gram Films Inc presents Laugh-O-grams, A Reel of Fun, Jack and the Beanstalk, cartooned by Walt. Disney." Next to it is the *Goldie Locks and the Three Bears* poster.

On the shelf on which the *Jack* poster rests, partially blocking it, are two bottles of what look like soda, and a certificate showing that Laugh-O-gram Films is a "Member, South Central Business Association," which operated out of the Alexander Printing Company, of which Laugh-O-gram was a customer. A framed certificate, which might be the company's articles of association, is on the shelf to the right of the *Goldie Locks* poster. The furniture includes an open file cabinet with visible files, an index card box, a typewriter, and a coat stand with two hats; a third hat is on the desk.

As they continued to animate, Walt and the others analyzed the cartoons of successful New York animators. Walt became friends with a woman Rudy dated at one time, twenty-six-year-old Nadine Simpson, who had worked at the Film Exchange. Nadine arranged to lend *Aesop's Fables* and Farmer Al Falfa cartoons to Walt and Rudy so they could study them. Nadine had also been a booker at Select Pictures Corporation and a bookkeeper at L. J. Selznick Enterprises before working as a stenographer for Phoenix Film Corporation. By 1922, she was a stenographer at George A. Adams & Co., and had moved from the Densmore Hotel (where she lived for three years, apparently after a failed marriage to a local car salesman) back in with her mother, but she kept up her connections with the movie industry in general and the film exchange in particular.

Rudy recalled that Nadine

had worked before at a couple of film exchanges. And we knew several people at the film exchanges. Universal didn't ship their film. They sold it to a guy who had the whole state of Missouri or the whole state of New York. They called it "states' rights." We knew several people down there, and they were the ones who handled the film, and they just rented it to all the theaters in Kansas City. [We would get their used prints when they discarded them]; when a print got scratched up they'd actually take it down to the city dump.

Rudy further explained that

> [s]ometimes Nadine would go down and get a couple of the cartoons, and the ones we got mostly, then, were *Aesop's Fables*. That's because we were concerned with how they got a quick turnover. They got a lot of live film, and then of course we got some cartoons. When Nadine would get us one of the *Aesop's Fables*, we'd run it, and we'd cut out a cycle. We'd cut out maybe a two-hundred-foot run section where Al Falfa would chase a lion—then the lion would chase him, and they'd repeat that back and forth. I'd cut out a whole repeat of the film and look at how they'd change it back. Then Nadine and I would splice it together again and put it in— everything was hand-spliced then. And we'd look at some of the timing of the animation.

◂ ◂ ◂

The Laugh-O-gram Films staff made numerous purchases in September 1922. On September 1, the company made the first of eight purchases that month from the Franz Wurm Hardware & Paint Company. The hardware supplies included nails, thumbtacks, turpentine, a hose, garbage cans, and a six-dollar watch. The company also purchased office forms from the Alexander Printing Company and two thousand business cards from Inter Collegiate Press.

Records from the *Kansas City Journal-Post* show that Laugh-O-gram placed numerous "Help Wanted" ads in September 1922, including three ads that each ran from September 1 through 5, a fourth ad that ran from September 6 through 9, a fifth ad that ran from September 14 through 16, and a sixth ad that ran from September 17 through the 19. If these records are accurate, Laugh-O-gram had one or more help-wanted ads running in the *Journal* (the morning daily), the *Post* (the afternoon daily), and the *Kansas City Journal-Post* (the Sunday edition) continuously from September 1 through 9 and September 14 through 17.

Only a few of these ads, however, have been located. For example, the "Female Help Wanted" classifieds in the *Kansas City Post* for September 1, 1922, included the following ad:

> SCENARIO writer for permanent position. Apply in person or write [and] submit samples. Laugh-O-Gram Films, Inc., 1127 E. 31st st. [*sic*].

A similar writer ad, but for a male, was found, as was an ad that stated, "Girls wanted—with artistic ability for mounting pictures, cartooning." Records from

Motion Picture News, Inc., indicate that Laugh-O-gram purchased another two-inch ad from *Motion Picture News* on September 2, 1922.

While Walt continued to build the Laugh-O-gram team and work on fairy tales, Leslie Mace remained in New York, where he tried to interest a distributor in *Laugh-O-gram* cartoons. Leslie stayed at the McAlpine Hotel and, as Jack recalled, the "bills were amounting to more than the amount of money that we had in the bank." Nadine Simpson recalled that Leslie "spent all the money [Laugh-O-gram] had for expenses. They didn't have much but he spent it all." Word reached the staff that, as Rudy remembered it, "nobody was interested [in distributing *Laugh-O-grams*]." Finally, Walt ordered Leslie to come home.

Before Leslie departed, however, he finally struck a deal with a Tennessee corporation named Pictorial Clubs, Inc. Walt recalled, "[W]e finally sold [several subjects] to a firm . . . called the Pictorial Club, a film distributing concern." Nadine explained that Leslie "sold this [series] to Pictorial [Clubs] to be shown in schools and non-theatrical places, but instead of getting the cash, he got a note[.]" The deal with Pictorial Clubs, Inc. of Tennessee was reached on Sunday, September 16, 1922. Pictorial agreed to pay $11,100 for six one-reel animated *Laugh-O-gram* cartoons. The contract called for Pictorial to put $100 down and pay the balance on January 1, 1924—over fifteen months later—after all six cartoons were delivered. It is unknown how Pictorial convinced Leslie, or Walt, to allow Pictorial to receive six films without paying for over a year.

The deal with Pictorial injected new excitement into the studio, where the twenty-year-old Walt was, in Max's words, "always full of fire and energy." Walt Pfeiffer said, "We used to eat, drink and sleep cartoons." Rudy recounted how Walt and his staff were "completely enthused with animation" and how they "used to sit around and make up our own stories, so those modernized fairy tales were not much like the [original] fairy tale, usually." Once there was a general story idea, "we'd start drawing some scenes." Hugh found it "easy to invent the little business, the little stuff, but to try to analyze certain actions at times seemed very, very difficult, because we had no reference to live action." The animators' main references remained the Lutz book and the films obtained from the film exchange.

At one point, Walt tried to improve the staff's abilities by conducting an art class for them. "We started an art class for a while back there," said Rudy. "Walt thought that we should all have more of a training in art and he got the idea of having a night class once a week, a life class. . . . [T]his was just where we put an ad in the paper and had ten or fifteen gals come to answer the ad, and I photographed them. I think we only needed one or two models during that period. It didn't last too long, the life class."

The young Laugh-O-gram staff members developed personal bonds as they labored together to produce Walt's cartoon fairy tales. "We were all under 25 back then," explained Rudy. "We sure had a lot of fun," Max agreed. Jack recalled the "happy spirit that existed. . . . [W]e all had many belly laughs when discussing a story or material and Walt would explode some wild gag to incorporate into the story." Walt Pfeiffer said that they got to the office at 9 a.m. and worked until midnight.

Evidence of the youthful exuberance permeating the air at Laugh-O-gram is evident in a number of gag photographs made by the young artists. In one, taken on the roof of the McConahy Building, Walt has wrestled Max to the edge of the roof and brandishes a gun at him. Ubbe holds a Laugh-O-gram Films director's megaphone while Jack pretends to film the scene with a fake movie camera. Rudy explained how the prop camera came into existence:

> [F]or publicity shots, we built a box that looked like a Debrie camera, as they called it at the time. One of those with the magazine. So we put some film cans together and painted the box and put the cans on it, and it looked real when we mounted it on the tripod. Then we went out and we'd "shoot" with it.

Walt and his staff also joked around on the streets of Kansas City. Max told a reporter, "I remember [that Walt] used to put a tripod and camera in the back of an open roadster and drive around Kansas City making like he was a newsreel photographer. Of course he never had any film in the camera but he liked the idea." On weekends, Rudy recalled, the gang would go "to Union Station . . . [and] Walt would turn his cap around and pretend to make a film. People would come up and pose and say 'Where are you from?' And we'd say 'New York.'"

They would go on trips to Swope Park, one the country's largest parks, which was located about seven miles southeast of the city, and take pictures at the cabin there called Buzzard's Roost. Max recalled that, "Hugh Harman and a friend of his . . . had built [the] log cabin in Swope Park and that was a favorite rendezvous." A Swope Park photograph they dubbed "The Fountain of Youth" shows Walt pumping Ubbe a drink from a fountain while Rudy, Max, and a friend look on. The same group is seen in the cabin in a photograph titled "Gang at Buzzard's Roost." Film clips survive that show Walt clowning around inside the cabin with Hugh Harman, his brother Walker, and three other friends, and outside, near a fence, with all three Harman brothers and one of the young men seen in the interior clip.

◂ ◂ ◂

By October, the fifth Laugh-O-gram cartoon, *Puss in Boots*, was nearly finished. Rudy recalled animating a *Puss in Boots* scene with "the king. He was eating popcorn in a theater, only he was in a box seat eating popcorn. I remember crowds coming in and out of the theater." Rudy's scene was part of a nine-minute, thirty-two-second cartoon, the earliest surviving *Laugh-O-gram* that includes the studio logo title card. The opening credits state that this film was "Cartooned by Walt. Disney, [and] Photographed by 'Red' Lyon."

The action in *Puss in Boots* takes place in Kingville, which appears to be like a small American town but for the presence of a king and his castle. A boy courts the king's daughter, but the king chases the boy away. He and Puss the cat walk to the Kingville Theater where they watch Rudolph Vaselino in *Throwing the Bull, In Six Parts*. The movie gives Puss an idea, which he will only share with the boy if the boy agrees to buy Puss a pair of flapper boots (on sale for $4.99 from a regular price of $5.00) the cat admired in the town Booterie. The boy agrees, and takes the cat's suggestion to stage a bullfight to impress the king.

The boy, as the Masked Toreador, makes his publicized appearance at the Kingville Arena, where, with the help of the cat's Radio Hypnotizer, the boy gets the best of the bull. The king, unaware of the boy's identity, gives his daughter's hand to the brave toreador. When the boy removes his mask, the king becomes angry and chases him. The boy, the princess, Puss the cat and James the dog (the king's chauffeur) escape in the king's car.

*Puss in Boots* features a parody of a then-current Valentino movie; a *Laugh-O-gram* inside joke in the form of a poster seen at the Kingville Theater for the upcoming *Laugh-O-gram*, *Cinderella*; the almost obligatory "cat's nine lives" gag; and the first of several instances of Walt using a bullfight setting (and related gags such as the hypnotizer and the victor blowing the vanquished bull away upon defeat). *Puss* also relied to a larger extent than in previous *Laugh-O-grams* on written dialogue inserts. For example, after the king throws the boy and Puss down the castle stairs, the boy asks the injured cat, "What's The Matter[,] Miss Your Step?" The cat responds, "No——I Hit 'Em All."

Though the studio's production capabilities were evolving, having expenses without income was taking a toll. Around this time, Red wrote to his mother, Margaret, in Moline, Illinois, that "It will take another five thousand to put the place over [and] an additional fifty or hundred thousand to put in a real production plant next spring. We originally capitalized only enough to get out four pictures of our series. Our fifth is nearly done." He added, "I am going to sit tight. I have the greatest opportunity I have ever had and I'm in for everything but my false teeth."

But the giddy atmosphere that must have existed at Laugh-O-gram from mid-September, when Leslie landed the Pictorial deal, through early October, when the staff back in Kansas City continued to make progress on the cartoons, quickly gave way to the reality that the company was out of money—and still well over a year away from receiving the $11,000 from Pictorial. It must have finally been clear to the young artists that the terms of the deal did not allow for income to the company, even though it continued to incur operating expenses such as production costs and salaries.

Rudy recalled that "Walt and I and a couple of the guys were still working for practically nothing for a long time." Walt Pfeiffer called the situation a "real challenge," and Red wrote his mother on October 16—just one week after his letter extolling the opportunity at Laugh-O-gram—that although Laugh-O-gram was "turning out some real pictures," the "company is worse than broke. We are about two thousand in the hole and going in about four hundred more each week. . . . We have the business in sight and orders to put this place over, but we lack the ready cash. . . . I am going to try and sell my stock—loan the money to the company [and] possibly quit and get me something more sure."

Perhaps because of the disastrous terms of the Pictorial agreement he negotiated, Leslie Mace quit Laugh-O-gram Films in mid-October, within a few weeks of returning from New York. On October 16 Leslie assigned to Dr. Cowles Leslie's claim against the company for salary due in the amount of $511.84. Dr. Cowles, in turn, paid Leslie his back pay plus interest. Dr. Cowles later transferred Leslie's claim to his wife, Minnie Cowles, who, according to her daughter-in-law, while not in charge of her husband's business affairs, was "by Doctor's side in everything he did."

Walt pivoted quickly and decided that the company would have to diversify if it were to stay in business. Walt got the *Kansas City Star* to help promote his latest idea, and the October 29 edition of the paper included an article titled "Recording The Baby's Life In Films," which described the newest "feature" of Laugh-O-gram Films: "photographing youngsters." The Company was in the "regular business of making animated cartoons," but was adding this service for the "admiring parent wishing to preserve the native graces of his progeny's actions[.]" Such parents should contact "'Red Lyon,' cinematographer, and 'Walt' Disney, president of the corporation and head cartoonist for the animated cartoons." Red would work the camera and "crank[] furiously for awhile, . . . wait[ing] with patience for the baby to 'look natural.'" The article suggested photographing "such momentous occasions as the first tooth, the first walk, the first word, birthdays and parties," and that such filming could be continued at limitless intervals.

The service included "projector service"—three showings at "the home" for each hundred feet of film. "In the future, projectors will be as common as phonographs are now," Red is quoted as saying, "and there will be no need to furnish private showings, as everyone will have one in his own home." The article began with a description of an imagined father-son argument in 1950, during which a father responds to the challenge about his own boyhood behavior by removing from a safe a reel of two thousand feet of film that "properly convinced" the "crestfallen" son of his father's perfection as a child. "[G]ad," the article concluded, "what a weapon!" (despite the fact that the films required "hours of waiting" to catch the child acting properly). The article suggested other purposes—convincing a suitor to "say the fateful words," recalling how you used to look once you "are old and gray," and the "historical importance . . . . of an embryo national [chief] executive."

Rudy, who was hired to help Walt animate, did not see an inconsistency in Walt's turn towards live-action filming. "[H]e had an idea," said Rudy years later. "[I]n fact he wanted to be more a live-action director like D. W. Griffith." In addition, recalled Rudy, Walt still had the acting bug: "Walt always wanted to be an actor, . . . more than he ever wanted to be a cartoonist; he wanted to be an actor and then a live-action director." Walt "wore puttees like DeMille and a cloth hat like D. W. Griffith used to wear. I think he really would have liked to have been in live pictures, but cartoons sort of overwhelmed him."

Perhaps Walt got the idea to start "photographing youngsters" from his proximity to the LeMorris Studio, which was initially located in Suite 206 of the McConahy Building but after a year moved two doors down to Suite 210. Photographers Lydia E. Morris and Peter Feldkamp ran the studio, and Walt had befriended one of their young portrait photographers, twenty-eight-year-old Siroon "Baron" Missakian.

Baron, of Armenian descent, was born in Turkey, immigrated to the United States in 1914 and settled in Kansas City the year before Walt formed Laugh-O-gram Films. A talented singer and photographer, Baron had been an apprentice to the official photographer of the Ottoman Empire. While performing with a boys' choir in Turkey, an American traveler heard him sing and was impressed enough that he offered to sponsor Baron by bringing him back to Boston to study opera.

Baron eventually quit performing once he concluded he was not tall enough to play leading roles. He served in the Army during World War I and sang for Liberty Bond campaigns. He then focused on photography and between 1917 and 1921 worked for White Studios and Bachrach & Chickering in Boston; a studio in Providence, Rhode Island; and the Moffett Studio in Chicago. Baron explained that he moved to Kansas City in 1921 "because he wanted to live in a small town and Kansas City was small then."

Baron sometimes photographed Walt and his Laugh-O-gram colleagues— he shot them at the lion statute in Swope Park, for example. Baron also made an interior portrait of Walt when Walt still professed to have acting aspirations. In that photograph, Walt wears a T-shirt and blazer, and the ends of his long combed-back hair fall slightly toward his temples as he assumes a brooding demeanor.

Ironically, as Laugh-O-gram's financial situation was dwindling in the fall of 1922, Walt kept spending on supplies and new employees. He bought cardboard imprints and twenty sheets of cels from Alexander Printing, eleven deliveries of office supplies from Franz Wurm Hardware, two hundred sheets of cels from E. I. du Pont de Nemours & Company, Inc., and made a purchase from the Kansas City Paper House. Additionally, three new employees joined the Laugh-O-gram staff.

The most noteworthy of the new hires was Ubbe Iwwerks, who finally quit his job at Film Ad and started at Laugh-O-gram on Saturday, November 4. Ubbe was hired to "perform work, labor and services in the drawing, etching, printing and manufacture of diagramatic or cartoon moving picture films and prints . . . [for] the sum of $50.00 per week[.]" By 1922, when Walt incorporated Laugh-O-gram Films, Ubbe had moved back in with his mother. Ubbe's granddaughter has written that Ubbe was hesitant to join Laugh-O-gram at its inception because it meant giving up the Film Ad salary that supported his mother and him. "Had it not been for his financial commitments to his mother," she wrote, "he would have preferred to join Walt [when Laugh-O-gram was formed], but this time he had to be sure[, so he stayed at] the Film Ad Service, where a steady income was assured."

Ubbe's granddaughter reasoned that, "The news of [the Pictorial] distribution was all Ubbe needed to be convinced that Laugh-O-gram Films, Inc. was finally on solid ground," yet by November 1922, Laugh-O-gram was on far shakier financial ground than it had been when the Pictorial deal was signed two short months earlier. Whatever Ubbe's reasons for joining Laugh-O-gram when its outlook seemed bleak, Walt's reasons for wanting him on board were clear to Rudy. Ubbe, said Rudy, "was really a lettering man. He didn't do much animation to start with, but he'd do all the titles. You know, in any picture you'd have the spoken titles all the way through. He was a hell of a good lettering man—always with a brush. . . . Yes, he did everything with a brush. He didn't animate with a brush, but he could have. That is where he got that beautiful swing that he had; he was great with a brush."

On November 11, Nadine Simpson, who had helped Walt, Rudy, and Hugh obtain and study other cartoons using her contacts at the Film Exchange, was hired as a "[s]tenographer-bookkeeper. That's what they called them in those days. Now they call them secretaries. But in those days they were stenos and secretaries.... [I was paid] $25 a week. That was good money though in those days. I mean for that time it wasn't bad." Nadine thought that Suite 218 was "very nice," and her office was "like a little reception room." Near Nadine, on the other side of a partition, was "Walt's drawing board. And we could see him sitting there at the drawing board all day, drawing." She also worked near "Mr. Kloepper [who] would say 'this space here was mine,'" and sat in an office that was not very wide.

One week after Nadine joined the company, Walt hired his second female employee. On November 19, twenty-year-old Aletha Reynolds was hired as an artist at a salary of $12 per week. Aletha was raised in Kansas City and lived with her father (a machinist with the Gille Manufacturing Company), her mother, and younger sister. She was still in school the year before Walt hired her. At Laugh-O-gram, she was brought in to do "general artwork ... including the inking in of films and the making of tracings, sketches and drawings of scenes[.]"

The staff most likely completed one of the last of the *Laugh-O-gram* fairy tales, *Cinderella*, during this time. (The studio also made a seventh reel called *Jack, the Giant Killer*; perhaps, in the end, Walt decided to exclude *Little Red Riding Hood* from the six shorts he agreed to make for Pictorial. *Giant Killer* apparently included an opening sequence in which a boy brags to a girl, followed by a segment showing how he and his cat destroyed four giants and rescued a girl imprisoned in a cage.) Like *Puss in Boots*, *Cinderella* opens with the *Laugh-O-gram* logo. The title card states that the production is "by Walt. Disney" and is "produced by a Laugh-O-gram Process."

The story begins with Cinderella washing dishes as a prince and his dog go bear hunting. The prince later decides to host a ball at the King's Palace, on "Tuesday Friday the 13th." After her stepsisters leave for the ball without her, Cinderella is visited by her Fairy Godmother, who provides her a gown and her cat a car. Cinderella is driven to the ball, dances with the prince, and leaves a shoe behind when she rushes out at midnight, when the "Clothes Will Change To Rags." The prince eventually locates Cinderella, and his dog romances Cinderella's cat. A final gag scene after the obligatory "And they lived happily ever after" title card shows Cinderella throwing a number of rolling pins at her prince.

Once again, some familiar Laugh-O-gram gags are employed in *Cinderella*. For example, Cinderella tosses the washed dishes to her cat who catches them with her tail before drying and throwing them into the cabinet. One of several dancing bears removes his tail and replaces it. The crowd at the ball creates a stampede when the butler announces dinner is ready. The prince uses a magnifying glass to track Cinderella's footprints, but the prints lead to a duck. Other gags include a scene in which the fat stepsister reads a book called "Eat And Grow Thin," while the thin sister reads "Beauty Secrets."

*Cinderella*'s ball scene is an example of how far Walt's cartoons had progressed since *Little Red Riding Hood* was animated about a year earlier. *Little Red Riding Hood* featured stark black and white characters against simple backgrounds. Even by *The Four Musicians of Bremen*, the animators incorporated more developed backgrounds and shadings of grey. In *Puss in Boots*, they tackled more complex scenes, such as the theater scene, where an orchestra plays beneath the Valentino movie—and the arena scene, which features crowds of people reacting to the bullfight. The ball scene in *Cinderella* is even more stylized: it features a tiled floor, dancers in detailed clothes, and even a wall with sconces. When Cinderella flees the ball, the shading reflects the nighttime's darkness.

By the end of November 1922, Walt's production and salary costs took their toll, and Walt turned to Dr. Cowles for a loan. On Thanksgiving Day, Dr. Cowles lent $2,500 to Laugh-O-gram. Walt executed a note, agreeing to repay the money to Dr. Cowles' Linwood State Bank account within ninety days at 6 percent interest. Walt signed the note as "Walter E. Disney, President." Dr. Cowles endorsed the back of the note, "Pay to the order of M. L. Cowles," and signed it "Dr. J. V. Cowles."

As the end of 1922 loomed, Laugh-O-gram Films was, as Rudy, Max, and Walt Pfeiffer later agreed, "down to the last penny," and the payment deadline for the $11,000 owed to the company by Pictorial, January 1, 1924, was still over a year away. In late November or early December, an unexpected opportunity presented itself to Walt when he was asked to make a live-action educational film. Dr. Thomas B. McCrum, forty-six, a dentist with the Deaner Dental Institute in Kansas City, asked Walt to produce a film that Dr. McCrum could use to educate children about dental care. Dr. McCrum offered to pay $500 for the film, but Walt's dire financial straits prevented Walt from agreeing to meet with Dr. McCrum:

[O]ne night the doctor called [Walt] to say, "I've got the money. Come on over and we'll set the deal." "I can't," [Walt] told him. "Why not?" the doctor asked. "I haven't any shoes," [Walt] said. "They were falling apart. I left them at the shoemaker's shop downstairs and he won't let me have them until I dig up a dollar and a half." "I'll be right over," Dr. McCrum said.

He paid the shoemaker, took [Walt] back to his office, and together they worked out an agreement to make the film he had in mind.

Rudy went with Walt and Dr. McCrum to the Benton School, the elementary school that Walt had attended, to get the school's permission to cast and film the movie there. Rudy recalled that Walt and Dr. McCrum "talked to the principal of the school. Dr. McCrum was a pretty well-known dentist there, and with his influence and Walt's gift for gab, they talked to the principal of the school. . . . [who agreed to] let Walt come out and interview children for this Dr. McCrum film[.]" Benton faculty members then preselected students as candidates for roles in the film, titled *Tommy Tucker's Tooth*. The story focused on Jimmie, a boy with bad dental hygiene, and Tommy, a dentist's dream patient. While the final film was mostly a live-action production, Walt decided to insert animated sequences, which could more easily show aspects of dental hygiene, such as how plaque affects a tooth's health.

Based on the faculty's recommendations, Walt interviewed what Rudy thought were "quite a few children" for the few roles in the film. Walt ultimately selected John "Jack" Records, eleven, a sixth grader, to play the part of Jimmie. Jack Records recalled that, even though "[t]here was no fooling around" with Walt, "we all liked him immediately."

For a few weeks in December 1922, while Rudy remained at the office and shot the still work on which the animated dental hygiene sequences would be based, Walt and his cameraman for the project, Walt Pfeiffer, another Benton alumnus, filmed the live-action sequences at the school. Because classes were still in session, filming was possible only a few days during the week. Jack Records remembered that "[e]verything went smoothly due to his easy way of directing us," even though Walt did not provide the children with their lines ahead of time:

> I don't recall any script—if he had a script, I didn't see it—but he always knew exactly what he wanted us to do. And he would act things out. I can't think of any specifics, but I do have a very strong recollection of how organized and prepared he was. It was all very informal—I mean, he liked children, it was obvious, and he knew how to handle us. I was impressed with that too, because the way he did it, why, it was fun.

*Tommy Tucker's Tooth* is a ten-minute, thirty-two-second educational film with live action and animation. The title card states that the story was "by Thos. B. McCrum, D.D.S., Kansas City, Mo." The film centers around a woman telling several children a story, "one [they] should never forget." Schoolmates Tommy

Tucker and Jimmie Jones are seen walking together to Benton School, but the children soon learn that, while Tommy had good health habits, Jimmie was "very careless" and "thought brushing teeth was only for girls."

The woman warns the children about brushing, to avoid cavities, experience better overall health, and be "better looking." Jimmie has not taken these lessons to heart, and when he and Tommy see a "Boy Wanted" sign, Tommy gets the job "[b]ecause Tommy's neat appearance and good teeth show that he takes pride in himself." Jimmie relents and gets an appointment with a dentist. He is subsequently hired by the employer who gave Tommy a job. The film concludes with a tutorial on brushing.

The surviving copy of *Tommy Tucker's Tooth* does not include the Laugh-O-gram name in the opening or closing credits, but its use of certain devices—animated alien-like creatures hacking at decaying teeth with pick-axes and a title card with a clock with wings that flies by over the caption "As the time flies" (also used in *Puss in Boots*)—makes the film recognizable as a Laugh-O-gram production.

After filming was completed, Walt invited Jack Records to visit Laugh-O-gram Films, where Jack saw "two men . . . at work on the animation over the big round glass drawing table lighted from beneath." Walt showed Jack his office and "gave me a substantial reward (either a five or ten dollar bill) for my cooperation." Walt, however, only made about $50 from *Tommy Tucker's Tooth*, and Laugh-O-gram's financial situation continued to deteriorate in the new year.

On Thursday, January 4, 1923, Laugh-O-gram Films was sued by E. M. McConahy for $384 in back rent. A hearing was scheduled before a justice of the peace for later that month. Meanwhile, Walt continued to fall behind in making the company's payroll, and a few of the studio's original staff members departed. Walt stopped paying Walt Pfeiffer, who was already owed almost $100 in back pay. By the middle of the month, Lorey Tague, who by then earned $80 per month but hadn't been paid since before Christmas, quit. Around this time, Red Lyon moved to California. Bills that Walt was never able to pay continued to arrive, including a subscription and advertising invoice from *Exhibitor Trade Review* and bills for the company's final purchases from Franz Wurm Hardware and du Pont (from which Laugh-O-gram bought another two hundred sheets of cels).

On Friday, January 26, Justice of the Peace W. J. Cairns ordered Laugh-O-gram to pay McConahy $384 plus $12.90 in interest, fees, and costs. It is unclear whether E. M. McConahy, who does not appear in city directories for the early 1920s and presumably lived somewhere outside the Kansas City metropolitan area, attended the hearing. Regardless, he continued to place tenants in his relatively new building in 1923, adding Mrs. M. F. Wood, a dress-maker, in Suite

202, and Mrs. Paul G. Brauer's beauty parlor in Suite 214. Walt turned to the Cowleses for help in paying the court's judgment. Minnie Cowles later claimed her husband paid the judgment at the "special instance [*sic*] and request" of Walt's company.

According to the Cowleses' daughter-in-law, "The Doctor" and Minnie continued to be supportive of Walt, frequently bringing sandwiches for the staff in the evening (although Rudy never remembered seeing "Doc" Cowles at the studio). The Cowles' son, John Jr., recalled that his parents even let "Walt live[] with us for a while in Kansas City." (He also lived in an apartment at 1325 Linwood Boulevard and by 1923 had an apartment at 3415 Charlotte.) Walt felt Dr. Cowles "showed more tenacity than the other investors. Once in a while [Cowles] told [him], 'Stay with it, Diz. Here's another few dollars. I hope it'll get you by for a little while.'"

The sandwiches provided by the Cowleses must have been especially appreciated since the staff was being paid sporadically, if at all, and therefore those who lived on their own had little money for food. Max recalled that "Things were really tough back then." He said, "We didn't ever have three square meals a day. My mom used to mail us a cake once in awhile and that was really something." Jack Kloepper recounted

> One day, when Walt and I went down to Dr. Cowles' office, on Grant Avenue in Kansas City at that time, to pick up the Friday payroll, we left Dr. Cowles' office and headed back to the studio on 31st and as we got to an intersection and just as we were ready to step off the curb, I think we both looked down at the same time and here was a dollar bill lying in the gutter. I think we both made a grab for it, but I got the dollar bill. And I held it up and I said, "Walt, we're going to have lunch." And we did, on the dollar bill. Because at that time I question whether we had a dollar between us.

An often-repeated anecdote told how Walt and his staff ate on credit at Jerry Raggos and Louis Katsis' Forest Inn Café on the first floor of the McConahy Building:

> When [Walt's] restaurant bill climbed past sixty dollars, [Jerry] came up to see him. "Walter," he said, "believe me, I'd give you unlimited credit, but my partner says fun's fun and we've got to cut you off." "All right, Jerry," [Walt] said. "I understand." ... [When Jerry later found Walt eating picnic leftovers of beans and bread from Baron's studio,] "Walt," he said, "I don't care what Louie says. You come down to our place and get something to eat."

Walt recounted this period as

> probably the blackest time of my life. I really knew what hardship and
> hunger were like. I remember a couple of Greeks who ran a restaurant
> below my office gave me credit to run up the food bills for a time, but
> even they grew hard-hearted in the end, and though they never really let
> me starve, they always made sure I got the cheapest food in the house and
> fed me on leftovers. It was a pretty lonely and miserable time of my life.

Nadine, like Jerry Raggos (who managed the restaurant and who Nadine
remembered as "a very nice little fellow, small[,]" with good food), also made
sure Walt didn't starve. Once Raggos stopped extending credit, Nadine recalled,
"I said, 'Why don't you tell him that I will type his menus for him in exchange
for your meals.'" Walt did so, and Raggos agreed; Nadine typed his menus and
Walt and "the boys" had their meals "down there at . . . Jerry's Café, on the first
floor." Hugh thought that Louie Katsis "was the world's greatest pie-maker; he
could make pies better than most good housewives."

One time, Nadine helped feed Walt, Rudy, and other staffers by giving them
tickets for her church's ice cream social:

> This is [at] the Annunciation Church at Lynwood [sic] and Benton. They
> had an ice cream social there . . . when the boys were starving: Rudolf,
> and Walt and them. And I gave them two dollars worth of tickets, because
> that's where I went to church. They had this ice cream social. They gave
> out tickets for prizes. I want you to know that they won a ham and all of
> the groceries. I think Monsignor Tierney must have just fixed that up so
> they could win. That's where they really struck it rich.

Nadine found Walt—although full of "drive and ambition"—was "always a very
humble, very unassuming, very pleasant person." She "never heard him say a
cross word" while working for him.

Walt urged Nadine to call on Baron at the photography studio down the
hall. Nadine finally "met Baron through Walt. He kept telling me to go to a good
young photographer he knew and have my portrait made. I said I didn't want
to and it was a long time before I finally went." Nadine and Baron eventually
began to date, and that enabled her to witness how Baron, too, took Walt under
his wing. "They were both very poor then," she said. "Baron used to buy a can
of pork and beans—they cost 10 cents then—and a loaf of bread for 5 cents and
he would share it with Walt. And that was about the only meal they had all day."
Roy's girlfriend, Edna Francis, would also look out for Walt. Edna invited Walt

to dinner on occasion, but he would get so involved with work that he would be a few hours late.

Edna was born in Kansas on January 1, 1890, making her three and one-half years older than Roy and twelve years older than Walt. She grew up near the Disneys in Kansas City. By the time Walt opened Kaycee Studios, the Francis family lived at 3025 Agnes Street, one block west of the Disney house on Bellefontaine. Edna lived with her widowed mother, Lettie, and her brothers, Edward and Bryan. Edna was a clerk with the Travelers Insurance Company. Edward was a bookkeeper at Kornfalfa Feed Milling Company, and Bryan was a clerk.

Edna and Roy met through Edna's other brother, Mitchell, who had been in the Navy with Roy and later worked with him at the First National Bank in Kansas City. Mitch used to play horseshoes in the backyard of the Disney home with Roy and his brother, Herb. "My brother brought Roy home," Edna said, "and they took my sister and me to a dance. Roy had only two dance lessons and he wasn't very good."

Edna met Walt not long after she and Roy started "going together[,]" several years before Walt went to Europe. Edna and Roy had played tennis and "stopped at the drugstore to get a soda." Walt came to the drugstore looking for Roy because Walt "wanted a quarter or a half dollar or something[.]" Edna found her future brother-in-law "a very cute" thirteen-year-old: "So good-looking: he had such big brown eyes, and [was] so interested in what he was doing." Edna recalled that Roy gave Walt the money: "Roy was always giving it to him, when he had it." Roy and Edna were going to marry in 1920, but Roy got sick with tuberculosis.

By the time Walt started Laugh-O-gram Films, Roy was out west, being treated for his condition in hospitals in Santa Fe, New Mexico, and the Sawtelle section of Los Angeles. Edna recalled how "Walt used to come out to our house. He was having a kind of struggle, financially, and when he'd get hungry he'd come over. We'd feed him a good meal and he'd talk until almost midnight about cartoon pictures, mostly, and things he wanted to do." Roy continued to support Walt from afar; Roy would send Walt blank checks, and write, "Kid, I have a hunch you could use a little dough so I'm enclosing a blank check. Fill it out for any amount you need—up to thirty dollars." Walt later said that he would fill such checks out for the full amount.

It is unclear exactly when Walt learned that Pictorial had gone out of business and that Laugh-O-gram Films would never receive the $11,000 that Pictorial owed it. Walt told a reporter that Pictorial, "soon after making the deal, went broke." He explained to another reporter that, "Immediately after the deal was made, the Pictorial club went broke[.]" Nadine's recollection was that once

Walt discovered that the Pictorial contract was "worthless," "[t]hen Dr. Cowles wouldn't put any more money into the business."

Dr. Cowles continued backing Walt in February of 1923 (when he paid a $13.50 phone bill), but Walt might have suspected that Dr. Cowles was not optimistic about a financial recovery for Laugh-O-gram Films. By early February, Walt turned to a new investor, hardware store owner John Fredrick Schmeltz. Schmeltz, fifty-five, was a Kansan and the son of German immigrants. He married his wife Lizzie in 1896, settled in Kansas City by the turn of the century and earned a living operating a hardware truck. By 1919 he had opened his own hardware store at 2410 East 15th Street, two and one-half miles northeast of the studio.

It is not clear how Walt—who was a customer of Franz Wurm's hardware store until the previous month—knew Schmeltz, but on Friday, February 9, according to Schmeltz, Walt "appealed to [Schmeltz] for advances" for "the purpose of enabling [Laugh-O-gram Films] to go ahead and to tide it over until the money would come in on the contract with the Pictorial Films[.]" That same day, Schmeltz wrote a check to Briggs Supply Co. for $482.51, the cost of lamps purchased from Briggs by Laugh-O-gram. It was the first of a number of loans and payments Schmeltz would make on Laugh-O-gram's behalf. In the end, Schmeltz would invest almost $2,500 in Laugh-O-gram. Although he paid the Briggs bill, however, Schmeltz was "unwilling" to advance Walt money without security.

On February 13, Schmeltz advanced the company $23.50 and paid a 75-cent "Express Item" bill in return for a note and mortgage from Laugh-O-gram for the amount of those expenses plus the amount of the Briggs lamp bill. The $506.76 mortgage was a Chattel Mortgage executed by Walter E. Disney, President, and A. H. Kloepper, Secretary, conveying to Schmeltz a mortgage on three "Perkins Hi-Power lamp moving picture machine[s]" with stands, and one Cooper-Hewitt tube. The accompanying note required repayment within six months at 6 percent interest. Walt approved this transaction without the authority of the Board of Directors. If the mortgage wasn't a sign that Walt's financial situation was getting desperate, another development was: by month's end, Walt stopped drawing a salary.

While Walt was working with Fred Schmeltz on the business front, he pivoted once again on the creative front, continuing Laugh-O-gram's expansion into other genres. Walt decided to release a series combining "animated cartoons and spicy jokes" and as early as February 10 was corresponding about it with a distributor, Inter-Ocean, as he would soon do with Universal and Commercial Traders Cinema Corporation. This series was not entirely new—it was a reworking of some of the *Lafflets* produced by Walt and Fred Harman at

Kaycee Studios. Walt had Aletha Reynolds provide "editorial work in the collection of squibbs reproduced . . . under the head or title of 'Lafflets,'" and the result was a number of new and recycled shorts, including *Golf in Slow Motion*, *Reuben's Big Day*, *The Woodland Potter*, *A Pirate for a Day*, *Descha's Tryst With The Moon*, *Aesthetic Camping*, *Rescued*, and *A Star Pitcher*.

Rudy remembered making two or three *Lafflets*, and that "a cat and a dog would crack a joke—it was all silent, of course—and then kill themselves laughing at it." Rudy recalled that he shot some of the new *Lafflets*, sometimes using matchstick animation, and that "Ub[be] was in one of them[:]"

> [Ubbe] went in and made a model of Warren G. Harding. It was sort of a takeoff on [Harding], and he was smoking a cigarette . . . . You made the model. After the model was finished, he smoked a cigarette. He had a cigarette in his mouth, and we blew the smoke with a pipe, that was shot full crank. Now what happened: the model was made, complete. Then he walked in backwards; everything was shot in reverse. He walked in backwards, but actually, when you ran it, he was walking away. He walked in to the clay model, turned around and started just really throwing this clay. I think we did a slow crank on that [to speed up the action on screen]. When it was over, we cut to the close-ups with the smoke coming out and whatnot. After that was done, he just had the pile of clay and he just walked backwards off the stage. So in reverse, the whole thing was that he walked in, he dumped the thing, set it up like that, and, when he was finished, turned around and walked off. . . . The cigarette was also done on a slow crank, but when he winked his eye or something like that, that was done in stop motion, on the model itself. Ub[be] was the artist on that.

Rudy also recalled that the *Lafflets* featured "a character with a music box crank. He would crank the jokes, and they would come out with a laugh."

Jack Kloepper sent a sample *Lafflets* reel to Universal in March, writing, "You will note that two of these reels are cartoon material and the other is clay modeling. In the series we will also introduce cartoons and live characters acting together in some productions. This will give you three separate and distinct types which can be released alternately. We are going to make arrangements for distribution for this series very soon." The following week, Jack wrote to Universal, "[W]ithin a very short time we will have several of these subjects available. [They] will be ideal to link with a screen magazine or any other short reel." While Universal and Commercial Traders Cinema Corporation liked the *Lafflets*, a distribution deal never came to fruition with either.

On Saint Patrick's Day, Saturday, March 17, according to a document executed by Walt, Rudy, and Dr. Cowles three months later, Walt held a stockholders meeting for which notice was "waived by the unanimous consent of majority of all the stockholders present[.]" The purpose of the meeting was a recapitalization of Laugh-O-gram stock, which was the latest attempt to prop up the ailing company. At the meeting, Walt was chosen to be the Chairman of the restructured company, and Rudy the Secretary. The proposal to raise the capital stock from $15,000 to $50,000 was passed. As a result of the restructuring, 1,000 shares worth $50 were to be issued, with Walt and Dr. Cowles each owning 350 shares.

The resulting "Statement of Increase of Capital Stock of Laugh-O-Gram Films, Inc." states that Laugh-O-gram had $20,000 in assets, $8,000 in liabilities, and that over half of the capital stock increase was paid in "money . . . [that] is in the hands of a Board of Directors . . . [or] in property." Elsewhere, the Statement lists $17,600 worth of Laugh-O-gram assets, including the Pictorial contract (worth $11,100), *The Musicians* cartoon ($2,000), *Lafflets* ($1,500), cash from Dr. Cowles ($2,000), and "services rendered" by Walt ($1,000).

A short time later, Walt decided to try to "crack the market" with a new series that was a variation of the popular *Out of the Inkwell* cartoons made famous by Max Fleischer. The *Inkwell* series featured an animated character in a live-action world; Walt's idea was to have a live-action character in an animated world. He believed he found just the young starlet who could help him pull it off in Virginia Davis.

Four-year-old Virginia was the daughter of Mr. and Mrs. Thomas Jefferson "Jeff" Davis of Kansas City. Thomas Davis was a traveling furniture salesman, who, as Virginia explained, "would be gone for a couple of weeks at a time. Mother had time on her hands," and sent Virginia to dancing school:

> [M]y mother took me to Georgia Brown Dramatic School when I was very young. And I was an only child, and that's sort of what she did; I was her life. She'd had a hard time having me and finally got me and, you know, she really did everything for me. But anyway, she took me to this Georgia Brown Dramatic School. I had ended up dancing. I was on my toes when I was three.

Virginia's hair was full of "long curls and I think someone had said I should get into modeling or something." Virginia began to model for ads that "they used to flash . . . on the screen . . . . in between motion pictures," including an ad for Warneker's Bread. The bread ad was "just a picture of me, smiling and looking like, 'Oh, yum yum!' and eating this piece of Warneker's Bread with a lot of jam on it."

As Virginia learned later, Walt saw one of her ads in a theater and realized he found the star for his new series. Walt found out Virginia's name and "called my mother and told her that he had this idea, and he came and talked to her." Virginia heard that Walt "already had this idea of doing a film about a little girl named Alice who goes to cartoon land" and "explained to my mother that he had this idea and he wanted to make a test film, and he would have to take it around to see if he could sell the idea."

Her mother, according to Virginia, "liked [Walt] a lot. He was quite charming." Mrs. Davis decided, "'Sure, we'll shoot a film and see what happens.'" Walt began negotiating with the Davises, and offered Virginia 5 percent of the receipts that *Alice* cartoons generated for Laugh-O-gram. The Davises accepted, and a contract was signed on Thursday, April 13, 1923.

As Walt was negotiating with the Davises, the studio still struggled. Aletha Reynolds quit her job on April 8 and was still owed $200 in back pay. A few days later, with the company "still unable to meet and pay [its] expenses," Walt again turned to Fred Schmeltz for help. Schmeltz wrote Laugh-O-gram a check in the amount of $46.55 on April 11. By the end of the month, Walt owed Max $170.50 in back pay.

Walt forged ahead with the reel he called *Alice's Wonderland* (both Hugh and Rudy recalled that it was initially called *Alice in Cartoonland*), filming the live-action scenes at the Laugh-O-gram studios and at the Davises' home. In the studio scenes, Walt, Rudy, Hugh, Ubbe, and two other men (possibly Alex and Otto) appear on-screen with Virginia, who wore her mother's favorite tam hat in these scenes. The bedroom scene, in which Mrs. Davis's sister, Louise, plays Alice's mother, was filmed in Virginia's bedroom. Walt directed Virginia by saying, "'do this' and 'do that'—of course, with no sound, he could be giving me directions at the same time [he was filming], and then he drew in everything [later]."

The remaining scenes would take place in Cartoonland, in which everything on the screen besides Virginia was animated. Rudy recalled, "We built the sets; they were actually just big sheets of 4 x 8 compo board. We cut out the train thing, and then painted a line around it." Hugh confirmed that the sets "were nothing more than white [backdrops] on which cartoon scenes were painted; a cartoon train, with an actual doorway in it, from which Alice, behind the flat [scenery], stepped out onto the [train] platform." For those scenes, Walt directed Virginia by "telling stories. All the work was done in pantomime. He'd say, 'A bear's chasing you!' Or 'Look sad—you've just been hit over the head.' He'd tell me these things and then I'd react."

As with *Tommy Tucker*, Walt dispensed with rehearsals. He would simply call out directions such as, "'Look frightened,' or 'Sit down and pretend this or that.'... Luckily I had a good imagination and took direction well so I was able to do what he wanted me to do." The twenty-one-year-old Walt struck the right demeanor with his four-year-old star, and she was under his spell. "Did you ever have a favorite uncle, someone you idolized who would . . . just light up your day?" she said. "That's where I was with Walt."

As 1923 wore on, Walt could no longer afford the $3 rent for his apartment. Nadine remembered that his "landlady kicked him out," and he moved into the studio, where he slept on a sofa chair in his drawing room. Jack recalled that Walt "slept there for quite some time in order to save money." Once a week, he bathed at Union Station, which was located west of the city's hospital district. He would walk to the station and pay a dime for soap and a towel and a bath.

Although the exact production dates are not known, around the time Walt was working on *Alice*, he earned some additional income when Carl Stalling, a local musician and theater organist, asked him to produce a sing-a-long film or, as Walt named it, a "Song-O-Reel." Stalling, thirty-one, was from Independence, Missouri. He attended the Kansas City Conservatory of Music and by the early 1920s was the musical director of the Isis Theatre at 31st Street and Troost Avenue, one block west of Walt's studio. Stalling explained that as musical director he "played the organ and had my own orchestra. This was music to accompany silent movies, and I played the whole afternoon and evening. When I wasn't at the organ, I'd be conducting, or playing piano and conducting. I had a pianist for a number of years, and then I just conducted." The organ that Stalling played at the theater was the $22,000 Hope Jones Organ, and in its newspaper ads, the Isis promoted the organ as well as Stalling, whom the Isis claimed was "Kansas City's Greatest 'Movie' Organist."

Stalling recalled meeting Walt when "Walt was making short commercials . . . and he'd have us run them for him." Rudy remembered that Carl knew Walt "because a couple of times in our . . . pictures with Walt, the [Laugh-O-gram] fairy tales, we would preview them at the Isis Theater, and Carl would play the organ for them. . . . We'd take a picture up [to the Isis] in the afternoon and run it for Carl a couple of times, so he could know what it was about, and then he'd play [the organ] for the preview." Later, Stalling asked Walt to work with him on a song film, in which "[t]he words would come on one at a time, with the music." The point of the song reel was to illustrate a song on film, and use the song lyrics as captions so that the movie theater audience could sing along as the organist played the melody.

The piece that Stalling hired Laugh-O-gram to work on was *Martha, Just a Plain Old-Fashioned Name*, a 1922 song by Joe L. Sanders of the Coon-Sanders Original Nighthawks Band. Stalling and Walt made an agreement with *Martha*'s publisher, the Jenkins Music Company of Kansas City, and Walt set out to write and cast a film based on the following lyrics:

[A] quaint old-fashioned girl that everybody knows,
Radiant as the poppy, lovely as the rose.
Martha, just a plain old-fashioned name like Mary or Molly or Rose.
She's just a plain old-fashioned girlie and everybody knows.

According to Rudy, Walt cast some models to appear in the film, and Ubbe played the male lead. Rudy said that "Walt was going to act in it," but Ubbe "finally played the disillusioned lover thinking back to this girl that he never did marry." Rudy recalled that he "shot it," with Walt directing, and that Laugh-O-gram "built the sets for that out in the alley at the back of the [McConahy] building." Nadine remembered that interior scenes were filmed inside the Laugh-O-gram offices. A photograph from a break in filming shows Ubbe in costume, dressed in a dinner jacket with grey powder in his hair, speaking with Jack on the sitting room set as Walt looks at the camera.

Some scenes were filmed on location, and Nadine also remembered that "Kansas City locations were chosen . . . and Walt and his crew roamed the city to find the proper atmosphere—homes, parks, wooded places in the suburbs, Troost Lake" and the "old Watts Mill"—"where Walt and the boys used to go so much." A photograph from the on-location filming—shot by Baron—establishes that Rudy and Walt Pfeiffer were part of the crew. (Red Lyon has been identified as the cameraman in this photograph, but he moved to California several months earlier; perhaps Alex manned the camera for *Martha*.) This photograph shows three women dressed in gowns on a wood-beam fence near a pasture and woods. Walt, sitting in a director's chair with "Laugh-O-gram Films Inc." on the back, wears a hat and holds a megaphone. Rudy, on a stool, and Walt Pfeiffer, on his knees, watch. A light reflector board and the movie camera are also labeled "Laugh-O-gram Films Inc."

Meanwhile, the production of *Alice's Wonderland* continued as the Laugh-O-gram crew began animating cartoon sequences. By the time the animation was begun, things were changing rapidly at Laugh-O-gram Films. Nadine, who was still owed $75.50, quit the company on Tuesday, May 1, recalling she had stayed with the company "[u]ntil they folded," although Laugh-O-gram continued to limp along after she left. Ubbe, who had a balance of unpaid salary of $1,003, left four days later, on May 5, and returned to his job at Film Ad. Said Hugh: Ubbe "quit . . . just for survival; he couldn't get along without money."

Walt continued to juggle the production of *Alice* around his collapsing company, and hoped that *Alice* would turn his fortunes around. On Monday, May 14, he wrote to Margaret J. Winkler, the New York distributor of the *Out of the Inkwell* and *Felix the Cat* series, and told her, with regard to *Alice's Wonderland*:

We have just discovered something new and clever in animated cartoons!

The first subject of this distinctly different series is now in production, and will require a few weeks more for completion. It is a new idea that will appeal to all classes, and is bound to be a winner, because it is a clever combination of live characters and cartoons, not like "Out of the Inkwell" or Earl Hurd's, but of an entirely different nature, using a cast of live child actors who carry on their action on cartoon scenes with cartoon characters.

These new subjects will be a full reel in length, and can be released at regular intervals of two weeks or a month.

However, before you go any further into the matter, we desire that you see some of our former work, so you may appreciate the quality of same. We ask that you get in touch with Mr. W. R. Kelley, of Pictorial Clubs Inc., 350 Madison Ave., New York City, and he will gladly screen several of our [Laugh-O-gram fairy tale] subjects for you. We will not try to explain or tell you any more about this new idea; instead, we will send you a print upon the completion of the first one, if you so desire.

At about that time, Walt sent the same type of letter to distributor Paul Cromelin of Inter-Ocean. Margaret Winkler responded two days later, writing, "I shall, indeed, be very pleased to have you send me a print of the new animated cartoon you are talking about." She also stated that, "If it is what you say, I shall be interested in contracting for a series of them."

Despite Margaret's prompt reply, Walt had to pull back, not only because he did not have a completed *Alice* to send her, but because his studio was continuing to fall apart. By May 16, the date of Margaret's reply letter, Walt owed Rudy $586.23 in back salary. Walt also owed Clifford J. Collingsworth $490.14 in back rent for the Laugh-O-gram offices in the McConahy Building. Collingsworth, who had been president and manager of the Great Northern Loan & Savings Company but by 1923 had become the president of Liberty Home Builders, must have purchased the building from McConahy earlier in the year, or otherwise came to have an interest in the Laugh-O-gram lease.

Sometime before May 19, Collingsworth locked Walt and his staff out of Suite 218 in the McConahy Building, and denied them the opportunity to remove their property and equipment from the office until the back rent was paid. Collingsworth went so far as to have a lien placed on Laugh-O-gram's movie equipment, office furniture, and other property. Walt turned to Fred Schmeltz for help, complaining that he could not rent other office space (needed to finish *Alice's Wonderland*) since Laugh-O-gram had no credit.

According to Schmeltz, when Laugh-O-gram "officers and officials[] again appealed to [him] for further [operating] funds," Schmeltz "refused and declined to advance any further sums or amounts whatsoever" unless Walt agreed to "secure the re-payment of said money with a further chattel mortgage upon all of [Laugh-O-gram's] property . . . and by an assignment of [the Pictorial contract.]" Walt acquiesced, but negotiated additional terms that would enable him, courtesy of Schmeltz, to rent new office space and secure the back pay he owed Nadine and Jack as well as the $2,500 Dr. Cowles lent Walt the previous November.

Pursuant to these negotiations, on Saturday, May 19, Schmeltz made a cash advance to Laugh-O-gram's bank account in the amount of $750 and agreed to pay Collingsworth the back rent on the McConahy lease. (With the funds Schmeltz advanced, Walt immediately paid Rudy and Max $15 each; neither employee was paid on the two previous paydays). Collingsworth then allowed Walt and his staff back into Suite 218 to remove their equipment and property, although Rudy remembered having "to move during the night [on two occasions] because we couldn't pay the rent." Schmeltz also guaranteed Laugh-O-gram's obligations under the new office lease that Walt had negotiated with his former Kaycee Studios landlord, Rudolph Peiser. On Tuesday, May 24, Walt signed a lease with Peiser to return to 3241 Troost Avenue, the second floor space above Peiser's Restaurant where Walt, Red, and Rudy had worked more than a year earlier when they were at Kaycee Studios. Rudy helped move Walt back into the office above Peiser's

On Tuesday, May 29, at a regular meeting of the Laugh-O-gram directors, the board authorized the execution of a mortgage and note to Schmeltz in the amount of $750. It also authorized the assignment to Schmeltz of the Pictorial contract. The meeting was recorded in the Laugh-O-gram minutes book. By Saturday, June 2, 1923, about one year after Walt left Rudolph Peiser's second floor office on Troost Avenue to start Laugh-O-gram Films in the McConahy Building, Walt returned to Peiser's building where, as "Walter E. Disney, President" of Laugh-O-gram, he executed a note and mortgage to Schmeltz in the amount of $750. The loan, plus 6 percent interest, was due on August 19, 1923.

The mortgage gave Schmeltz an interest in all Laugh-O-gram office furniture and movie equipment, including a roll top desk, stenographer's desk and chair, filing cabinet, coat rack, Cooper-Hewitt Lights and Reostadts, movie camera, tripod, and printer. Walt also, and allegedly "with the authority and order of the Board of Directors[,]" assigned the Pictorial contract to Schmeltz, in order to secure the re-payment to Fred Schmeltz of any and all indebtedness which the Laugh-O-Gram Films, Inc. now owes to him . . . and also to secure the payment of the sum of Five hundred forty-seven dollars ($547.00) . . . to A. H. Kloepper, also the sum of One hundred twenty-five dollars ($125.00) to Miss N. Simpson, also Twenty-five hundred dollars ($2500.00) to Mrs. M. L. Cowles[.]

The assignment was attested to by the latest Laugh-O-gram Secretary, C. E. Hamilton, who lived in the New Francis Hotel and oversaw a mineral water venture out of an office in the same building Dr. Cowles' medical office was located.

On June 4, Walt summoned Balthaser Electric to install "service and [a] box," run ground wires, and inspect the electrical system at the Peiser location; despite its financial and personnel setbacks, Laugh-O-gram had a film in production, and Walt and the others had to get back to work. Hugh recalled that he worked on *Alice* along with Walt, Rudy and others. Max remembered working on *Alice* in the Peiser space, "taking turns with Walt on the camera stand for a long session shooting a circus parade."

On June 18, Walt finally responded to Margaret Winkler's favorable letter of a month earlier, writing

Owing to the numerous delays and [setbacks] we have encountered in moving into our new studio, we will not be able to complete the first picture of our new series by the time we expected . . . . However, it will be finished very soon, and the writer expects to be in New York about the first of July with a print of same, and an outline of our future program.

Walt sent a similar letter that same date to Paul Cromelin of Inter-Ocean. Margaret wrote back a week later about meeting with Walt in New York, but neither the trip nor the meeting took place.

While June appears to have begun with a sense of a fresh start, within a few weeks, the lack of income dealt Laugh-O-gram additional blows. Walt must have seen them coming; on Friday, June 22, in what was likely a preemptive strike, Walt, Rudy, and Dr. Cowles signed the Statement of Increase of Capital Stock that had been drafted on March 17. Walt may have been referring to the recapitalization when he said in a speech decades later, "I tried my best to salvage something out of the company and to obtain new financing so I could remain in Kansas City, but I wasn't successful." As a result, Walt could not take advantage of Margaret Winkler's interest in *Alice*; on June 23, Margaret had written Walt, asking if his new cartoon "is completed yet as I am making my plans for next year's product. Also let me know how soon I could see a sample of this cartoon."

Walt's upbeat attitude made an impression on the members of his staff, even though, one by one, they realized that they were not going to be able to make a living working for Walt. Jack Kloepper recounted that

> [d]uring those lean times, I never once heard Walt say anything that would sound like defeat. He was always optimistic about his ability and about the value of his ideas and about the possibilities of cartoons in the entertainment field. Never once did I hear him express anything except determination to go ahead, because he believed in himself and he believed in what he was trying to accomplish.

The day after the recapitalization was Rudy's last at Laugh-O-gram. He felt that "[o]ur ideas were great, but we were in the wrong area. Kansas City wasn't the place for this kind of work." Walt owed Rudy $711.23 in back salary. One week later, on Saturday, June 30, Walt prepared Statements of Account for Walt Pfeiffer and Max, as he had previously done for Rudy. Laugh-O-gram still owed Walt Pfeiffer the same amount it owed him six months earlier, $96.50, and it owed Max $220.50. Max received his last pay, in the amount of $15, that same day, his last day at the studio.

In one of his final efforts to save Laugh-O-gram, Walt revived an idea he and Fred Harman had pursued early on at Kaycee Studios—that of a news series produced under the banner of a local paper—and decided to approach the *Kansas City Post* with a proposal. "I spent a number of weeks," he recalled, "working on a plan to make a weekly newsreel for the *Kansas City Post*[.]" He also completed *Alice's Wonderland*. Hugh recalled that he and Walt made it "almost all by ourselves. We had part of it done with Rudy and others working on it. . . . But then the [company] blew up and Walt and I finished it up completely by ourselves." Hugh said that his father "spoiled" him by continuing to send him money, which Hugh used during this period to support Walt and him at the Elsmere Hotel and its restaurant.

Rudy, however, recalled that he completed the film along with Walt and Hugh. The young filmmakers had to reshoot some scenes because hot weather caused the emulsion to run and the first negative was ruined. When they first saw the spotted negative, said Hugh, "It nearly killed us."

The completed *Alice's Wonderland* ran twelve minutes and twenty-five seconds. The surviving version does not include the *Laugh-O-gram* logo, but the opening credits state that, like *Cinderella, Alice* was "Produced by a Laugh-O-gram Process," with "Scenario and Direction" by Walt, photography by Ubbe and Rudy, and "Technical Direction" by Hugh and Max. The final opening credit sets up the live-action beginning and also introduces Walt's star: "Little Alice, chuck full of curiosity pays her first visit to a cartoon studio, [is] Played by Virginia Davis."

In the opening scene, Virginia, wearing her mother's tam but with plenty of curls showing nonetheless, opens the McConahy studio door, marked "Studio, Private," and peers in at Walt as he draws a doghouse on an easel. Walt's hair is slicked back and he wears a tie, white shirt, and dark vest that matches his trousers. Virginia comes in and watches as the easel drawings come to life (like in Walt's and Fred Harman's *The Little Artist* of nearly two years earlier): the Laugh-O-gram white dog keeps trying to enter the doghouse, but each time he does, a fight ensues, and he retreats. Finally, his nemesis follows him out of the doghouse and we see who has caused the commotion: the Laugh-O-gram black cat.

Walt and Virginia walk to another part of the office, where they see five animated black cats on a live-action Laugh-O-gram desk. Two of the cats dance on the desk (in between some office supplies and the telephone) while the other three play a sax, a violin, and a drum. In another room of the studio, three artists work while an animated mouse jousts with a live-action cat on a desktop. In this scene, the mouse, who stands on an easel on the desk, brandishes a sword and harasses the live-action cat until it jumps down from the desk.

In the background, the three artists continue to work. The middle of the three artists is Ubbe, who sits at an easel and paints. To the left is an older man with a moustache, probably Otto, who works at a desk. To the right is a young man, possibly Alex, in a cap and overalls. At the end of this scene, Hugh enters in from the left, walks behind the desk where the cat had been, speaks with Otto for a moment, and then turns and exits.

In the last of the office scenes, Hugh sits in front of an easel on which the animated dog and cat fight. On the wall behind the easel are a few framed pictures of cartoon characters, including one of the king from *Puss in Boots*. Hugh calls to people who are off-screen, and Ubbe, Otto, and Alex enter from the right and stand around the easel to watch the animated fight between the cat and dog. Rudy then enters from the right and joins the other four as they cheer and hoot while the animated dog and cat continue to fight. Hugh, still seated in front of the easel, waves a piece of cloth. Rudy, at left, uses a pocket watch to time the fight and, in place of a referee's bell, taps a mallet against a glass filled with pens.

A card possibly lettered by Ubbe before his departure from the studio marks the transitions to Alice's bedroom and sets the stage for the animated dream that comprises the remainder of the film. The card reads, "What Alice saw would make any little girl's heart flutter—so that night when the sandman came[. . .]" Alice's mother is then seen tucking her into bed in the scene filmed in Virginia's bedroom at the Davis home.

In the cartoon dream sequence in which everything except Alice is animated, Alice arrives by train in Cartoonland, where its citizens—animals such as an elephant, ostriches, giraffes, hippos, rabbits, and mice—welcome her with a band and a parade. Alice rides the elephant in the parade and then performs a dance while a band of five black cats plays music. Lions escape from the Cartoonland Zoo and chase Alice, and in a frequently used Disney gag, one lion removes its teeth and sharpens them before rejoining the chase. Alice eventually runs to a cliff and falls, as her mother wakes her and her dream ends.

◂ ◂ ◂

By Friday, July 6, Jack Kloepper quit the studio. That same day, he sued the company for the $499 in back salary the studio owed him. The next day a Kaw Township constable served Jack's summons on Laugh-O-gram, setting a hearing for 7 a.m. on July 26. When the constable arrived at Laugh-O-gram that Saturday, the only person present was Max, whose last paid workday was the previous week. Perhaps Max returned to the office to help Walt on a voluntary basis, or maybe he stayed on at Laugh-O-gram later than existing documents reflect. The constable served the summons on Max, "in the absence of the President [of Laugh-O-gram] and other chief officers[.]" Also on July 7, Schmeltz paid Rudolph Peiser $75 for Laugh-O-gram's July rent.

By then, Laugh-O-gram was in its last gasps. After a few weeks of talking to the *Kansas City Post* about a newsreel series, "that deal fell through, too," said Walt. "That seemed to wash up all the prospects in Kansas City," and forced Walt to do some soul-searching. He had hoped *Alice's Wonderland* would lead to a distribution contract that could save Laugh-O-gram, but the studio was collapsing and he had yet to fully complete *Alice*. The failure of Laugh-O-gram Films was a hard blow for the normally optimistic and resourceful twenty-one-year-old, who Hugh said was now "really disconsolate . . . just completely dejected." Walt had told Hugh, "I've got to get Laugh-[O]-grams started again." Hugh explained that Walt "felt he shouldn't let down Doc Cowles . . . [and] Schmeltz . . . and quite a few others."

Walt spent almost two and a half years trying everything he could think of to capitalize on the initial success of *Newman Laugh-O-Grams*. He attempted to parlay that first success into a series. A short time later, he started his first movie studio. At Kaycee Studios, he attempted to sell the *Kansas City Journal* on a film companion series, animate *The Little Artist*, market his and Fred Har-man's Film Ad experience to local movie theaters, use aerial filming to break into the news footage business, jumpstart his animation portfolio with the *Laf-flets* series, and, with Red's and Rudy's help, animate modern versions of the fairy tales *Little Red Riding Hood* and *The Four Musicians of Bremen*.

Later, at Laugh-O-gram, he sought to build a thriving business by selling a series of animated fairy tales, marketing home movies of children, producing an educational film, revising and remarketing the *Lafflet* series, experimenting with a mix of live action and animation through the proposed *Alice* series, pro-ducing a Song-O-Reel, and trying to again entice a local daily newspaper into a joint newsreel series. At one point, Walt even tried to sell a mail order course on animation. After all of these efforts, he now realized that there were no more avenues open to him—his efforts to make it as a film producer in Kansas City had failed.

Rudy recalled that Walt "was seriously considering going . . . to New York" to work on *Felix the Cat*. But, as Walt later explained, "I finally came to a great conclusion. I had missed the boat. I had got in[to the animated cartoon field] too late. Film cartooning had been going on for all of six or seven years." Walt shared his predicament with his brother, Roy, who agreed that his younger brother should leave Kansas City. Roy felt that, had his brother stayed in Kansas City

> Walt would have gotten mired down with the crooks [like Pictorial].
> That was his problem in Kansas City. He made some nice little pictures.
> They were sold . . . on a silly thing of a sixth-month trade acceptance. . . .
> It was stupid. So in six months time he delivered the pictures, and when
> the first one came due, the damn company went into bankruptcy. . . . So
> it was a pathetic, interesting little story. If Walt had gone on like that in
> life, he never would have gone anyplace. Because there are always slick-
> ers to take you.

Roy wrote Walt, "Kid I think you should get out of there. I don't think you can do any more for it." Roy suggested that Walt move to Los Angeles, pointing out that he could stay with their Uncle Robert, who left Kansas City and bought a home in Hollywood and who also encouraged Walt to move west. "My only hope," Walt concluded, "lay in live-action movies." Thus, Walt "finally turned my eyes to Hollywood, where I decided I would go and try to become a director."

Walt left for California to "take my chances in the movie game" in late July 1923, but he spent the two weeks before he left earning money to pay for his train ticket. He bought an "antiquated" movie camera and made films of babies to fund his trip. In one account, Walt explained that he purchased the camera with profits from the *Martha* Song-O-Reel. In another, he said he lacked the money to purchase the camera, so asked to try it out, and quickly made a baby film so he could return to the seller with money to conclude the purchase.

Walt claimed that he traded one of his hand-drawn cartoons for a haircut before dressing neatly and going door-to-door in a comfortable residential neighborhood of Kansas City, offering to film babies for $10 or $15. Walt remembered that his first customers were Dr. and Mrs. Leland Viley, who had him film their six-month-old daughter, Kay. The Vileys received two hundred feet of film of their infant, and other jobs followed. When Walt had enough money, he sold the camera to a "movie fan" for twice what Walt paid for it. "This," he recalled, "gave me a little extra money"—enough for a train ticket to California and $40 to spare.

There is no record of what day in late July was the date of Walt's departure. On Friday, July 20, and Monday, July 23, Schmeltz forwarded the company $50 and $25, respectively. Schmeltz later indicated that the first of these two checks was for "operating expenses," although it is not clear what expenses were paid (or even if Walt was present and was the one who decided what bills to pay). Perhaps Walt needed more travel money than he later recalled.

At 11:30 a.m. on July 26, after the failure of the appearance in court of any representative from Laugh-O-gram Films, the Kaw Township Justice of the Peace entered a judgment in favor of Jack Kloepper in the amount of $499 plus $14 in interest. The following day, Schmeltz wrote a check to Clifford Collingsworth in the amount of $367.61 "in payment of back rent" owed by Laugh-O-gram on the McConahy Building lease.

Walt did not dismantle the Laugh-O-gram Films offices above Peiser's Restaurant before he left town. According to Rudy, "the studio as such was still set up, he just left everything there." Walt, said Hugh, "put in a good word for me at the Film Ad, so I got a job there[.]" Rudy was not as lucky; he "went there to look for a job, [but] I never got to sit in the office."

Meanwhile, Walt simply "packed all my worldly goods in a pasteboard suitcase" and prepared to leave home "with that wonderful audacity of youth[.]" The night before his departure, Walt had dinner with Edna Francis. The next day, Walt's brother Herbert's mother-in-law gave Walt food for the trip, and her son drove Walt to Union Station, where he boarded the California Limited train to Hollywood.

Walt bought a first-class ticket and, with all the lower berths taken, rode west in an upper berth. He later described his mood on that "big day, the day I got on that Santa Fe, California Limited," saying that he was "just free and happy."

It was a hot day in August of 1923 when Walt, just twenty-two years old, arrived in Los Angeles. Years later, he told his daughter that, as he left Kansas City, he was sure that his hopes would be fulfilled in California. Perhaps the locale had changed, but the dream and his confidence in it had not. "Walt always said," recalled Max, "even back then [in Kansas City,] that he would make it big."

Walt in his Red Cross uniform, 1918 or 1919. This is how the sixteen- or seventeen-year-old Walt Disney looked the year before he embarked on his storied career.

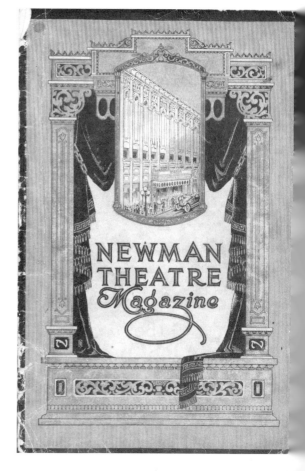

A *Newman Theatre Magazine* cover on which Walt worked as an apprentice for twenty-seven-year-old Lou Pesmen and twenty-four-year-old Bill Rubin at the Gray Advertising Company between October and December 1919. Frank L. Newman, twenty-nine, owned several theaters in Kansas City. The art apprenticeship at Gray Advertising was Walt's first job after his return from France.

The cover of the February 1920 edition of the *Leather Workers Journal*. Walt worked on this cover with his friend, eighteen-year-old Ubbe Iwwerks, with whom he started the Iwwerks-Disney commercial art agency in January 1920. Ubbe and Walt likely worked on this cover while their agency was located in an unused bathroom in the offices of the National Restaurant Association, located a block from the Gray Building. Walt landed the *Journal* job through John Pfeiffer, forty-nine, a neighbor and the father of Walt's schoolmate and friend, Walt Pfeiffer.

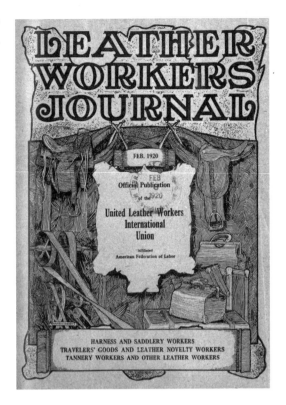

In February 1920, Walt was hired as an artist for the Kansas City Slide Company, which was renamed the Kansas City Film Ad Service and moved to 2449 Charlotte Street. This picture shows the Show Card and Title Men team at work at the Film Ad. Walt is in the back row, wearing a visor. Fred Harman, about nineteen, is to Walt's right. Walt's tormentor, forty-one-year-old "Art Boss" James MacLachlan, sits at the near end of the middle row, and Ubbe sits to MacLachlan's left. At Ubbe's left is MacLachlan's seventeen-year-old daughter, Marjorie.

Three young Kansas City swells employed at the Film Ad. Walt is in the middle. Ubbe is to Walt's right, and Fred is to Walt's left. Ubbe is probably twenty years old in this photograph, and the others are probably nineteen.

Walt's cartoonist logo, which he probably created in early 1921 when he began what he called his "home experimenting" in the garage behind his family's home at 3028 Bellefontaine Street, southeast of downtown Kansas City. Walt's address was crossed out when Walt opened a studio on Troost Avenue that year. Walt later used this logo in the *Newman Laugh-O-Grams* title card (March 1921) and a *Motion Picture News* ad for Laugh-O-gram Films, Inc. (July 1922).

Walt as seen in the *Newman Laugh-O-Grams*, which premiered at Frank Newman's Newman Theatre on Sunday, March 20, 1921. Walt's cartoonist logo appears over his right shoulder.

The *Newman Laugh-O-Gram* lightning sketch about Kansas City street potholes, made by Walt in early 1921. The hand and pen can be seen at the bottom of this photograph.

Walt, left, and Fred outside Kaycee Studios. Kaycee was located at 3241 Troost Avenue, a second-story office initially above the Standard Phonograph Company, 3239 Troost (and later above Peiser's Restaurant at that address). Prior to this location, Kaycee was in an office above a car barn located at 30th and Holmes, seven blocks from the Troost Avenue location, and Kaycee may have been located in another office before it moved to Troost. This photograph was probably taken in the second half of 1921.

Walt wearing a hat, with Fred Harman and their camera.

By the end of 1921, Fred Harman apparently left Kaycee Studios when twenty-eight-year-old Red Lyon, a former Film Ad colleague, was brought into the partnership. For six months, spanning from late 1921 to early 1922, Walt animated *Little Red Riding Hood*, a six-and-one-half-minute, single-reel modernization of the classic story. Red acted as Walt's cameraman until Red left Kaycee. Eighteen-year-old Rudy Ising joined Kaycee Studios as a cartoonist in February or March of 1922 and took over as cameraman once Red left the studio.

he McConahy Building, located at 1127 East 31st Street, Kansas City, was the first and longest ome of Laugh-O-gram Films, Inc., which Walt formed after Kaycee Studios disbanded and 'alt left the Film Ad in May 1922. The building, at the southwest corner of 31st Street and Forest venue in the heart of the city's South Central Business District, was one block east and two and e-half blocks north of Kaycee Studios' Troost Avenue office. Walt, Red Lyon, and Rudy Ising oved into Suite 218 on the building's second floor by Sunday, May 28, 1922, ten days after Laugh- -gram was incorporated. Suite 218 included three rooms at the front of the building, overlooking st Street (the four second-story windows at the far right of this photograph denote these oms), and two rooms across the hall, at the rear of the building. The three rooms in the front of e building included the offices of Walt, his twenty-six-year-old secretary Nadine Simpson, and enty-five-year-old business manager Jack Kloepper. The two rooms in the back of the building cluded the camera room and the animator's room. The LeMorris photography studio's labeled ndows are also seen in this picture. LeMorris was in Suite 206, the second-story corner suite. ry Raggos and Louis Katsis' street-level Forest Inn Café is seen in this picture as well.

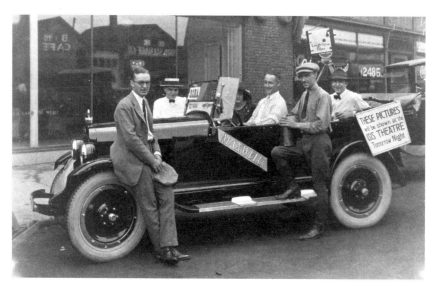

Walt (seated in the back seat) and Laugh-O-gram Films participated in a South Central Business Association parade, likely held before mid-August 1922, or between late September and mid-October 1922. To Walt's right is a mock Laugh-O-gram camera and tripod. To his left is a sign proclaiming that the footage filmed during the parade would be shown in the following evening at the Isis Theatre, which was located at 31st and Troost, one block west of the McConahy Building. To the driver's left, holding a Laugh-O-gram megaphone, is twenty-four-year-old Leslie Mace, the studio's general sales manager. Behind the hood of the car, wearing a bow tie, is Rudy Ising. The other two men in the picture could be twenty-five-year-old animator Lorey Tague, twenty-one-year-old poster artist Alex Kurfiss, or Red Lyon.

The animators' room in the southwest corner of the McConahy Building. The artists in this photograph could by Rudy, eighteen-year-old Hugh Harman, nineteen-year-old Max Maxwell, Lorey Tague, or Alex Kurfiss (or Walt if he had walked across the hall from his own office). On the shelf are framed posters of *Jack and the Beanstalk* and *Goldie Locks and the Three Bears*.

Jack Kloepper in his office with Rudy Ising. Jack's narrow office was next to the reception room where Nadine Simpson worked. Nadine could see into Walt's office from the reception room. On the wall is Alex Kurfiss' poster for *Little Red Riding Hood*. Alex's name is seen in the poster's lower right-hand corner. The poster was likely made by Alex in the poster's summer or fall of 1922 at the Laugh-O-gram studio, even though the film was made in late 1921 and early 1922 by Walt, Red Lyon, and Rudy Ising at Kaycee Studios.

A scene from *Puss in Boots*, completed in October 1922. The movie poster seen at left is an inside joke; *Cinderella* was put into production by the Laugh-O-gram studio not long after *Puss* was completed.

Walt filming home movies of Kansas City children, probably in the fall of 1922. Based on an article about this part of Laugh-O-grams' work that appeared in the October 29, 1922, edition of the *Kansas City Star* (titled "Recording the Baby's Life In Films"), the person to Walt's left is probably Red Lyon.

In the spring of 1923, Walt was hired to make a sing-along film for a song published the previous year, *Martha, Just a Plain Old Fashioned Name*. Walt called the film a "Song-O-Reel." Walt hired models to play the female roles in *Martha* and Ubbe played the male lead. Nadine recounted how Walt and the crew, which included Rudy and Walt Pfeiffer, roamed Kansas City to find the homes, parks, and woods from which he chose his exterior location sites. The crew also filmed at Troost Lake. The crew and several models are seen here. From left: Rudy (sitting and watching), Walt (holding the Laugh-O-gram megaphone that Nadine would return to the Disney studio some forty-five years later), twenty-two-year-old "Scenario Editor" Walt Pfeiffer (kneeling), and an unknown cameraman behind the camera bearing the studio's name. The cameraman has been identified as Red Lyon in the 2002 book *Walt Disney's Missouri* by Brian Burnes, Robert W. Butler, and Dan Viets, but Red Lyon's death certificate states that he moved to California early in 1923. If that is correct, the cameraman could be Alex Kurfiss or Jack Kloepper.

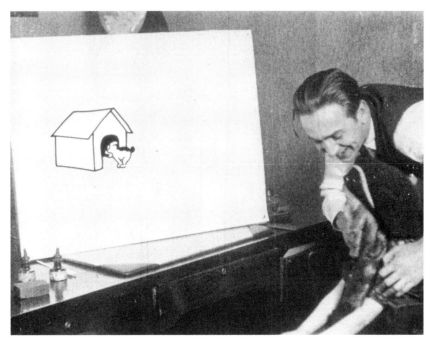

Twenty-one-year-old Walt and four-year-old Virginia Davis in a scene from *Alice's Wonderland*, filmed sometime after April 13, 1923, in Suite 218 of the McConahy Building.

Another scene from *Alice's Wonderland* filmed inside Suite 218. From left: Rudy, Ubbe, unknown (perhaps Alex Kurfiss), unknown (given the age, probably Otto Walliman, forty-seven), and Hugh Harman. Most of the animated scenes for this short were made in June and July 1923, after Laugh-O-gram Films moved from the McConahy Building back to the second-story location at 3241 Troost Avenue where Kaycee Studios had been located from at least late 1921 to May 1922.

Walt behind the camera not long after he arrived in Los Angeles in August 1923.

Margaret Winkler, who was twenty-eight when she sent Walt a telegram October 15, 1923, offering him a cont for a series based on *Alice's Wonderl* Late that night, Walt and his thirty-year-old brother Roy agreed to beco business partners. They formed Disr Brothers Studio the next day. By Aug 1924, Margaret's husband, Charles Mintz, thirty-four, took over the Winkler company's relationship wit the Disney brothers.

Virginia Davis and her parents, Margaret, thirty-four, and Jeff Davis, forty, moved to California in early November 1923 so that Virginia could continue to play Alice in Walt's new series. The first short made in Los Angeles, *Alice's Day At Sea*, was produced that November. Some scenes were filmed on the beach in Santa Monica. In this picture, the cast and others take a break. From left: unknown (who played a sailor in this short), Virginia, Walt, unknown (who played another sailor), Margaret Davis, unknown (possibly sixteen-year-old inker and painter Kathleen Dollard, the first Disney Brothers Studio employee and the only other studio employee besides Walt and Roy until December 8, 1923), and Jeff Davis.

At work on the set of *Alice's Spooky Adventure*, which was in production in January and February of 1924. From left: Jeff Davis, Walt, Virginia, and Roy.

Virginia and the black cat that would eventually become known as Julius in a scene from *Spooky Adventure*.

Virginia and some of her co-stars (including Uncle Robert Disney's German shepherd, Peggy) from *Alice and the Dog Catcher*, which was produced in April and May of 1924. Walt and his first Disney Brothers Studio animation hire, twenty-five-year-old Rollin "Ham" Hamilton, appeared in this film as the dogcatchers. Here, the cast is on Hollywood Boulevard, two blocks south of Kingswell Avenue. *Dog Catcher* was the first of three Alice Comedies with live-action scenes filmed by thirty-six-year-old Harry Forbes; Roy still manned the animation camera. This was the last film with animation done by Walt. *Dog Catcher* marked the end of twenty-two-year-old Walt Disney's three-year career as an animator. After this film, Walt focused on writing, directing, and producing.

A scene from *Alice the Peacemaker*, apparently filmed on the sidewalk near the Kingswell studio. To Virginia's right is ten-year-old Leon Sederholm, a San Francisco native who moved with his widowed mother and siblings to Los Angeles and whose stage name was Leon Holmes. Leon appeared in seven *Alice* shorts. To Virginia's left is thirteen-year-old Walter "Spec" O'Donnell, who appeared in two Alice Comedies. *Peacemaker* was made in June and July of 1924.

The staff of Disney Brothers Studio, taken outside its 4649 Kingswell Avenue location, where it moved from its original location next door, at 4651 Kingswell, in February 1924. Based on the hire and termination dates of the studio's staff, this photograph was probably taken between March 26, 1925, and May 23, 1925. From left: twenty-two-year-old cameraman Mike Marcus; inker and secretary Lillian Bounds, twenty-six, who was likely by then Walt's fiancée; producer, director, and writer Walt; animator Thurston Harper, twenty-two; animator Ubbe; animator Ham Hamilton; and business manager Roy.

The Disney Brothers Studio staff, probably taken not long after Hugh and Walker Harman and Rudy Ising joined the studio in June of 1925. Hugh was hired as an animator, Rudy as a cameraman, and Walker, nineteen, as an inker. Walt took this photograph in front of the 4649 Kingswell Avenue location. From left: nineteen-year-old painter Irene Hamilton; Rudy; inker Hazelle Linston, age unknown; Ubbe; Ham; Thurston; Walker; Hugh; and Roy. Thurston painted the gold "Disney Bros. Studio" lettering seen here. Studio artwork was displayed below the lettering.

Margie Gay as Alice, with Julius, in *Alice's Mysterious Mystery*. This short was produced in January 1926, making it one of the last films made at the Kingswell Avenue studio. The following month, Walt and his staff moved to the new studio on Hyperion Avenue. The six-year-old's real name was Marjorie Gossett, and she replaced Virginia Davis as Alice in February 1925, when Margie was five and one-half. But for a single appearance as Alice by Dawn O'Day in a short produced in March 1925, Margie remained in the role through the end of 1926.

2719 Hyperion Avenue, a few years after Walt and Roy built the studio in 1925 and in February of 1926 moved their staff there. This photograph was probably taken in 1929 or 1930. By then, the front wall of the studio was moved six feet forward, bringing it to the sidewalk, and additions were made to the front, rear, and side of the building.

A publicity shot showing Walt and Margie Gay and their animated friends, including Julius, moving into the new Disney studio at 2719 Hyperion Avenue. Since Walt suggested this type of photograph to Charlie Mintz in June 22, 1926—four months after the move—this publicity shot was probably made in the summer of 1926.

A Walt Disney Studio staff photograph at the new Hyperion studio. Based on staff hire dates and the clothes worn by those in the picture, this photograph was probably taken sometime between February 1926 and mid-September 1926. Based on Hugh's recollection, this was one of a series of photographs from the summer of 1926, after the rainy first few weeks in the Hyperion building "finally dried out, and the summer was beautiful." Here, from left, are Ham, Roy, Hugh, Walt, Margie, Rudy, Ubbe, and Walker.

Twelve-year-old Lois Hardwick, a veteran child actor who was the fourth and final Alice, poses in front of, from left, Walker, twenty-two-year-old animator Friz Freleng, Rudy, Roy, Hugh, Ubbe, Norman Blackburn, Paul Smith, and Walt. Norm, twenty-three, was an animator who joined the studio on February 5, 1927. Paul, twenty, was a cel painter hired on December 8, 1926. Based on staff hire dates, this 1927 Disney staff photograph and others taken the same day were taken at the Hyperion studio between Saturday, February 5, and Thursday, February 10, 1927. Said Friz of this series of photographs: "Everybody is wearing their California clothes, and I'm still Kansas City. I didn't think I belonged."

A Universal publicity photograph trumpets its new series, *Oswald the Lucky Rabbit*. Charlie Mintz hired the Disney studio to animate this new series requested by Universal. Here, an early version of Oswald (who changed significantly by the time he appeared on-screen) appears with, from left, Charlie and Robert H. Cochrane, the vice president of Universal. The deal for the new series was consummated in early March 1927 and announced in the trade papers on March 12, 1927. In the weeks that followed, the last Alice Comedy, *Alice in the Big League*, was produced, and it was released in August of 1927.

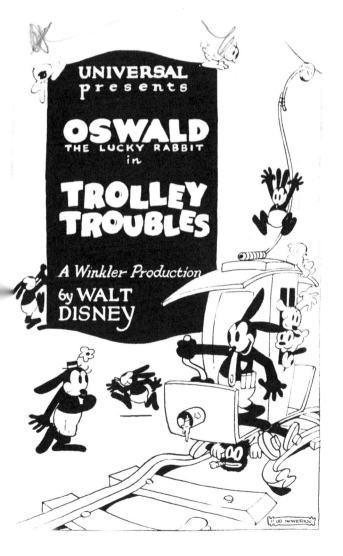

Ubbe's lobby card for *Trolley Troubles*. Ubbe's signature is seen in the lower right-hand corner. This short was the second Oswald produced, but the first released. It received positive reviews after its premiere on September 5, 1927. Six months later, Walt and Lilly were in New York for meetings with Charlie Mintz that resulted in Walt's ouster as the producer of the Oswald series. On the evening of Tuesday, March 13, 1928, Walt and Lilly boarded their train back to Los Angeles, on which they began to discuss a new series that would replace Oswald. This marked the end of twenty-six-year-old Walt Disney's life before Mickey Mouse.

# Book Two
# Los Angeles

# Disney Brothers Studio
## *1923–1926*

When twenty-one-year-old Walt arrived in Los Angeles, he was met by his brother, Roy, who recalled, "I met [Walt] at the station. He was carrying a cheap suitcase that contained all of his belongings." Walt explained, "I landed in Hollywood in August, 1923, with a two-year-old suit of clothes, a sweater, a lot of drawing materials and $40. . . . Also in my suitcase was [*Alice's Wonderland,*] the last of the fairy tale reels we had made [at Laugh-O-gram Films]." The print of *Alice* may not have been entirely finished.

Walt seemed content with his decision to forgo a move to New York or even stay in Kansas City. "The pull toward Hollywood," he said, "became strong. Animation was big there, and if I couldn't be successful at that, I wanted to be a director or a writer." With fifty-eight motion picture studios and 250 production companies, Los Angeles of 1923—a city of almost 950,000 and the fifth largest city in the United States—certainly seemed the place for Walt.

Once he arrived in L.A., however, Walt did not stay with Roy, who still suffered from tuberculosis and lived west of the city at the Veterans Hospital in Sawtelle. Instead, Walt moved in with his uncle, Robert Samuel Disney, who had left Kansas City for Los Angeles upon his retirement a few years earlier. Walt's father recalled that "my brother . . . took care of him for awhile." Robert lived in the Los Feliz section of the city, about six miles northwest of downtown Los Angeles and two and one-half miles east of Hollywood. He dabbled in real estate; he was sixty-two, stocky, and liked to smoke cigars.

Robert lived in a bungalow at 4406 Kingswell Avenue with his second wife, thirty-year-old Charlotte Ann Hussey Disney (who was then five months pregnant with their son, Robert, Jr.), and their German shepherd, Peggy. Charlotte is recalled by one relative as a "rather stiff" woman, and by another as "a little bit on the strict side but, underneath the exterior, she had a heart of gold." The Disney home, described by Walt's daughter as "[n]othing remarkable" and "very typical of homes of the time[,]" was located one house west of the southwest corner of Kingswell Avenue, an east-west residential street, and North Commonwealth Avenue.

Despite Robert's hospitality, Walt was not enamored of his uncle. While Robert's grandson described Robert as a "very loving, gracious individual," Walt felt his uncle "meant well" but was "kind of pompous." Walt thought that Robert "demanded a lot of respect and he didn't think I gave it to him." The two argued soon after Walt arrived in Los Angeles. Walt recalled,

> Our first argument was about how I'd come West. As everyone knows, the Santa Fe Railroad is really the Atchison, Topeka and Santa Fe Railroad. When I arrived, Uncle Robert asked, "Did you come through Topeka?" I said, "I didn't go through Topeka." "If you came on the Santa Fe you did," he said. "Not the train I was on," I said. "It bypassed Topeka." Uncle Robert got hot under the collar at that but I wouldn't give in. He had his wife call up the Santa Fe and when he found out the train on which I'd arrived hadn't gone through Topeka, he was sore at me for weeks.

Walt paid Robert and Charlotte rent in the amount of $5 weekly, but relied on Roy—and Roy's government pension—for financial support. Walt liked to joke that "[t]he government did play a part in subsidizing [my early career efforts in Los Angeles] because my brother was discharged from the service with a partial disability allowance. I think it was about $65 a month. My brother and I lived on that[.]"

Roy did not hesitate to encourage Walt to find work, however, even if it meant returning to cartooning. But Walt rebuffed his brother, saying, "No, I'm too late [for cartoons]. . . . I should have started six years ago. I don't see how I can top those New York boys now." Walt later explained, "When I got to Hollywood, I was discouraged with animation. I figured I had gotten into it too late. I was through with the cartoon business."

Although he was "fed up with cartoons," Walt decided that he still wanted to be a part of the motion picture industry. "What I wanted to do," he said, "was get a job in a studio—any studio, doing anything." His "ambition at that time was to be a director," even though he was open to accepting any job a studio would offer him. He would take "[a]nything. [I wanted to just g]et in. . . . Be a part of it and then move up." His goal was to "learn . . . . the picture business[.]"

During his first week in Los Angeles, Walt went to Universal City and showed his Universal News newsreel press credentials from Kansas City, and was able to get onto the lot. The credentials were cards that said, "Walter Disney, representing Universal News and Selznick News Representative in Kansas City Missouri," and Walt handed them to studio representatives. Walt stayed at the studio all day and evening, making the adventure "one of the big thrills I had." Walt would arrive early and stay late, examining the sets and lingering where filming was underway. His efforts to parlay the visit into a job failed, though, when he visited the studio employment office the following day.

In addition to Universal, Walt took a red Pacific Electric trolley to Culver City, where he saw the *Ben-Hur* set. When Walt's cousin, Alice, visited L.A., they toured the Vitagraph studio together. Walt walked past Charlie Chaplin's studio on La Brea Avenue, and he visited Metro Goldwyn Mayer and Paramount, where a friend from Kansas City was working as an extra and got Walt a job riding a horse in a Western. The friend said, "I got a job in a picture called *The Light That Failed*. . . . They need more extras. You can ride a horse, can't you, Diz?" Walt said that he could, and "went [to the studio] and hung around and got signed." He was selected to appear in a cavalry scene, but the weather did not cooperate. "Well," Walt said, "it rained like hell. So I didn't get to go. And that was the end of my career as an actor. When they started all over again, they hired a whole new bunch."

Walt was certainly enjoying his time on the studio lots, although it frustrated Roy. "I kept saying to him, 'Aren't you gonna get a job?'" Roy recalled. "'Why don't you get a job?' He could have got a job, I'm sure, but he didn't want a job. But he'd get into Universal, for example, on the strength of applying for a job, and then . . . he'd just hang around the Studio lot all day . . . watching sets and what was going on. . . . MGM was another favorite spot where he could work that gag."

Walt worked that "gag" through August and September, job hunting while spending his days at the studios. He recalled, "I didn't figure on setting the town on fire—at least, not for a year or two. But I had to start with a job. For two months, I tramped from one studio to another, trying to sell myself as a writer, a director, a day laborer—anything to get through those magic gates of bigtime show business. But nobody bought." He "went from one studio to another and I went to the personnel departments and it was pretty cold."

At the same time, Walt tried to make money by selling the *Alice's Wonderland* pilot that he brought with him from Kansas City. He called on distributors, bringing with him his copy of that film. "I tried to sell . . . [*Alice*] in Hollywood without any luck," he said. "With the print of that cartoon under my arm, I tramped the streets of Hollywood for several weeks," Walt recalled, "trying to interest someone in my picture. I couldn't make a sale[.]" Walt also pitched, without success, his old comic strip, "Mr. George's Wife." This was one of several strips he drew in January 1920 between jobs at the post office and Iwwerks-Disney.

Heeding distributors' advice that he would have better luck in New York, Walt, as he had in Kansas City three months earlier, wrote New York distributor

Margaret Winkler about his *Alice* reel. On Saturday, August 25, he wrote to Margaret on letterhead that read, "Walt Disney, Cartoonist," and included his Uncle Robert's home address of 4406 Kingswell Avenue. The letter bears the dictation-typist legend "WD.C" in the lower left corner, suggesting that perhaps Walt's Aunt Charlotte typed the letter for him.

In the letter, Walt wrote that he and some of his Kansas City staff were launching a studio in Los Angeles, where they would be better suited to start their new series:

Dear Miss Winkler:

This is to inform you that I am no longer connected with the Laugh-O-Gram Films, Inc., of Kansas City, Mo. and that I am establishing a studio in Los Angeles for the purpose of producing the new and novel series of cartoons I have previously written you about.

The making of these new cartoons necessitates being located in a production center that I may engage trained talent for my casts, and be within reach of the right facilities for producing.

I am taking with me a select number of my former staff and will in a very short time be producing at regular intervals. It is my intention of securing working space with one of the studios, that I may better study technical detail and comedy situations and combine these with my cartoons.

Walt went on to describe what he found wrong with earlier attempts at combination live action-animation reels, but he could have been describing the way he and his own staff produced *Alice's Wonderland*:

In the past all cartoons combining live actors have been produced in an amateur manner with cartoonists doing the acting, photographing, etc. It is my intention to employ only trained and experienced people for my casts and staff that I may inject quality humor, photography and detail into these comedies.

Walt concluded by lowering expectations for *Alice's Wonderland*:

The first picture of this new idea, [*Alice's Wonderland,*] which I have just completed, was made in Kansas City under big difficulties owing to lack of necessary equipment and experienced talent.

I would appreciate an interview with your representative here that I may screen several comedies and explain my new idea.

Unbeknownst to Walt, the timing of his August 25th letter to Margaret Winkler could not have been better. By the time Walt was in California, Margaret was twenty-eight years old. She, her parents, and her three brothers were born in Hungary, and came to the United States in 1904, when Margaret was nine years old. Her father, Leopold, was a tailor in New York. In 1915, when Margaret was twenty, she went to work for producer Harry Warner at Warner Brothers' New York office. The job gave Margaret good experience in the motion picture industry. She explained, "I was secretary to Harry M. Warner and as such traveled from New York to the West Coast and around to film conventions meeting film people and learning much." Warner respected and trusted Margaret, and believed she could succeed on her own in the motion picture industry.

Margaret finally became a cartoon distributor after serving as Warner's executive secretary for seven years. Margaret's own company came about when, in 1921, Pat Sullivan, the producer-director of Paramount's *Felix the Cat* series, approached Harry Warner about distributing *Felix*. When Margaret expressed interest in the samples that Sullivan brought to the office, Warner suggested that Margaret distribute *Felix*. Warner also thought that Margaret should distribute *Out of the Inkwell* after Warners' distribution contract with *Inkwell's* producers expired the following year.

Margaret followed Warner's counsel—as she would throughout her career as a distributor—and in December 1921 she and Sullivan signed an agreement for *Felix the Cat*, which she first distributed in January 1922. Margaret started distributing *Out of the Inkwell* on a state's rights basis in either late 1921 or in 1922.

When Margaret announced in trade journals in February 1922 the formation of her own distribution company, called simply, "M. J. Winkler," she had become, at twenty-seven, the first female distributor and producer of animated cartoons. Margaret felt she was well qualified for the distinction, noting that "I had . . . years of good training for it . . . working for Warner Brothers." It was at this time that Margaret added to her name the middle initial, "J" (which did not stand for anything), not only because she liked the sound of a full name, but also so that she could go by "M. J. Winkler," and thus let industry people believe she was a man.

By the time Walt moved west, Margaret had been in business for over a year, and *Felix the Cat* remained a big hit. Although *Felix* animator Otto Messmer found Margaret the "the great live-wire saleslady of Warner Brothers," Pat Sullivan's relationship with Margaret began to deteriorate. In August of 1923, just as Walt got settled in Los Angeles, Margaret was worried about her ability to hold on to the *Felix* series since her contract with Sullivan expired within a few months.

Even though her original arrangement with Sullivan gave her an option to renew *Felix* for a second season, Margaret was afraid that Sullivan would use *Felix*'s popularity to negotiate a much higher price than that called for by their contract. Moreover, Max Fleischer was forming his own production company, so Margaret would no longer have *Out of the Inkwell* in her portfolio either. Unbeknownst to Walt, it was while Margaret wrestled with renewing *Felix* and losing *Inkwell* that she received Walt's August 25 letter inquiring about her interest in *Alice*—which must have struck her as a possible replacement series for *Felix* in the event she and Sullivan could not agree to terms for a new season.

In an effort to lock Sullivan into producing *Felix* at the original contract price, Margaret wrote Sullivan on August 29 that she was, under their 1921 contract, picking up *Felix* for another season. Sullivan took offense to the letter, and the two became involved in a contract dispute. On August 30, Sullivan responded that the contract only gave Winkler an option for a second series of shorts if the reels were similar in number and length to those of the first series. Sullivan wrote to Margaret that he was considering a new series of *Felix* that would be different in number and length, and would thus not fall within the specific terms of Margaret's contract. As a result, he was not bound to Margaret as his distributor.

The week after receiving Sullivan's veiled threat to take *Felix* to a different distributor, Margaret wrote back to Walt about *Alice*. Specifically, on Friday, September 7, Margaret wrote Walt on M. J. Winkler company stationery (adorned with illustrations of *Felix the Cat*) and told him she was ready to consider adding his series to her lineup:

> Dear Mr. Disney:
>     We have been corresponding with each other since your first letter to me of May 14th. It seems that this is about all it has amounted to.
>     Your letter of August 25th interests me. . . . At present I am handling FELIX the CAT and OUT OF THE INKWELL . . . . You will note that each one of these subjects is of a very high standard. I can handle only just one more of the same standard.
>     If your comedies are what you say they are and what I think they should be, we can do business. If you can spare a couple of them long enough to send me so that I can screen them and can see just what they are, please do so at once. . . .

Margaret's closing line would have made more sense to Walt if he knew that she was in a precarious position with both the *Felix* and *Inkwell* series:

It is necessary for me to have this information without delay so that I can lay my plans properly for immediate and next year's contracts.

Walt did not have to take Margaret's suggestion to mail her a copy of *Alice's Wonderland* since he had followed the L.A. distributors' advice and sent the reel to New York. The Hollywood distributors to whom he showed *Alice* "told me to go to New York and sell it. I didn't have the money, so I mailed the reel to an agent in New York" and then "awaited developments." When someone—such as Margaret—showed an interest in *Alice*, Walt instructed his agent at Lloyd's Film Storage in New York to take the reel to the distributor for a showing. Margaret screened *Alice's Wonderland* sometime after her letter to Walt of September 7.

Whether it was because of Margaret's continued interest, or his own recognition that "I just couldn't get anywhere" with his efforts to become a director, Walt found a renewed commitment to animation. "Things looked pretty black at that time," he said. "I was flat broke and I heard nothing encouraging from New York." He recalled, "I couldn't get a job, so I went into business for myself." Specifically, given the "shortage of directorial opportunities," Walt "decided to give cartooning another whirl and to put off being a director till things loosened up." Because "[t]hings didn't look any too good," he explained, "[b]efore I knew it, I had my animation board out."

Just as Elias Disney let Walt use the family garage in Kansas City as an animation studio two years earlier, Robert let Walt set up a studio in the garage behind 4406 Kingswell. Walt purchased an "old dilapidated" used Pathé camera for $200 from John W. Peterson. Peterson, forty-four, was the proprietor of the California Camera Hospital, which had been at 356 South Broadway in downtown L.A. for nearly a decade. Peterson's shop was in Suite 321 of the O. T. Johnson Building, and he specialized in "Shutter Repairs" and "Expert Cinematograph, Kodak and Camera Repairing[.]" He also mounted lenses and was "Equipped with Precision Machinery for Accurate Work." Walt built a camera stand for the Pathé in Robert's garage.

Another long-time L.A. businessman on whom Walt called that fall was Alexander Pantages, who owned the Pantages Theatre located two blocks from Peterson's camera shop, at the northwest corner of Hill and 7th Streets. Pantages, forty-six, came to the United States from Greece in 1888, when he was eleven years old. As a young man, Pantages worked as a waiter in the Klondike and as a bootblack in Seattle, where he purchased his first theater, the Oaks Theatre, at the age of twenty-eight. Five years later he married Lois Mendenhall, a violinist who played at the Oaks.

By 1915, Pantages owned the Los Angeles theater that he named after himself; it was managed by Carl J. Walker. Pantages also owned an office building next door to the theater. The businesses in the Pantages Building included a surgeon, dentist, tailor, property manager, and theatrical exchange. In the fall of 1923, Pantages, Lois, their teenage sons, Rodney and Lloyd, and their two younger daughters lived on North Vermont Avenue, almost three miles south of Uncle Robert. But it was Pantages' office in Room 211 of the Pantages Theatre Building at 411 West 7th Street where Walt came calling that fall.

"Finally I managed to sell Alexander Pantages on the idea of me making a special little joke reel for his theaters on the order of 'Topics of the Day,'" Walt recalled. At first, he tried to sell Pantages' assistant—possibly Carl Walker—on the "special little joke reel" with "the name of Pantages splashed all over it, to add prestige and keep the name Pantages before his theatre patrons." Pantages overheard Walt's pitch to the assistant as he explained his idea of "turn[ing] out a weekly joke reel, a sort of 'Topics of the Day' affair." The assistant was not convinced by Walt, but Pantages was. "He was interested," Walt recalled, "but wanted to see more of my work." He told Walt, "I think you have a good idea . . . . Make up a sample and if it's all you describe, you've got a deal." Walt returned to Robert's garage, where "I set about drawing up a sample reel."

Walt began to work on the Pantages joke reel, using what he called "my little stick figures" with heads that had mouths and eyes. The characters told each other jokes, which were written in type above them. The settings were simple; the figures appeared near a tree or under a sky with a moon. "The best way I can describe these," Walt said, "is to say that they looked like white matchsticks on a black background."

Walt realized that he could not sustain an animation enterprise out of his uncle's garage, and on Monday, October 8, rented space in the back of the office of McRae & Abernathy, a real estate company located at 4651 Kingswell Avenue, two and one-half blocks west of Uncle Robert's house. James A. McRae, seventy-six, was born in Indiana, and was a realtor who also lived on Kingswell Avenue, a half-block east of his real estate office. His partner, Claude C. Abernathy, forty-four, a former insurance agent and messenger originally from Ohio, lived less than a mile from Kingswell, on North Kenmore, where he resided for almost a decade. Abernathy was married and lived with his wife Blanche, son James, fourteen, and daughter Dorothy, eleven.

Walt recalled that he "rented the back end of a real estate office for $5 a month," but the rent was actually double that amount. Walt found the space by speaking with Abernathy, who ran the office, and offering to pay him for enough space to "swing a cat in." Abernathy laughed at Walt's offer, and agreed to rent Walt the space. Walt borrowed $75 from his Kansas City friend, Carl Stalling, around this time, possibly in order to finance his makeshift studio at McRae & Abernathy.

After one week as a tenant in the McRae & Abernathy office, "[w]hile I was busy making that [Pantages] reel," recalled Walt, "I received an offer from Margaret Winkler, an independent distributor in New York, for a series of pictures like my sample [*Alice*] reel which I had sent back East." Five months after he first wrote Margaret, among other distributors, looking for a contract, Walt finally had an offer—his first one since the Pictorial Films deal almost two years earlier. The telegram was sent to Uncle Robert's house on Monday, October 15, and in it Margaret stated:

> BELIEVE SERIES CAN BE PUT OVER BUT PHOTOGRAPHY OF ALICE SHOULD SHOW MORE DETAIL AND BE STEADIER THIS BEING NEW PRODUCT MUST SPEND LARGE AMOUNT ON EXPLOITATION AND ADVERTISING THEREFORE NEED YOUR COOPERATION.

Not only had Walt heard from an interested distributor, he also received firm financial terms that must have made his eyes pop:

> WILL PAY FIFTEEN HUNDRED EACH NEGATIVE FOR FIRST SIX AND TO SHOW MY GOOD FAITH WILL PAY FULL AMOUNT ON EACH OF THESE SIX IMMEDIATELY ON DELIVERY OF NEGATIVE.

In full, Margaret offered Walt a series of twelve *Alice* cartoons (six cartoons with an option for six more), and would pay $1,500 for each of the first six and $1,800 for each of the second six. Walt was to deliver the first reel by December 15, just eight weeks away, along with the negative and a poster sketch. Margaret added that "Alice must be used in all subjects" and that she "[w]ould like to keep [*Alice's Wonderland*] for sample."

Walt was elated, but also caught off guard. While he immediately wired his acceptance (but stated that he could not deliver the first short until January 1), he said of Margaret's offer that "I was surprised myself." Late that evening, after wiring Margaret, he took a bus to Sawtelle to talk to Roy. Walt found Roy asleep in what Roy described as a "[t]ypical porch type of a ward out there in the old Sawtelle Hospital. Numbers of beds all in a string. . . . He wasn't allowed in, but when you know the place, you can always get in." Roy recalled that Walt "found his way to my bed . . . . It was eleven or twelve o'clock at night, and he shaked me awake and showed me a telegram of acceptance of his offers. He said, 'What can I do now? Can you come out of here and help me to get this started?'" Walt recalled sitting on Roy's bed and saying, "We're in! It's a deal. . . . Fifteen hundred smackers a reel" and "Let's go, Roy."

But Roy's reaction was one of caution. He wondered whether they could actually produce the series. Yet Roy wanted a job so that he could marry Edna Francis, and he knew that his tuberculosis prevented him from working in a normal office setting. Walt used his selling skills to convince Roy to go into business with him. Walt explained, "I talked . . . Roy into going in with me." Roy "always had been in sympathy with what I was trying to do. . . . So, although Roy didn't know anything about the motion picture business, we went into partnership to fill the Winkler order for my cartoons." They agreed to a 50-50 split, with Walt doing the artwork and Roy acting as the business manager. "So," said Roy, "I left the hospital the next day[.]"

Walt's situation, like Roy's, changed dramatically overnight. On Monday, he went to the back area of McRae & Abernathy to continue work on a sample reel that he hoped would lead to work for Alex Pantages. The next day, he and Roy were partners in a studio that had an order for a series of cartoon shorts. That Tuesday, Walt explained, "I dropped the Pantages idea and went to work on the *Alice* series." Also that day, while Margaret was in New York signing and mailing the contract to Walt, Walt and Roy got busy: they looked for financing, asked their original "Alice" to move west to reprise the role, and hired the first employee of their new studio.

Margaret prepared and sent an outright sale contract that required delivery of the first *Alice* by January 2, 1924, and enlarged the option to twenty-four additional cartoons (i.e., a series of twelve reels for 1925 and a series of twelve reels for 1926). She also asked Walt for photographs and biographies of Virginia Davis, whom Margaret presumed would continue to play "Alice," and him. Margaret wired Walt that she had mailed him the contract, and had accepted his January 1 delivery date (the contract's delivery date of January 2 was probably a typographical error). Margaret also gave Walt the name of Harry Warner as a reference: "Inquire of Harry M. Warner of Warner Bros[.] Hollywood."

Meanwhile, Roy applied for bank loans, but was unsuccessful; the *Alice* series was deemed too much of a risk. Roy and Walt then went to Uncle Robert for a loan, but Robert was unwilling because he had heard that Walt never repaid a $60 loan made by another older brother, Ray Disney. Robert did, however, ultimately witness the signing of the contracts for his nephews.

As for Walt, he wrote to Margaret Davis, asking if she would bring Virginia from Kansas City to California to star in *Alice:*

> I have at last succeeded in arranging for distribution of a series of "Alice" productions—twelve in all—with a very reliable distributor in New York.
>
> I screened "Alice's Wonderland" several times in Hollywood and every one seemed to think that Virginia was real cute and thought she

had wonderful possibilities—and I was wondering if you would arrange
to come out here so I could star her in this series—It would be a big
opportunity for her and would introduce her to the profession in a manner that few children could receive . . . .

[I]f Virginia was used in the series it would be the making of her . . . .
so you see the big possibilities that await Virginia . . . .

If you desire to come out and let me star Virginia in this series it
will be necessary that you answer immediately as in all probability I will
have to start production within fifteen or twenty days so I will know
wheather [*sic*] or not I will use Virginia or have to get a little girl here in
Hollywood—If you decide to come answer immediately so I can count
on you—I will want a year[']s contract with option on further services at
a very reasonable salary . . . . [M. J. Winkler] demands that who ever I star
in the series must be under contract to me for a series of twelve pictures
with option on further services . . . . therefore you understand the neces-
sity of a contract. However if Virginia can secure other work between
pictures she can do so without any complications and I believe I can
secure her work myself—In all probability I will do most of my shooting
in one of the studios near here—I am now dickering with several[.]

Walt offered Virginia a one-year contract. Virginia recalled, "My mother was
very excited about the letter that came from California. Walt wrote that he had
a distributor and proceeded to do a great selling job to my mother, that this
would be a great opportunity for Virginia, and so forth."

In all likelihood, Walt did not need to sell too hard to Mrs. Davis. Just after
he arrived in L.A., Walt received a letter from her, written on August 6, in which
she explained she had taken Virginia to Hollywood earlier in the summer to
break into movies but could not get an appointment at the studios. Margaret
Davis wrote Walt that she planned on returning to Los Angeles in November to
try again.

By the end of October 16, the venture that Walt and Roy decided to call
Disney Brothers Studio was in operation. While they lacked financing and were
unsure whether their star would sign with them, they had a series. They also
had an employee: Miss Kathleen G. Dollard, a sixteen-year-old young woman
who lived about two miles from the studio who was hired that day to ink and
paint cels. Walt claimed that, with Disney Brothers Studio, he and Roy "established the first animated cartoon studio in Hollywood." Walt told his father, "I'll
make the name Disney famous around the world."

Margaret Winkler continued the flurry of letter-writing on Wednesday,
October 17, when she asked Walt for a "short history of [Alice's] work in the
picture." In addition, she wrote,

I would also like to have any sketches or information that you may have
regarding her or the reel. If you have a photograph of yourself, will you
please also send me that together with a short history of your activities in
the motion picture business.

Walt responded that, "I am now preparing a brief synopsis of Alice and my
screen activities and will forward same to you at an early date."

That Saturday, October 20, Walt wrote a follow-up letter to the Davises
and included the terms of Virginia's contract. Walt offered Virginia a graduated
yearly contract that included a monthly salary of $100 for the first two months
and a raise of $25 every two months until month nine, when her salary leveled
off at $200. He also offered a monthly salary of $250 for the second series of
cartoons. Walt explained that the relatively "low salary at start" was the result of
publicity costs. On Sunday, he wrote to Harry Warner, asking for information
about Margaret's "responsibility and standing."

On Tuesday, October 23, Warner responded:

Miss M. J. Winkler was my secretary for a number of years, and since she
has gone into business for herself, she has done very well, and I believe
she is responsible for anything she may undertake.

In my opinion, the main thing you should consider is the quality of
goods you are going to give her, and if that is right, I don't think you need
have any hesitancy in having her handle your merchandise.

Walt conducted other research into Margaret's background, and the financial report he received shortly thereafter also indicated that she had a good
reputation.

The next day, October 24, Walt mailed the contracts back to Margaret and
wrote her that "[t]he first of this series, the title of which has been changed
from 'Alice's Sea Story' to 'Alice's Day at Sea' is now in production and in all
probability I will have this subject to you by December 15th. But on account of
the many details attached to the starting of a series of this nature it may require
a week longer." Walt also wrote Margaret Davis that day:

In my last letter to you I said that final signing of contracts had not
been completed—However everything is complete now and my proposition to you can be put in force.

However before I can go ahead and do any work in the publicity line
it will be necessary for me to have a letter from you accepting my proposition and later when you come out we can sign contracts—You can plan

on being here by Nov 15 ready to start work—I am already working on the first picture—please send letter of acceptance at once[.]

By the last weekend in October, the Davises decided to move west, and on Sunday, October 28, Virginia's mother wired Walt to accept his offer. "Walt found a distributor for *Alice's Wonderland* and we packed up and moved to Hollywood," recalled Virginia Davis. She explained, "There were two reasons we went to California. I'd had double pneumonia and almost died. The doctor told my mother that I would be better off in a drier climate. So I think when all this came up, it was another incentive that brought us to California. . . . It was, 'Virginia could do this, and you, Jeff, can sell from there' since he was a traveling salesman, and healthwise it would be better for me. It was a combination of factors." Virginia later suggested that another factor might have been her mother's regret at not appearing in movies herself. Regardless, Margaret Davis wanted to bring her daughter back to Hollywood in November even before Walt relocated there, and she got her wish.

By late October or early November, production of *Alice's Day At Sea* was underway, and would last for about a month. Margaret Winkler advised Walt "to have the photography, both in the cartoon and the actual shots, much sharper and steadier than it is in the sample reel. I supposed you recognize this yourself but please do not lose track of it."

Meanwhile, the Davises arrived in California by train. After the move, Jeff Davis "went into real estate," his daughter recalled, "and I can remember my mother being so angry because he'd sit and read the paper and have his feet up, and he wasn't making any money!" Within a year, Davis returned to selling furniture, which he did for Overell's—the J. M. Overell Furniture Company, "The Mecca For Shrewd Buyers"—which was located at 7th and Main Streets downtown and offered its customers, "Homes Furnished Complete, [and] Liberal Credit."

Like the *Alice's Wonderland* pilot Walt created six months earlier in Kansas City, *Alice's Day At Sea* began and ended with a live-action sequence. In *Day At Sea*, the live-action bookends framed an animated undersea romp by Alice. The live-action scenes showed Alice and her dog sneaking out of the house for a visit to the beach, where they meet two sailors before Alice falls asleep and dreams about being under the sea. The animated portion, like that of the pilot, showed Alice dancing and playing with animated animals. Walt later explained his penchant for using animals in cartoons by saying that "they look so much like humans" and "everybody loves animals[.]"

Uncle Robert's house probably doubled as Alice's house in *Day at Sea*, and the busy street Virginia Davis crosses as she heads to the beach might be

Commonwealth. The seaside live-action scenes were filmed on a beach in Santa Monica, where two fishermen appeared as extras. Virginia's parents and, possibly, Kathleen Dollard attended the shoot. "I'd never seen the sea," Virginia recalled. "That was a big experience for a youngster, all these waves. It was wonderful[.]"

Robert Disney's German shepherd, Peggy, also appeared in *Day At Sea*. The dog appeared in the opening scene and shared the remainder of the live-action segments with Virginia. Virginia believed that Peggy appeared in the reel not because it was "a family enterprise as much as it was [Walt] didn't have any money to hire a dog. . . . Walt would be inspired by what was around, and here was this nice police dog that I liked very much. He would spin his stories around what was available."

Virginia found the atmosphere on the set "very informal. We used to have a lot of people gathered around. . . . [W]e would have a lot of the curious children and the neighbors come around to watch what was going on." Walt wrote and directed *Day At Sea* and also "did all the drawings myself . . . I did—I had no help at all, I was all alone." The film required a few hundred drawings per day—thousands in all. One source claimed that each film required 10,000 drawings. One of the clever combination scenes showed the animated face of Peggy's live-action alarm clock getting annoyed at Peggy sleeping through the alarm. Walt animated the film in the back of McRae & Abernathy, and dry goods cartons became his animating desk. Walt said the boxes were "swiped from an alley off Hollywood Boulevard" and he and Roy "rigged up a camera stand and animating tables" out of the boxes "and a little lumber we bought."

Roy remembered that, while "Walt did all the animation, . . . I cranked the old-fashioned camera" used to film the live-action footage. Walt confirmed that "In order to save money I tried to break . . . Roy in as a cameraman. He'd never had anything to do with a camera, but I did my best to teach him the even rhythm that had to be used in cranking an old-time silent movie camera. I set the exposures for Roy and he'd crank away."

Around the same time, Uncle Robert finally agreed to lend Walt and Roy $500 at 8 percent interest. Roy recorded this loan and other company finances in small, meticulous handwriting in a Standard School Series notebook. Ledger #1 shows that the first installment of Robert Disney's loan, in the amount of $200, was made on November 14. The second installment, $150, was made the last week of the month.

Other expenses Roy recorded included the rent due McRae & Abernathy (which had by now gone up to $15 a month), a desk, a light bill, and costumes, possibly for the hats worn by Virginia or the costumes worn by the sailors in *Day At Sea*. The Western Costume Company featured "Costumes and

Properties, [and] Military Equipment," and was located in the 900 block of South Broadway in downtown Los Angeles.

The studio also paid for an ad in the *Los Angeles Examiner*, a daily newspaper published by William Randolph Hearst. Given that the Disneys hired a new employee in each of the next three months, the ad might have been a "help wanted" ad similar to those that Walt used to hire his animation staff in Kansas City. Roy also recorded, by year's end, an expenditure for a $200 camera, perhaps the one Walt had purchased from John Peterson.

While *Alice's Day At Sea* was in production, the Disney brothers may have moved out of their uncle's house to the Olive Hill, an apartment complex near the studio. Roy's physical condition still left him tired, so he would return to the apartment in the afternoon, sleep, and then prepare dinner, which the brothers would eat once Walt got home. Roy recalled, "we got an apartment" to which he "used to go home in the afternoon and take a sleep because I was convalescing." Walt confirmed that, after living with Robert, "as soon as we got our studio going we rented a room near the [studio] where we could do light housekeeping. Roy did the cooking while I drew as late as possible every night."

Meanwhile, back in New York, Margaret Winkler got married. Her new husband, Charles B. Mintz, thirty-three, was born in York, Pennsylvania, to Austrian immigrants who later moved to New York. Charlie first met Margaret in 1915, when he was twenty-five years old and she was twenty. Within two years, he was living on Madison Street, New York, and employed as a film solicitor for Monmouth Film Corporation.

After working at a jewelry store, possibly with one of his brothers (a second brother was a watchmaker), Charlie became a Warner Brothers booking agent and executive. He joined Margaret Winkler's company in 1922—she handled marketing and he oversaw the transactions. Charlie was described by a veteran animator as a "grim-faced man, with a pair of cold eyes glittering behind a pince-nez . . . [who] never talked to the staff. . . . [which he looked] over like an admiral surveying a row of stanchions." Margaret's brother, George Winkler, was the office manager and supervised productions on the west coast.

Margaret and Charlie were married on Saturday, November 24, 1923. That month, they continued to meet with Pat Sullivan to discuss their *Felix* contract dispute, although they still had not reached a resolution.

In December, around the time of Walt's twenty-second birthday, the Disney brothers found a cheaper room at 4409 Kingswell Avenue, directly across the street from Robert's house, for $15 a month. They moved into the room— what Roy called "just a single room in a house"—in a boardinghouse owned by Charles and Nettie Schneider.

Charles (fifty-nine) and his wife Nettie (fifty-eight) were from Iowa and born to parents who had emigrated from Germany. Charles and Nettie married in their early twenties, and lived with their five children in Plymouth, Iowa, where Charles was a farmer. By the time their children reached adulthood, the Schneiders had moved to Le Mars, Iowa, where Charles became a real estate agent. Their youngest child, Lester, an auto mechanic, still lived at home, as did Nettie's eighty-three-year-old father.

Within three years, the Schneiders retired to California, and purchased the house on Kingswell. While the Disney brothers cooked and ate their meals in the first apartment they shared, they did not cook at the Schneider house. "Later," Walt recalled, "[after living in an apartment,] we took just a sleeping room and got our meals at a cheap cafeteria to save time. We worked out a system in that cafeteria. Roy and I always went in together. One would get a meat order, the other a vegetable. When we reached our table we would divide up." The cafeteria was "inexpensive" and "dreary." Walt recalled, "there was many a week when Roy and I ate one square meal a day—between us."

The cafeteria may have been the Garden Cafeteria, around the corner (on North Vermont, less than a block south of Kingswell) and managed by Harry W. Marshall who, with his wife, Laura, lived about a block west of Uncle Robert on Kingswell. Within a year, the Garden had competition when George F. S. Marsh opened a restaurant directly across the street, and Annie Ivey and Rosa Golan opened the Ivey Cafeteria one block north. The Disney brothers liked to go out for ice cream, and for dessert likely walked along North Vermont three doors north of the Garden to The Chocolate Den, owned by confectioners Peter Ladas and William Chagalakes, or six doors north of the Den to an ice cream and candy store owned by A. L. Farris.

That December the Disneys also hired their second employee: Ann B. Loomis, a part-time inker and painter. Ann began work at the studio on December 8, 1923, and stayed for eight months. That month, Walt and Roy also rented a lot for exterior filming. They wanted to rent space from a studio in town, but the cost was too expensive. Instead, they rented a lot at 4589 Hollywood Boulevard, at the intersection of Hollywood Boulevard and Rodney Drive, one block east and two blocks south of the studio. The rent for the lot was $10 a month.

The company records for December show that the brothers' latest purchases included cigars for their Uncle Robert, tools, $30 worth of lumber likely used to construct their sets, and a $50 curtain that might have been used as a background tarp.

Virginia Davis recalled filming at Hollywood and Rodney: "We'd film in a vacant lot. Walt would drape a white tarpaulin over the back of a billboard and along the ground, and I'd have to work in pantomime. They would add the animation later." She was happy that "Walt was always pleased with my performances even in just one take." Walt would "lead me into pretending there was a big bear there or something like that, and that's what he'd do. He would say, 'Pretend there is a very big bear—look scared!' Walt did all of the directing and storylines."

Meanwhile, behind the scenes, Robert Disney continued to make loan installments to his nephews. He gave Roy and Walt $75 early in December and another $75—the last payment of his $500 loan—on December 14. Walt and Roy also borrowed $200 from Carl Stalling, $200 from Margaret Davis, $50 from another uncle, and $25 from Edna Francis. Roy told Walt not to write Edna for money, but Walt wrote her anyway, saying, "Don't tell Roy I wrote, but we need money. Can you lend us some, and if so, how much?" Roy himself put a "few hundred dollars" into the company. Roy and Walt's parents helped by taking out a $2,500 mortgage on their house in Portland, Oregon.

*Alice's Day At Sea* was completed and shipped on Saturday, December 15, its original due date (and two weeks earlier than the due date Walt subsequently negotiated). Thus began the period that Walt later described as "producing one series after another on a shoe-string budget for the state rights market[.]" The studio then put into production *Alice Hunting in Africa*, which, except for Ann Loomis, was made by the same team that made *Day At Sea*: Walt animated and directed the reel, Roy filmed it, Kathleen Dollard and Ann Loomis inked and painted it, and Virginia Davis starred in it.

Because the live-action sequences from *Hunting in Africa* no longer exist, it is unknown who else, if anyone, appeared with Virginia in this reel, although a poster for this short featured an African American boy, perhaps the same young actor who appeared in four subsequent reels in the series that became known as the Alice Comedies. Once again the animation was shot at McRae & Abernathy, and the live-action scenes were filmed in the lot at Hollywood and Rodney against the white tarp hung on the billboard there.

While things seemed to move smoothly on the west coast, on the east coast, Margaret Winkler and Charlie Mintz still had difficulties with Pat Sullivan. On December 19, the Mintzes ran an ad in *The Film Daily* that essentially threatened legal action against Joe Brandt, a distributor with whom Pat Sullivan had entered into a new distribution agreement for *Felix*. In the ad, Margaret stated that she exercised her contractual right to option another series of *Felix* reels the previous August. The ad worked: the threat of litigation caused Brandt to cancel his deal with Sullivan.

◂ ◂ ◂

On Wednesday, December 26, Margaret Winkler received *Day At Sea*, wrote Walt her reaction, and wired him his $1,500 fee. In the wire Margaret stated,

"DAY AT SEA RECEIVED TODAY SATISFACTORY MAILING TODAY DRAFT ON LOS ANGELES BANK WITH DETAILED LETTER." In her letter, Margaret asked Walt to send her the raw footage made for the film, both positive and negative, explaining that, "All our films are recut in New York." Margaret told Walt, "We believe [*Day At Sea*] can possibly be improved by re-editing here."

Margaret also wrote:

> While Alice's Day at Sea is satisfactory, still I think you will agree with me that there are some improvements to be made along general lines. . . .
> I am confident, however, that as we go along, each subject will grow better. . . . The progress that I have made in the film industry has been due to the fact that I know just what my people want and I always try to give it to them with the assistance of my organization.

Roy confirmed that "[B]y Christmas we delivered our first picture." When he and Walt got paid, said Roy, they "[t]hought we were rich." The brothers had spent $750 on the film, and received $1,500 for it; thus their profit was $750—and they went out and each ordered meat.

Two weeks after receiving *Alice's Day At Sea*, Margaret wrote Walt that

> We agree with you when you say that this subject is not all that it was expected to be, but as it stands it is a good picture. Of course, there is no use in going into details. I guess you know as well as I do, just what improvements it can stand. One big thing that I would suggest is that you inject as much humor as you possibly can.
>    Humor is the first requisite of short-subjects . . . . I think that you can appreciate that your product being a new one, will of necessity, require a great deal of plugging. Therefore, it is vital that each subject be good.

Margaret also asked Walt for a photograph of his cast since "[a] customer wanted to have an oil painting made of Virginia Davis and 'Peggy' to hang in his private office."

The next day, January 10, 1924, Margaret asked what "the very lowest price" was that Walt would accept for the first Alice short, *Alice's Wonderland*, which she wanted as an emergency backup reel. On January 12, Margaret made her second payment to the Disneys (presumably an advance for *Africa*), and the brothers repaid their Uncle Robert's $500 loan—with interest, for a total of $528.66—that same day, although they subsequently had to come back to Robert for another $100 loan. As they continued to work on *Hunting in Africa*, the brothers saw their production costs rise. Walt recalled that while "[t]he first [Alice] cost $750, . . . I managed to spend more on the second."

Sometime that week, Walt interviewed another young woman who had applied as the studio's third inker and painter. The woman—who in eighteen months would become Mrs. Walt Disney—got the job after Walt and Roy asked Kathleen Dollard to recommend someone for the position, and Kathleen suggested the younger sister of her friend, Hazel Sewell.

Hazel Bounds Sewell, twenty-six, was from Idaho and one of ten children raised on the Nez Perce Native American reservation in Lapwai, where her father Willard was a federal marshal and blacksmith. Hazel's mother, Jeanette, had been a schoolteacher. The Bounds family worried about putting food on the table and the children sometimes did not have shoes that fit properly. They were poor, but happy.

At the age of eighteen, Hazel Bounds married twenty-two-year-old Glenn O. Sewell, a pharmacist from Illinois. The couple lived in Lapwai, Idaho, and had one daughter, Marjorie. After eight years of marriage, the Sewells and seven-year-old Marjorie moved to Los Angeles, where Glenn worked for Frank Sohn, who owned a pharmacy. The family lived on North Vermont Avenue, about two miles south of the Kingswell studio.

In late December 1923, Hazel's twenty-four-year-old sister, Lillian Bounds, left Idaho to live with the Sewells in Los Angeles. Lillian was the youngest of the ten siblings. She was born in Spalding, Idaho, on February 15, 1899, making her nearly three years older than Walt. Lillian recalled, "I was a visitor in Hollywood from Lewiston, Idaho," where she had attended business college. She moved to Los Angeles "[t]o live with my sister." Lillian "got a job working for Walt. . . . [when] [a] girlfriend of my sister [Hazel] was filling in celluloids . . . and told me they needed someone else."

The friend "said [the Disneys] were going to hire another girl to do the inking and painting. Since [the studio] was within walking distance from where I lived, I applied for the job." She went to the "tiny office" in the "little studio" at McRae & Abernathy on Kingswell to apply for the job, and "[t]hat's when I met Walt." She recalled, "He didn't even have a suit." He "was wearing a brown coat, sweater, raincoat and pants." Regardless of what Lillian thought of Walt at that first meeting, Kathleen warned her: "I have a job for you, but I'm telling you about it on one condition: don't vamp the boss."

Lillian interviewed for the position and "got the job at $15 a week," the same as Kathleen earned. Lillian decided "to work for [the Disneys] because . . . I didn't have to take the bus" to get to work. Instead, she had only to walk approximately two miles north on Vermont, turn right on Kingswell, and then a half-block to the Disney Brothers Studio. Lillian recalled, "I went to work right away." Her first day was Monday, January 14, 1924, and her niece, seven-year-old Marjorie Sewell, joined her for the walk to the studio so Lillian would not get lost.

The courtship between Walt and Lilly began almost immediately and came about when Walt gave Lilly and Kathleen rides home from the studio. "We used to work nights," Lilly recalled. "He used to take us home after work." Walt drove the girls home in the Ford "runabout" he and Roy had purchased. Lilly recalled that the "Ford roadster [had] one seat and an open back." "When he started taking me home from work then I began to look at him like he was somebody," said Lilly. Walt must have felt the same way: as Lilly recalled, "He took the other girl home first."

Lilly felt Walt was "[a] wonderful man in every way—kind, gentle, brilliant, lots of energy and humility." As for Walt, he found Lilly "a good listener. I'd talk to her about what I hoped to do, and she'd listen." Lilly agreed: "He was always talking about what he was going to do. He always wanted to do the talking." "His work," she explained, "was [his conversation]." She also admired his outlook and his curiosity, exclaiming, "Did he ever [have a lot of optimism]! Enthusiasm and optimism together. He was enthusiastic about everything. He never thought anything would turn out badly." "If he didn't know about something," she said, "he would ask. Walt always remembered everything."

Walt's lack of a proper automobile and proper clothing, however, made him hesitant to meet Lilly's family. "When he got to my sister's he was embarrassed to stop in front of the house," Lilly recalled, "One night he asked, 'If I get a suit, can I come and see you?'" Lilly said he could, and remembered that "Roy and Walt both went to Foreman and Clark's downtown." The brothers agreed that they would only spend $35.00 each on their new suits. Walt bought a two-pants suit, and Roy's had one pair of pants. Roy's cost $35.00, but Walt's cost $40.00. Walt, Lilly explained, "always got the best,"

Lilly recalled that, "When he came to my house [he wore the suit]. It was gray-green and double-breasted, and he looked very handsome." As he met the Sewells, Walt "stood up and said, 'Well, how do you like my suit?' My family liked him immediately. There was never any embarrassment about Walt. He met people easily. He was completely natural." One night, Walt and Lilly were working late and Lilly was taking dictation. "Suddenly," Lilly said later, Walt "leaned over and kissed me." In response, Lilly blushed, which she said "was customary in those days."

◆ ◆ ◆

On Monday, January 21, with the third Alice Comedy, *Alice's Spooky Adventure*, in production, the Disney brothers shipped the second reel, *Alice Hunting in*

*Africa,* to Margaret Winkler, and Walt made clear that he was taking to heart his distributor's suggestions about humor. Walt wrote Margaret that, "I sincerely believe I have made a great deal of improvement on this subject in the line of humorous situations and I assure you that I will make it a point to inject as many funny gags and comical situations into future productions as possible." He thanked Margaret for the inquiry from what might have been his (or his characters') first fan, writing, "I wish to thank you [o]n behalf of little Virginia and 'Peggy' for the very unusual compliment paid them by your customer. I will send photo as you requested[.]"

Walt also replied to Margaret's offer to purchase *Alice's Wonderland* for $300. He wrote, "I believe your price of three hundred is very low and I doubt if it will be acceptable[ to Pictorial, the reel's owner]. However, I will do the best I can and notify you at once."

Margaret explained that she offered "such an extremely low figure" for the negative since she would receive no financial return on the reel, and only wanted it "as an emergency reel where another shipment, for some reason, may be held up." Walt replied that Laugh-O-gram Films "has been thrown into bankruptcy" and the bankruptcy trustee, Receiver Joseph Jones, sold the reel to Pictorial Clubs. Walt "had quite a time getting this information as the Receiver is very close mouthed and I had to secure it through other channels." Perhaps understating his role in Laugh-O-gram Films, Walt told Margaret that he "did not file a claim for my back salary and therefore I have no interest in *Alice's Wonderland*[.]" Walt suggested that Margaret contact W. R. Kelley of Pictorial if she still wanted to obtain that reel. Walt heard a few days later from Joseph Jones, who confirmed that the "*Alice's Wonderland* negative [was] disposed of" by the bankrupt estate.

*Hunting in Africa* was completed by January 21. The *Los Angeles Times* commemorated the event by reporting that "Virginia Davis, 5-year old film newcomer, has just completed the second of a series of twelve short-subject cartoon films in which she is featured by Walt Disney, local cartoonist and producer."

While Margaret wrote of *Hunting in Africa* that Walt made "great improvement on . . . timing" and that viewers found "the subject is nice and clean and they like Alice very much," she found that "[t]he comedy situations, however, are still lacking and I wish you would do your utmost to see that this end of the series be improved." Margaret claimed that this "lack of humor" was "the only hitch . . . in the selling of this series to various territories[.]" Margaret asked Walt to "see what you can do to improve that situation. . . . Please again let me impress upon you that future productions must be of a much higher standard than those we have already seen. By this I mean only the comedy situations. The other parts being satisfactory."

It is unknown how, if at all, Winkler's critique of *Africa* affected Walt's current production, *Alice's Spooky Adventure*, because it was already underway, and with a much larger cast and a more involved live-action plot than *Day At Sea*. The live-action sequences of *Spooky Adventure* focus on a dozen or so children playing baseball in a field. When one of the children hits the ball through a window of a supposedly haunted house, it is Alice (wearing the same plaid dress seen in *Day At Sea*) who steps forward to retrieve it. Inside the house, she comes across a black cat and falls asleep. In the animated sequence she dreams that she and the cat visit ghosts at a concert in Spookville. When she awakens, a police officer finds her and jails her for trespassing.

Because the live-action sequences of *Hunting in Africa* have not survived, it is *Spooky Adventure* that introduces the modern viewer to the gang of children that appears in several of the first six Alice Comedies. Walt cast these roles by using neighborhood and other children, and he paid them 50 cents a day. Even when he persuaded some of the kids to appear simply for fun, he paid them a token amount so that Roy could get them to sign payment vouchers—and a legal release.

The gang included ten-year-old Leon Sederholm, a large, chubby youngster whose frustrated efforts to hit an animated trick baseball open the *Spooky Adventure* reel. Leon—whose stage name was Leon Holmes—and his family lived on North Hudson Avenue, about two and one-half miles west of the Kingswell studio. The Sederholms had recently relocated to Los Angeles from San Francisco, and the move signaled a fresh start for a family that struggled to survive the untimely death of its father and husband.

Leon was born in 1913 in San Francisco to immigrant parents. His father, Alfred Sederhulden, thirty-eight years old at Leon's birth, was a watchmaker from Russia. Leon's mother, Rose, then thirty-three, was also Russian-born. The Sederhuldens lived on Eddy Street in San Francisco with Rose's mother and two brothers. Leon was the youngest; his older brothers were Norvin and Robert, and his older sister was Isabel. Alf died a few years after Leon's birth, and Rose was forced to place the children—who now went by the last name of Sederholm—as "inmates" in the Pacific Hebrew Orphan Asylum on Divisadero Street in San Francisco while she worked to support them.

Rose got a job as a bakery clerk and continued to live with her mother and a brother in the Eddy Street house, a half-mile from the orphanage. By the time Leon was cast in *Alice*, he, his siblings, and his mother were reunited under one roof in Los Angeles. Norvin, then eighteen, supported the family by working as a salesman at the Broadway Department Store downtown.

Freckle-faced Walter D. "Spec" O'Donnell also appeared in *Alice's Spooky Adventure*. Spec, thirteen, was the son of John O'Donnell, a lumber mill laborer from Maryland. Walter's mother, like his older siblings, Jack and Minnie, were native Californians. Several years before working for the Disneys, the O'Donnells lived in Madera, California.

Another cast member was thirteen-year-old Ruth S. Tompson, who was born in Maine, the home state of her mother, Athene—Ruth's father was from Massachusetts. By 1924 the Tompsons had divorced, and Athene married commercial artist John E. Roberts. The Roberts family lived at 4449 Kingswell, about ten houses west of the Schneiders and in the same block as Robert Disney. Ruthie met the Disneys because "a neighbor down the street . . . had a new baby boy, so I went in to see the new baby, and the name of the people that lived in that house [was] Disney, but it was Walt's [u]ncle, Robert."

Ruthie ended up appearing in the Alice Comedies after meeting Walt and Roy at their studio. She recalled

I met Walt, Roy, . . . and others while their studio was on Kingswell Avenue. I was nosey and saw girls [inking and] painting. I walked in and everyone was really nice. They were great with us kids, very patient, letting us look around. I knew Roy best. I used to sit on the bench by him when he was shooting. I stopped in often on my way home from grammar school. Going into the 'animation lab' was a wonderful experience—watching the drawings being made and later traced onto celluloid with pens, and then painted. What kid wouldn't be fascinated!

According to Ruthie, her sister, Dorothy, twelve, also appeared in the Alice Comedies, as did her cousin, Junior Allen. Other local children who might have appeared in the series included Paulie Grade, Tubby Vogel, and the Phillips brothers, Jimmie and Frankie. Paulie's father may have been Carl Grade, a casket company owner who lived in the 4400 block of Kingswell. Ruthie remembered playing with the neighborhood children near the local "hills where we all chased rabbits . . . near Vitagraph Studios[,]"located on nearby Talmadge Street, four blocks east of the Disney Brothers Studio.

Virginia Davis enjoyed having other children appear with her. "It was such fun. Kids in the neighborhood would act as extras," she recalled, "and Walt paid them fifty cents apiece." She "played with the children that were on the set and what have you. I was young enough that we didn't need a tutor or anything like that[.]" Her mother, however, did not let her overdo it. Virginia remembered, "We'd have our box lunches, but my mother used to keep me off to the side. She didn't want me to get too tired or overexerted."

Virginia's feelings about the other children were not always mutual; Ruthie Tompson later confessed she was jealous of Virginia: "I hated her! Wouldn't you be jealous of a little girl, yes you would, I mean if you were a little girl and this little kid came with all her little bouncing curls and everything? Cute little girl. She was getting all the attention."

Virginia recalled that Walt played a little with the children, but "he and Roy were under a great deal of pressure deciding what sequence to shoot next" because they had to meet "tight distribution deadlines. They worked very, very hard. They were the whole Studio crew—set makers, carpenters, cameramen, writers, and directors. Money shortages dictated that all live-action shots be completed in one take."

The only adult in *Alice's Spooky Adventure*, the policeman, was played by Joe Allen, a thirty-six-year-old "photo player" whose brother, David was a casting agent with Screen Talent Company, located on Hollywood Boulevard about a mile west of the studio. Perhaps Allen's brother cast any child actors in *Spooky Adventure* who were not from the Kingswell neighborhood.

The baseball scene in *Spooky Adventure* was filmed in an empty lot near a busy street along which many cars are seen driving. It was probably the lot rented by the Disneys at Hollywood Boulevard and Rodney Drive. The prison scene was filmed on an outdoor set built behind a large brick building, possibly the Kingswell studio building. Jeff Davis visited the prison set and the vacant house interior set, and surviving photographs shows Roy filming Virginia in those scenes while Walt directs and Jeff Davis looks on.

In February 1924, while *Spooky Adventure* was still in production, Rollin Clare Hamilton started at Disney Brothers, earning $15 a week as well as the distinction of being the first in a long line of Hollywood animators to be hired by Walt. Upon being hired, "Ham" Hamilton, twenty-five, helped Walt animate *Spooky Adventure*.

Ham was born in South Dakota; his parents were both natives of Iowa. The family later lived in Edgely, North Dakota, where Ham's father worked at a pharmacy to support his wife, daughter, and two sons. Ham still lived with his family at twenty-two—now in Grand Forks, North Dakota, where Ham's father remained a "druggist"—but within a few years, Ham left for Los Angeles. He started at Disney Brothers on Monday, February 11, 1924.

On February 22, at the end of Ham's second week on the job, the studio shipped *Spooky Adventure* to Margaret, after a live-action filming delay caused by fog and clouds. Walt wrote Margaret, "I am trying to comply with your instructions by injecting as much humor as possible and believe I have done better on this production. I have had professional critics at all pre-views and have been informed that we are making big improvements on each one. However, they seemed to be well pleased with all of them at that. It is my desire to be a little different from the usual run of slap stick and hold them more to a dignified line of comedy."

By the time the studio shipped *Spooky Adventure* to Margaret, it started production on the fourth Alice Comedy, *Alice's Wild West Show*. This reel featured an animated segment in which Alice's tale of the old West comes to life. Instead of teaming with a black cartoon cat, as she did in *Spooky Adventure*, Alice's animated co-star in *Wild West Show* is a white dog.

The live-action sequences of *Wild West* feature Alice and her friends putting on a western show for the neighborhood kids. This was Virginia's favorite Alice Comedy, "because I was a tomboy. . . . That was my favorite, because I loved to dress as a boy. I loved it[.]" Leon Sederholm's character—who gets a name, Tubby O'Brien, in this reel—plays the villain of the piece, leading a group of bullies who mock Alice and her fellow performers. Lilly's niece, Marjorie, appears as a member of the audience. The closing live-action sequence shows an indignant Alice wrestling her chief heckler, Tubby, on the lawn of a home. In the background across the street is a storefront that could be the Kingswell studio or one of the stores near the intersection of Kingswell and Vermont.

On Sunday, February 24, Disney Brothers Studio left the McRae & Abernathy real estate office. The staff—the Disney brothers, Ham, and inkers and painters Kathleen, Ann and Lillian—moved next door to the corner store at 4649 Kingswell. A future Kingswell animator recalled that the new studio was "in a little building that housed cleaning shops, that kind of thing, and had about a 20 or 25 foot frontage." The Disneys also rented a separate garage they converted into an office. The studio rent was $35 a month, and the garage rent was $7 per month.

The Disneys rented their new studio from a man named Gulstrand. Perhaps their landlord was Hans E. Gulstrand, who lived nearby (on Franklin Avenue, three blocks north and a block west of the new studio) at the time that the Disneys moved to 4649 Kingswell. A short time later, two brothers named Gulstrand lived on Prospect Avenue, one block south and a few houses east of the new studio, and either of them could have owned the building as well. Harold N. Gulstrand, who was five years older than Walt, was a paint salesman who lived at 4622½ Prospect Avenue with his wife Helen and their young daughter Louise. The Gulstrands were from Illinois, and Harold's parents were from Sweden. Harold's younger brother Herman lived next door, at 4622 Prospect. He was two years older than Walt, was a paper salesman, and was also born in Illinois.

By the end of February 1924, Disney had completed and delivered to Margaret the first three Alice Comedies: *Day At Sea*, *Hunting in Africa*, and *Spooky*

*Adventure.* On Saturday, March 1, Alice finally made it to a theater, as *Alice's Day At Sea* was released by M. J. Winkler Productions via state's rights distribution. *Motion Picture News* said *Day At Sea* was a "novel idea . . . very unique and entertaining enough to satisfy any sort of audience."

Walt's efforts to improve his shorts must have been working—whereas Margaret was somewhat critical of the first two Alice Comedies, she wrote Walt on March 4 to tell him she liked *Spooky Adventure.* She asked Walt to

> allow me to compliment you on "Alice's Spooky Adventure." As long as you have reached that standard please try your utmost to maintain it and if possible go a little bit better. . . . I will be frank with you and say that I have been waiting for just such a picture . . . before using every effort to place it in all the territories throughout the world. It may make you feel good to know that on the strength of this last one I was able to place the series in Southern New Jersey, Eastern Pennsylvania, Delaware, Maryland and District of Columbia. I am very optimistic about the future and believe that we have something here of which we will all be proud. . . . In the meantime, I might just say, keep plugging along on the subject[.]

Perhaps Margaret was praising Walt because she still worried about losing the *Felix* series—earlier that month, Pat Sullivan went to court to challenge his contract with Margaret. Despite her compliments, Margaret asked Walt to redo some of *Spooky Adventure's* combination animation/live-action scenes, and she edited out a live-action sequence where a policeman is seen carrying Alice down the street en route to jail. Margaret added that she was leaving for Los Angeles within a month, and was "sure that it will be a pleasure to meet you personally and when I do there will be so much which we will have to talk over."

Margaret decided to release one Alice Comedy per month—on the first of each month—but because she felt that *Hunting in Africa* was not good enough to distribute, her next release was *Spooky Adventure,* which premiered on Tuesday, April 1. She seemed as pleased with *Wild West Show* as she was with *Spooky Adventure*: even though Walt asked for "more criticism on each picture . . . as we feel you can point out faults and chances for improvement that we cannot see[,]" Margaret found *Wild West Show* "a very good subject." If Walt could make all of his shorts as good as *Wild West Show,* she ventured, "there will be absolutely no fault to find." Her editors even added back into the reel a bar room scene that Walt had cut from the animated sequence. As for Walt's cast, Margaret thought "it an excellent idea to use the children you have had in your last two pictures[, *Spooky Adventure* and *Wild West Show*]."

While Margaret thought *West* was a technically good reel, she suggested that Walt "improve a little on your comedy." In addition, perhaps because she still worried about losing *Felix*, Margaret thought Walt should use "wherever possible" in his "cartoon stuff" a cat and "don't be afraid to let him do ridiculous things." Walt was open to the idea, and Margaret appreciated his reaction to constructive criticism: "I am happy to see the spirit in which you take any criticism that is sent you. I think you can appreciate as well that we are both striving toward one goal—to make a cracker jack single reel."

Walt had utilized an animated cat as early as *Little Red Riding Hood* two years earlier at Kaycee Studios. The cat appeared in all seven fairy tale reels he made, collectively, at Kaycee and Laugh-O-gram Films. A black cat also jousted with some mice in the Alice *Wonderland* pilot. Walt followed Margaret's advice and, after appearing in *Spooky Adventure*, the black cat returned for the fifth Alice Comedy, *Alice's Fishy Story*, which continued the use of extended live-action sequences featuring Virginia Davis, Leon Sederholm, and the others.

In *Fishy Story*'s opening scene, Alice is frustrated when she cannot go fishing with her friends because she has to practice the piano. She gets Peggy the German shepherd to bang on the keyboard while she sneaks out the window and joins her friends. Alice's unsuspecting mother appears to be played by Robert Disney's wife, Charlotte, and the living room scene was likely filmed at Robert and Charlotte's home. This was the second and final time Alice's mother was seen in the series. As Alice's mother listens to Peggy play the piano, Alice goes fishing with her friends. After the animated sequence, Alice and her live-action friends' outing ends when the children are caught fishing in a prohibited area.

*Fishy Story*'s fishing scenes were likely filmed on a creek bank in Griffith Park, one of forty parks in Los Angeles and, at 3,751 acres, the largest municipal park in the country. It is located south of the Santa Monica mountains and north of Los Feliz. Walt had a clear recollection of filming on location there because—much like Alice and her friends in *Fishy Story*—he was chased away: he and his film crew were pursued by the authorities "for not having a license," he said, which he could not afford. "So we used to keep an eye out for the park policeman, and then run like mad before he got to us. We would then try another part of the park, and another." The crew on *Fishy Story*, like that which produced the recent Alice Comedies, included Walt, who directed; Roy, who filmed it; Ham, who animated the reel along with Walt; and Kathleen, Lillian and Ann Loomis, who inked and painted it.

◀ ◀ ◀

A unique problem delayed production of the sixth Alice Comedy. *Alice and the Dog Catcher*, which featured appearances by several dogs, was filmed in April and May (a "coming soon" poster advertising the upcoming date of May 19 is seen on a fence in the live-action sequence), but production was halted when an outbreak of foot-and-mouth disease in five California counties resulted in an animal quarantine. Walt wrote Margaret that the staff was "almost half through with it when we were forced to stop." By early May, the "quarantine had slackened," and Walt figured that two more weeks would be needed to complete and ship the reel.

*Dog Catcher* was the last Alice Comedy on which Walt worked as an animator, and thus the last of several Alice Comedies Walt and Ham animated together. The pair takes a bow of sorts on screen: they both play the heartless dog catchers thwarted by Alice, Peggy, Tubby, and the gang. In this reel, Walt and Ham are seen picking up dogs in their dog catcher truck and are involved in a lengthy car chase. In one scene Walt and Ham chase Virginia and her co-stars near Samuel J. Douds' grocery store at 1852 North Vermont Avenue, about two blocks north of Kingswell. A production still shows the children driving the dog catchers' car past the A.B. Strode Co., a real estate firm owned by Anxious Strode at 4705 Hollywood Boulevard, two blocks south of Kingswell.

While Roy still manned the Pathé camera and filmed the animated sequences of *Alice and the Dog Catcher* (which featured the cartoon dog seen in *Wild West* rather than the cat from *Spooky Adventure* and *Fishy Story*), its live-action sequences were filmed with a rented Bell and Howell camera by thirty-six-year-old Harry W. Forbes, who had worked as a cinematographer for almost a decade by the time he was hired by the Disneys as their new live-action photographer. Forbes moved to Hollywood from Ohio with his wife Bertha and had filmed movies at the Fox and other studios. Forbes came to Disney Brothers through George Winkler, and photographed the live-action sequences for *Dog Catcher* and two subsequent Alice Comedies.

*Alice's Wild West Show* was released on May 1 to good reviews. *Motion Picture News* stated, "Walt Disney, the cartoonist, produced a novel combination of an actual acting cast and cartoons in this single reeler and it is highly amusing and wholly entertaining." *Moving Picture World* wrote,

> In this reel, . . . produced by Walter Disney and distributed on the state right market by M. J. Winkler, clever use is made of photography and cartoon work in combination. There is considerable novelty in which this is handled, the photographed characters and cartoon characters working together against a cartoon background; there are also a number of scenes in which straight camera work is employed. A pretty and talented little tot, Alice, is the featured player, and she will make a hit with almost any audience.

Also on May 1, Pat Sullivan and the Mintzes settled their contract dispute. Their trial had been scheduled for late April, but Sullivan and the Mintzes resolved the matter and signed an agreement that would keep *Felix the Cat* with the Mintzes for at least another year.

Though Walt's staff was now six, as he looked ahead to the next six Alice Comedies, Walt's thoughts were with members of his former Kaycee and Laugh-O-gram colleagues. Earlier in the year, Walt had written to Ubbe Iwwerks, who was still working at Film Ad, and asked him to consider moving to California to join Disney Brothers. In May Ubbe wrote Walt he was ready to accept. Walt later explained his recruitment of Ubbe this way: "Trying to do all the drawing myself was too big a task. Finally I got Ubbe Iwwerks to come out and throw in his lot with us."

Hugh Harman, Rudy Ising, and Max Maxwell were also on Walt's mind, and Hugh remembered that he and his friends "heard from [Walt] frequently" after Walt went to California. On Friday, May 9, Walt did a favor for his three former staffers by putting a good word in for them to Margaret Winkler. Hugh, Rudy, and Max were still in Kansas City, where they continued to work together at night—using the Laugh-O-gram camera stand and other Laugh-O-gram equipment—in an effort to get their Arabian Nights Cartoons studio off the ground.

Just as Walt came to Kaycee at night after working at Film Ad, Hugh, Rudy, and Max had day jobs to support their after-hours work at Arabian Nights. Rudy recalled, "I had a Kodak finishing business, and Maxwell was going to college, and Hugh was working at the Film Ad," and "then Hugh, Max and I would work on this [Arabian Nights] film at night." Walt wrote in his May 9 letter to Margaret (a letter typed by Lillian), "The boys in Kansas City inform me[ ] that you seem interested in the 'Arabian Nights' series they are planning on making. I would like to say a word or two for them, as they are three very clever, clean-cut, young fellows and I would like very much to have them out here with me." Indeed, Rudy stated that Walt wanted his former staffers to "come out, right from the beginning [of Walt's time in California]." According to Hugh, the Arabian Nights sent a film to the Mintzes, but Hugh said it was "advanced technically" but "not very funny."

About three weeks later on Sunday, June 1,—the same day that Margaret Winkler left New York for her first meeting with the Disneys—Walt wrote to Ubbe to confirm that Ubbe, like Margaret, was heading west:

> Dear Friend Ubbe,
>     I'll say I was surprised to hear from you and also glad to hear from you. Everything is going fine with us and am glad you have made up your mind to come out. Boy you will never regret it—this is the place for you—a real country—to work and play in—no kidding—don't change your mind—remember what ol' Horace Greely [*sic*] said: "Go west young man—go west"—

We have just finished our sixth comedy for M. J. Winkler [*Alice the Dog Catcher*] and are starting tomorrow on the seventh [*Alice the Peacemaker*] of the first series of twelve. Miss Winkler is well pleased with them and has given us some high praise—she is leaving New York for here June 1st, and I believe we will be able to start a twice a month schedule instead of our monthly schedule—

I can give you a job—as artist-cartoonist and etc. with the Disney Productions. Most of the work would be cartooning—Answer at once and let me know when you want to start and I will write more details—At the present time I have one fellow [Ham] helping me on the animating, three girls [Kathleen, Lillian and Ann Loomis] that do the inking etc. while Roy handles the business end—I have a regular cast of kids that I use in the picture and little Virginia is the star.

I was talking with Mr. Davis last nite [*sic*]—told him you were figureing [*sic*] on coming out and he wants you to drive his car out—it is a seven pass[e]nger Cadillac—he will pay all expenses on the car—such as gas, oil and up keep—I think it is a dandy proposition and the best way to come out—You could have a nice trip—

Mr. Davis says it is a good car—an old model but has not been driven very far—he wants you to go over to the Much More Garage [at] 3220 Troost (under Georg[i]a Brown[']s Dramatic school) and take a look at it[.] Just tell them you are figureing [*sic*] on driving it out for him—

Then write and let me know what you want to do and how soon you can come out—if you can leave before the first of the month all the better—of course you would sell all your furniture and also your car? Wouldn't you?—I believe it would be best if you did—Anyways write and let me know all the details—Give my regards to every one at the Film Ad and the boys at the Arabian Knights [*sic*]—and also to your mother—

as ever your old friend—
Walt

Don't hesitate—Do it now—
P.D.Q. [Pretty Darn Quick]

P.S. I wouldn't live in K.C. now if you gave me the place—Yep—You bet—Hooray for Hollywood!

Margaret Winkler arrived in Los Angeles shortly after Walt wrote Ubbe, and she stayed for at least a week. On Tuesday, June 10, Walt wrote Ubbe again:

Received your letter yesterday and was glad you answered at once, as I wanted to make my plans for the future as soon as possible.

I have seen Mr. Davis and let him read your letter. Everything is O.K. with him and he is going to drop you a letter this evening and give you details about car. He will obtain a California license and forward same to you. . . .

Well, Ubbe, I am glad you are coming out and feel sure you will like it here after you are settled, and believe you will enjoy your trip out here, after you get across Kansas.

Our Big Boss, M. J. Winkler, is here. . . . [W]e have been making arrangements with them for the future. We are trying in every way to improve our picture as intend to make them the most popular single reel on the film market. I suppose you know that M. J. Winkler handles "Felix the Cat", and used to handle "Out of the Inkwell", but dropped it for our stuff. They are well satisfied with our stuff and are figuring on taking them twice a month, instead of once a month. I talked with them about the [Arabian Nights] boy's stuff. They seem interested and said if they had the right pep and humor they might talk business. So tell the boys to forget unnecessary detail and cram it full of ridiculous and impossible comedy. It[']s what they like. We have had to learn that by degree and at the present are doing everything impossible in the[m] that we can.

It will take you about ten days to drive out here so why can't you leave a week earlier, which would land you here around the first of July. The sooner the better.

Well Ubbe give my regards to your Mother and the bunch at the [F]ilm Ad., also say hello to the boys at Arabian Knights [*sic*]. Let me hear from you.

While Walt and Roy had meetings with Margaret, and Ubbe was preparing to join Disney Brothers Studio, the rest of the staff—Ham, Kathleen, Lillian and Ann, Harry Forbes, and newcomer Mike Marcus—worked on *Alice the Peacemaker*. For the first time in four years, Walt was no longer animating; with this reel, and going forward, he focused exclusively on writing, directing, and producing. The twenty-two-year-old Walt's three-year career as an animator was over.

About this transition, Walt said, "I was able to eventually build an organization. And it reached a point that I had so many working with me, and there was so much time and attention demanded that I had to drop the drawing end of it myself. But I've never regretted it, because drawing was always a means to an end with me." Roy felt that "Walt was never a good artist in execution. He was a Rube Goldberg type of an artist. Walt always put a meaning in his pictures, but the technique was not [as good] ... He was always conscious of it and would certainly turn to a better artist if he had one around."

At this time, twenty-two-year-old Mike Marcus replaced Roy as the animation cameraman. Walt explained that Roy "never could master the cranking rhythm a cameraman must learn. As a result, we ended up with a fluctuating tempo on the screen, so finally I had to hire a real cameraman and that did cost more money." Mike Marcus was born in Minnesota to Romanian-born parents, Aron and Fannie, who came to the United States in 1899. Mike lived with his family in Minneapolis until at least the age of eighteen, when he was a cigar store salesman. His father was a wholesaler, his older brother was a retail grocer, and his younger brother was a department store errand boy. Within four years, Mike moved to Los Angeles and eventually lived at 4634 Prospect Avenue, one block south of the studio.

Mike's first Alice reel, *Alice the Peacemaker*, experimented with a technique that employed, during the animation sequence, a photograph of Virginia Davis rather than the use of a live-action film clip of her. Recalled Virginia, "They only did that in one scene where I ran. I remember that in one picture where I would run and spread my legs like the animated animals as though they were sailing through the air, and they did use photographs for that, yes. They took the pictures against the whitedrop and then inserted them in those spots and you can certainly see where they were inserted." Another noteworthy thing about the animated sequence in *Peacemaker* is that the cat who appears in it, who was named Mike, fights with a mouse named Ike who looks very similar to a certain future Disney cartoon mouse.

The live-action sequences in *Peacemaker* featured, besides Virginia, only Leon Sederholm and Spec O'Donnell. In one scene, newspaper boys Leon and Spec argue over a customer on what appears to be Kingswell Avenue, a few doors from the studio. In another, it appears to be the intersection of Kingswell and North Vermont that can be seen behind Leon.

◂ ◂ ◂

As the summer of 1924 got in full swing, Walt must have been content. He received more press attention and Ubbe, his friend and collaborator, would soon be on his way to California. Over the Fourth of July weekend, the *Los Angeles Times* ran an article about Walt and his series. In "Actors Mix With Cartoons," the paper stated that "In Hollywood a young cartoonist by the name of Walt Disney is making a series of twelve animated cartoon productions. Real people are seen acting with pen-and-ink actors. They are known as the 'Alice' series and 5-year-old Virginia Davis, de luxe child dancer, has the big part. M. J. Winkler of New York is releasing the comedies."

As for Ubbe, although Walt had tried to get him to come west the previous month, Ubbe did not leave until July because of the time it took to sell his car and household goods. Ubbe and his mother, Laura Iwwerks, left Kansas City in Jeff Davis' Cadillac in late July, almost exactly one year after Walt made the same journey. During the trip Ubbe took many photographs, and his grand-daughter later wrote about a series of pictures that showed Ubbe's "dour-faced" mother. The drive took seven days.

When Ubbe and Laura arrived in L.A., they rented a house, possibly the one they lived in six months later, at 4334 Russell Avenue, which was a half-mile— or five blocks—north and east of the studio. Ubbe began work on Wednesday, July 23 at a weekly salary of $40—$10 less than the salary he left behind at Film Ad, but the highest salary at the Disney Brothers Studio. In addition to animat-ing, Ubbe worked on posters, titles, and lobby cards. Ubbe's arrival must have been good news for Ham, who got a raise from $15 to $20 a week at that time.

It is unclear whether Ubbe worked with Ham on *The Peacemaker*, which appears to have been completed around the time of Ubbe's arrival, or whether his first reel was the next one, *Alice Gets in Dutch*, which went into production in August. *Dutch* was the final of three reels filmed by Harry Forbes, and—but for one episode made six months later during the series' second season—the last one to feature a live-action cast other than Alice. The live-action scenes fea-ture a woman known as Mrs. Hunt in the role of Alice's teacher. Spec O'Donnell and Peggy the dog also appear. Another student is played by Marjorie Sewell, who said of her experience: "I know one thing. I was absolutely fascinated to see Walt using a megaphone. That excited me, because I thought, oh, that's a real director! Using that megaphone, that was keen!"

*Gets in Dutch* marks the start of the regular appearance of the animated black cat seen earlier in the Alice Comedies. In fairly short order, the cat, even-tually named Julius, became Alice's co-star, and Walt's first real recurring car-toon character. Up until this point, the cat (unnamed in the early episodes, in which he seemed to alternate in the co-starring role with an animated white dog, and named Mike in *Alice the Peacemaker*) seemed like a generic response to the popularity of the popular Felix the Cat. From this point on, however, Julius developed his own mischievous personality—along with a friendship with Alice, and he would remain a mainstay of the series throughout its run.

Ubbe's arrival also meant that the Davises were reunited with their Cadil-lac, which they loaned to Walt for dates with Lillian. Virginia recalled that Walt "borrowed my mother's [car] to court his wife." Virginia said, "Well, he didn't have a car, and he would ask mom if he could borrow the car." By early August, Ubbe purchased his own car. "Ubbe has been with us now for over a week," Walt wrote Dr. McCrum, "and we are certainly making use of him . . . He has bought a big Cole Eight roadster. After driving a big car, he couldn't go back to a small one."

By August, Charlie Mintz, now thirty-four, seemed to take over the Winkler company's relationship with the Disney brothers. Walt, twenty-two, and Roy, thirty-one, must have been glad that Charlie appeared to like the studio's latest reel. On August 7, Charlie wrote Walt that *Alice the Peacemaker* had arrived in New York that morning, and established that Walt's films had "progressed quite a little. Please see that all future subjects are up to at least the standard of this one." Charlie, however, complained about an old reel; he wrote that the Winkler company lost money whenever it showed *Hunting in Africa*, and that "our people will positively not accept that subject." Charlie dispatched his brother-in-law, George Winkler, to Los Angeles, and he advised Walt to work with George to "fix up this subject" so it could be distributed.

Like Margaret Winkler, her brother George, twenty-two, was born in Hungary and he came to the United States sometime before the age of eight. One longtime animator described George Winkler, who seemed nervous and suffered from a stutter, as Charlie's "hatchet man." Yet George was knowledgeable about filmmaking and was respected by Charlie, which is why he sent George west to help edit the Alice Comedies.

While *Peacemaker* earned a compliment from Charlie Mintz, it lost Disney Brothers Studio $45.54, but Walt chalked such losses up to the cost of quality. He said that he and Roy "took a lot of bumps along the way, but we always kept striving for the same goal: How could we best use this medium of the film? How could we use this artistic talent we had developed? We were never interested in how much money we could make, only in how good a job we could do on film." With regard to the industry, he said, "It was a fight first to get in, to crack the ice." Then, said Walt, "it was a fight to survive." Walt's focus on quality, no matter the cost, caught up with him, and by August the studio was in dire financial straits, causing Walt to provide Virginia Davis' parents with a promissory note in lieu of her salary.

On August 15 Walt wrote Charlie that he and Roy were "in a very tight place" because they were "[g]oing to expense almost equal to the selling price," and asked that Charlie advance the Disneys $900 for their next reel three months early in exchange for a discount of $40. Things got so bad that Walt tried to get work from Dr. McCrum, who had commissioned Walt to produce *Tommy Tucker's Tooth* almost two years earlier. On August 29, Walt pressed Charlie again:

We need money. . . . We have been spending as much as you have been
paying us for [the films] in order to improve and make them as good as
possible, and now that we are receiving only $900.00, it puts us in a "ell
of a 'ole." I am not kicking about that, however, I am perfectly willing to
sacrifice a profit on this series, in order to put out something good, but
I expect you to show your appreciation by helping us out. As you know,
we haven't had the money to spend on them, we will have to skimp, and
at this time, it would not be best to do that. So please, for our sake as
well as your own, give this more consideration and instead of sending us
$900.00, make it the full amount [$,1800] excepting a fair discount which
will enable us to pull through this period.

Walt also vouched for his improved quality; his staff was making the "girl
stand out plain and distinct when she is acting with the cartoons" and would
"make nothing but sure-fire laugh-getters." Camera work would be "good, if
not perfect[.]"

Walt tried to handle the financial pressure, as he had in Kansas City, by
asking employees for help. Lilly recalled, "When I first went to work for Walt, I
made $15 a week. And sometimes he'd say, 'Lilly, have you cashed any checks?'
I'd say, 'No,' and he'd say, 'Well, hold off for a while, will you?' So I'd keep [the
checks]. I didn't need 'em. I'd put them away and he and Roy would use that
little bit of money to pay their expenses." Lilly said that Roy was in on it, too:
"Roy would tell [Walt], 'Now don't let Lilly cash her checks.'"

Perhaps as another means of cost-cutting, Walt asked Charlie if he could
do away with the live-action opening and closing segments in the next reel,
*Alice and the Three Bears*, and Charlie approved and was happy with the result.
He wrote Walt how "very much satisfied" he and "Mrs. Mintz" were with *Three
Bears*, "and [I] can say the same for the last couple previous to that one." He
thought Walt was "doing a wise thing by sacrificing some of the little details of
the story and going more after laughs and funny little gags."

Given Charlie's positive reaction to the Alice Comedies, it is not surprising
that, with only a few reels left to be made under their contract, Charlie wanted
Walt to speak with the Winkler company's west coast representative because
"[t]his may not be a bad time to talk over plans for the future[.]" But Charlie
continued with some complaints as well. For example, he continued to push
Walt to remake *Hunting in Africa*, which Walt had avoided by invoking his
precarious financial situation. Charlie wrote Walt,

I might say that we are selling some territory and in order not to kill the
entire series, we are still holding off on releasing "Hunting in Africa." For
your future good as well as for ours, something must be done on this

subject very soon as there are several exchanges who are now up on their releases and we can use this subject to very good advantage. As it is however, we are compelled to hold off.

George Winkler confirmed Walt's financial circumstances for Charlie, however, and Charlie finally agreed "to wait, let you fix up this subject and release it as the twelfth of the series."

Almost three weeks later, Charlie reiterated his praise for *Three Bears*, and complimented *Alice Gets in Dutch* as well. "I hope you will pardon me," he wrote, "for not having written you sooner about 'Alice Gets in Dutch' and 'Alice and the Three Bears.' These are both excellent subjects." *Gets in Dutch* was "so well liked" that the manager of the new Piccadilly Theatre, "the newest of the first run Broadway houses[,]" booked the reel himself.

Charlie was concerned, however, about the "unanimous" opinion of purchasers of the Alice series that "the subject is actually better when you use a gang of kids than when you don't use them. . . . Please use a gang of kids in your future pictures." In addition, the manager of the Piccadilly had pointed out "one radical fault" of *Gets in Dutch*, a problem that "would keep him from running any future ones unless a very great improvement is made." Specifically, Alice "is always very light" and "there is more or less of a jump all the way through when the combination [of Virginia Davis with cartoons] is used."

By the time that production was underway in October on a retelling of the Pied Piper fable entitled *Alice the Piper*, the Disneys hired a third animator, Thurston Harper, to assist Ubbe and Ham. Carl Thurston Harper, Jr., twenty-one, was from Texas. His father was a general practice lawyer. Both Thurston's father and his mother, Jennie Webb Harper, were born in Texas. By the age of seventeen, Thurston lived with his parents, his older sister, Clothilde, and his younger brothers, Paul and Webb, in Madisonville, Texas. But within four years, Thurston moved to Los Angeles.

A Disney Brothers colleague recalled that Thurston had "a big, almost perfect Jack Dempsey type of build, and [was] a hell of a nice guy until he lost his temper. He was okay with pals and with us, he never got too rough." While Thurston hit it off with Roy Disney, whom Thurston found to be "a very wonderful and level-headed man[,]" there was soon "little love lost" between Thurston and Walt. Thurston blamed the tension on "a clash of personalities [that] occurred quite often."

Ubbe, whom Thurston also befriended and thought was "a multi-talented person and . . . very fine man" but "taciturn and retiring," suggested that Thurston just ignore Walt. Thurston recalled that Roy "always acted as peace-maker and resolved any difficulties" with Walt, and that Roy and Ubbe made it possible for Thurston to remain at the studio. About Walt, he later wrote, "I didn't hate Walt. I just didn't number him among my favorite people."

That same month, Walt finally ceded to Charlie's demand that he remake *Alice Hunting in Africa*. Walt removed part of the original live-action sequence and had Ubbe, Ham, and Thurston rework some of the animation. *Alice the Piper* was completed the next month, and Walt decided to use that reel to convince Charlie once and for all to drop the live-action opening and closing sequences.

Walt wrote to "Mr. Mintz" in a letter typed by Lillian that *Piper* was a "very good subject" that "received laughs from the very first title to the end" when it previewed at Bard's Hollywood Theater. "In fact," Walt wrote, "every little scene got at least a chuckle from the audience." Walt was not exaggerating, he said, and George Winkler would back him up. Further, "[a]fter George cuts this picture down to its proper length, it will be a corker of a laugh getter without a dead moment in it." Walt hoped that, after Charlie viewed *Piper*, he would agree that the live-action opening and closing sections were unnecessary:

> If we had to figure a live action opening and closing on each picture, it would necessitate our cutting down on the cartoon expense in order that we could spend the money on the live action and instead of doing this, I have been wanting to put on another cartoonist, in order to improve the cartoon work still more. I sincerely hope you will drop this idea of the two kinds of action and allow us to show you what can be done without the gang of kids.

In truth, Walt had already hired Thurston. Walt also tried to leverage his relationship with George to sell Charlie on a completely animated series:

> We have talked this over with George and believe that after you have talked it over with him, you will see the advantage of leaving out the gang of kids, because after all these are cartoon comedies and not kid comedies. . . . [I]f we have to put a live action opening and closing [in the story we are now working on,] I am afraid it will just be another one of the ordinary. There [are] not enough logical live action opening and closings to go around and besides, the public would soon tire of them.

George returned to New York soon after and talked to Charlie "about doing away with the gang of kids in the openings and closings." George told Walt that "we can bring [Charlie] around to your way of thinking," but only if "each subject should be 100% good." George took responsibility for authorizing Walt to make the next reel, *Alice Cans the Cannibals*, without live-action opening and closing scenes, but needed Walt to "stand back of me and give me your thorough cooperation by sending a good picture East, [or] Lord help me!! So it's up to you."

Meanwhile, it appears that Lilly's career as an inker and painter stalled, as did her back-up role as Walt's secretary. Lilly recalled, "I was not very artistic at all and I was never very good at inking and painting. Later Walt made me his secretary, but I made too many mistakes when he was dictating." Thus, even though "[t]hey tried to use me as a secretary, . . . I wasn't very good at it." Lilly's job, however, seemed secure: she was still dating the boss. "He was fun, even if he didn't have a nickel. We would go to see a picture show or take a drive up to Sunset Boulevard sometimes."

By now, Walt said he "went Hollywood" and bought a used but "ostentatious" dark gray Moon roadster. He adored the car, which had steel wheels, an exposed radiator, running boards, and hood ornament. "We used to take rides in it out to Pomona and Riverside," recalled Lilly, "driving through the orange groves. And Walt would take me out to dinner at tearooms on Hollywood Boulevard. He also would like to take me to shows."

If there was a star on Walt's artistic staff at this time, it was Ubbe. He eschewed the pose method of animation endorsed by the Lutz book he and Walt had studied in Kansas City. Over time, he prepared for the animators sketches made from rushes of Alice's scenes. After Mike Marcus filmed Virginia, Ubbe would watch the film, and then draw a guide to the proposed animated sequences based on Virginia's location in each scene. Ubbe also reworked Walt's hand-crank Pathé camera. Specifically, as Thurston recalled, Ubbe "converted the hand cranked camera to motor drive, utilizing a telegraph key for its operation." This change improved the exposure of the animated scenes.

As for Walt's on-screen star, Virginia Davis had become a local celebrity of sorts and made "many" Saturday appearances at local theatres. "[I]t would be Little Virginia Davis appearing in person, . . . They would introduce me, and then I did a dance and took a bow and that was it," she recalled. "[I]t would be mainly just locally, you see, wherever they showed [Alice Comedies] in the theaters. They used to put out little [lobby] cards. . . . They had an orchestra." She would appear at matinees, before such audiences as Shriners and groups of children. She never stayed to watch her films. "I didn't care. It didn't mean anything to me, because I was doing whatever I was told to do. Kids don't care that much, you know, they're not that vain. I had fun doing it, and that was it."

In early December, three days before Walt's twenty-third birthday, Lillian typed a letter from Walt to Charlie in which Walt appears to be nudging Charlie into offering the Disney brothers another contract:

Dear Mr. Mintz

By the time you receive this letter you will, no doubt, have screened "Alice Cans the Cannibals". In this subject we have endeavored to have nothing but gags, and the whole story is one gags [*sic*] after another. You will, no doubt, notice a great improvement in the cartoon photography. This is due to the fact that we have equipped our camera with a motor drive, which will give us A-1 photography throughout. . . . In Georg[e] Winkler's letter of Nov. 13th., he spoke of the action of little Alice being too slow. We have snapped this up by our cranking when photographing her. The twelfth subject "Alice the Toreador" is well under way and prom-ises to be the best yet.

Finally, Walt got to the point: "We would appreciate hearing from you in regard to the future, so that we can arrange things accordingly." Walt also defended his preference for animated characters over live-action child actors by claiming that "animals afford a bigger opportunity for laughs than people." George got Charlie to agree, finally, to drop the live-action sequences from all future Alice Comedies.

On Monday, December 8, Charlie replied, "We have gone over the situa-tion very thoroughly and while things are not 100% rosy, still there is a whole lot that looks favorable. George knows all these things, knows just how we feel about it and will take up with you among other things, the making of a new contract for next year's product."

George left New York that Wednesday, and arrived in Los Angeles on Sunday, December 14. The Disney Brothers Studio that George visited in late 1924—with its staff of eight, including the Disneys, animators Ham, Ubbe and Thurston, inkers Kathleen and Lillian, and cameraman Mike Marcus—is memorialized in a layout diagram made by Thurston. He estimated that the Dis-ney Brothers building was 18 feet across and 36 feet deep. The diagram shows a front door entrance on Kingswell Avenue, to the left side of the large storefront. The inside of the storefront window was used to display Disney Brothers ani-mation art—cels and scenes from various Alice Comedies. A hallway inside the front entrance took up half the length of the space, and led back to the camera room. A three-foot high gate was between the hallway and the camera room. The Pathé camera run by Mike Marcus sat in the center of the camera room and a sink and unused film were in separate corners of that room.

To the right of the front hallway was a large table. Roy's desk (which held the company's books and records) sat to the right of the large table, and desks for the inkers and painters—Kathleen and Lillian—sat to the left side of the large table. Thurston recalled that "The chairs were inexpensive straight-backed ones, as were the desks, tables and cabinets for storage, etc." Roy used the large table to "punch holes in the cels and animation paper by use of a hand-operated machine." The table "had two levels, [and] the lower level [was] used to store clean cels." Ubbe also used the table to "set up his special drawing board to do all the posters, backgrounds, letter all titles, sub-titles, etc."

Along the right wall of the studio, behind the large table and leading almost all the way to the back of the building, was a series of animators' boards. The first of these was Walt's, which was closer to the front of the studio so Walt could communicate with Roy, Mike Marcus, and the two inkers and painters, Kathleen and Lilly. The rest of the animators' tables were used by Ham, Ubbe, and Thurston. In the back right corner of the studio was the restroom. It was accessible through the back of the camera room, and the restroom was also used as a darkroom. All of the furniture was "inexpensive and utilitarian."

That month, Charlie proposed a new contract, offering to pay Walt $1,800 each for eighteen additional Alice Comedies. Walt and Charlie signed the new contract on December 31, 1924, perhaps a date that allowed Walt to believe, for the first time, that his multi-year efforts to build a thriving animation studio had succeeded.

The possibility of a new contract led Walt and Roy to finally start paying themselves a salary of $50 per week, which they took on an irregular basis. Prior to that, they only took small amounts of money as needed, and continued to rely on loans from Uncle Robert for their payroll and their $30 rent at the Schneiders' house at 4409 Kingswell. Lillian recalled, "At that time [when I started] Walt and Roy weren't allowing themselves much more [than $15 a week], for nearly everything they made went into the pictures or to pay back money Walt borrowed to start the business." While Walt and Roy frequently passed on their salary or took less than the full amount, they permitted staff members to take advances on their salaries.

1925 began as 1924 ended: with Alice getting good reviews. A review of *Alice and the Three Bears* in London's *Kinematographic Weekly* stated, "The artist's work and the living player are capitally united." *Alice Cans the Cannibals*, which was released on New Year's Day, earned praise from *The Moving Picture World*, which wrote, "Each one of these Walt Disney cartoons ... appears to be more imaginative and clever than the preceding, and this one is a corker."

But the new year brought changes as well. The first new reel that went into production in January of 1925, *Alice Gets Stung*, was noteworthy for two reasons. First, it was filmed by a new live-action cameraman. Second, *Alice Gets Stung* was the last Alice Comedy filmed with Virginia Davis in the title role.

At the suggestion of George Winkler, who was by now the secretary-treasurer of M. J. Winkler Productions Inc. (Margaret was still the company's president and Charlie its vice president), the Disney brothers hired Century Studios cameraman Philip Tannura as its latest cinematographer. Tannura, twenty-seven, was born in New York, the son of Giusepe Tannura, a shoemaker who came to the United States from Italy five years before sending for his wife, Mattea, and Philip's older two brothers. The Tannuras had three more children, two daughters and Philip, after the family was reunited in the Bronx, New York. Tannura began working as a cameraman in Hollywood in 1917, eight years before his stint with Walt and Roy. For reasons unknown, Tannura lasted at Disney Brothers for only one Alice reel.

Ironically, Virginia Davis' last Alice Comedy was produced just as Walt redid *Alice's Day At Sea*, the first Alice Comedy she made in California over a year earlier. Walt was not happy with some of the animation in *Day At Sea*, and had Ubbe, Ham and Thurston reanimate some of those scenes. While improving the old reel, however, Walt and Roy worried about cutting the costs of future reels. One way to do so, they concluded, was to pay Virginia for the days she was filmed rather than pay her monthly, as they had done during the first season of the Alice Comedies.

"The reason my mother took me out of it after the twelfth Alice picture," Virginia recalled, "was that when my contract came up, they didn't want to put me under another contract as such." During the first season of the Alice series, Virginia reported to the Kingswell Avenue studio "once or twice a week. It wasn't very much, and I think this is why . . . Mintz didn't want to pay me on a monthly basis. He was more sold on the cartoon gags rather than the human interaction." Walt and Roy estimated that they could film all of Virginia's scenes for the eighteen-second season films in eighteen days. Virginia explained, "They wanted to pay me for each day where perhaps I would be photographed for two or three different stories." She recalled, "My mother said, 'Never mind.'"

The Davises, however, did not blame Walt. While they did not socialize with Walt (he was twenty-three; Jeff Davis was forty-one and Margaret Davis was thirty-five), Margaret, in particular, was partial to Walt. Virginia felt that her parents and her boss had "nothing in common. He was a bachelor, and also he was working most of the time, too[.]" But Virginia maintained that her mother "always loved him. I mean, she loved Walt. She was very fond of Walt."

And Virginia herself had had no ill will towards Walt: "It was Mintz. Walt never had any ill feelings toward me." Virginia believed that the Disneys had to rework her compensation because they were "having money problems because Mintz kept cutting [the] budgets . . . . [Also,] Mintz had a big ego and wanted things his way. . . . He threatened to replace me if I wouldn't appear under the new terms of the contract. He wrote that he still wanted me, but under his terms. . . . and Mother would not accept the terms."

Thus, the Davises, Virginia recalled, "were mostly upset with Mintz and they felt he was not being fair with anybody. He later intimated that there was a little friend of theirs that got into the films after I left. Whether that's true or not I don't know. He wanted someone a little more like Clara Bow and I had those long curls. . . . I think Mother was smart enough though to realize that the live action that Walt was doing was being put aside in favor of the cartoon gags, so it really wasn't doing me any good." While the Davises may have blamed Charlie for Virginia's exit from the series, a letter written by Jeff and Margaret to Walt on January 7, probably written while *Alice Gets Stung* was in production, showed a straining relationship between Walt and Jeff and Margaret Davis.

With an increased number of Alice reels to produce in the series' second season, Walt and Roy realized they could not afford to lose their star animator. So, even before they found their new Alice, they gave Ubbe a raise to $50 a week. This meant that Walt, Roy, and Ubbe all earned the same amount. Ham also got a raise, from $20 per week to $30 per week. By February, when the next reel, *Alice Solves the Puzzle*, went into production, Walt and Roy still had not found their new Alice. While they kept looking for Virginia's permanent replacement, they hired five and one-half-year-old Margie Gay to play Alice in *Solves the Puzzle*.

Margie Gay was born Marjorie Teresa Gossett in Oklahoma in the summer of 1919. She was born to eighteen-year-old Ruth Gossett, a native of New Jersey, who by then worked as a telephone company clerk operator in Muskogee, Oklahoma. Ruth alternately stated that she had been widowed by and divorced from Marjorie's father, and that he was from Missouri and Oklahoma.

By the time Marjorie was one, Ruth boarded the baby at a home in Muskogee while Ruth, who lived elsewhere, worked to support her. Within a few years, the Gossetts relocated to Los Angeles, and Ruth gave her toddler the stage name of Margie Gay. Ruth called herself Mrs. Ruth Gay and got a job as a typist.

By February 1925, Walt had more than a new Alice on his mind. He continued to hope, nine months after writing to Margaret Winkler about his desire to get Hugh Harman, Rudy Ising, and Max Maxwell to L.A., that his former staff members would join Disney Brothers. On Friday, February 27, Walt wrote Hugh that, "You have'nt [*sic*] much chance for big stuff where you are[.]" Almost a month later, on March 30, Walt wrote Rudy about "things that can only be learned by actual experience with experienced people." Walt told Rudy, "After you see Los Angeles, Hollywood and the surrounding country, you will feel ashamed of yourself for not coming sooner."

Despite the tension between Walt and Thurston, Walt's existing staff experienced light moments at work. Photographs that Walt took in front of 4649 Kingswell in late 1924 or early 1925 show Roy, Ubbe, Ham, and Thurston having fun with some empty liquor bottles. In one of the photographs, explained Thurston, "We are engaging in a little horseplay with the [studio] props. Roy is oiling me up for the day's work. The rear of Ham's T Model and front of Ubbe's Cole 8 are shown. Walt was driving a Moon roadster at the time. Also [in the photograph is] part of the gold leaf sign I painted reading Disney Bros. Studio [on the front window]."

Walt and Lilly continued to date. One of their "big date[s]" Lillian recalled was their trip "downtown" to "go see *No, No, Nanette*," which made its L.A. premiere on March 9, 1925. Walt loved the theater, especially musicals, and *Nanette* was a big hit at the time. The musical "sensation[']s" seventeen-week run at the Mason Theater was its west coast debut, and it had just played in Chicago, where it ran for forty-two weeks. Walt and Lilly saw the show between its March 9 premiere and Fourth of July closing night. The *Los Angeles Times* described the show as "written with a pen dipped in fun. There is a man who has so much money that he cannot spend it fast enough. There is his wife, who refuses to help him distribute gold. There are the pretty girls whom this man engages to act where his wife failed. And there is dancing and song and comedy galore."

Although the show would not make it to Broadway until the following summer (it played in San Francisco and other west coast locales from mid-1925 to mid-1926), it featured a New York cast, including leading man Taylor Holmes and leading lady Nancy Welford, who sang, "Tea For Two," "I Want to be Happy," and other selections from the score. The Los Angeles premiere warranted two expansive opening eve articles in the Sunday *Los Angeles Times*, and its run set a city theater attendance record.

In March, the Disneys produced *Alice's Egg Plant*, in which a Moscow hen leads a pro-union frenzy among the hens that Julius is trying to get to lay eggs. *Egg Plant* is the first short in which Alice's feline friend is referred to on screen (at least on a title card) as Julius. It also marks the replacement of Margie Gay in the lead role with Dawn Paris, the third Alice in as many months. Walt and Roy apparently hoped that five-year-old Dawn would be the permanent replacement for Virginia Davis. Paris went by the stage name, "Dawn O'Day," and had worked in movies for a few years under Cecil DeMille's brother, William, and other directors.

Dawn Evelyeen Paris was born in New York in 1919 to forty-six-year-old Henry Paris and his wife, Mimi, thirty-five. Henry was a storehouse clerk. He, too, was born in New York, the son of German immigrants. Mimi came to the United States from England at the age of twenty-four. By the time Dawn was one-year-old, the Parises lived on 136th Street in New York. Dawn was photographed by commercial artists as an infant, and began acting at three. Within a few years, Dawn and Mimi moved to Los Angeles where Dawn, under the stage name Dawn O'Day, became a "photoplayer." It is unknown whether Henry died or left Mimi. It is possible he moved to Los Angeles separately and pursued a career in advertising.

The terms the Disneys had offered to Jeff and Margaret Davis in January were ultimately not acceptable to Mimi Paris (who Dawn supported) and, after a month on the job, the O'Days and the Disneys quickly parted ways. As a result, *Egg Plant* was O'Day's one and only appearance as Alice. Of this phase in her life, O'Day later recalled, "Sometimes there was a part, there was a bit, there was extra work, there was a large part. It went up and down, and there were terrible times where you didn't pay the rent and little things like that."

The month of March saw renewed tension between the Mintzes and *Felix*'s Pat Sullivan. Their current contract ran from May 1924 to May 1925. With two months left on that contract, Sullivan's attorney negotiated a new deal with an English distributor. The lawyer, over lunch, told Charlie of the deal so that Charlie could bid for worldwide rights outside of England. Charlie declined, and he and Margaret decided to sue Sullivan. Perhaps the possibility of losing *Felix* led Margaret Winkler to, once again, see the Alice series in a different light: on March 26, she filed a copyright registration for the Alice Comedy trademark, stating that the trademark, in which the "A" in Alice formed an underscore to the rest of the series title, had been in use "since January 2, 1925."

Walt was still experiencing tensions of his own. While disagreements with Charlie and Thurston seemed to be a recurring fact of life for him, he certainly must not have enjoyed parting ways with the Davises, who were not only instrumental in the making of *Alice's Wonderland* before Walt left Kansas City, but also followed him to California and played a prominent part in his first successful cartoon series.

In addition, Walt and Roy appeared to be getting on each other's nerves after fifteen months of sharing a room at the Schneider house, where the rent in early 1925 was still $15 per month. One night, after a disagreement with Walt over one of Roy's meals, Roy sent a marriage proposal to his fiancée of five years, Edna Francis. (It is not known if the bedroom they shared at the Schneider house had a kitchenette, or if Roy otherwise on occasion prepared a meal in the room.) As Roy recalled, "It came to the point where Walt didn't like my cooking.... Well, he just walked out on my meal one night, and I said, 'Okay, to hell with you. If you don't like my cooking, let's quit this business.' So I wrote my girl in Kansas City and suggested she come out and we get married, which she did."

Walt later joked, "When Roy told me he was going to be married I realized that I'd need a new roommate, so I proposed to Lilly." Roy made a quip, saying that his marriage to Edna "left Walt alone," and his quick engagement to Lillian showed that "apparently he didn't like living alone, even though he didn't like my cooking."

Lilly said that she, too, "teased Walt that the reason he asked me to marry him so soon after Roy married Edna . . . was that he needed somebody to fix his meals." Lilly gave other joking explanations for their engagement. Lilly recalled that Walt "said he married me because he got so far in debt to me" and "Walt always used to say I was such a bad secretary he had to marry me."

Regardless of the explanation, Walt ignored his own advice that he should not marry until he was twenty-five years old and had saved $10,000, and proposed to Lilly. Walt recalled that he and Lilly were going to buy a car together, but the plan went awry when Walt asked her, "Which do you think we ought to pay for first, the car or the ring?" Lilly chose the ring.

Edna, thirty-five, and her mother traveled to California for her marriage to Roy, and they arrived in Los Angeles on Tuesday, April 7. The following day, Rudy wrote Walt from Kansas City, and his letter referred to a new look Walt would sport for Roy's wedding: Walt had grown a moustache. Roy explained that Walt did so because Walt had "a complex for a while of trying to make himself look older because he was so young." Lilly recalled that Walt grew it because he and "Ub[be] . . . , the Harman boys and Rudolf Ising made a bet. They all grew moustaches. Walt wanted to shave it off later but we didn't let him."

Edna presumably met Lilly for the first time after arriving in L.A. Edna remembered that Lilly "was already working for [Walt] when I came out here. And he and Lilly were talking about getting married and he just thought about her and about his work." Edna and Roy married on the Saturday after Edna got to California. She recalled, "Roy and I were married on April 11 at Uncle Robert's house. Mother, Father, and [Roy's brother] Herb came down from Portland. Walt was the best man, and Lilly was maid of honor." The couple—with Edna's mother—honeymooned at the Hotel Del Coronado in San Diego.

Meanwhile, *Alice Loses Out* went into production. After Dawn Paris didn't work out, Walt and Roy went back to Margie Gay, and not only cast her in *Loses Out*, but kept her in the role for an additional twenty-nine episodes. The thirty-one reels Margie Gay made for the Disneys were more than double the number of episodes in which Virginia Davis appeared, making Margie Gay the most prolific of Disneys' Alices.

That month, *Alice Stage Struck* also went into production, under the working title of *Alice's Uncle Tom's Cabin*. It was a noteworthy episode of the Alice series since it was the first Alice in eight months with live-action bookend sequences and probably the last Alice episode to include them.

One of the children who appeared in *Stage Struck* was Lillian's niece, Marjorie Sewell, who returned for her second Alice Comedy. Marjorie, now eight, was enamored of her new co-star, Margie Gay. Said Marjorie, "I thought she was so cute!" Virginia Davis, however, thought her successors, "[i]n all honesty, . . . didn't have all that much to do because the cartoon characters were taking over. The comedies started going downhill after Mintz began dictating to Disney and demanding more gags and more films for less money." She said, "[T]he girls who followed me just stood there and waved their arms and jumped up and down rather than having to do any emoting to follow the storylines." Appearing with Marjorie Sewell—and star Margie Gay—were Spec O'Donnell, an unidentified African American boy, and two other children.

April, May, and June of 1925 brought numerous studio developments on the personnel front. The size of the studio, which had dropped back to seven after the Disneys' first hire, Kathleen Dollard, left earlier in the year, almost doubled by the middle of the year. By the end of April, after extensive negotiations, Hugh Harman, his younger brother, Walker, and Rudy Ising decided to move to California and join Disney Brothers, which they did eight weeks later. Hugh explained, "Rudy and I decided that it would be a good thing to come [to California], and find out what the Hollywood scene was like, because we intended it anyway, and we thought we'd work for Walt for a while, quit, and form our own company." Inker and painter Hazelle A. Linston joined the studio on May 23, and worked there for seven months. In May, perhaps in anticipation of the Kansas City animators' arrival in Los Angeles, the Disneys gave Ubbe a raise from $50 a week to $55 a week, and Ham an increase from $30 a week to $35 a week.

Lillian, probably because of her upcoming marriage to Walt, stopped working at the studio on June 1. "I quit work when we married," she said. Afterwards, she only worked for Walt in an emergency. Lilly's and Walt's original wedding date is not known, but after Edna's and Roy's wedding, Lilly and Walt moved their wedding date up to mid-July because Walt was alone in the apartment that he had shared with Roy and, according to Lilly, "Walt didn't like to be alone."

Ham's sister Irene Hamilton also joined the studio as a painter, on June 30. At nineteen, she was seven years younger than Ham. She lived with her brother at 1447 E. 73rd Street and worked at Disney Brothers for six months. Studio records show that Walt's sister, Ruth Disney, twenty-two, started as an inker and painter one week before Irene, and remained on the staff for seven months, but Ruth denied ever working for Walt and Roy.

The most significant of these personnel changes, however, was the addition of Hugh Harman, Walker Harman, and Rudy Ising. Hugh recalled, "We came out here in 1925 in June, Rudy, my brother Walker and I and joined Walt and Roy at their Studio on Kingswell[.]" Hugh and Rudy started at the studio on Monday, June 22, immediately upon their arrival in California, and probably started work on *Alice's Tin Pony*, which began production the previous Thursday. Hugh was hired as an animator, Rudy as a cameraman, and Walker—whose first day was June 24—as an inker. The Harmans and Rudy lived with Uncle Robert during their first week in Los Angeles until they found an apartment.

Walt explained the addition of the Harmans and Rudy: "I was able to get some of the boys that had been with me in Kansas City to come out. So then, . . . I had some help." Rudy found the Disney Brothers Studio very similar to Kaycee Studios and Laugh-O-gram Films. "Nothing [was different]. I mean, as far as our work. The new man in the organization then was Roy. We never knew Roy back in Kansas City. . . . He was a hell of a nice guy, that got along great with people . . . . He was the only new person. We knew Ub[be] and Walt. Hamilton we met when we came here, and Ham's sister used to do the painting. . . . Walker Harman inked the whole thing, on the drawings." Rudy found that, in addition to the "same group," Disney Brothers Studio used "almost the same equipment" as Disney's Kansas City ventures.

Rudy's animation and photography experience led Walt to use him in a few different ways. Rudy explained, "I did assistant animation and some animation, and camera work. Principally it was the camera and the editing and the printing." A few days after Rudy's arrival, Mike Marcus left Disney Brothers and became a cartoonist. Rudy manned the Pathé camera that was used for animation and the rented Bell and Howell camera to film Margie Gay.

Walt and Roy paid Hugh $45 a week ($10 less a week than Ubbe) and Rudy $35 a week (the same amount as Ham and Thurston). Walker Harman earned $20 a week. As a result, by June 1925, Ubbe was the highest paid person at Disney Brothers ($55 a week); Roy and Walt were the second highest ($50 a week); Hugh was the third ($45 a week); and Ham, Thurston, and Rudy were fourth ($35 a week).

Early July found Walt putting a number of affairs in order, probably in anticipation of his upcoming nuptials. First, the day before the Fourth of July holiday, Walt gave himself a raise from $50 to $75. Roy's salary remained at $50 a week. This meant that Walt was now the highest earner at the studio ($75 a week), Ubbe the second highest ($55 a week), and Roy the third highest ($50 a week).

Second, on Monday, July 6, Walt and Roy acted on their intention to move to a new studio, and put a $400 deposit on a vacant lot at 2719 Hyperion Avenue, south of Griffith Park, in L.A.'s Silver Lake region. The lot was one and one-half miles east and slightly north of the Kingswell Studio, and was near the fabled studio of Mack Sennett. The Disney brothers no doubt felt that their growing staff warranted the increased space. The brothers planned to build a new animation facility on the 60-by-40-foot lot.

Sometime that week, Lilly and Walt took a steamer to Seattle and a train to Lewiston, Idaho, probably using $150 in cash that Walt withdrew from the studio before their departure. On Monday, July 13, the couple was married in the home of Lilly's brother, the fire chief of Lewiston. Lilly, twenty-six, wore lavender and laughed nervously during the ceremony. Walt, twenty-three, was, in the words of his daughter, "very fascinated and very crazy about [Lilly's] family. They were a big family. I think he always liked the thought of a big happy family." The couple honeymooned at Mount Rainer National Park and in Seattle, and it was early August before they returned to L.A.

In Walt's absence, production was underway for *Alice Chops the Suey*, which used scenes featuring the lightning sketch animation technique Walt had employed in some of the *Newman Laugh-O-Grams* he made in Kansas City. Like those earlier films, *Chops the Suey* showed a photograph of a human hand that appears to quickly sketch such things as an ink bottle, into which Alice and Julius jumped. The photograph of the hand was provided by the Ries  Brothers. Paul L. Ries and Park J. Ries ran a commercial photography business for most of the 1920s. Their office was located at 6036 Hollywood Boulevard, almost two miles west of the Disney studio and about a half-mile north of the home the brothers shared. Around this time, the Rieses worked on about three Alice Comedies for Disney Brothers Studios.

Another special effect seen in *Chops the Suey* and numerous other Alice Comedies is the use of an animated Alice in place of the actress playing her where Alice is called on to perform a stunt (like jumping into an ink bottle, as in *Suey*) that the actress could not realistically perform. This animated effect would be spliced in between live-action shots of the actress playing Alice. Hugh believed Ubbe typically handled this effect because Ubbe "was a very good artist. He was capable . . . of rendering a drawing of Alice that would look so photographic that the comparison would be simple."

Around the time of Walt's marriage to Lilly, the New York Supreme Court heard the Mintzes' case against Pat Sullivan. The Mintzes argued that their original 1921 contract with Sullivan, and the second contract they entered into with him the following year, bound Sullivan from contracting with another distributor for the *Felix* series. In late July, while Walt was on his honeymoon, the Court sided with Sullivan, and the Mintzes later appealed the ruling. On August 3, Pat Sullivan took an ad in *The Film Daily* announcing his legal victory and the name of *Felix*'s new distributor, the Educational Film Corporation of America.

In August, after visiting Walt's parents in Portland, Walt and Lilly returned to Los Angeles. Although they had looked for a home to buy prior to their wedding, they were not successful and, upon their return from their honeymoon, settled into an apartment in the Ray Apartment complex located at 4639 Melbourne Avenue. Before the wedding, Walt still lived with the Schneiders, across the street from Uncle Robert's house, and Lilly still lived with Hazel Sewell and her family on Hollywood Boulevard. Walt and Lilly's new one-room honeymoon apartment had an alley view. It was one block north of the studio.

The rent for the small kitchenette apartment was $40 a month. Lilly recalled that she was "so unhappy because I had never lived in an apartment before." She explained that, "I was used to homes in Idaho where you could step out of your front door and be in the open."

Roy had also moved from the Schneiders' house to a honeymoon apartment on Melbourne. He and Edna lived a block east of Walt and Lilly, at 4535 Melbourne. Edna recalled, "On Melbourne [is where we lived after we were married]. We rented a little furnished duplex or something there. It wasn't our furniture. We just stayed there until we got settled, and then we bought our own furniture and started housekeeping in a court [apartment]. Just a small place. We lived there a year or two."

Walt returned to a studio energized by the arrival of the Harman brothers and Rudy. According to a veteran animator who later worked for Hugh and Rudy, Hugh "was sincere, high-minded, and very talented[.]" He "was a handsome man" and had "a genuine ambition to raise cartoons to loftier heights." Rudy "drawled and spoke with great and gradual deliberation. Working on his own, he would stay up all hours and was extremely creative, but, when he was working with others, he seemed acutely afflicted with an inability to make a decision."

Another veteran animator who became close friends with Hugh and Rudy found them "amiable" and that "their good-humored, optimistic belief in a bright future in animation production filled . . . [other animators] with the same hopeful expectations." Yet they were a "study in contrasts." Hugh was "the artist of the two, a very good animator with an outgoing personality." Rudy was "leisurely warm and unpretentious[.]" He was a "very quiet and private man who preferred to come into the studio in the afternoon and work late into the evening alone developing the story material for the cartoons."

As for how Hugh and Rudy found some of their new colleagues, Hugh thought that Ham Hamilton's "drawing was very poor, notably poor, but the guy was one of the greatest animators who ever lived. He got such great quality of feeling and expression in his stuff." Hugh recalled that Ham "was always interested in science—always, anything that was unusual or bizarre." Rudy also thought that Ham "couldn't draw very much" but had "fine, sketchy lines," was an expert on motion and timing, and "was able to turn out some great animation scenes." "He'd have made a hell of an actor, [or] a great comedian," Rudy concluded.

Conversely, Rudy felt Ubbe "was really a genius at animation. [But] he never would have made an actor . . . . He was a mechanical genius, but emotion-wise, he didn't have much." Hugh agreed: "Ubbe was never emotional, and he could never grasp anything that was interior within a character. Nothing of the mind of that character, what he was thinking, and how he was acting to make you think what he thought, and was going to do. That was beyond Ub[be]. He just did not think that way. . . . But he tended to be the craftsman rather than the artist."

Regarding the way the Disney Brothers Studio functioned, Rudy recalled that "Alice was shot in an area that was the size of [a small anteroom approximately eight feet wide], and the canvas came down from a height of maybe ten feet. It came down and then rolled out. . . . [W]e used to shoot Alice behind a billboard down on Hollywood Boulevard, in the daylight." He said that

> Walt would direct her, and she would have to play a closeup or a long shot or run across the camera. Sometimes there were full shots. . . . We'd shoot about three pictures on one day. . . . We would always shoot about three at one time. Then we picked the prints we wanted and that would be put in the camera. . . Then you traced the girl, you traced the area on each film. . . . [F]rom that tracing . . . they were filled in black on the white paper. And we shot that and got a negative made, and that was bipacked in the camera and then we shot the animation.

Rudy recalled that Walt "was the one who really sort of put the story together[.]" "He was always thinking and acting pictures," Rudy said.

> [W]e would sit in the office and would have story meetings, Walt, Ham, Hugh and me would all work over various gags. Walt would have an idea: let's let Alice be a fireman in this one, or let's let Alice go fishing, or what-ever it was. Then we'd work up fire gags or fishing gags. And then Walt would put them all together to tell the story.

Hugh remembered that the "general story meeting . . . usually was at night, we'd invent the story at night, in a session where Roy and Walt would sit with us around a table—it was called a gag meeting. They'd always bring a bowl of candy, just simple candy, we'd eat candy and think of gags. . . . [The meeting included] Walker, usually, and Walt and Roy, . . . Sometimes Rollin Hamilton was there."

The story would then go into animation. "An idea would come up and as fast as we'd think about it, we'd have it animated," Walt said. Hugh remembered that Walt made "very, very little" changes to the animators' work, except to add "flicker marks" that signaled when a character had an idea or was beaming with happiness. "We got so we put them in to save him the trouble," Rudy said. Rudy also remembered that the live-action scenes of Margie Gay were filmed—as they had been with Virginia Davis—"outside. . . . [on] a vacant lot on Hollywood Boulevard, just below Vermont. There were billboards there, and we would string this [big white canvas] on the back of the billboards." Rudy recalled George Winkler helped "doing the camera work" at this location.

The reunion of Walt and Ubbe with several of their other former Kansas City colleagues seemed a happy one and, as they had done in Kansas City, the young artists spent much of their free time together. It is unclear to what extent, if any, Walt was aware that Rudy and the Harman brothers were not committed to the Disney Brothers Studio in the long term. Hugh and Rudy went to California hoping to launch their own series; working for Walt was simply a step along the way. On August 7, probably around the time that Walt returned from his honeymoon, Rudy wrote his and Hugh's friend Ray Friedman in Kansas City, "We think that in a year we will be able to begin production on our own pictures with the experience and information we are gaining here [at Disney Brothers]."

In the meantime, the Harmans and Rudy enjoyed spending time with Walt and their other studio colleagues. For their first two years in Los Angeles, Hugh, Rudy and Walker (and, a year after their arrival, Rudy's brother, Louis) lived at 1801 North Alexandria Avenue, less than a mile west of the studio. By then, Ubbe also lived near the studio; he and his mother lived a half-mile from the studio on Russell Avenue. Both Disneys lived on Melbourne, within walking distance of the Kingswell studio. Thus, it is no surprise that the group spent a lot of time together. "You saw them," Rudy explained, "night and day, so to speak." This began "when [Walt] first got married, [and went on] for a couple of years." Rudy recalled,

> [W]e used to all get together nights and weekends. It was just a little closed group, so to speak. We'd go to Walt's house and they'd come to our apartment. We never went to Ub[be]'s house, because Ub[be] had his mother living there. She did not approve of any of us, because at one of the parties Ub[be] got drunk and she always blamed us for that.

Rudy also remembered how the group "used to play tennis in the morning, and [Thurston Harper] would take that racket and bang it on the iron posts or on the ground, and completely ruin it, and then come over and say, 'Rudy, can I borrow your racket?'" Hugh confirmed that "[w]hen we first came out here, nearly every evening we were at Roy's house, with Walt and his wife, and the three of us, Walker and Rudy and I. Or they were at our apartment; or we were at Walt's apartment. Always at ten o'clock, if it were at Roy's, he'd say, 'Well, get the hell outa here.' It was so funny, we'd all laugh. But he had to [end the night], because of his health; he was recovering from TB. We used to play tennis in those early days, every morning, including Saturdays and Sundays. Every morning, up at 6, playing tennis."

While there were other forms of entertainment the staff certainly pursued (according to Edna, Walt spent his free time going to "picture shows"), in the evenings, according to Hugh, the young artists would mostly discuss work. Hugh said, "[W]e would do nothing after dinner but start thinking of stories and acting them out. We got to thinking to ourselves, well, here are cartoons, they've never acted. We resolved we were going to make them act."

Walt was still entirely focused on work. His bride would often accompany Walt to the studio; he frequently told her on evenings when he was not socializing with the others, "I've just got one little thing I want to do at the studio." Even a night out could lead them back to the studio on Kingswell. "We'd go out for a ride," Lillian recalled, "we'd go any place—he'd say, 'Well, I've got just one little thing I want to do.'"

Lilly would sleep on the sofa in Walt's office, and it would suddenly be 10:30 p.m. or 2:00 a.m. "When we were first married my gosh, he didn't know what it was to go to sleep until two or three in the morning. I used to get so mad at him because he was in the habit of working so late at night." When asked about Walt's work ethic, Edna replied, "[Energetic?] Oh, yes. He never thought of anything, except his work and Lilly." Sometimes Lilly waited at home: "Once, soon after we were married, . . . . [w]hen it came dinnertime he wandered out of the studio to the corner beanery for a bowl of soup and then right back to the studio to continue with his idea. It wasn't until far into the night that he woke up to the fact that he had a bride at home who had cooked dinner and was waiting[.]"

◂ ◂ ◂

Walt had a full plate in the summer of 1925. He got married, went away for several weeks, and started building—for the first time—a new studio facility from scratch. Disney Brothers soon fell behind in its production schedule. By the fall, however, Walt was intent, he informed Charlie, on getting the Alice Comedies back on track. To do so, he had to motivate his employees.

Thus, he and Roy gave a raise to Ubbe, still the second highest paid staffer after Walt, from $55 a week to $60 a week. Ham and Rudy were given raises from $35 a week to $40 a week (but Thurston remained at $35 a week). Walt and Roy offered a bonus to his staff for films completed ahead of time.

The increase in staff and payroll might have given Walt the need for extra income. He wrote to Carl Stalling, his "Song-O-Reel" partner in Kansas City, and suggested that Disney Brothers make Stalling another song reel, but nothing came of the idea. He attempted to cut costs on his latest reel, *Alice in the Jungle*, by using live-action footage—featuring the now-departed Virginia Davis—trimmed from *Alice Hunting in Africa* when Margaret Winkler rejected *Africa* as unusable eighteen months earlier. Thus, Virginia Davis was seen in another Alice Comedy—eight months after she left the series. Ironically, while the studio turned this used footage of Virginia into a new reel, Margaret Davis (still angry over the Disneys' final contact proposal to Virginia) wrote to Charlie Mintz, without success, to see if her daughter could return to the series and play Alice again.

While *Jungle* was in production, a disagreement between Walt and Charlie erupted when Walt began delivering his films ahead of schedule. When Walt wired the Winkler company on September 26 about "further holding up" his check for *Alice the Jail Bird*, Charlie responded,

> Don't you think it is about time for you to put on your brakes? We are supposed to get one picture from you which is satisfactory to us every three weeks. When we get your pictures we always send you a check. This applies not only to the present Alice's but to the very early ones on which you were experimenting and on which we had nothing but grief and aggravation since we first took them.
>
> "Alice Chops the Suey" reached here Aug. 28th. You were sent your check. "Alice the Jail Bird" reached here Sept. 12th which is fourteen days after "Chops the Suey". This, as you know, is positively contrary to all our arrangements and we may as well tell you now rather than later that we cannot handle your pictures in that manner....
>
> If every one with whom you deal will pay you as surely and as promptly as we do, take my word for it, your life will be one sweet song. There is nothing further that I have to say to you, excepting please use a little of the common sense which you displayed when I met you on the Coast last summer.

Walt replied, in a letter sent via registered mail,

> First, let me say, that it is my intention to live up to the contract and I
> expect you to do the same. The contract calls for delivery of the eighteen
> pictures between the dates of Jan. 15, 1925, and Jan. 1, 1926, "at intervals
> not exceeding three weeks". . . . The important point is that, according
> to the contract, we must make final delivery <u>not later than January 15,
> 1926</u>. However, there is positively nothing in the contract which prevents
> making final delivery before that date. . . . I intend to continue shipping
> pictures to you as fast as completed, which is about every sixteen days. I
> will expect you to take them up as delivered and remit immediately. Your
> failure to do so will constitute a breach of contract and will force me to
> seek other distributors.

On October 6, 1925, Charlie wrote a long reply. He was offended that Walt sent
his last letter via registered mail since Charlie "would not have denied receiving
it any how." He accused Walt of relying on a lawyer; Charlie could tell "from the
language in your letter that it was written by neither you nor by your brother
Roy[.]" He catalogued for Walt the Mintzes' kindnesses, from offering an inex-
perienced animator like Walt a contract, to overlooking the low "class" of *Alice's
Day At Sea*, to paying Walt significant sums.

Ignoring the fact that Margaret Winkler had complimented *Spooky Adventure* and *Wild West Show*, and that Charlie himself praised *Peacemaker* and
*Gets in Dutch*, Charlie wondered if Walt realized that "had any of the first seven
pictures that [he] made . . . been given to any other Distributor in the whole
world that they would have thrown them out bodily and that they would not
have anything to do further with you or with anyone who made pictures of that
kind." Charlie went on, referring to the Mintzes' loss of *Felix the Cat*,

> Haven't you a single spark of appreciativeness in your whole soul or are
> we going to face the same situation which we faced after having put a cer-
> tain other short subject on the market only to have it prove a boomerang
> to us? Don't you appreciate further that the only reason that you are mak-
> ing pictures today is because we sent our George Winkler out and, at our
> expense, taught you what it was necessary to know to produce the kind of
> pictures you are now making[?]

Charlie claimed that the first seven Alice reels were "an absolute total loss to us
and . . . we have not made one single dollar on any picture that we have ever
gotten from you." Charlie and the Winkler company worked with Walt because

it figured that Disney Brothers Studio, and the *Alice* series, "would eventually be made" if Walt cooperated with the Mintzes. Charlie told Walt that he "should whole-heartedly be ashamed of yourself[,]" but recognized that Walt knew "his rights and no one [was] stopping [him] from going ahead" with enforcing those rights. Charlie thought that Walt was "man enough so that we will get a square deal in the same manner as we have given you."

Walt countered,

> Our contract calls for <u>final delivery</u> by January 15, 1926, with your option calling for twenty-six pictures the following year. I have built up my organization to where I can complete my deliveries on this contract by the specified time and be able to make deliveries of every two weeks, the following year, should you choose to exercise your option. With my present payroll, on a three weeks schedule, I would absolutely be loosing [*sic*] money, and to cut down my force is out of the question. You well know, yourself, how hard it is to get men trained in this line of work. My artists are all experienced, capable men, difficult to replace at any salary. How can I afford the loss which a delayed schedule would mean?

Hugh felt that the tension between Walt and Charlie existed because "Walt resented the very implication that Mintz was the producer, that . . . George [Winkler] would attempt supervision in any sense, even by mild-suggestion. That was Walt's constitution, to resent such things. He wanted to do everything himself. I don't blame him, but he was that way, and thus a friction developed between them."

Around this time, Walt was also experiencing renewed tension with Thurston Harper, whose temper—he ripped up half of his scenes—led to an outburst that ultimately caused his departure from Disney Brothers. Rudy explained,

> One time [Thurston] was animating a scene, and I was sitting next to him, and Ham on the other side. . . . Walt wasn't there, he was in the office in front with Roy. Harper had a scene I think he'd almost finished. But he would sharpen his pencil, and then he'd go to draw and pretty soon nothing, no lead, he probably got the bad pencil in the bunch. "Goddamn," and he'd sharpen the thing, have his hands clenched and he'd go back. Pretty soon nothing was happening and "Godammit!" He went through this about four times getting madder and madder and madder. Finally he got up and broke the pencil in half, took the pencil sharpener and broke the thing right off the drawing board and threw it in the wastepaper basket.

He took the scene that he was working on in both hands, it was almost finished, and he just tore the hell out of it, threw it in the wastebasket, got up and walked off, like that. Walt heard him, finally—it was only from the back door to the front door . . . . The next day Harper came back in. By this time Walt knew what he'd done and he said, "I want to talk to you, Harp." Thurston said, "What about?" And he said, "You know, you're costing us too much money, we're going to have to let you go," and Harper said, "Let's talk about it out in the alley after work." There was a back door, and of course half of us used to leave out through the alley. Walt had to leave early that afternoon himself, so Harp was sitting around, at least one or two months. And Walt didn't dare, because if he'd really gone out there he knew Harper was liable to beat the hell out of him.

In November, Walt and Roy made their last employee hire at Disney Brothers when they hired a part-time janitor named John Lott. Part of the impetus behind the hiring of a janitor was that Roy needed help washing used cels so that they could be reused by the animators. Thurston recalled, "The sink was used for washing cels which Roy attended to until he hired a part-time worker when his tasks were too many and varied." John R. Lott, forty-two, started work at the studio on Monday, November 2, 1925. He was born in Texas and had already been working as a janitor in Los Angeles by the time he was hired by the Disneys.

That same month—with contract renewal season approaching—Walt and Charlie struck a friendlier tone with each other. Walt wrote to Charlie:

We are striving to make all future Alice comedies of the highest standard, and are figuring on incorporating as much novel and clever live action as is possible to put into each picture without sacrificing laughs and gags. . . . I wish to send my best regards to Mrs. Mintz, and congratulate you on the fine looking and good natured baby you have; as I have noticed by the set of photos George brought back with him.

Charlie responded by sending a telegram to Walt about the Winkler company's plans to sign with a national film distributor, which would give films distributed by Winkler greater exposure than they had received while Winkler distributed films on a "states' rights" basis to local theaters.

Specifically, Charlie revealed that he had been in negotiations with the Film Booking Office, a national distributorship owned by businessman Joseph P. Kennedy of Boston. Charlie proposed to Walt a new contract, offering $1,500 per film, with $900 due upon delivery, $600 due within ninety days of delivery, and an equal share of profits over $3,000. Charlie even invited Walt to New York ("I will pay half your expenses") to

> make new arrangements for the forthcoming series due to the fact that we are forced to give national organization our production on a straight percentage basis which means that we will not get any real returns for about nine months. Am certain that in a personal conference we can make some arrangements satisfactory to both of us.

On November 17, 1925, Charlie wrote Walt that the possibility of a deal between Winkler and the Disney brothers "rests entirely with you." Like the first Alice series, claimed Charlie, the second series was "a great distance from breaking even." Not only has the "[i]ndependent [cartoon] market gone to smash[,]" Charlie wrote, its prospects for 1926 were even worse. Charlie announced that, "[My] negotiations [with a national organization] have come to a close and we have accepted each other[']s terms." Charlie's new national distributor had agreed to release fifty-two Winkler productions starting on September 1, 1926, and half of them would be *Krazy Kat* shorts.

If he and Walt could "get together on a good healthy basis," then Charlie would fill the remainder of the order with twenty-six *Alice* shorts. But Charlie wanted Walt to "work along with me" and "not insist on too much." While Walt was still pushing to deliver shorts to Charlie regularly and even ahead of time, given the September 1926 start-date of Charlie's new distribution arrangement, if Walt persisted on early delivery, Charlie "would have about 15 pictures on hand before I can even give [the new distributor] one [short]."

If Walt agreed to wait until June 1, 1926, to make deliveries, Charlie would advance him $1,500 per picture ("$900.00 payable on receipt of the negative, $600.00 in 90 days. This, I am sure, will take you off the nut. After I have received the $1500 advanced [to] you plus $1500 for myself, we are to share 50-50."). Charlie asked Walt, "before making a definite decision," to "digest this letter thoroughly, talk it over with Roy and your Uncle or with whomever you wish, and don't make any hasty decisions."

Walt wrote back on November 22, and the letter was friendly and collaborative in tone. Charlie was "indeed happy at the attitude [Walt was] taking[,]" and called *Alice* a subject "that we admit is very very good" and one he intended to make "the leading subject of its kind in the entire world[.]" Charlie stated that "Mrs. Mintz and the baby are quite well and want to be remembered" and sent his "personal regards to you and Roy."

Charlie was aware, through George Winkler, that Walt was willing to wait and not start delivery of any new reels until March 1, 1926. (Hugh described

George as "the intermediary; he had full contact with Walt, and an authorization for such from the Winkler organization.") Charlie therefore offered a seven-year contract in which the Winkler company would take delivery of thirteen reels at three-week intervals for $900 per negative, to be paid upon receipt, with an additional $600 to be paid sixty days later—and then take delivery of an additional thirteen reels at two-week intervals for $900 per negative with an additional $600 to be paid ninety days later. Walt would also get an equal share of any profits over $5,000—a sum Charlie thought "should be the easiest thing in the world" to reach.

Charlie explained that his own deal with the distributor was for a minimum of $3,500 per reel, and 60 percent of gross receipts above $3,500. Charlie calculated that his minimum of $3,500 would cover the $1,500 advance to the Disneys and $2,000 in overhead costs. Walt balked, and the negotiations continued into December, when the studio started production on *Alice's Little Parade*, which was the last reel Thurston Harper worked on before he became the first ex-Disney Brothers Studio animator.

Thurston left by year's end. Meanwhile Walt's other antagonist continued to vex him, as the Disneys' contract negotiations with Charlie dragged on. Charlie wrote Walt, "If you think this is a fair arrangement, you have another think coming." But Walt, who had just turned twenty-four, was not so consumed by Charlie that he did not get in the holiday spirit. That Christmas, Walt sent Rudy and the Harmans a Christmas card that cleverly played off of their last names. Hugh recalled, "At Christmas time in 1925 Walt drew a Xmas card to Rudy Ising, my brother Walker Harman and myself. He had a drawing of the three of us singing a Christmas Carol—not caricatures, but figures representing us. And he titled it 'THE HARMAN-ISING TRIO.'"

By year's end, Walt countered to Charlie with $2,250 per reel. On New Year's Eve, Charlie wrote Walt that he thought a new contract with Disney Brothers Studio was "a hopeless task" since he and Walt "wasted just about enough time, energy and money in trying to get together." Charlie threatened that if he and Walt could not "get together, . . . this is my last letter to you, [and] I don't intend to argue any further." Walt's counter offer of $2,250 per reel was unworkable for Charlie because, if a reel earned $5,000, Walt's take of $2,250 plus overhead of $1,500, left only $1,250 for the Winkler company. Charlie would "positively not work along those lines."

Charlie offered Walt two options: $1,500 per reel plus half of profits in excess of $3,000, or $1,750 per reel plus half of profits over $4,500. Charlie was running out of patience, and needed Walt's answer "very, very quickly . . . as soon as you receive this letter." Charlie was through arguing, and offered to release Walt from their contract if he had a better offer elsewhere. Charlie preferred

not to do business with Walt if Walt had "a doubt in your mind as to my inten-
tions[.]" Charlie pointed out that Walt's advances, and Charlie's delayed profits
pay-out, meant that Charlie "must keep paying money and holding the bag for
fourteen months, while you are happily working along getting your earnings
as you finish your pictures. If you have not considered this angle of it you have
been unfair."

The Disney Brothers Studio staff spent New Year's Day, 1926, in Tijuana.
Walt drove part of the group south in his Moon roadster, and Roy drove the
rest in his Oakland. A week later George Winkler sent Walt a letter setting
forth the Winkler company's latest offer: $1,500 per reel for twenty-six *Alice
Comedies* ($900 upon delivery, $600 in ninety days), with thirteen reels to
be delivered every three weeks starting on March 1, and an additional thirteen reels to be delivered every two weeks. Once profits reached $4,000,
Walt was entitled to $350, and he would share equally in profits thereafter.
The Winkler company had an option for "six like series to extend over a
period of six years."

The next day Walt responded that those terms were acceptable. But in
addition to the right to inspect the Winkler books, Walt also asked to "have
embodied in the contract . . . the understanding which we had verbal[l]y, that
all pictures are to be a minimum of 600 ft., that all matters regarding making
of comedies are to be left to me. I agree to make each picture in a high class
manner and of a standard equal to that of the series of 1925." Walt also was to
share equally in any profits from "toys, novelties, newspaper strips, etc."

Charlie rejected Walt's demands, and Walt sent him a telegram ending
their negotiation and informing Charlie that their professional relationship
would be ending:

MY OFFER IS THE LIMIT I CAN GO STOP YOUR PROPOSITIONS
ARE ALL UNACCEPTABLE TO ME STOP THEREFORE UPON THE
DELIVERY OF THE NEXT SUBJECT THE FINAL ONE OF THE
NINETEEN TWENTY FIVE SERIES I WILL CONSIDER ALL MY
CONTRACTUAL OBLIGATIONS FULFILLED.

But on Monday, February 8, Walt sent another counter offer to Charlie: $500
to Walt after the first $4,000 in profits; the next $500 to Charlie; then an equal
share of profits. Charlie accepted this offer. Under the terms, Walt would provide twenty-six new Alice films for a third series of Alice Comedies. The first
thirteen would be delivered every three weeks; the second thirteen every two.
The price was dropped from $1,800 per film to $1,500 in exchange for a share
of the profits.

As the contract came together, so did the Disneys' new Hyperion studio. On Tuesday, February 9, the concrete flooring was put in. It was probably between Friday, February 12, and Tuesday, February 16, on what Rudy described as a "rainy day in mid-February[,]" that the Disney brothers left Kingswell Avenue. Hugh confirmed that it was "in February . . . [that] we moved to Hyperion. It was raining that day, . . . and we all pitched in and did the moving. Walker, Rudy, Walt, Roy and I."

Hugh explained that Walt and Roy "rented an old Ford truck and we moved the stuff in that." "We hauled all the equipment down ourselves, down to Hyperion," said Hugh, and "I guess we must have made a number of trips." Hugh remembered that he and the other animators "were glad to pitch in and help. All of us [helped with the] move[]." Walt and his brother, with some old colleagues from Kansas City (Ubbe, the two Harman brothers, and Rudy) and some new ones from Hollywood (the Hamilton siblings and John Lott), moved from Kingswell Avenue to Hyperion Avenue—from the Disney brothers' first Los Angeles venture to the Walt Disney Studio, the home of the Golden Age of Disney animation.

# Walt Disney Studio
## *1926–1928*

In mid-February 1926, twenty-four-year-old Walt Disney moved his studio one and one-half miles east to the Silver Lake district several miles northwest of downtown Los Angeles, at the eastern border of Hollywood. The area, according to a longtime Disney employee, "was mainly a residential development, a section of town which [by the late 1920s] had been laid out with streets and curbs, but which had very few homes at that time. . . . [T]he grass and weeds were very tall and they were growing up through the sidewalk in places" and the main street in the area was not "very much used at the time."

Within a few years of the Disneys' move there, a visitor characterized the new studio as "a quiet little building, one story high, a spot you would hardly notice as you drive along Hyperion Avenue." A future Disney animator agreed that the building was "hardly noticed on a quiet street that meandered down a small valley." Walt described the new studio at 2719 Hyperion Avenue as a "little green and white structure with a red tile roof, and a nice little plot of grass in front of us." It was, according to another employee, a "little square building" made of stucco, about 1,600 square feet in size. Hugh Harman thought that the new studio "wasn't much bigger than the one on Kingswell." The building was situated on a 60-by-40-foot lot three properties to the east of the northeast corner of the intersection of Hyperion Avenue and Griffith Park Boulevard, a main intersection in the area.

Griffith Park Boulevard is the north-south axis at that intersection, and Hyperion Avenue runs east-west. The two streets do not meet at a right angle, thus the Disneys' new property was not a rectangular lot, but rather the shape of a trapezoid. The first property east of Griffith Park Boulevard, on the north side of Hyperion Avenue, was a gas station located at 2701 Hyperion. The second property in was a pipe organ factory, located at 2711 Hyperion. The third property from the intersection was the new Disney studio, at 2719 Hyperion. The fourth property in, to the east of the studio, was a vacant lot.

Between the studio and the organ factory was, as one animator remembered it, "Walt's little shed . . . where he kept all his old film[.]" The vacant lot on the other side of the studio, along with the space in the back, provided privacy for the studio employees. The back was so private that Walt had a stage for the Alice Comedies built there.

The studio was still a work in progress when the staff of nine (the Disney and Harman brothers, the Hamilton siblings, Ubbe, Rudy and John Lott) settled in. On Tuesday, February 20, plasterboard partitions were installed, and stucco and additional plasterwork was added five days later. It was another month before landscaping and interior and exterior painting was completed, and a month after that the offices were decorated.

Unlike the Kingswell office, where the main entrance was at the left of the storefront, at Hyperion, the front door was situated in the middle of the façade. Walt's office was to the left of the main entrance, inside the three windows to the left of the front door, and Roy's office was to the right. Like Kingswell, however, the camera room where Rudy shot the animation was located in the left rear section of the office. The dark room was behind the camera room, and rest rooms were behind the dark room.

Rudy described Walt's office as being like that of a bank president's "loafing room.... [with a d]esk and chairs in walnut, large overstuffed divan and chair, floor lamp etc." Between Walt's office and the camera room were tables used by the animators, Ubbe, Hugh, and Ham. On the building's western wall, near the camera and dark rooms, was a "long table for painting backgrounds."

On the east side of the building, between Roy's office and a rear storage area, were tables used by the inkers and painters, Irene and Walker. Against the center hallway wall was a counter and sink where John Lott washed cels. Behind the studio was the outdoor set Walt constructed for the Alice series, which Rudy remembered as a "big 2 x 4 structure on the back of the lot." Hugh added that the stage "was a platform with a curve [that went] into the back wall [of the Hyperion building]." Rudy complained about the set, saying, "We had to whitewash it every time we used it."

Differing accounts relate how, at the time of the move to Hyperion, the "Disney Brothers Studios" was rechristened "Walt Disney Studios." According to one of the brothers' biographers, "Roy reasoned that a single name could have more box-office appeal and identification, and so the Disney Brothers Studio became the Walt Disney Studio." Roy told that biographer that the name change "was my idea. Walt was the creative member of the team. His name deserved to be on the pictures."

Roy's son, however, later said that Walt suddenly told Roy of the change. Roy's son claimed that his father agreed because he didn't like attention, although it bothered him a little bit. According to his son, Roy always kind of defended [the change in name], by saying "it's better to have one person out there in front than it is to try to sell two brothers." Walt was good at that, although he said he wasn't, he could be when he had to be. My father [Roy] would rather not have been the front man anyway.

Hugh also recalled that the change was Walt's idea, but one which caused a heated argument with Roy. "When we came out here[ to California the previous year], Walt had already established [a studio] with Roy and they called it the 'Disney Brothers Studio.' But, now [at the time of the move to Hyperion], I started hearing some heated arguments going on." Harman said the arguments were "between Walt and Roy. . . . [Walt] ranted and raved . . . . He was having a fight with Roy over changing the name from 'Disney Brothers' to 'Walt Disney Studio.' It was like a three-day argument. And Roy gave in. The new Hyperion building was called 'Walt Disney Studio' from the first."

Later, Roy is said to have told a longtime Disney employee, "One evening when Walt and I were discussing our move [to the new studio], Walt said to me, 'Roy, when we move to Hyperion, I'm going to have a large neon sign erected, reading 'Walt Disney Studios['] . . . . He looked at me as if expecting an argument. I said, 'If that's the way you want it.' And Walt said, 'That's the way I want it and that's the way it will be!' And that's the way it was."

The new year also brought a new apartment for Walt and Lilly, although the exact date of their move is not known. The Disneys moved—at least by the fall of 1926—from their apartment on Melbourne, one block north of the Kingswell studio, to an apartment at 1307 North Commonwealth Avenue, nearly a mile and one-half southeast of the new Hyperion Avenue studio.

As the artists got settled into their new studio after a rainy moving day, they discovered that the furniture had gotten so soaked that it would not dry. Hugh recalled that, "the plaster was wet. . . . It was rainy all that February, [like] it rained the day we moved in there. Next door [on the vacant lot to the east of the studio] was an excavation, a cellar excavation; I guess they'd planned to build there, but never had. It collected water, and it was a lake when it rained. It was about five feet deep. Everything was just wet, wet, wet; I thought it would never end." Even the animation paper got wet, and Hugh found drawing on it was "just like drawing on a wet blotter . . . until summer came."

Nevertheless, the staff quickly returned to the production schedule called for by the new Winkler contract—and to dealing with Charlie. *Alice's Monkey Business* and *Alice in the Wooly West* were both in production that February. Meanwhile, Charlie complained about *Alice's Mysterious Mystery*, the last Alice

Comedy to be distributed through the state's rights market: "'Alice's Mysterious Mystery,'" said Charlie, "was received and looked at. It is just another picture and has nothing in it whatever that is outstanding." Charlie thought that Walt would "concede that I probably know a little more about what the market wants than you do," and offered the following advice:

> The Alice Comedies, what little success they have attained have been bought because they are cute and because the public likes the double stuff. I think we will both be a little better off if you try to put just a little more live action in it even if you must put in a close-up here and there with Alice having a little smile or some such piece of business.

Charlie wanted Walt to use "special efforts" on the first reels in the new season "so that we can really call them knock-outs, because on these first few will hang the success or failure of the ALICE COMEDIES."

Within a few weeks after moving into the new studio, the contract resolution that appeared to have been reached just before the move seemed to unravel. After George gave Walt the final contract, Walt "found several things that I think should be changed or rewritten[,]," although he was confident that the issues could be worked out and thus was going "ahead with production, and will have the first picture of the new series ready for shipment as soon as the main title sketches are approved and can be made."

Charlie's reaction was swift:

> I received your letter of March 1st which made me feel quite optimistic. Yesterday, I received the contract which you gave George Winkler and .... I am sorry to tell you that the receipt of this contract changed all my [optimism] to extreme pessimism. I was definitely certain that we would get together on what was meant to be a good proposition for both of us. I am afraid, however, that there is some danger of a proposition between us not being consum[m]ated.

Walt's renegotiating notwithstanding, Charlie may have been hesitant to sign a new contract with Walt because, by March, Charlie seemed to suspect that Walt did not own the rights to the Alice series and might not have leveled with Margaret Winkler when they entered into their first contract two and one-half years earlier. The Mintzes retained Asher Blum of the Mock & Blum law firm to advise them. Either Charlie or Margaret, or one of their employees, drafted a "Statement Of Facts" that explained the situation, and Charlie asked Blum to read the document and advise whether Walt had a legal claim to the "Alice Comedies" name.

Charlie's confusion no doubt arouse from the fact that, while Walt had indeed created the Alice series, the ongoing bankruptcy proceedings involving Laugh-O-gram meant that Joseph Jones, the court-appointed bankruptcy trustee—and not Walt—now controlled all of Laugh-O-gram's remaining assets. These assets included the Alice pilot, *Alice's Wonderland*, as well as the other Laugh-O-gram fairy tale cartoons Walt made in Kansas City under the Laugh-O-gram Films banner in 1922.

When the trustee successfully demanded that Laugh-O-gram Films' would-be distributor and debtor, Pictorial Films, pay the Laugh-O-gram estate the money owed it, Pictorial wanted in return the benefit of the original contract, and claimed it had the right to distribute the Laugh-O-gram fairy tales. The trustee agreed. In exchange for Pictorial's payments under the original contract, the trustee allowed Pictorial to purchase several films in the estate's possession, including the Laugh-O-gram fairy tales *The Four Musicians of Bremen* and *Jack, the Giant Killer*, the *Lafflets* series—and *Alice's Wonderland*.

By 1926, the Mintzes became aware that Pictorial was distributing *Alice's Wonderland* and other Laugh-O-gram reels, and concluded that Pictorial was distributing its own series of Alice reels. Apparently not realizing that Walt founded—and indeed *was*—Laugh-O-gram films, the Mintzes thought Walt, in dealing with Margaret in 1923, misrepresented his role in creating the Alice Comedies, and was merely "employed" by the series' producer, Laugh-O-gram Films.

The Mintzes' "Statement Of Facts" document claimed that, "While we were distributing pictures bearing the name 'Alice Comedies,' an assignee of Laugh-O-Gram [sic] Films Inc., produced several 'Alice Comedies' and was also distributing a number of these pictures, meaning that there were two people distributing pictures bearing the same names, the rights for which were obtained from two separate sources." Blum's opinion was that—with regard to the name, "Alice Comedies"—that "Mr. Disney has no right to this name at all."

Perhaps Charlie thought that putting Walt in a legal bind would give the Winkler company leverage as Charlie and Walt continued to negotiate the third season contract. On Sunday, March 21, Charlie left New York to meet with Walt. He arrived in Los Angeles on Thursday, and met with Walt on Friday. By the end of March, Charlie and Walt ironed out their differences, as set forth in a letter agreement (on old Disney Brothers Studio stationery) from Walt to Charlie, dated Tuesday, March 30:

Qualifying the contract into which we entered yesterday, our understanding is as follows:

First: We are to retain our interest as provided in the contract in Alice and are to be paid our share after F.B.O. ceases distribution from whatever source there may be any revenue at all time thereafter.

Second: If you exercise the options, as provided for, for all of the six years spoken of in the contract, then the right and title to the name ALICE COMEDIES shall be and become your property and my property in common, each of us owning fifty per cent, together with all trade mark registrations, copyrights, and all other protections.

Charlie, by then president of the Winkler Film Corporation (soon referred to on company stationery as Winkler Pictures, Incorporated), signed the document, and the third season contract was finally concluded.

By spring, with that long negotiation behind them, Walt and Charlie's relationship seemed to improve. For example, on Thursday, May 20, Charlie wrote Walt to compliment him about the latest reel sent to New York, *Alice the Fire Fighter*:

You asked me some time ago to be fair with you and tell you when you made a good picture. Now, I will tell you that I think 'Alice the Fire Fighter' is as good as anything you have turned out and perhaps a little better. I will also be fair with you a little more when I tell you that making good pictures as you are, you are your own worst enemy by either taking unqualified advice or refusing to take advice with a certain amount of past performances and sincerity behind it.

Walt replied,

I want to thank you for the compliment on 'Alice the Fire Fighter', and want to say right here that I will not be satisfied until I am able to make them all as good, or better. I am putting every effort toward this end and hope that in a very short time our average will be above them all. (Including Krazy Kat.) I sincerely believe you are a well qualified Judge of what a good cartoon is and will expect you to give us your opinion, from time to time, as to what you think is best for the good of all.

While Walt was still striving for a high quality product, he also increased his efforts at studio publicity. Sometime during this period, he and members of his staff, including Ham and Irene Hamilton, Ubbe, Hugh, and Rudy, posed for a series of photographs in which the men wear golf knickers and are frolicking, prancing, and striking silly poses. Based on Hugh's recollection, this series of photographs may have been taken in the summer of 1926, when the weather—and the studio—"finally dried out, and the summer was beautiful. They were going to build something next door [to the east of the studio], and they'd thrown up great mounds of earth. We stood there and took pictures that day. [W]e're on Walt's lot, and there's a big white backdrop against which Alice was shot, and Ubbe [had] a fireman's hat on, [and we were] clowning, and . . . [doing] crazy stuff." The animators, Ubbe, Hugh, Rudy, and Ham, also posed during this session for a formal photograph in front of the new studio with the Disney brothers, Walker Harman, and Margie Gay.

In the summer of 1926, Walt suggested to Charlie that their publicity should take advantage of the recent move to the Hyperion studio. Specifically, Walt asked Charlie to "write me in regard to the nature of the future stuff you want in this line[,]" such as the Alice characters walking into 2719 Hyperion "to represent our moving into our new location[.]" This idea likely led to a studio still showing Walt, drawing board in tow, Margie Gay, and an assortment of cartoon animals who populated the Alice Comedies, including Julius, walking into the doorway of the new Hyperion studio.

But while Walt and Charlie finally seemed to be getting along, some of Walt's staff considered taking their skills elsewhere. Even as the photographic record showed a close and fun-loving team of animators, Hugh and Rudy continued to contemplate their departure from the Disney studio. As Rudy said later, "We were always thinking of starting our own studio again, ever since we came out from Kansas City." On Sunday, August 1, Hugh and Rudy, who by then were talking to producer Jesse Lasky about opening their own studio, wrote Max Maxwell in Kansas City about the difficulty their leaving the Disney studio would cause for Walt. They wrote that their departure "will leave Walt in a mellava hess but business is business."

In August Walt took a break from the Alice Comedies and started production on a sequel to *Tommy Tucker's Tooth*, the educational film he made almost four years earlier for Dr. McCrum. *Clara Cleans Her Teeth* was directed by Walt and based on a story by Margaret E. Greenwood and Eleanor M. Fonda. Ubbe did the animation, and the cast included professional actors George Morrell and Lillian Worth, Lilly's niece, Marjorie Sewell, and, in her fifth and final appearance in a Disney production, Uncle Robert's dog, Peggy.

August also saw another new production: the construction of Walt's and Roy's neighboring houses on Lyric Avenue. These were the first houses owned by the brothers, and they were several blocks from the new Hyperion studio. Two months earlier, Walt and Roy had each put $200 down on the lots in Silver Lake, at the edge of the Los Feliz hills. Roy recalled, "In '26, we bought this lot, about 50 by 150 feet, on Lyric Avenue near St. George Street; it was on a side street. . . . We built two houses. They were the ready-cut type of houses. The lot and the houses cost us $16,000." The "kit" homes were Pacific Ready-Cut models. The houses each contained two thousand square feet, and Walt thought that the cost was "exorbitant[.]"

◂ ◂ ◂

Although the Walt Disney Studio had been diligently producing the third season of the Alice Comedies since it relocated to Hyperion Avenue in early 1926, none of those new episodes were released to theaters until the fall of 1926 due to the terms of Charlie's contract with Joe Kennedy. Finally, on Monday, September 6, seven months after the last "states rights" Alice Comedy was released to theaters, FBO released *Alice Charms the Fish*, the first Disney cartoon to be distributed nationally. Not long after, Walt added to his staff a new inker and painter, twenty-two-year-old Robert Edmunds, a British seaman who had jumped ship before coming to Los Angeles.

Bob had sometimes stayed with the Harmans and Rudy after meeting Walker Harman at dancing school and had worked in a grocery store. Hugh recalled that Bob "virtually lived with us; he was broke at the time, couldn't get a job here. We were supporting him, so we figured it would be better to get him a job." Bob's first reel was *Rodeo Story*, which was eventually renamed *Alice's Rodeo*. Hugh remembered that Bob was not an artist but "was the first . . . story man in the cartoon business, starting with [the] Disney [studio] . . . . He would just write his ideas for gags and stories; that was his whole job. Nobody else there had such a job." Bob left the studio after almost three months when, on Hugh's recommendation, Bob "went up north to work in the woods, as a lumberjack."

That month, in the midst of all of this activity, Walt closed his new studio for two weeks of vacation. Unbeknownst to Walt, during the studio shutdown Ubbe, Hugh, Rudy, and Ham made a cartoon of their own. Rudy recalled, "We made one [additional *Arabian Nights*] film out here [in California] called *Aladdin's Vamp*, I think. We were on vacation from Walt for a couple of weeks, and Ubbe, Hamilton, Hugh and myself made this one film."

Although the moonlighting animators could not get their cartoon released, perhaps Walt sensed their interest in branching out on their own, and on October 16, Walt gave Ubbe another raise, from $60 to $70 per week. Walt still had the highest salary, at $75 a week, and Hugh, who was paid $60 a week, now out-earned Roy. Cel painter Paul Smith, twenty, who later became an assistant and then an animator, joined the studio a short time later for $18 a week. Paul found that "Walt Disney just lived cartoons, that was his whole life. . . . He talked of nothing else, ever." Hugh felt that Paul became a "pretty good" animator: "He wasn't a great [animator], but he could animate."

The cordial relationship between Walt and Charlie continued during the second half of 1926. At one point Charlie ended a letter to Walt by stating that, "Mrs. Mintz, the baby and I are enjoying the best of health. I hope this finds you, your brother and your wives the same." The Disneys' recurring financial problems also persisted in late 1926. Throughout the year, Walt and Roy made no more than $300 profit per short, but by year's end, as the third Alice contract reached its halfway mark, their profit was as little as $100 per film. Yet, the Disney brothers were receiving between $1,800 and $2,000 per reel. The overhead costs that concerned Walt two years earlier still prevented Roy and him from realizing large profits.

Two days after Christmas, Walt, now twenty-five, mentioned in a letter to Charlie that the studio was

> in very tight circumstances at this time. I am spending the limit on my negatives and I have been on a two week schedule since last October while you only recently started accepting on the two week schedule. This has cramped me to such an extent that I have borrowed to my capacity and have to squeeze very hard to make things come out right.

The studio's overhead decreased by at least one salary a few days later, however, when Ham Hamilton left the studio on New Year's Eve after a dispute with Walt.

That same day, as *Circus Story* (eventually released as *Alice's Circus Daze*) went into production, Walt hired his fourth and final Alice. For reasons unknown, George Winkler, now Winkler Pictures' Supervisor of Production, decided to replace Margie Gay, who had played the part for two years, with another veteran child actor, Lois Hardwick.

Lois Eleanor Hardwick, twelve, was the daughter of William Hardwick, forty-eight, a native of Missouri, and Frances Hardwick, forty-three, of Texas. William Hardwick worked as a laborer and, later, a grammar school janitor. Lois, like her older brother, Frederick, nineteen, was born in California. At the time Lois was hired by the Disneys, the Hardwicks lived on E. 57th Street, twelve miles south of the studio.

Within a few weeks of Lois' hire, however, Charlie, still the President of Winkler Pictures (his brother, Nat, was now Manager of Production), complained about Lois—or at least about the fact that she was hired without his approval. Walt replied,

In regard to your recent letter in which you pan me for using the new
girl without your permission: I believe it is all a misunderstanding. In
the first place, George and Nat [Levine, the west coast representative for
the Winkler company] picked her. They made a screen test and George
told me to go ahead and use her. I would not have done so, had I not
tho[ugh]t George's word was sufficient. Personally, I think she is the best
yet. She is full of life and expression and I have hopes of getting some
good stuff with her. However, if you want us to go back to the other girl,
I will do so. . . . I would appreciate your immediate reply . . . in regard to
the girl as we want to shoot again next week.

Charlie backed down:

. . . I certainly did not mean to pan you. I have since then received a letter
from George in which he tells me that he took up the matter of the new
girl with me and that I told him if the girl looked good to him that it was
okay to go ahead. I remember now that I did say that and I have taken
another look at her. My only objection to her was that her legs seemed
kind of heavy. She does, however, look like a good little trouper so lets go
ahead and use her. You fellows are out there on the ground and, of course,
are in a better position to size up matters than I am.

Charlie told Walt that George Winkler felt undermined by Charlie's intervention. Charlie felt that it "might just be better for you [and George] to go along as
you have been doing. That method has certainly proved satisfactory and I don't
want to take a chance by spoiling anything by changing it." Charlie had soft-
ened towards Lois, and one of her predecessors, Virginia Davis, complimented
her as well. Virginia recalled that "Lois Hardwick[ ] . . . . was a lot older, about
11 years old, and had a lot more training. You can tell if you look at the photographs that she would always have her knee bent to make herself seem shorter.
You catch those things, they're all tricks of the trade. She was very good."
    Early in 1927, Walt and Lilly, and Roy and Edna, moved into their respec-
tive homes on Lyric Avenue. Walt's house was the corner lot, at 2495 Lyric; Roy
was next door at 2491. "Each one," Lilly recalled, "had two bedrooms, a dining
room, a living room and a kitchen." Walt said that Lilly thought the small and
dark house was wonderful. Whatever Walt felt about the house, he was not
crazy about tending to its property. "One of our first arguments," Lilly recalled,
"was over the lawn. Walt said he was never going to take care of any lawn."
    Living as next-door neighbors kept Walt and Roy, and their wives, close.
Unless they had to work late, Walt and Roy left the studio together and they,
Lilly and Edna had dinner at one home or the other. Lilly's mother moved in

with Walt and Lilly a short time after the move. Of Walt's relationship with his mother-in-law, Marjorie Sewell recalled, "Walt was so good to my grandmother. He treated her like she was a queen."

Another of Walt's staff members experienced changes on the domestic front in early 1927. On Friday, January 5, 1927, Ubbe Iwwerks got married after a one-year romance. Ubbe's friend, Santa Fe Railroad employee Ed Wehe, fixed Ubbe up with a railroad comptometer operator named Mildred Henderson, who was originally from Topeka, Kansas. Ubbe and Mildred's courtship included weekend trips to Santa Barbara with Walt and Lillian.

While Ubbe was away on his two-week honeymoon, a new animator—another Kansas City native who came to the Disney studio via Film Ad, and someone who would replace Ham and succeed Thurston Harper as Walt's on-staff antagonist—joined the team. On Monday, January 15 Isadore "Friz" Freleng began work with the Walt Disney Studio. As Hugh recalled, "I got [Friz] out here [to California]. It was my suggestion to Walt that brought [Friz] here. He had worked with me a little at the Film Ad." Friz knew Ubbe and Max from Film Ad, as well. Max recalled that "everybody [at the Film Ad] picked on" Friz, who Max described as "this little red-headed . . . guy[.]"

Friz, twenty-two, was a year younger than Hugh and was a year behind him at Westport High School:

> Well, when I was in high school, I did some drawings for the annual. There was another name that appeared . . . a fellow that I never met who was going to school then and drawing for the annual by the name of Hugh Harman. And then there was a contest given by *The Kansas City Post* for students of high school age for cartoonists. So I entered a drawing and sent it in. I won the contest. But there was second and thirds and one of them was Hugh Harman, whose work I admired very much. I didn't see how I could win and he didn't.

Friz sat next to Hugh at Film Ad. When Hugh left for California in the summer of 1925, Friz told him, "'Well, you can't leave me here alone, because I don't know enough about animation.' [Hugh] said, 'Well, get a book in the library called Lutz's book of animation,' which I did, and I studied the book." Eventually, Hugh mentioned Friz to Walt. Hugh recalled, "I'd told Walt about [Friz] because [he] had worked at the Film Ad with me." Friz confirmed that "Hugh recommended that Walt write to me. So he did, and we corresponded." Walt made Friz "different offers." "I told Walt at the time, I said, 'Well, I don't know anything about [animation]—all I've learned is what I've learned here, self-taught.' And he said, 'Well, you come on out and we'll teach you.'"

And so, Friz—like the Davises, Ubbe, the Harmans, and Rudy before him—agreed to make the trip from Kansas City to Los Angeles to work for Walt. Friz explained, "Walt was one of the first ones to come out to California to work in animation." But, "[b]eing the first one, he didn't have any other animators to work with, so Kansas City was his source of supply."

Friz took the train to California, and "Walt met me at the Santa Fe station there. It was a little station in Los Angeles, and it was a rainy day. So anyhow, Walt picked me up; he had a Moon roadster, and drove me down Sunset Boulevard to this little studio on Hyperion where I met all the boys. I knew practically everybody there except Walt; I had never met Walt or Roy."

In early February, not long after Friz arrived at the studio, Walt brought in a photographer to take formal pictures of the staff. Friz joined his new bosses (Walt and Roy), his Film Ad friends (Hugh and Ubbe), and his new colleagues (Rudy, Walker Harman, and little Lois Hardwick) as they posed for the camera in front of the Hyperion studio. Paul Smith and new assistant animator Norman Blackburn, twenty-three, appear in another photograph from this session. "Everybody is wearing their California clothes, and I'm still Kansas City," Friz recalled. "I didn't think I belonged."

Friz might have been too new to feel at home on the Disney animation staff. Meanwhile, Rudy, who by then had first worked for Walt five years earlier, apparently felt he had been there long enough. A few weeks earlier, Rudy wrote his sister Adele, "We have a secret shop all equipped and can start immediate production on our own pictures in event of obtaining a contract. I hope this will be soon as we shall not make a name and fortune for ourselves working for Walt." Not long before that, Rudy and Hugh wrote Max that they were "quite confident of securing a contract, as we are corresponding with Metro Goldwyn, Fox, Universal and Paramount."

On Wednesday, February 23, while Rudy was contemplating his departure from the Disney studio, Walt hired Les Clark, a twenty-year-old artist who a few days before had graduated from nearby Venice High School. Leslie James Clark was born on November 17, 1907 in Ogden, Utah, the oldest of twelve children of James Elliott Clark, a carpenter of English-Irish descent, and his wife, Lute Wadsworth Clark, who was of Welsh-English descent. The family lived in Idaho before moving to Santa Monica. When he was seventeen, Les passed the entrance exam to the University of Southern California, but his father was injured from a fall off a roof, and Les had to go to work.

Les recalled that he got a job "working a part-time summer job at a lunch counter and confectionary store on Vermont and Kingswell[,]" a half block from the Disney Brothers Studio on Kingswell Avenue. It was during the summer of

1925 that Les, working at the shop as a soda jerk, met Walt, who came in for ice cream. While Les described the restaurant as "a malt shop, confectionary store . . . [it also] served lunch and other meals[,]" and the Disney brothers "used to come over there for lunch." At one point, Walt "used to come in . . . almost every day" and, on one occasion, he praised the lettering that Les used when he wrote the shop's menu on its wall mirror. Les likely worked at A. L. Farris, an ice cream and confectioners located on the east side of North Vermont Avenue, a few stores south of the intersection of North Vermont and Kingswell, one-half block from the Disney Brothers Studio. The shop's owner, Albert Lawson Farris, lived nearby, on North Vermont, one block north of his store.

By early 1927, almost two years after meeting Walt, Les had returned to school, was nearing graduation, and looking for a job. "While I was still in high school, I asked Walt for a job. He said, 'Bring some of your drawings in and let me see what they look like.' Well, I copied some cartoons out of *College Humor* and showed them to him" at the Hyperion studio on Saturday, February 19. Les "told him I had copied" the drawings. Walt liked Les' "swift, deft" lines and offered him a job, although he warned Les that it "might just be a temporary job." Walt "invited me to start work the following [week,]" and Les accepted.

Les and Norm Blackburn were two of three animators hired that month. The other was Ben Clopton, twenty-one. Rudy recalled, "You see . . . the studio was getting to where the little group [of original animators] was beginning to bring in other people. Norm Blackburn, and a bunch of new people started coming in. Even more so when we [had to produce] . . . . twenty-six [reels] a year, so we had to find some new help too." Hugh felt that Ben "had some very fine training with Ub[be]." Ben worked as Ubbe's assistant, and Hugh recalled that "Ben developed this facility, under Ub[be]'s tutelage. He was not really as flexible or good as Ub[be] . . . But he was a very excellent assistant[.]"

Meanwhile, Friz settled in at the studio. He commuted to work with Hugh, and worked alongside Ubbe:

> I rented a room in a house on Vermont Avenue, which was about a mile or a mile and a half from the Studio, and we could walk to work and walk back. Then I sat right next to Ub[be]. . . who was teaching me how to animate. He was an expert at it; it was easy for him and it was hard for me, because I was just learning. Roy Disney would pick up Hugh and me in the mornings—none of us had cars—and he'd drive us to work. But after work we had to walk home, because he didn't care when we got home, but he did care when we got to work! So every morning Roy would pick us up at the restaurant, we'd have breakfast and Roy would pick us up.

Friz continued to look to Hugh as a mentor:

> Well, Hugh Harman was my ideal and practically my teacher. Of course, Rudy was kind of secondary. He kind of followed along with Hugh, Hugh was more the leader. I don't think [Hugh] was as creative [as Walt] . . . . What he did was follow Walt, whatever Walt did, he did the same kind of thing.

One person that Friz was not getting along with, however, was Walt. "I'd become very sensitive as a child, because I was much smaller than other kids, and I was always defending myself, because they'd pick on me. Walt picked this up, and he used to rib me quite a bit, maybe size, or whatever it was[.]" Friz felt that he "made mistakes and Walt—even though he expressed patience in his letters prior to my joining him—didn't show any. He became abusive and harassed me." Friz said, "I don't think he really meant any harm. [But] when he'd make a remark, I'd take exception, and I'd make a nasty remark back to him."

In March 1927, not long after Friz, Les Clark, Norm Blackburn, and Ben Clopton started at the studio, Rudy left. Excluding Walt's pre-Kaycee Studios jobs, Rudy was the animator who had been with Walt the longest—since early 1922—and he was fired (although Rudy later described it as an amicable parting) for an unusual reason:

> How did I leave Walt Disney? [I had a problem with falling asleep.] It took me about three or four years to get over that sleeping problem. The change in coming from Kansas City out here, I don't know just what it was. Camera work was pretty monotonous once you started to photograph, and I used to fall asleep between frames. Then we had a motor drive—you'd pull the cord and it would click, and the motor was kind of noisy, and every once in a while I'd fall asleep. Walt told me one day, "It's too costly, if you're going to keep falling asleep." My brother had the same malady. In those early days I was interested as much in photography as I was in being an artist. But the thing I wanted to do in photography was portraits. I was as much interested in that as I was in being an artist or a cartoonist. So actually I said, "Look, Walt, why don't I just leave, and you can get somebody else for your camera." And he said, "No, I don't want to do that," and I said, "Yeah, but I'd just as soon, why don't I leave." And that was it.

Said Hugh: "I don't blame Walt [for firing Rudy], because Rudy would sleep during the day, when he should have been working[.]"

✦ ✦ ✦

On Saturday, February 26, Walt wrote Charlie about the Alice series, stating:

> [u]p to the present time, I have felt we have sort of been in a rut in regard
> to the st[y]le and general construction of our plots and gags. I tried every
> way possible to find out just what was lacking and now I believe I have
> found "IT". Wish you would take special notice of the future pictures and
> let me know just what you think. I will surely appreciate having you give
> me any constructive criticism in regard to bettering the future pictures.

Ironically, if Walt found a new formula for the Alice series, he did not have much
time to employ it, as the developments of the next few days put him on the path
to the series that would replace the Alice Comedies. Charlie's March 3 letter recognized that Walt's "later pictures . . . are very good," but Charlie's thoughts were
on the new series, not Alice. Charlie would be in Los Angeles in a few days, he
wrote Walt, and "[a]t that time I will go over many things with you."

Among them was the fact that, before leaving New York, Charlie, concluding
a few months of negotiations, signed a contract with Robert H. Cochrane, the
vice president of Universal, for a series of twenty-six reels based on a new character named Oswald the Rabbit. Cochrane's boss, Carl Laemmle, the founder
and president of Universal Pictures, had decided that he wanted a new animated
series. According to a reporter, when the "Universal Film Company wanted some
animal cartoons. . . . [t]hey asked Mintz to submit samples." Margaret Winkler
thought that Walt could work on the proposed series as a follow-up to the Alice
series and, as Rudy recalled, the "Winklers talked to [Walt] about it."

About five weeks earlier in late January, pursuant to Charlie's request, Walt
had pictures of rabbits made for a new series that Charlie told Walt he was
discussing with a "national organization[.]" "So," according to Rudy, "everybody
got together and tried to draw a rabbit." Hugh recalled that the Disney animators "just sat down and drew a few sketches. Each of us would draw one . . . .
Ub[be] would draw some, I drew some, others would draw some, and from
that evolved this character." Walt sent "several rough pencil sketches of different
rabbit characters" and told Charlie, "If these sketches are not what you want, let
me know more about it and I will try again."

Upon receiving the sketches sent by Walt, Charlie replied,

> I received the rabbit characters and, of course, don't know just at the
> moment whether they will prove to be what we want. It isn't so much
> what I want because if it were up to me I would say leave everything

stand just as it is. I am negotiating with a national organization and they seem to think that there are too many cats on the market.... As long as they are doing the buying, we must try to sell them what they want.

Universal liked the Disney rabbits and concluded a deal with Charlie. Only then did Walt learn that the Winkler negotiations were with Universal. As for the new character's name, a committee at Universal had decided that the rabbit would be named Oswald.

Charlie arrived in Los Angeles in mid-March, and met with Walt about their new venture. Charlie agreed to advance the Disney Studio $2,250 each for twenty-six Oswald shorts, the first of which would be delivered in time for a September 1 release. On Saturday, March 12, at least one trade journal broke the Oswald story. *Moving Picture World* reported:

> "U" to Release "Oswald," Universal has signed a contract with Charles Mintz, president of Winkler Productions, for the addition of a series of 26 "Oswald the Rabbit" one-reel cartoon comedies to the Universal short production line-up.

Others reported that George Winkler was going to relocate from New York to Los Angeles permanently to oversee the "Oswald the Rabbit" series, and that

> Universal Announces Release of "Oscar [*sic*] the Rabbit" Cartoons.... [A] contract was entered into between Universal and Winkler Pictures for twenty-six .... cartoons drawn by Walt Disney about the fortunes of a rabbit named Oswald, an exclusive creation of the artist, which the sales force is already designating as the Welsh Rabbit or the Lucky Rabbit. They will be released under the brand name of Snappy Comedies.

By that time, the Disney staff had designed Oswald and had begun preliminary work on the first reel. Hugh recalled,

> It was announced to us one morning, when we went in, that we were starting Oswalds. So the time was right now to think of an Oswald story. We all got together in Walt's little office ... and dreamed up this first story .... [W]e began to build on it, and about 11 o'clock, Walt said, "Why don't we start animating?" He said, "Hugh, the first part of that is pretty well worked out; you know what it is, don't you?" I said, "Yeah, that's enough to start on." So I went in and started Oswald pacing up and down on the ridge of this roof.

As to the rest of the reel, "[i]t was decided," said Hugh, "that Ubbe would take roughly half the picture."

By late March, the last four Alice shorts, including *Alice in the Big League*, the fifty-sixth and final Alice Comedy, were in production, but the focus now was on Oswald. On Monday, March 28, Charlie wired Walt that he had arrived back in New York "safely [to] find everyone enthusiastic about Oswald. Universal wants Oswald sketches [which] I requested soon as possible." Within a few days, Charlie was anxious about getting the first Oswald reel completed:

> I guess I needn't urge you to shoot the first picture along as soon as possible—I know you will do it yourself. Please keep sending me all sketches, etc., that you can think of and let me know by return mail the names of the first three subjects. Also let me know how soon I will receive the poster sketches on these subjects.

The excitement of a new project brought a new informality to Charlie's letter; he addressed it to "Walt" and signed it "Charlie."

The development of a different series also led Walt and Roy to take some actions on the personnel front. On Saturday, April 2 Walt hired his sister-in-law, Hazel Sewell, to oversee the inking and painting. That same day, to replace Rudy, the Disneys rehired cameraman Mike Marcus, who had been replaced by Rudy at Disney Brothers Studio nearly two years earlier. In addition, at about this time, and no doubt in recognition of the importance of Ubbe to the success of the Oswald series, Walt and Roy raised Ubbe's pay "in steps from seventy dollars to one hundred twenty dollars in just two months' time."

The first Oswald reel, entitled *Poor Papa*, took two weeks to produce, and it was finished and shipped on Sunday, April 10. "The theme of the thing," said Hugh, "was that Oswald was fretting because of the arrival of storks carrying new little rabbits. He was on the roof of this house, with a shotgun, trying to keep the stork away. . . . I animated that [scene]." Five days later, Charlie wired his, and Universal's, less than enthusiastic reaction to Walt:

> Oswald arrived today and [I] am disappointed. I thought it was understood between us that the early pictures particularly would show more of the rabbit itself than this one does. There are so many other characters [that] at no time is Oswald outstanding. [I] presume you have already finished animation on [the] second picture and will therefore request that [the] third one carry more story, less characters and show Oswald to

better advantage. My contract with Universal [is] subject to their approval of [the] first two pictures and this is their criticism. . . . Please also avoid all repetition unless you are absolutely certain of its humor. Also make Oswald young and snappy looking with a monocle.

Universal was more pointed and prepared a list of complaints:

(1) Approximately 100 feet of the opening is jerky in action due to poor animation. (2) There is too much repetition of action. Scenes are dragged out to such an extent that the cartoon is materially slowed down. (3) The Oswald shown in this picture is far from being a funny character. Sometimes there are hints that something is going on underneath, but it is buried too deep to bother about. He's just flat. He has no outstanding trait. Nothing would eventually become characteristic insofar as Oswald is concerned. (4) The picture is merely a succession of unrelated gags, there being not even a thread of story throughout its length. (5) Why is Oswald so old, sloppy and fat? Audiences like their characters young, trim and smart. This one is practically decrepit.

According to his notes, Walt apparently intended to tell Charlie that he was

[s]orry [that] we were both disappointed—I changed type of character and story immediately after seeing first Oswald—I am working for less story and more gags and believe you will agree with me after seeing future pictures . . . . I tried to tell you plot of first picture but you said go ahead and make it any way only use a rabbit—please let me know just what you mean by repetition [and] forget the monicle [sic].

As he worked on the second Oswald, *Trolley Troubles*, Walt continued to refine Oswald as Charlie requested, but Walt also pushed back a bit. Walt conceded to Charlie that Oswald could be "neat and trim" and a "younger character, peppy, alert, saucy, and venturesome," but Walt did not want his new star to be "shown in the same light as the commonly known cat characters." Rather, Walt wanted Oswald to be "peculiarly . . . OSWALD." And he did not agree that *Poor Papa* was padded with repeat action, or needed narrative. "[B]y the time you have a story really started it is time to iris out, and you have failed to make the audience laugh." Walt felt that his "poorest pictures have been the ones where we went into story detail."

As for the animation, Ubbe was "a man of experience whom I am willing to put alongside any man in the business today." Walt wasn't the only one with the highest regard for Ubbe's work. Said Hugh: "We [animators] had a difficult [standard to measure up to], and that was Ubbe's animation. I've never seen anybody like him. He could do this: he would sit down with a pile of paper, and put one paper on, and draw Oswald . . . . I've never seen such facility in drafts-manship. Before you knew it, within a half hour, he would have maybe 20 or 30 drawings of Oswald, running off into perspective."

*Trolley Troubles* was based on a 1917 Harold Lloyd short called *Luke's Trol-ley Troubles* and, given the disappointment over *Poor Papa*, was eagerly antici-pated by Universal. In this short, Oswald drives an out-of-control trolley. Friz recalled how *Trolley Troubles* came to be:

> Well, Walt would come up with an idea. He'd say, "Let's have Oswald and his little girl on a trolley car, you know, and the trolley car runs away or something and Oswald saves the day. And if you guys come up with any gags, I'll give you five dollars," if they used the gag, or something. And that's the way, you know, we'd throw little gags or ideas at it. And what he used, you know, if he used it, why, sometimes he'd pay you five dollars or something like that. . . . But it was just kind of a get-together where Walt was the leader, and he just wrote the ideas as we went along, and stretched it out so it was six or seven minutes long, that's about all it was. There was really no story. There was a situation we'd create, and we'd throw in gags: what would happen if a streetcar ran down a hill, ran away, and the little things that might happen, you know. And then we'd always have a villain in it, and the villain would either try to kidnap the little girl or something. There was always a conflict created somehow.

Hugh helped animate the scene that showed Oswald's perspective as his trolley raced towards, and into, a tunnel. "Walt," said Hugh, "thought that [scene] was the most wonderful thing in the world, and so did I. As it turned out, the ani-mation [and use of perspective] was so effective[.]" According to Hugh, it was his younger brother, Walker, who "thought of the idea of this car running wild and running into a tunnel . . . in advancing panorama."

Friz also remembered animating scenes from *Troubles*. "It was a rabbit on a streetcar, and the streetcar ran away down a hill and the little rabbit was on it. He took off his foot and rubbed it on his back, like the old gag of the lucky rab-bit foot—he was Oswald the Lucky Rabbit." The reason this scene was memo-rable to Friz is that

> when the rabbit took his foot off to rub on the back of his neck, I was questioning, "What do I show when his foot's taken off?" You know, "what

do I show, do I show a bone in there or what?" And Walt made an issue of it because I didn't know what to do. And of course he never thought of it either, at the time. But when I said, "what do I show, do I show a bone?", then everybody started laughing, and nobody knew, really, what do to.... Well, we just showed a white spot there, of course, just a circle where—it was like putting a plastic character together.

Friz was also making strides in his work on the final Alice reels. He added some action to a scene from *Alice's Picnic*, featuring Julius' wife, "Mrs. Julius," that captured the personality animation for which Walt strived, and Friz's work drew very high praise from Walt:

> I remember one scene that Walt liked very well that I did, and it wasn't written into the script or anything. He said, "A mother cat is bathing her little kittens. Do a scene with the mother cat bathing the kittens." So I did the scene, and I added one little kitten crawling out of the tub, and he's hanging—he was so small he had to hang on the edge of the tub and then drop down. And then the mother grabbed him and put him back into the tub, and a couple of them were trying to escape. This was just ad-libbed in there, because all the script said was, "A mother cat bathing the kittens." And then Walt called that to everybody's attention. He says, "I want you to see this scene." He says, "That little kitten didn't just jump out of the water, he climbed up and hung there and dropped down like a little kid would do." He says, "Friz did it this way and made him act like a little kid. That's what I want to see in the pictures, I want the characters to *be* somebody. I don't want them just to be a drawing." And he was the first guy that recognized that you had to put personality, build character into it, and they weren't just drawings moving around.

When Walt shipped *Trolley Troubles* to Charlie around May 1, Walt wrote,

> This picture is far from being what I am working for in the future. I want to make Oswald have more personality and really create a likeable character, and I believe that with a little time and patience on the part of you and Universal, that we will be able to develop a knockout series. We are changing the rabbit still more from the way he looks in this picture. We have eliminated the suspenders and changed his face considerably in the third one. I am also installing a new motor-drive on the camera to eliminate a certain unevenness in the photography that has been noticeable

in the past. I believe this will give much cleaner and better stuff in the future.

That month, Walt continued to expand the number of animators he wanted on Oswald. Ham Hamilton returned after a five-month absence, although his sister, Irene, left a month later. Ironically, Ham became "the very best of friends" with Friz, who was initially hired to replace Ham. Walt and Roy also hired Laugh-O-gram alumnus Max Maxwell, who moved from Kansas City to Los Angeles and started at the studio on Monday, May 23. Twenty-one-year-old animator Ray Abrams started a week later. Ray, and Paul Smith, Hugh thought, "started as beginners[ and] . . . . just did what they could, and worked rather as assistants [to the animators]."

Max recalled this time as "the period when Walt was very intrigued with off-color gags, such as cows with swinging udders and little characters running into outhouses." Paul Smith agreed. "We'd all be called into Walt's office and hash over notes that he had made on the next picture. What did we think of this gag, was it too risqué . . . he was always putting in gags where a cow would get her udder caught in something."

By the beginning of the summer, Universal was mobilizing its publicity department to prepare the market for the upcoming debut of its new animated star. *Universal Weekly* featured an inside cover ad, with a primitive-looking Oswald, that proclaimed,

> Something NEW from Universal! Here I am Folks!—I am the LUCKY Rabbit. I bring laughs, profits, money, gelt, gold, simoleons. . . . I'm the animule Universal discovered after two years' experimentation and preparation seeking the Krazy Kartoon Knockout that would set the industry on its rabbit ears. I'll be with you 26 times this year. One reel each time.

A five-cent candy bar, the "Oswald the Milk Chocolate Frappe Bar," was released by the Vogan Candy Company of Oregon. According to *Universal Weekly*, "F. F. Vincent, the Universal exploitation man in the Pacific Northwest, has tied them [Oswald Comedies] up in such a way that they have been sold to practically everyone in his territory before they ever reached the screen, and their fame is rapidly traveling eastward."

"The Vogan Candy Company of Portland, Ore., . . . snapped up Vincent's suggestion that they put an 'Oswald' candy bar on the market." The extensive advertising campaign included truck banners, window stickers, newspaper ads, counter cards. "The bar immediately 'took' and is providing the biggest seller the company has ever had. Already shipments have been made to Honolulu and Alaska." Because of the wrapper, with its depiction of Oswald, "his face as well as his name is fast becoming familiar to fans." Oswald was also used for a button made by the Philadelphia Badge Company and a stencil set from Universal Tag and Novelty Company.

Due to its discontent over *Poor Papa*, Universal decided that *Trolley Troubles* would be the first Oswald released, and it premiered at the Criterion Theater in Los Angeles on Monday, the Fourth of July, 1927, alongside MGM's *Flesh and the Devil. Troubles* made its New York debut eleven days later at the Roxy Theatre, alongside 20th Century Fox's *Singed*, and was released nationally on Labor Day.

The critics were impressed. According to *The Film Daily*, "As conductor on a 'Toonerville' trolley, Oswald is a riot. This . . . you can book on pure faith, and our solemn word that they have the goods." In its "Timely Reviews of Short Subjects" column, *Moving Picture World* claimed that Oswald was "good for a lot of smiles and real laughs. 'Trolley Troubles' presents Oswald as the skipper of a dinky little trolley on a wild ride over mountains."

*Motion Picture News* wrote

> If the first of these new cartoon comedies for Universal release is an indication of what is to come, then this series is destined to win much popular favor. They are cleverly drawn, well executed, brimful of action and fairly abounding in humorous situations. Oswald the Lucky Rabbit is all of that. Some of his experiences are hilarious and breath taking. He is the conductor of the suburban trolley in this one and it is a trick car that provides plenty of humor. Oswald and the car encounter all sorts of obstacles. They flatten out to run under a cow and they hurdle others, much to the consternation of the bewildered passengers. The laughs are spontaneous and there are plenty of them.

Seemingly unnoticed in the studio's and press' enthusiasm over the new series was the quiet end of the Alice Comedies. On Monday, August 22, the last Alice reel, *Alice in the Big League*, was released. A few years later, Walt said of Alice, "she was terrible." Maybe he had soured on Alice because of her dwindling profit margin; Walt lost money—$61.25—on *Big League*. Roy was more measured, saying, "The Alice cartoons didn't make much of a splash[.]"

◂ ◂ ◂

The fresh start signaled by Oswald led Walt to, for the first time, divide his staff into separate animation units. One unit was led by Ubbe and Friz (whose younger brother, twenty-year-old Allen Freleng, was hired as an inker and painter for a few weeks in the summer of 1927), and Hugh and Ham led the other. A new animator, Johnny Cannon, twenty, was hired to join Paul Smith, Ben Clopton, Norm Blackburn, and Les Clark in the animator pool. Walt now offered bonuses to the animators not only for gags, but when a short finished on time. Story meetings were held in the evenings approximately every two weeks, and a one-page synopsis of the resulting story would be typed the next day.

But the rejuvenation signaled by Oswald masked discontent that threatened the end of the Walt Disney Studio. By the summer of 1927, whether because of personality conflict or the desire for personal autonomy and individual success, a number of the Disney animators contemplated leaving Walt. Hugh, for example, could not stand Walt's heavy-handed personality and felt that "[u]nless you were 100% for Walt, unless you were doing for him, working for him, he thought you were double-crossing him." Hugh claimed that Walt had agreed in the summer of 1923 to form a partnership with Hugh once Hugh arrived in California, but later reneged to form Disney Brothers with Roy.

Walker Harman left the studio that July. Others, too, wanted to break out on their own. Friz recalled that "[e]verybody was conspiring against the other one. . . . Everybody had ambition; everybody wanted to be a producer and there was no one to work with." Friz himself continued to experience friction with Walt. On one occasion, Friz called Walt at home,

> telling him I had something on my mind which bothered me. . . . It took
> him just a few minutes to drive over to where I was living in a boarding
> house. He wouldn't let me say a word until he arrived at the studio and
> opened the door. He got behind his desk and took out a cigar. He asked
> me to sit opposite to him, and said, "Now start talking." I told him how
> much he upset me emotionally, and reminded him of his letters to me
> expressing his patience in my learning animation. He apologized, and
> complimented me for having the nerve to speak my mind. He said he
> had a great respect for me, but I don't think really, truthfully he did,
> because after that, things became somewhat more unbearable.

Rudy, now gone but still friendly with Hugh (who still—"even though Rudy wasn't working for Disney"—"asked Rudy to help me with my [Oswald] stories[]") and the others, found the studio to be a "den of strife and vexation." In Rudy's view, Walt wanted the animators to believe they were overpaid and had "a lot to learn" from the Disneys.

Thus, the atmosphere at the Walt Disney Studio was already charged when, sometime during mid-1927, Charlie Mintz had George Winkler, who would go to the studio to bring checks to Roy and pick up the next short and poster, approach Hugh about taking over the production of Oswald. But, as Paul Smith recalled, it did not end there; the Winkler people also "made telephone calls and arrangements to talk with us." Paul and other animators met with Charlie "at various places" outside the studio. When Charlie and his staff made over-tures about setting up a new studio to make Oswalds, Hugh recalled, "I was interested right away, because I was very disappointed in Walt, and wanted to get away from him. I would have quit anyway, one way or another. . . . Rudy and I had been planning to go into production for ourselves for quite some time, and I saw this as a possibility. Against that, I didn't want to be in a position of stealing the deal with Walt, so I thought I'd just go to work for Winklers[.]"

George Winkler came to Hugh in mid-1927, and "told me frankly they were going to break with Walt," Hugh said. George "asked me if I would come to work for his company . . . . He had sworn me to confidence before that; . . . I would've told Roy, but [George] had sworn[n] me to confidence. At first, I thought, here's Rudy's and my chance to set up our own business." But Hugh "didn't want to undercut Roy. . . . I didn't want to steal the [Oswald] deal from [Roy]. . . . [although] I could have kicked the carpet from under [Walt] without any qualms[.]"

As for Ubbe, by now, even he intended to leave the studio. Rudy said that Ubbe planned "to engage in a private enterprise," although history has not recorded what Ubbe had in mind late in the summer of 1927. Perhaps Ubbe realized that he had developed into the studio's star animator and contemplated branching out on his own. But as for most of the others, they were interested in accepting Charlie's offer to work for Winkler Pictures. By the end of August, Rudy wrote a friend of Hugh's and his in Kansas City that the "Winklers have made us a definite offer for a next years [sic] release. Winklers are thoroughly disgusted with the Disneys and with the expiration of their present contract will have no more dealings with them. Their present contract expires in April, 1928."

As for Friz, on Thursday, September 1, after almost eight rocky months with Walt, he quit the studio. The previous day, he skipped work out of frustra-tion and went to the movies on Wilshire Boulevard. As Friz rode home on the upper level of a double-decker bus, he was seen by Walt, who happened to be riding right behind the bus in his Moon roadster. The next day, Friz went to the studio and found that his desk had been emptied, and another argument ensued. Friz collected his paycheck and returned to Kansas City.

In assessing his difficult relationship with Walt, Friz recalled, "Walt and I had personalities that clashed." As a result, "I couldn't take him any more and decided to quit." Friz felt that "Walt was just a hard person to work for. I think a lot of people have said the same thing, you had to please Walt, you couldn't please yourself. I guess I was one of those people who just had to do my thing, you know, and I couldn't do his thing. That was in the back of my mind all the time, I guess, I just couldn't do the other guy's thing."

Hugh, who had his own complaints about Walt, did not feel that Walt picked on Friz, whom Hugh said "was the best animator we had." In fact, Hugh thought that "Walt was very generous and kind with him. . . . I don't think that [Walt] harassed him in any sense[.]" Hugh admitted that "We used to tease [Friz] a lot." The staff thought Friz worked too intensely, and used to torment Friz by building fires under his chair "almost every other day," said Hugh, but Friz would "never catch onto it, because his concentration was so deep." Finally, Friz would scream for help and Hugh and the others would put out the fire. As for his part, Walt later conceded that "I used to be less tolerant in those days because there was more pressure of that payroll and getting that picture out, and I guess I was a pretty tough guy at times . . . I can look back and [realize] I used to get mad and blow my top[.]"

Two weeks after Friz left, the second Oswald release, *Oh, Teacher*, premiered and also garnered favorable press. In this reel, Oswald fights a cat bully in order to reclaim his stolen bike and his rabbit girlfriend, eventually named Fanny. *Moving Picture World* wrote that *Oh, Teacher* "lives up to the promise of the first . . . as a clever, peppy and amusing series of cartoons that should prove popular in any type of house. This one deals with Oswald as a school kid and introduces a cat as his rival. It contains some of the best gags we have seen in cartoons."

The next three Oswald releases, *The Mechanical Cow*, *Great Guns*, and *All Wet*, each featuring Fanny, were released in October. In *Mechanical Cow*, a robot cow helps Oswald deliver milk. Describing *Cow*, *Moving Picture World* said that inventor Oswald "has a wild and amusing time with his ingenious milk producer." Hugh recalled that he and Rudy created the story for *Mechanical Cow*. They, Hugh said, "figured out a gag that set off a whole series of followups, and that was the cow-udder gag. Oswald was chasing this mechanical cow, trying to catch it, and he took a long dive, leaping for the cow, missed the tail but grabbed the udder, and the milk shot him in the face, and he had to let go. . . . That started that whole splurge of cow-udder gags that Walt persisted in[.]"

Commenting on *Guns*, a *Moving Picture World* columnist wrote that Oswald is a "hero in action in the trenches and [in] a situation where two planes fight each other like pugilists." *Motion Picture News* found *Guns* was "chock full of humor" and wrote, "This series is bound to be popular in all types of houses if the present standard is maintained." In *All Wet*, Oswald is a lifeguard who rescues Fanny.

Subsequent Oswald releases continued to receive good notices. *Moving Picture World* wrote of the series, "In addition to striking a new note in cartoon characters by featuring a rabbit, these Disney creations are bright, speedy and genuinely amusing. . . . The animation is good and the clever way in which Disney makes his creations simulate the gestures and expressions of human beings adds to the enjoyment. They should provide worthwhile attractions in any type of house." Another stated, "Oswald looks like a real contender. Walt Disney is doing this new series. Funny how the cartoon artists never hit on a rabbit before. Oswald with his long ears has a chance for a lot of new comedy gags and makes the most of them. Universal has been looking for a good animated subject for the past year. They've found it."

Oswald was a hit. It played in the best movie houses and brought in "larger and larger bundles of money[.]" In October and November, presumably with some of their profits, the Disney brothers purchased ten acres of land in the desert. They also invested in an oil-drilling venture overseen by Uncle Robert and Dr. Cowles. Ubbe invested his income during this time as well, and bought several stone mills to crush paint pigment he used to make paint formulas that were utilized by animators for decades.

Meanwhile, as Walt and Roy hired inkers and painters Esther Benson, a former maid, and twenty-six-year-Mary Tebb (Lilly's cousin, Ruby Bounds, also worked as an inker and painter for a few weeks that fall), some of the staff still considered quitting. By November, Rudy and several of the Disney animators with whom he remained friends set their sights on getting hired by Cecil B. DeMille. On Tuesday, November 15 Rudy wrote to Friz, now back in Kansas City, that a friend was trying to get Rudy and the others such a contract. Specifically, Rudy wrote that Ray Friedman was "at present working on the general manager of Cecil DeMille Studios. . . . Ray is putting all of his time towards the securing of a contract and getting everything in shape for starting production. It shouldn't be long now."

The November Oswald releases featured a trans-Atlantic plane race (*The Ocean Hop*) and a bank robbery and chase (*The Banker's Daughter*). The December reels focused on a holiday visit by Oswald to an orphanage (*Empty Socks*) and a bootleg liquor-fueled flirtation with a nurse (*Rickety Gin*). In the midst of these December releases, Walt turned twenty-six. By year's end, *Moving Picture World* proclaimed that Oswald had "accomplished the astounding feat of jumping into the first-run favor overnight."

The series' success "enabled the [Disney] firm to save about fifteen thousand dollars and hire some help," according to a reporter. By this time, the staff of the Walt Disney Studio had grown to almost twenty. Walt's weekly salary was

$100 and Roy's was $65. The brothers cleared $500 per Oswald cartoon and split the year-end profits, with Walt getting 60 percent of the profit, or $5,361, and Roy getting 40 percent, or $3,574.

◂ ◂ ◂

In early 1928, as Walt and Roy prepared to ship the nineteenth of the twenty-six Oswald shorts called for by their contract—and anticipated the renewal of the Oswald the Lucky Rabbit series—Charlie kept plotting behind Walt's back to take the series away from him. George Winkler continued conferring with Hugh and other Disney animators about entering into a contract directly with Charlie. Ubbe's granddaughter wrote that Ubbe suspected George's motives and confronted him.

Ubbe also explained to Walt that George was doing more on his "fortnightly" visits to Hyperion Avenue than picking up the latest Oswald short. Ubbe told Walt that several of the staff—Ubbe called them "renegades"—were signing with Charlie, and that Ubbe was asked to join but refused.

But with Oswald a hit, perhaps Walt wanted only good news. He must have thought he found it when, on Thursday, February 2, Charlie signed a new three-year contract with Universal that would continue the Oswald series into 1931. In reporting on the renewal, *The Film Daily* called the series "one of the best sellers of the 'U[niversal]' short subject program," adding that, "Charley [*sic*] Mintz's organization has been delivering and how."

But now that Charlie had his new Universal contract in place, he moved to secure the animators he hoped would make the series directly for him rather than for the Disney brothers. On Friday, February 10, Rudy, perhaps referencing his run at the DeMille Studios of a few months earlier, wrote Friz: "Our plans to get a contract to make our own pictures this year fell through, so we are taking the next best thing. Hugh, Max, Ham and I are signing a one-year employment contract with George Winkler to make 'Oswald the Lucky Rabbit.'"

Meanwhile, in the wake of the Universal contract renewal, the Disney brothers talked and agreed that Walt would travel to New York to ask Charlie for a raise to $2,500 per reel. Walt told a reporter eight years later that his motivation for the price increase was to invest more in the shorts and improve their quality. He told another, "At the end of the first year with Oswald, because of his success, I expected to be allowed a little more money to build the series up to a higher standard."

Years later, Walt explained that his mission was not just about improving Oswald, but related to what he saw as the overall lethargy in the industry:

The [Oswald] series was going over. We had built up a little organization. Roy and I each had our own homes and a "flivver." We had money in the bank and security. But we didn't like the looks of the future. The cartoon business didn't seem to be going anywhere except in circles. The pictures were kicked out in a hurry and made to price. Money was the only object. Cartoons had become the shabby Cinderella of the picture industry. They were thrown in for nothing as a bonus to exhibitors buying features. I resented that. Some of the possibilities in the cartoon medium had begun to dawn on me. And at the same time we saw that the medium was dying. You could feel *rigor mortis* setting in. I could feel it in myself. Yet with more money and time, I felt we could make better pictures and shake ourselves out of the rut.

Perhaps because of Ubbe's warning, Walt did not consider it inevitable that Charlie would agree to a new contract. While he intended to get Charlie to agree to a raise from $2,250 to $2,500 per short, if Charlie declined, Walt believed he could interest another distributor.

Walt asked Lilly to travel with him to New York. She recalled that the purpose of the trip was so that Walt could convince Charlie that the Disney brothers "couldn't break even" at the current price he paid them for Oswald. Lilly said that Charlie "was paying them $2,250 a film [but it was] not as much as it sounds when you take the costs out, but still quite a sum of money to us in those days." Lilly agreed to go with Walt: "I went along, too, for a second honeymoon. It didn't turn out that way."

Walt left for New York with two Oswald prints and favorable Oswald press clippings, which he hoped would earn him an offer from a distributor other than Charlie, if need be. Walt and Lilly stopped in Chicago, which was cold, windy, and snowy, before arriving in New York on Tuesday, February 21, 1928. They checked into the Hotel Knickerbocker at 120 West 45th Street in Times Square, "The Hotel With A Heart" and "400 Rooms [and] 400 Baths." Walt did not plan on meeting with Charlie right away—he wanted to "find how things stand [with other distributors] before seeing Charlie[.]"

Upon his arrival in New York, Walt first went to see John W. Alicoate, the publisher of the *Film Daily*—"The Newspaper of Filmdom ... All The News All The Time"—at his office six blocks north of the Knickerbocker at 1650 Broadway. Jack Alicoate, thirty-eight, was the manager and secretary of the *Daily*. He had served in the army and graduated from the law school at Georgetown University. He became the automobile editor of the *Washington Post* and was later that paper's first motion picture editor. He wrote screenplays for one-reel shorts and eventually went to work for the *Film Daily* where, by 1926, he was promoted to president and publisher.

Prior to coming to New York, a friend of Walt's gave him a letter introducing him to Jack. When Walt got to the *Daily* offices on February 21, Jack was not yet in, and Walt did not see him until three that afternoon. Walt found Jack to be "a dandy fellow—kind of reserved and dignified but very obliging and willing to give me all the help and advice that he can[.]" Jack advised Walt to "not get too rough" with Charlie Mintz, since the Disneys might ultimately need him. Walt wrote Roy that "Alicoate said that Charlie couldn't do us any harm as regards the other companys [*sic*] and seemed to think I ought to see [Charlie] as soon as possible[.]"

With regard to the short subject market, Jack told Walt that it was in poor shape. Jack said that MGM, Pathé, Educational, and others were having difficulty with their short subjects. Jack thought that Walt's best bet in terms of finding a distributor other than Charlie was either MGM or Fox, and asked Walt to come back two days later, on Thursday, to update him on progress with other distributors (Wednesday, February 22, was George Washington's birthday, a federal holiday).

Walt left Jack and immediately phoned the "heads" of MGM and Fox. Salesman Frederick C. Quimby, forty-two, of MGM agreed to see Walt at 2:30 p.m. on Thursday, but Walt's contact at Fox was away. Wednesday, the Disneys' first full day in New York, was a long one, and, like the day before, was "very cold[.]" Walt was no doubt anxious to meet with other distributors, and he wrote Roy that "Wednesday was a holiday and I couldn't see anyone—Lilly and I bummed around town and spent a very miserable day[.]"

Thursday was more mild; Walt called it "a dandy day[.]" Walt placed the two Oswald prints under one arm and the press reviews under the other, and—feeling "like a hick"—marched one half-block north on Broadway to MGM to see Fred Quimby. Walt told Roy that Fred was "not a bad sort[,]" but Fred was not interested in Oswald since MGM's theatre department felt that cartoons were "on the wane." Nor was Fred interested in reading the Oswald clippings, but he agreed to screen the prints later if Walt would agree to leave them for a few days. Fred thought he had recently been shown a few Oswald shorts by someone who Walt suspected was one of "the Boys." Fred asked Walt to call him two days later on Saturday. Walt left MGM and went back to the *Daily*, but Jack Alicoate had a bad cold and was out of the office and would remain out until the following week.

Walt then went to the offices of Winkler Pictures to speak with Charlie. The Winkler company was located in Room 660 at 220 West 42nd Street, three blocks south of the Knickerbocker and just west of Seventh Avenue. Charlie, now thirty-eight, was "very nice" and invited Walt and Lilly to join Margaret and him for lunch the next day at the Astor Hotel. Walt, twenty-six, and Charlie did not "talk business" at the time, but Walt could tell from "what remarks were dropped" that Charlie "had something up his sleeve."

On Friday, which was cold once again, the Disneys and the Mintzes met at the Astor on 44th and Broadway. During lunch, the Mintzes invited Walt and Lilly to come to their home for dinner the following Monday night. Red Kahn, editor of the *Film Daily*, was also eating at the Astor that day, and Charlie waved Kahn over to the table so Kahn could meet Walt. Walt recalled that

> "Red" accidentally dropped a remark that Charlie didn't like—
> he said "Oswald—oh yes—I have heard a lot of nice things about
> them—especially the nice grosses."—Charlie didn't say any thing
> but acted kind of funny—I let on like I didn't notice it[.]

As the Disneys and the Mintzes finished lunch and walked out of the hotel dining room, Charlie asked Walt to come by the office the following afternoon so that they could talk.

On Saturday morning, Walt called Fred Quimby, whose screening of the Oswald prints confirmed Fred's sense that he had been shown Oswald shorts before. MGM, however, would not be interested in "so short a subject," and preferred titles that would gross $25,000. Walt then phoned Fox, and was able to get an appointment there for the following week. That same day, back in Los Angeles, Max Maxwell left the Disney payroll. Roy sent Walt an air mail letter explaining that Roy had given Max "the 'go by'" and that it gave Roy a measure of satisfaction to do so.

Walt presumably had follow-up discussions with Charlie on Saturday and during dinner on Monday. But whether it was due to their anxiousness over getting a new distributor agreement, or because they were away from home, Walt and Lilly did not seem too happy in New York. They found it "very cold and windy and not at all agreeable[.]" Walt wrote Roy that they were "homesick ever since we left" and that "every night we get home sick for our little house and puppy[.]" (Walt had given the puppy, a Chow named Sunnee, to Lilly in a hatbox the previous Christmas.) Perhaps Walt and Lilly cheered themselves up by attending the premiere of the latest Oswald short, *Rival Romeos*, which made its New York debut on Sunday, February 26, at the Colony at 53rd and Broadway, along with *The Leopard Lady*, a DeMille-Pathé film.

On Tuesday afternoon, February 28, Walt met Charlie again, and Walt characterized their discussion as "THE SAME OLD STUFF—rug chewing[.]" Walt began the negotiations by asking for $2,500 per reel. Charlie offered the Disneys their costs plus an equal share in the profits, but Walt explained that he and Roy wanted a more definite offer, one consisting of "more <u>credit</u> [for mak-ing the shorts] and <u>cash</u>." If the Disneys continued to do business with Winkler Pictures, Walt told Charlie, they wanted to be treated as equals. Charlie may have acted disinterested, for Walt wrote Roy that, "the way he took what I said plainly shows that he is bluffing."

Walt wired Roy that he didn't like Charlie's "percentage deal" and would "try for larger cash advance and percentage[.]" Walt also asked Roy to "please be patient[,]" and he promised Roy that he would wire him "all important news[.]" Walt also followed up with Jack Alicoate, who was now feeling better and back in the office. Walt thought about offering a percentage of his profits to Fox or MGM if he got traction with either studio, but must have worried that such an offer would make him seem desperate. "Hell no," Jack told him. It was a good idea to offer them money, said Jack, because "that's what talks[.]" He told Walt that Fox might be the Disneys' best option.

That night, Walt took Lilly to see *Gentlemen Prefer Blondes*, the well-reviewed film version of Anita Loos's book, starring Ruth Taylor and Holmes Herbert and directed by Malcolm St. Clair. *Blondes* had opened in mid-January at the Rivoli, along with a *Krazy Kat* cartoon. By the week the Disneys saw the movie, it appeared at alternating Loew's theaters including Loew's Lexington at 51st and Lexington; Loew's Sheridan in Greenwich Village; and, just one and one-half blocks from the Disneys' hotel, Loew's New York Theater at 44th Street and Seventh Avenue.

After the movie, when he and Lilly got back to their room at the Knicker-bocker, Walt wrote Roy about his game plan for the remainder of the week. His conversation with Jack that afternoon motivated Walt to reach out to MGM and Fox again. The more Walt thought about Fred Quimby, the more he became convinced that Fred had not "definitely turned me down" and was actually "waiting for some kind of a proposition[.]" Following Jack's advice, however, Walt decided to "hang onto Charlie" until—"IF I should be so lucky"—Walt signed a contract with Fox or MGM. Walt also realized that he and Roy needed to "have our entire crew under contract" before he broke with Charlie because Charlie "would try harder than ever to get [the crew] if he knew we were going to break" from him.

On Wednesday, February 29, Walt made another offer to Fred Quimby but "definitely found out that they are not going to release another cartoon this year." Fox, which was about a mile north and west of the Knickerbocker, at 56th Street and 10th Avenue, also turned him down because it only distributed what it produced itself. After striking out with both studios, Walt went back to see Jack Alicoate, who Walt marveled "has sure been dandy [and] is always glad to help me and do any thing he can for me[.]"

After hearing about Walt's disappointing runs at Fox and MGM, Jack advised Walt to "bluff Charlie" because the "entire industry is topsy turvy and it would be another year before it is straightened out[.]" That night, Walt, who was apparently not convinced that Charlie was his best option, continued to contemplate a break with the Winkler organization. Walt still felt that he and Roy needed to get "the gang" under contract before such a break, either to get to the staff before Charlie did, or to find out if Charlie had gotten to them first.

Walt wired Roy that night about the staff's contracts. Specifically, Walt wired Roy that a "Break with Charlie [is] looming" so "contracts with boys [are] necessary to prevent [Charlie from] undermining" the Disneys by hiring away their staff. Walt instructed Roy to get a lawyer to prepare "ironclad" staff contracts for a one-year term with a 10-percent raise after six months, and options for two additional years with a 10-percent raise each year. Walt wanted the contracts to require his signature—even though he was not there to provide it—so that the contracts gave him and Roy "protection without responsibility[,]" although he wanted things to be "absolute[ly] legal[.]" Walt told Roy not to present the contracts to the staff until Walt gave Roy the word to do so, and reminded Roy that "absolute secrecy [is] necessary" but that "everything [is] OK[.]"

The next day, Lilly and Walt had lunch with animator Bill Nolan, thirty-four, who was the producer of Winkler's *Krazy Kat* series. Nolan told Walt that Charlie was looking for an animator to move to California and "take charge" of Walt's staff, and that George Winkler would supervise the operation. According to Nolan, Charlie had even shipped one of Nolan's old cameras to George in California. Nolan said that he would find out more by talking to one of the animators whom Charlie had approached.

Nolan gave Walt a tour of the *Krazy Kat* studio (of which Walt said, "it is sure a dump"), where the crew was "glad to see me and treated me royal." Nolan had no commitment to Charlie beyond the current year and did not refuse when Walt asked Nolan to work for him and Roy. Perhaps Walt invited others from the *Krazy Kat* crew to join him in Los Angeles, since when he wrote Roy about Nolan, Walt added that he could "get plenty of good men."

That same day, Walt met with Charlie and "pulled bluff" on him. Walt told Charlie that the Disneys had two offers, unsolicited, that they would be forced to consider if they could not come to terms with the Winkler company. Charlie "was very nice" in response. He told Walt that he wanted an agreement, but could not afford to pay more than $1,750 per short—the cost of making the negative—plus 50 percent of profits, and asked Walt to think it over. In response, Walt "offered to compromise because I said I hated to leave Oswald after getting it started[,]" but said that he could not accept that price.

Walt, wanting to flush Charlie out, tried a different tack. He offered to accept Charlie's terms if Charlie would show Walt the contract immediately. Charlie could not do so and said that Walt would have to take his word. Then it was Charlie's turn to call Walt's bluff. When Walt said that he was going to "quit fooling around" with Charlie and entertain his other offers, Charlie encouraged him to do so, and even asked Walt to let him advise Walt on the other offers. Walt thanked Charlie, but declined, which prompted Charlie to say "Ah! [G]o on home to your wife and come back and see me tomorrow and lets [sic] get down to business." The meeting ended on "very friendly terms," but Walt concluded that it was over with Charlie, and that night he wired Roy to "sign [the] boys to contracts[.]"

Actually, that night Walt sent Roy two wires, one that was for Roy's eyes only, and another that Walt wanted the "present crew"—more so the six animators whose loyalties were questioned (Hugh, Ham, Paul Smith, Norm Blackburn, Ben Clopton, and Ray Abrams) than the three who were seen to be loyal (Ubbe, Les Clark, and Johnny Cannon)—to see. In the first wire, meant only for Roy, Walt instructed his brother to have the "boys sign contracts . . . immediately because if given time [the possible break with Charlie] may get to George [Winkler, who may try to] rob [the] deal[.]" If any of the crew refused to sign, Walt wanted to "know [the] reason before allowing them to leave[.]" Walt added he intended to complain to Universal if Charlie continued to pose a problem. Walt also explained to Roy that he would be "sending another wire for [crew's] benefit[.]"

The second night wire, the one that Walt wanted the staff to see, projected an air of calm and played up the possibility of Bill Nolan's arrival at the studio. It also let the artists know that Walt was aware of the pending defection to Charlie. Walt wrote that he "[l]unched with Bill Nolan today [and I] may be able to bring him out[ to California and join the staff. H]ave those of present crew that are going to stay sign contracts[.]" Walt said that, if some of the crew were leaving, it was "necessary [that] I close [on contracts] with others [in New York] at once[. E]verything OK."

The next day, Friday, March 2, Ubbe signed a new contract. Les Clark stayed too. Les recalled, "I was approached by the animators who did leave. . . . I said, no, I was working for Walt. He hired me and I liked him regardless of what happened. . . . I think Ub[be] and I were the only ones left in the organization except the girls." Johnny Cannon remained as well.

Meanwhile, in New York, Walt again met with Jack Alicoate and told Jack that he had broken with Charlie, but that he would "let it ride" to give Charlie time to rethink things. If Charlie didn't call him by Monday, Walt told Jack, Walt was going to go over Charlie's head and complain to Universal. Jack replied, "Well—don't worry—I was to the fights with 'Manny Goldstein' of Universal last nite [*sic*] and I told him about you—he said Mintz got $3,000 advance [per Oswald short] and he wants to see you." Jack called Emmanuel H. Goldstein, the treasurer of Universal, who said to send Walt right over.

Walt went to Universal at 57th Street and Fifth Avenue, about eight blocks north and east of the *Film Daily* offices, where Manny Goldstein took him into "some big bugs [*sic*] office"—"some swell office"—although Walt found Manny to be "a pretty big bug hi[m] self." Walt did not know the name or title of Manny's colleague, but wrote Roy that "from his office he must own the dump[.]" The "big bug" could have been Universal's vice president, Robert Cochrane, or its secretary, P. D. Cochrane, both of whom had been involved in the Oswald contract.

Robert H. Cochrane, forty-nine, and his older brother, Philip D. "P. D." Cochrane, fifty-one, co-founded Universal Pictures, Inc. with Universal president Carl Laemmle more than fifteen years earlier. Robert and P. D. were reporters for, and Robert the city editor of, an Ohio newspaper called the *Toledo Bee*. In 1904, the brothers moved to Chicago and opened, with a third brother, Witt K. Cochrane, the Cochrane Advertising Agency. One of the agency's clients was the Stern Company store in Oshkosh, Wisconsin. The store's manager, Carl Laemmle, was interested in the motion picture business.

In 1906, Robert and P. D. invested with Laemmle in three Chicago movie theaters in which they reportedly screened "Paul Rainey's wild-animal picture, . . . The first movie shown in legitimate theatres[.]" The two Cochranes and Laemmle subsequently purchased a film exchange and a New Jersey production facility, thereby establishing the Independent Motion Picture Company. By 1912 the company merged with other production companies to form the Universal Film Manufacturing Company, which was later known as Universal Pictures, Inc. Together, Laemmle and the Cochranes pioneered the studio star system, billing their $1,000-per-week leading lady, Florence Lawrence, as the "Queen of the Screen."

Regardless of the identity of the Universal executive with whom Walt met, Walt found that the "big boy was sure nice." He gave Walt "advice and got very friendly[.]" The unnamed Universal executive, along with Manny, expressed surprise at Walt's inability to get a new contract with Charlie, and they wished they had known the situation sooner. They also told Walt that "they want good pictures and that they won't stand for Mr. Mintz cutting down costs in any way that might lower the standard[.]"

The conversation turned to a potential arrangement between Universal and the Disneys, and Manny and his colleague, said Walt, "were tickled at the possibility of dealing direct[ly with Walt] next year." However, since Universal had a contract with Charlie, they encouraged Walt to see the year through with Winkler Pictures, and they would "call [Walt] in on the deal" in 1929. They offered to intercede if Walt and Charlie could not come to terms, and asked Walt to keep their meeting a secret. They told Walt that discretion would better enable them to work with Walt directly once their contract with Charlie was up the following year. Thus, they advised Walt to take the best offer he could get from Charlie and "work like hell" in 1928 so that they could "talk business" the following year.

That night, a flurry of wires went back and forth between the Disney brothers. Roy sent two wires and an airmail letter to Walt, and Walt wired Roy twice before going back to his hotel room at 10:30 p.m. and writing Roy on Knickerbocker stationery. In one of his wires, Roy wrote Walt that the crew members in question would not sign new contracts. According to Hugh, he gave Roy notice he would leave the studio in one month, and Roy stopped speaking to him. Ultimately, six animators, Hugh, Ham, Paul Smith, Norm Blackburn, Ben Clopton, and Ray Abrams, decided not to sign. While Hugh was close to Roy, Hugh (and Rudy Ising, who by now had been gone almost a year) later "ma[d]e it clear, in their remarks about [Walt], that they felt they owed no special loyalty to him; Walt, they say, was too obviously devoted to the advancement of Walt Disney to inspire such feelings." Walt knew that those six animators' refusal "means only one thing—They are hooked up with Charlie . . . . I know how the rest of the market is and they haven't a smell." Walt was wounded by his staff's departure and later wrote, "That hurt!"

In the letter he wrote at 10:30 that night, Walt expressed optimism about the Disneys' future even as he recognized that Universal wanted them to deal with Charlie and they might have overestimated their ability to line up another distributor. Walt wrote, "I feel very confident that we will come out allright [sic] even if it is a bit disillusioning [sic]—we were shooting too high[.]" Perhaps recognizing he might not be able to cut a deal with Charlie, Walt wrote to Roy that Hugh and Ham "will find them selves out in the cold" because Universal would not want Oswald to be in "entirely new" hands. This made Walt feel sorry for Ham: "I hate to see him [lose] out."

At this point, Walt hoped that Universal would save the day. He believed that Charlie's deal with Universal was worthless if Charlie could not give Universal "the same Oswalds they have been getting[.]" Walt thought he could convince Universal that they would not get the same product "unless I make them." He wrote that he was not worried ("I feel fine over everything") and he exhorted Roy to follow suit. But in reality, Walt was worried; he just wanted to spare Roy until he got home and could explain the situation.

The next day was Saturday and Walt called Charlie, but he was not at home and Walt missed Charlie's return call. Walt spent Sunday with Bill Nolan, and they had "quite a talk[.]" Nolan was "very anxious" to work for the Disneys, and he told Walt he could start by the first of June. Nolan thought "he and Ubb[e] would make a good team[,]" and Walt agreed that he "could get some dandy stuff with Ubb[e] & Bill[.]" That night Walt wired Roy to get his thoughts about Nolan. While Walt was frustrated that "Charlie [was] trying to control Oswald[,]" he was glad that "Universal understands[,]" and he thought the "future looks bright[.]"

By Monday, March 5, Walt and Lilly had both come down with colds. Nevertheless, Walt returned Charlie's call that morning and agreed to a noon meeting, presumably at Winkler Pictures. Walt summarized his final negotiation with Charlie by saying that, "per Universal[']s instructions I tried to do business with him but found it impossible." Charlie's strategy was to offer Walt unacceptably low terms so that the only alternative was for Charlie to take over production of the series himself. Walt wrote Roy that Charlie "insisted on taking over the entire orginazation [sic] even to paying our taxes on [the] shop." As for terms, Charlie offered Walt $1,400 per negative plus a weekly salary of $200 and 50 percent of the Winkler company's profits, which would yield the Disneys about $450 for each short. "But that's impossible," Walt told Charlie. "We couldn't make a profit." Walt recalled that Charlie replied, "[T]here was no sense giving Oswald more running room; he was good enough as he was, [and] the animated cartoon industry looked like it couldn't go much farther, anyway."

Walt "tried every way possible to get him to a reasonable amount but he wouldn't listen." Years later, Walt recounted that Charlie told him, "Either you come at my price, or I'll take your organization from you. . . . I have your key men signed up." Walt added that he then told Charlie to protect himself from the animators: "If they'll do this to me, they'll do it to you too, if they get a chance[.]" At the time, however, Walt wrote Roy that, after the discussion over finances, Walt "left [Charlie] with a good bye and wishes for luck in his new venture."

Walt then went to the *Film Daily* to say goodbye to Jack Alicoate, who was leaving for California. Walt phoned Manny Goldstein, and got a 5:30 p.m. appointment at Universal. When Walt "mentioned [to Manny] that Charlie wanted to take over the entire orginization [sic], [Manny] smiled and nodded his head" and told Walt he would call Charlie and report back to Walt. Walt showed Manny the current contract with Winkler Pictures, and as Walt left, Manny "immediately went into the big boy[']s office."

Walt returned to the Knickerbocker and, as Lilly recalled, told her "that [Charlie] owned the rights to Oswald and intended to go on making Oswald shorts without Walt if he refused to knuckle down to the cut price." Walt explained that "he was out of a job" and that the bottom had fallen out of the studio. Lilly remembered Walt saying that he was glad about what happened, "because he would never again work for anybody else." At ten that night, Walt wrote Roy by hand a letter update and, perhaps referring to his belief he would ultimately work directly with Universal, Walt told Roy to "[k]eep up your [c]hin [because] we will be able to laugh last—that[']s the best laugh after all[.]" Walt asked Roy to give Lilly's and his "regards to all [and] include Ubbe and Mildred."

Walt did not expect to hear from Universal as soon as Tuesday, but he "stuck around close waiting for a call" anyway. Not wanting to pester Manny and Universal, Walt "waited all day" on Wednesday, March 7, although he got together with Bill Nolan to screen the Oswald prints for him (Nolan told Walt that they were the "[b]est cartoons he has seen in a longtime"), and they had lunch together. Nolan told Walt that all the animators he knew watched the Disney shorts "with open eyes[,]" and that he was anxious to join Walt's staff. He and Walt even agreed on a salary, although Walt wanted the salary proposal kept quiet, and not shared with Ubbe, whose $120 weekly salary would be less than the $150 weekly package proposed for Nolan. Walt and Nolan also talked about a starting date. Walt continued to think that Nolan would be "a dandy fit[.]"

Just as he had at their previous lunch, Nolan told Walt what he had heard about Charlie. Specifically, Nolan repeated that Charlie shipped to George Winkler in California a Pathé camera that Nolan had used, and that Charlie had been planning to take over Walt's staff for a long time. In addition, Charlie apparently tried to dissuade an animator, who eventually joined the Disney studio almost two years later, from going out to California.

Walt's time with Nolan no doubt took his mind off of Manny Goldstein and Universal, but at 5 p.m., Walt's patience ran out and he telephoned Universal. Expecting Manny or his colleague to say, "I am sorry but I cannot do anything" ("you know how it is—many things can run through a fellow[']s mind in affairs like this," wrote Walt, perhaps wondering if Manny and the Cochranes were conspiring with Charlie), Walt was pleasantly surprised to be asked to meet at Universal the following day. Given the satisfying conversations that Walt had at Universal, he hoped Universal would "take advantage of the situation and give Charlie the air and deal direct with us—But I guess that is hoping for too much." At the least, he believed that Universal would "insist that Charlie give us a decent break."

Later that day, Walt wrote Roy that he and Lilly were "feeling fine except for a couple of colds" and that they were "still hanging around this Hell Hole waiting for something to happen." Walt complained that he couldn't bring the distributor situation to a head faster but said that he "WILL FIGHT IT OUT ON THIS LINE IF IT TAKES ALL SUMMER and all our jack[.]" Walt wrote Roy that, while Charlie's attempt to take over their staff and series was turning into a "fight to the finish[,]" Charlie didn't realize that the Disneys had "a stronger power than he on [their] side"—presumably either the artistic vision and commitment to quality that made Oswald a hit in the first place, or the support of the "big bugs" at Universal.

It is unknown if Walt was able to see Manny or anyone else at Universal on Thursday. On Friday, March 9, Walt wrote to Roy and complained, "Well it looks like another week in this damned town[.]" Walt was frustrated that he could not "rush thing[s] any faster[.]" He had told Roy earlier in the week he was "so absorbed in everything" that he could not think of gags for the Oswald short then in production, *The Fox Chase*, but by Friday he provided three paragraphs of ideas. For example, Walt thought the film should get to the fox chase right away, and suggested that Ham and Hugh could help Ubbe "pull as many of the gags with Oswald as you can so [Oswald] will be brought into the story more[.]" As to specific gags, though, Walt was "helpless to make any suggestions as my mind is not on gags at this time[.]"

That weekend, the last of the Disneys' three-week stay in New York, Walt met with Universal and Tiffany-Stahl, a 1920s studio that released its films through, and was located at, the same address as MGM. Neither visit was productive, however, and Walt finally had it with what he later called an "out-and-out cutthroat business" where one would be "putting a knife in your back and he'll be laughing and having a drink with you."

On the evening of Tuesday, March 13, Walt wired Roy that Lilly and he were leaving New York. "LEAVING TONIGHT STOPPING OVER KC ARRIVE HOME SUNDAY MORNING SEVEN THIRTY," Walt wrote. "DON'T WORRY[,]" he added, "EVERYTHING OK WILL GIVE DETAILS WHEN ARRIVE." Walt later explained that "Roy was running the studio out [in California]. I didn't want to worry him so I wired him that everything was all right." Perhaps Walt's concern for Roy was well founded; Lilly later stated that, "[e]ven my husband's astute older brother, Roy, . . . has shared my jitters at times."

But, as the Disneys' stay in New York ended, Lilly was worried. She recalled, "I was scared to death. Walt didn't even tell Roy what had happened, but wired him that he was coming home with a great new idea." Walt had told Lilly, "Let's get the first train out of here. I can't do any good in New York. I have to hire new artists and get a new series going. I can't sell a new series with talk. I've got to have it on film." As Walt told a reporter a few years later, Charlie "took Oswald, [and] a few men from my organization and started his own studio. This left me with two or three loyal men and nothing to do." In addition to those three animators, Ubbe, Les, and Johnny Cannon, the staff who remained with Walt and Roy included inkers and painters Hazel Sewell, Esther Benson, and Mary Tebb, and the janitor, John Lott (Mike Marcus left the studio not long after the six defecting animators did).

While Walt joked later that Oswald's loss was not a big deal ("I never liked that damn rabbit, anyway."), Lilly told a reporter that Walt was like a "raging lion" on the train ride west. Lilly recalled, "He had gambled everything we had—which wasn't much, but seemed a lot to us—on the Oswald series. All he could say, over and over, was that he'd never work for anyone again as long as he lived; he'd be his own boss. I didn't share his long-range viewpoint. I was in a state of shock, scared to death."

As Walt and Lilly boarded their train that March Tuesday in New York in 1928—the train on which they began to discuss a new series that would replace Oswald—the curtain came down on twenty-six-year-old Walt Disney's life before Mickey.

# Epilogue: After Mickey

## Walt Disney

In the wake of his disastrous meetings with Charlie Mintz in New York in February and March of 1928, Walt, with the assistance of Roy, Ubbe, and the remaining studio staff (supplemented by Lillian and Edna, who helped with the inking and painting, and a new animator), created the first Mickey Mouse reel. *Plane Crazy* was completed about two months after Walt and Lilly's return from New York. Unable to find a distributor for the first two Mickey cartoons, Walt—providing Mickey's voice—set the series' third short, *Steamboat Willie*, to sound and in the process created one of the earliest cartoons with synchronized sound. *Willie* premiered at the Colony Theatre in New York on Sunday, November 18, 1928. Mickey Mouse became an international phenomenon, and earned Walt a Special Academy Award in 1932.

The year after creating Mickey Mouse, Walt launched the Silly Symphonies series of animated shorts. One 1932 entry in this series, *Flowers and Trees*, was one of the first full-color cartoons. Another, 1933's *Three Little Pigs*, became almost as big a hit as Mickey. A Silly Symphony won the Cartoon Short Subject Oscar every year but one from 1931 to 1939—the only exception was 1938, when the Silly Symphony entry (along with Mickey Mouse and Donald Duck cartoons) lost to another Disney cartoon short, *Ferdinand the Bull*.

In December 1937, Walt unveiled his latest innovation: the first full-length color animated feature. *Snow White and the Seven Dwarfs*, like Mickey and the Three Pigs, took the world by storm. It set a box office record, becoming the highest grossing feature in history until *Gone With the Wind* surpassed it a few years later, and won Walt another Special Academy Award.

Walt never stopped redefining the boundaries of family entertainment. While he continued in the 1930s to release classic shorts (such as the Mickey Mouse, Silly Symphonies, Donald Duck, and Goofy series) and put into production other animated features (*Pinocchio, Fantasia*), he branched out in the 1940s after an acrimonious strike and a focus on World War II–related projects, to combination live-action/animated features (*The Three Caballeros, Song of the South*); and in the 1950s to live-action features (*Treasure Island, 20,000 Leagues*

*Under the Sea*); nature films (*True-Life Adventures*); television (*Davy Crockett, The Mickey Mouse Club*); and even a theme park (Disneyland).

By the mid-1960s, almost a half-century after starting his career at the Gray Advertising Company, Walt Disney still worked with a number of people from the early years of his career, including colleagues from Film Ad (Ubbe Iwwerks); Laugh-O-grams (Walt Pfeiffer); Disney Brothers Studio (Roy Disney, Ruthie Tompson); and the early Hyperion era of the Walt Disney Studio (Les Clark, Mary Tebb). By then, Walt still produced cartoon shorts (*Winnie the Pooh and the Honey Tree*), animated features (the Oscar-nominated *The Jungle Book*), live-action/animated features (Oscar winner *Mary Poppins*), live-action features (*The Parent Trap*), television shows (*Walt Disney's Wonderful World of Color*), and theme park attractions (the New York World's Fair 1964–1965 attractions "it's a small world" and the State of Illinois' "Great Moments with Mr. Lincoln"). By then he even envisioned creating the ideal community, his Experimental Prototype Community of Tomorrow, or EPCOT.

Walt Disney was diagnosed with lung cancer in early November 1966. After surgery, he underwent postoperative cobalt treatments and was released from the hospital. On Tuesday, November 22, despite Walt's prognosis, the Disney company issued a press release stating "there is no reason to predict recurrence of the problem" and that Walt would resume a full work schedule within six weeks. On Friday, November 25, the day after spending Thanksgiving with his family, Walt and Lilly flew to their vacation home in Palm Springs, where he took a turn for the worse. On Wednesday, November 30, he was flown back to Burbank and taken directly back to St. Joseph's, where he spent his sixty-fifth birthday on Monday, December 5.

Of his daily hospital visit of Wednesday, December 14, Walt's older brother, Roy, wrote, "Walt lay on the hospital bed staring at the ceiling. It was squares of perforated acoustical tile, and Walt pictured them as a grid map for Disney World, which he planned to build in Florida. Every four tiles," recalled Roy, "represented a square mile, and he said, 'Now there is where the highway will run. There is the route for the monorail.'" Roy's visit that night confirmed that Walt "drove himself right up to the end."

Walt died of acute circulatory collapse the following morning, forty-seven years after returning from France and going to work at the Gray Advertising Company, and thirty-eight years after creating Mickey Mouse. A private service was held for his family the next day at the Little Church of the Flowers at Forest Lawn Cemetery, where Walt's ashes were interred. The Disney family asked that, in lieu of flowers, contributions be made to the California Institute of the Arts in Los Angeles, which Walt had been developing.

By the time of his death, Walt had received over nine hundred awards and citations from governments, institutions, and organizations around the world (including the Presidential Freedom Medal), honorary degrees from Harvard and Yale, and thirty-two Academy Awards, more than any other individual in entertainment history. But his greatest reward, he told an interviewer a few years before he died, was that he was "able to build this wonderful organization[,]" which by then had four thousand employees and was a "$100-million-a-year entertainment empire." When the interviewer wondered what Walt would do differently if he had it to do over again, Walt Disney laughed and—perhaps thinking of the long road from Gray Advertising to Mickey Mouse—replied as he chuckled, "If I had it to do over again, no, I don't think I would. . . . I hope I don't have to do it over again!"

## His Studios

**Kaycee Studios** ceased operation shortly before Walt incorporated Laugh-O-gram Films, Inc. in May 1922. The Peiser building was demolished by the city of Kansas City in 1992 and 1993.

**Laugh-O-gram Films, Inc.** was still in existence when Walt left for California in late July 1923. In early August, as Walt was settling in at his uncle's house in Los Angeles, things might have seemed normal at the Laugh-O-gram studio; Walt had left the studio intact (although he later wrote Jerry Raggos that he instructed Hugh Harman to sell the office property so creditors, including Raggos, could be paid) and, on Tuesday, August 7, Fred Schmeltz made the studio's monthly rental payment of $75 to Rudolph Peiser. Perhaps former Laugh-O-gram employees even came to the office to plot their next steps.

For Rudy Ising, Hugh Harman, and Max Maxwell, the next step was the formation of their own studio, Arabian Nights Cartoons, for which they wanted to use Laugh-O-gram studio equipment. By the end of August, however, Schmeltz, acting on his mortgage on Laugh-O-gram's equipment, had removed the Laugh-O-gram equipment and furniture from the office above Peiser's restaurant. Rudy recalled that, "Hugh, Maxwell and I . . . went out to talk to . . . Schmeltz, who . . . . had a big warehouse and had moved all the furniture plus the camera stand, the camera and some animation boards into it . . . So we talked him into letting us buy the equipment[.]" In September 1923, Rudy, Hugh, and Max paid Schmeltz $302 for two animating booths, a camera, a camera stand, one inking table, and some other equipment and furniture.

Less than six weeks later, on Thursday, October 4, Ubbe filed a request in federal court in Kansas City to have Laugh-O-gram Films declared bankrupt so that its assets could be liquidated and its creditors paid. Ubbe claimed that the June 1923 assignment to Schmeltz of the Pictorial contract was fraudulent. Walt's recollection that "[b]ack in Kansas City were plenty of debts which took me two to three years to clean up" suggests that Walt was monitoring the Laugh-O-gram bankruptcy from the west coast, although his claim that there were about $200 worth of debts significantly underestimated his creditors' claims, which were, collectively, about $10,500.

On Tuesday, October 16, 1923—while Walt and Roy scrambled to form Disney Brothers Studio in the wake of Margaret Winkler's contract offer the day before—Laugh-O-gram employees and investors met for what Nadine Simpson called the studio's "final wake." The meeting was the result of Ubbe's court filing. The "wake" was attended by five animators (Ubbe, Rudy, Max, Lorey Tague, and Otto Walliman), three other staff members (Jack Kloepper, Nadine Simpson, and Aletha Reynolds), and two investors (Dr. Cowles and one of the Hammonds). Dr. Cowles offered to serve, without pay, as the liquidation trustee. Two days later, Schutte Lumber and Schroer Brothers Machine Works joined in Ubbe's court petition. On Tuesday, October 30, United States District Judge Albert Reeves declared Laugh-O-gram bankrupt.

In December 1923, the liquidation trustee appointed by the court, Joseph M. Jones, interviewed Dr. Cowles, in his capacity as the Secretary of Laugh-O-gram, and made a demand on Pictorial for the $11,000 owed to Laugh-O-gram under their original contract. When Pictorial ignored this demand, Jones sent his lawyers to Chicago and New York to confront Pictorial's New York corporation, which eventually agreed to assume the debt of the Pictorial Tennessee corporation that made the contract with Laugh-O-gram. Pictorial of New York agreed to pay the Laugh-O-gram estate $11,000 within six months, or by July 1924.

Pictorial paid less than half that amount over the next six months, and sporadic additional payments in late 1924 and early 1925 garnered a total of $8,000 of the $11,000 owed to the estate. In May of 1925, Referee Jones resigned; the court accepted his resignation rather than make him answer allegations that had arisen about his fiscal management of a number of bankrupt estates. Jones was replaced by William E. Kemp.

One of Kemp's first acts was to contest Schmeltz's claim that, due to the two notes that Walt executed in Schmeltz's behalf in February and June of 1923, Schmeltz's debts should have preference over other debts owed by the Laugh-O-gram estate. The court rejected Schmeltz's claim of priority. Schmeltz appealed the court's ruling to Judge Reeves, who denied the appeal and agreed that Schmeltz's debts were to be treated the same as any other creditor's. In particular, Reeves found the February note was not authorized by the company, and that the June note and the assignment of the Pictorial contract to Schmeltz were made when Schmeltz knew that Laugh-O-gram Films was insolvent.

Another of Kemp's first acts was to send a lawyer back to New York to pressure Pictorial to pay the remaining $3,000 it owed Laugh-O-gram. Pictorial resumed payments in October 1925. By mid-August of 1926, Pictorial paid off its $11,000 debt, plus an additional $1,000, presumably in interest. Kemp produced a list of proven debts, and a dividend of 25 percent, or 25 cents on the dollar, was approved at a creditor meeting held in July 1926. A supplemental dividend of 20 percent, or 20 additional cents on the dollar, was approved in January 1927. Thus, in the end, Laugh-O-gram creditors were paid a total of 45 cents on the dollar.

Kemp issued his final report on August 23, 1927, and the court's final certification and report discharging the bankruptcy was issued on December 28, 1927—more than four years after Walt left Kansas City, and two months before Walt traveled to New York and lost the Oswald series to Charlie Mintz. Less than a year after the Laugh-O-gram bankruptcy discharge order was issued in Kansas City, Mickey Mouse premiered in New York, and the journey to fame and fortune that seventeen-year-old Walt Disney started when he returned to Kansas City almost a decade earlier was over.

The McConahy Building, home to Laugh-O-gram films from May 1922 to May 1923, still stands today. After Laugh-O-gram went out of business, its offices in Suite 218 were shared by two new tenants, the King Building Company and Paul L. Davis, an architect. The LeMorris Studio and Mrs. Brauer's beauty parlor remained in their offices on the second floor, and the King-Moore Investment Company moved into Suite 216. The building fell into disrepair in the second half of the twentieth century. In 1993, a nonprofit group, "Thank You Walt Disney," purchased the building, which it is renovating to become a museum.

**Disney Brothers Studio** continued under a new name and location as of mid-February, 1926, when Walt, Roy and their staff of seven moved to Hyperion Avenue as the Walt Disney Studio.

The McRae & Abernathy real estate office at 4651 Kingswell Avenue, which housed the Disney Brothers Studio from October 1923, to February 1924 (and for a week before that was where Walt worked on his sample reel for Alexander Pantages), did not operate long after the Disneys moved out. By 1925, the McRae & Abernathy partnership appears to have ended, but Claude Abernathy, who continued to sell real estate, remained in that location for a few years. By

1929, 4651 Kingswell housed fabric weaver Kathy Hiestand, and the Colonial Upholstering Shop was located there by the mid-1930s. Different health food markets occupied the store in the late 1930s and early 1940s.

4649 Kingswell Avenue, the storefront next door to the McRae & Abernathy realty company and the site of Disney Brothers Studio from February 1924 until February 1926, became a hardware store in the mid-1930s, and it housed different bakeries in the late 1930s and early 1940s.

4651 and 4649 Kingswell Avenue still stand today.

**Walt Disney Studios** remained at 2719 Hyperion Avenue from February 1926 to January 1940, when, using the profits from their smash hit, *Snow White and the Seven Dwarfs*, Walt and Roy moved the studio six miles north and west of the Hyperion site to a new state-of-the-art facility in Burbank. The fourteen years at Hyperion are recognized as the Golden Age of Disney animation. During that time, Walt and his staff animated over a hundred Mickey Mouse shorts; seventy-five Silly Symphonies; nearly twenty Donald Duck shorts; a few Pluto, Goofy, and other shorts; the feature *Snow White and the Seven Dwarfs*; most of the feature *Pinocchio*; and parts of the feature *Fantasia*.

From 1929 to 1940, the Hyperion studio expanded far beyond the original building the Disney brothers built in late 1925 and early 1926, and where Walt, Roy, Ubbe, Les Clark, Johnny Cannon, Hazel Sewell, Esther Benson, Mary Tebb, and John Lott worked as the Oswald era gave way to the Mickey Mouse era in the spring of 1928. Additions to the front, rear, and side were made in 1929 and 1930. In 1930, the front wall of the studio was moved six feet forward, bringing it to the sidewalk. A large two-story animation building was built behind the original building in the spring of 1931, and a sound stage was built at the back of the lot. Eventually, the Disneys purchased and incorporated into the studio the property of J. W. Klein Organ Builders, the pipe organ company that had been owned by Joseph W. Klein and located to the left of the studio at 2711 Hyperion. This building eventually housed Roy's office, a conference room, and the accounting and administrative offices.

In 1934, as the studio geared up for *Snow White*, the animation building was expanded again, and soon after, an ink and paint building was erected and neighboring apartment houses and other small buildings were acquired by the company. Eventually, the staff outgrew the Hyperion campus, and Walt and Roy moved the company to the forty-four-acre site at 500 South Buena Vista Street in Burbank in the San Fernando Valley. The move took place between December 26, 1939 and January 5, 1940, although some employees worked at the new site as early as August 1939 and others moved in there as late as September 1940.

Of the fifty-five colleagues who worked with Walt, collectively, at Kaycee Studios, Laugh-O-gram Films, Disney Brothers Studio, and the Walt Disney Studio between 1921 and February of 1928, only four made the move with Walt from the "old" Walt Disney Studio on Hyperion Avenue to the "new" Walt Disney Studio in Burbank: Roy, Ubbe, Les Clark, and Johnny Cannon.

Walt and Roy moved several Hyperion buildings to the new site in Burbank. For example, the Hyperion Bungalow conference room building just inside the main Burbank gate was formerly the Hyperion comic strip department. The nearby Burbank studio store was the Hyperion training annex. The Burbank Shorts Building, which is just around the corner from the studio store, on the other side of Sound Stage No. 1, and now a studio operations building, is the combination of two Hyperion animation buildings. In addition, the current Sound Transfer building came from the Hyperion lot, as did various Hyperion ink and paint buildings that were eventually torn down.

In 1941, the year after the Disneys moved to Burbank, they sold the one-acre Hyperion lot and its 20,000 square feet of office space for $75,000 to vitamin manufacturer William T. Thompson, who by 1956 located several companies there, including the Thompson Chemical Corp., the William T. Thompson Co., and Thompson Vitamin Manufacturers Co. By then, the property was renumbered 2727 Hyperion Avenue. Thompson was still at that location as of 1960.

The Hyperion studio was eventually demolished, and today the Silver Lake-Los Feliz branch of the Gelson's Market grocery store chain sits in its place, now with the address of 2725 Hyperion Avenue. A Los Angeles Cultural Heritage Board Point of Historical Interest sign is the only evidence the Disney studio once stood at that location. The sign, ignoring Uncle Robert's garage as well as both Kingswell Avenue studios and Walt's first three years in Hollywood, states that the area was the "[s]ite of Walt Disney's original animation studio in Los Angeles, 2719 Hyperion Avenue, 1926—1940."

The gas station to the left of the old Klein organ factory continued to operate from the late 1920s through the 1960s. It was a Shell Oil station from the late 1930s to the early 1960s, and doubled as an A-1 trailer rental center in the late 1950s and early 1960s.

As for the Disney company itself, it was a partnership between Walt and Roy (and, for a short time, Ubbe) until 1929, when the Walt Disney Studios incorporated as Walt Disney Productions. The company went public in 1940. In 1986, the company changed its corporate name to The Walt Disney Company. As of this writing, this Fortune 100 company employs approximately 150,000 people worldwide. In 2008, eighty-five years after Walt and Roy went into business as Disney Brothers Studio, the company had revenues of over $37 billion. The Walt Disney Company defines itself as a "leading diversified international family entertainment and media enterprise" and is currently divided into four segments: The Walt Disney Studios, Disney Consumer Products, Parks and Resorts, and Media Networks.

## His Colleagues and Others

**Claude Abernathy** continued to work as a realtor at 4651 Kingswell for about two years after the Disneys moved their studio from his real estate office to the store next door. Abernathy later became an insurance salesman. He died in Van Nuys, Los Angeles, in 1970. He was ninety-two years old.

**Ray Abrams** worked for the Winkler company after leaving Walt. During the course of his long post-Disney animation career, he animated *Oswald the Lucky Rabbit*, *Woody Woodpecker*, *Secret Squirrel*, and *Scooby-Doo*. Abrams died in San Bernardino, California, in 1981 at the age of seventy-five.

**Jack Alicoate** became the editor of the *Film Daily* in 1929, and eventually co-published the *Film Daily* and the *Radio & Television Daily* with his brother, Charles. Alicoate died in Englewood, New Jersey, in 1960. He was seventy years old.

**Joe Allen** continued to act in the late 1920s and the 1930s, appearing in Mack Sennett shorts (alongside Carole Lombard in one), and a drama written by Billy Wilder. He got married, remained in Hollywood, and by the 1940s was a "studio worker." Allen died in Hollywood in 1955 at the age of sixty-seven. He had been ill for some time, and died four weeks to the day after his sixty-eight-year-old brother, Dave. By 1925, Dave Allen ran the Services Bureau, which provided extras for movies. The next year, Allen founded Central Casting Corp., which "handle[d] the employment of film extras[,]" and he remained there for almost a decade. He left what was by then known as Central Casting Bureau—"Hollywood's clearing house for extra players"—as the result of a 1934 sex scandal involving two young extras, Gloria Marsh and June De Long. The scandal cost him his job and his wife. Dave Allen eventually joined Columbia Pictures, where he worked from 1936 until he was laid off in 1954. He died the following year.

**Lawrence Baer** remained a realtor in Kansas City until his death there in 1937 at the age of fifty-one.

**Esther Benson** stayed with the Walt Disney Studio for eighteen months after Charlie Mintz took over the Oswald series. By 1936, Esther was a masseur on South Vermont Avenue, and she still lived in Los Angeles in 1938.

**Norm Blackburn** became a newspaper cartoonist and a writer, and later worked on the *Our Gang* comedy shorts. By the 1940s he was an executive at the J. Walter Thompson advertising agency in Hollywood and later an NBC program director. He helped create the TV series *You Bet Your Life* with Groucho Marx and *The Dinah Shore Show*. Blackburn died in North Hollywood in 1990. He was eighty-six years old.

**Ruby Bounds** left the studio after less than a month, and the Disney family heard very little about her thereafter.

**Johnny Cannon** was an animator at the Disney studio until 1940. He and his wife Evelyn lived in Los Angeles while he worked on such classic Mickey Mouse shorts as *Orphan's Benefit* (1934), *The Band Concert* (1935), and *Thru the Mirror* (1936). Cannon died in Los Angeles in 1946 at the age of thirty-nine and was buried at Forest Lawn.

**Al Carder** and his family relocated to Evanston, Illinois, where he owned a restaurant.

**Joe Carder** continued to live next door to the former Disney home on Bellefontaine Avenue until his death in 1937 at the age of seventy-nine.

**Vern Cauger** continued to run the Film Ad for years after Walt's departure. It remained in operation until Cauger finally sold the company to a competitor. By the 1940s, Cauger still distributed, but did not produce, film ads. Cauger and his family kept in touch with Walt over the years. In February 1942, when Walt visited Kansas City to unveil at his alma mater, the Benton School, murals of Disney characters made by a Works Progress Administration project, Walt recognized Cauger at a luncheon as the man who gave Walt his first job in motion pictures, and Cauger stood up as the crowd applauded. Nearly three years later, on December 28, 1944, a reunion of Cauger's former employees was held at the Roosevelt Hotel in Los Angeles. In attendance besides Cauger and his wife, daughter and son-in-law, were Walt, Fred Harman, Ubbe Iwwerks, Jimmy Lowerre, Rudy Ising, and Max Maxwell. Cauger died nine months later. He was sixty-seven years old. His *Variety* obituary called him a "pioneer animated film maker."

**Les Clark,** along with Ubbe Iwwerks and Johnny Cannon, were the three animators who remained with Walt and Roy when the studio's six other animators defected to Charlie Mintz. Clark must have stayed in touch with ex-Disney staffers Mike Marcus and Paul Smith since they, like Clark, lived at the Mount

Holly Hotel in the late 1920s. (Clark lived with ex-Disney animator Friz Freleng in the late 1930s). Clark was an assistant to Ubbe Iwwerks on Mickey Mouse's debut, *Steamboat Willie* (1928), and made his own debut as an animator a year later on the Silly Symphony *The Skeleton Dance* (1929).

Clark animated on such Mickey Mouse classics as *The Band Concert* (1935) and *The Sorcerer's Apprentice* sequence from *Fantasia* (1940). Prior to becoming a sequence director with *Sleeping Beauty* (1959), he animated on such classic features as *Snow White and the Seven Dwarfs* (1937), *Pinocchio* (1940), *Song of the South* (1946), *Alice in Wonderland* (1951), and *Lady and the Tramp* (1955). Clark was the earliest hire by Walt among the select group of animators and directors that became famously known as Walt's "Nine Old Men;" the others were Marc Davis, Ollie Johnston, Milt Kahl, Ward Kimball, Eric Larson, John Lounsbery, Woolie Reitherman, and Frank Thomas.

Clark's father eventually worked at the studio as a security guard, and his sister got a job there in the ink and paint department. Two of his brothers worked at the studio, one in production and another in finance. Clark retired from the Walt Disney Studios in 1975, forty-eight years after Walt hired him for what Walt thought might be a "temporary" job. When he retired, Clark was Walt Disney Productions' longest serving employee. He died in 1979 at the age of seventy-two. Ten years after his death, Clark was given The Walt Disney Company's highest honor, and was named a Disney Legend in the field of Animation.

**Ben Clopton** worked for the Winkler company after leaving Walt, and animated on *Oswald the Lucky Rabbit* and, later, *Looney Tunes* shorts. He also worked on the 1939 animated feature, *Gulliver's Travels*, the Fleischers' answer to *Snow White and the Seven Dwarfs*. Clopton married and eventually relocated to Helena, Montana, where he died in 1987 at the age of eighty-one.

**P. D. Cochrane** commuted between New York and Los Angeles as Universal grew, and he played a key role in the establishment of Universal City on the edge of Hollywood. He worked to promote early Universal serial and horror movies, including such classics as *Frankenstein*, *The Phantom of the Opera*, and *The Hunchback of Notre Dame*. As a result, Cochrane helped further the careers of such stars as Boris Karloff and Lon Chaney, as well as non-horror stars Carole Lombard and Deanna Durbin. By the time he resigned from Universal in 1936 at fifty-nine, Cochrane was the vice president of advertising, publicity, and exploitation. He died at age eighty-one in New Rochelle, New York, in 1958.

**Robert H. Cochrane** remained vice president of Universal until 1936, when Carl Laemmle sold his share of the company. At that time, Cochrane became the president of Universal, a position he held until he retired in 1938 at the age of fifty-nine. He also served as the director of the Motion Picture Producers and Distributors of America and was a member of the Code Authority of the Motion Picture Industry. Cochrane died in 1973 in New Rochelle, New York. He was ninety-four years old.

**John V. Cowles, Jr.** became an architect and helped design buildings at Disneyland, a soundstage on the Disney lot in Burbank, and a barn Disney built at his Holmby Hills home in 1950. Cowles died in 2001 at the age of eighty-two.

**Dr. John V. Cowles, Sr.** continued to practice medicine in Kansas City and maintained sporadic contact with Walt. At times, Walt asked Cowles for additional backing, and once Cowles turned to Walt for financial assistance. Cowles died of leukemia in 1943 at the age of seventy.

**Minnie Cowles**, according to her son, John, Jr., was the inspiration for the name of Mickey Mouse's girlfriend. Upon Dr. Cowles' death, Minnie Cowles moved to California to live with John Cowles, Jr. She remarried and died in California in 1961 at the age of seventy-two.

**Margaret and Jeff Davis** remained in Los Angeles, where Jeff died around 1950. Margaret predeceased him by a few years.

**Virginia Davis** returned to the Disney studio on occasion to do voice and ink and paint work. She auditioned for the title role in *Snow White and the Seven Dwarfs* and did voice work for *Pinocchio*. Virginia appeared in several movies in the late 1920s and 1930s, including *The Greater Glory* with Boris Karloff, *Street Scene* with Beulah Bondi and directed by King Vidor, and *3 on a Match* with Bette Davis and Joan Blondell and directed by Mervyn Le Roy, the director of *The Wizard of Oz*. In *3 on a Match*, which also featured Humphrey Bogart and Jack Webb, the main characters, played as adults by Joan Blondell, Bette Davis, and Ann Dvorak, were played as young girls by Virginia, Betty Wescot, and Anne Shirley, respectively. Anne Shirley was the stage name adopted by Dawn Paris, thus Virginia Davis' co-star in *Match* was one of the girls who followed her in the role of Alice in Disney's Alice Comedies.

Virginia appeared in a handful of films in the 1940s. Her last movie was the 1946 classic, *The Harvey Girls*, starring Judy Garland, Ray Bolger, Angela

Lansbury, and Cyd Charisse. Virginia played one of the Harvey Girls. Virginia Davis McGee was married and became the mother of two adopted daughters and the grandmother of three children. In 1998 Virginia was named a Disney Legend in the field of Animation. She died in Corona, California, on August 5, 2009, at the age of ninety-one.

**Edna Francis Disney** survived Roy by thirteen years. Her brother Mitch—Roy's best friend, who moved to California to work at the studio as a purchasing manager—died a short time before Roy. Edna remained in her and Roy's house in Toluca Lake, and she stayed active in her later years. She frequently visited Disneyland, and a granddaughter (she and Roy had one son, Roy E. Disney) recalled that "[s]he drove [her] giant car into her nineties.... She used to drive the Hollywood Freeway forty miles an hour in the fast lane. People honked their horns, and she'd say, 'I don't know why everyone is in such a gol-darned hurry.'"

In December 1984, Edna became ill and was hospitalized at St. Joseph's hospital (across the street from the Walt Disney Studios), where Walt and Roy had died. She was visited in the hospital by Lilly's niece, Marjorie Sewell Davis. On December 18, Lilly visited Edna, and promised to visit her again the next day. Edna predicted, "I won't be here." Edna died on December 19, 1984, at the age of ninety-four. Edna was named a Disney Legend by The Walt Disney Company in 2003.

**Lillian Bounds Disney** played a key role in the creation of Mickey Mouse after Walt lost the Oswald series during their trip to New York in February and March of 1928. When Walt initially decided to name his new mouse Mortimer, Lilly had a "violent reaction" and told him, "Mortimer is a horrible name for a mouse!" Walt quietly suggested Mickey. "I said it sounded better than Mortimer, and that's how Mickey was born," recalled Lillian.

Like Edna, Lillian helped ink and paint the first Mickey reels, but during Mickey's heyday, Lilly focused on raising the Disneys' two daughters, Diane Marie, born in 1933, and Sharon Mae, born in 1936. Lilly continued, however, to assess Walt's latest projects, and he appreciated her honesty. She recalled, "Walt said I was the only person he could count on never to 'yes' him. He had to have a sounding board. I had to listen carefully because when he had something he wanted to ask me, he would expect me to be listening." She joked that she was his "Severest Critic" and that she had a mixed record of advising Walt: "I tried to stop him [from making *Snow White and the Seven Dwarfs*] because I didn't think people would go see a motion picture about [D]warfs!"

Lilly and Walt were married for forty-one years at the time of Walt's death. Roy said that their marriage succeeded because "Lilly was the kind of girl who let Walt have his way. Walt was a dominating person. And she was the kind that just went along with him in what he did. She worshipped him, and anything he wanted to do was all right with her. She had a lot of patience with him, and they used to fuss at each other in their own kind of kidding way."

After Walt's death, Lilly made appearances from time to time at events related to her husband's legacy. In the fall of 1968, less than two years after Walt's death, Lilly traveled to Marceline, Missouri, where Walt lived as a young boy, for the release of the U.S. Postal Service's first class stamp honoring Walt. She was accompanied by Diane and Sharon and their families, and Roy and his family. She went to the White House in 1969 to receive, on Walt's behalf, a medal presented by President Nixon. In October 1971, two months before the fifth anniversary of Walt's death, she joined Roy and Edna and their respective family members at the opening ceremonies at Walt Disney World near Orlando, Florida.

In 1973 she made an appearance with Mickey Mouse at Disneyland, as part of the Disney Studio's yearlong commemoration of the Walt Disney Studios' fiftieth anniversary (the studio considered its opening to be October 16, 1923—the day Walt and Roy started Disney Brothers Studio). Specifically, Lillian presided over the Disneyland debut of *The Walt Disney Story*, a new attraction at both Disneyland and Walt Disney World that featured a film about, and a walk-through exhibit with memorabilia from, Walt's life and career.

Lillian's philanthropic works included a 1987 gift of $50 million for the construction of the Walt Disney Concert Hall in Los Angeles, which opened sixteen years later, and the 1993 remodeling of the Walt Disney Modular Theater at California Institute of the Arts. In announcing her Concert Hall gift, Lillian stated, "I have always had a deep love and admiration for my husband, and I wanted to find a way to honor him, as well as give something to Los Angeles which would have lasting qualities." In 1993, Lillian released a statement criticizing a negative biography of Walt. In that statement, she said, "We shared a wonderful, exciting life, and we loved every minute of it.... He was a wonderful husband to me and [a] wonderful and joyful father and grandfather."

Lillian was married to real estate man John L. Truyens from 1969 until his death in 1981. Lillian suffered a stroke on December 15, 1997, the thirty-first anniversary of Walt's death. She died the following day, at the age of ninety-eight. She was survived by one of her daughters, Diane Disney Miller, ten grandchildren, and thirteen great-grandchildren. Lilly was named a Disney Legend in 2003.

**Robert and Charlotte Disney**, because of their son, Robert, Jr., were featured in the *Los Angeles Times* shortly before Mickey Mouse was created. It was probably the last time during Walt's life that another Disney commanded more press attention than he. On New Year's Eve, 1927, the *Times* ran a story on Walt's four-year-old "[f]air-haired and blue-eyed" nephew, Robert S. Disney, Jr. Alongside a photograph of the toddler writing on a blackboard was an article claiming that young Robert "is the possessor of powers of observation and a memory which are the wonder not only of his parents, Mr. and Mrs. Robert S. Disney of 4406 Kingswell [A]venue, but also of psychologists who have studied him." The piece, with a headline proclaiming, "Child Marvel At Memory Baby's Case Studied by Psychologists," explained that Robert could name all the state capitals and explain why Washington, Lincoln, Theodore Roosevelt, and Coolidge were the four best presidents. The article confided, however, that, in the words of Charlotte, young Robert was full of "the old nick" and was as rambunctious as any other four-year-old.

Robert and Charlotte continued to live in their house on Kingswell for several years. A letter from Roy to his parents from the fall of 1931 provides insights to the relationship between Walt and Uncle Robert: "Right now [Robert] has quite a peeve against Walt because [Robert] has never been invited up to the new [Lyric Avenue] house. But Walt takes the attitude that they never cared to come down to the old one, so why invite them to the new one? Edna and I have made two attempts lately to keep on cordial relationships with [Robert and Charlotte], having visited Uncle Robert twice. We, too, never see them at our house. They are funny that way. Uncle Robert is still as rabid on politics as ever. I 'dared' not to agree with him the other night on some of his views, and a clash almost ensued. In fact, we had to go to our car escorted by only Aunt Charlotte and Robert Jr., big Robert peevishly walking away from us. Ain't life funny?" All seemed to be forgotten by that Christmas, however, as the family members gathered to celebrate the holiday together. In the 1930s, Robert and Charlotte moved next door to the corner house located at 4400 Kingswell.

Robert died in 1953 at the age of ninety-one. Charlotte stayed at 4400 Kingswell until the mid-1970s. Around that time, she fell and broke her hip, and her son, Robert, Jr., moved her out and sold her house. Charlotte died a few years later in 1979. She was eighty-seven. Robert, Jr., survived his mother by about twenty years. He died in Merced, California, in 1996 at the age of seventy-three.

**Roy Disney** remained at the studio until his death in 1971. In his forty-eight years with the company, Roy provided many invaluable services. To offset the cost of the Mickey Mouse and Silly Symphonies series, Roy rented to other producers the Disney sound trucks. In 1929, Roy realized that Pat Powers, the man who succeeded the Mintzes as the Disneys' distributor, was withholding money. While Powers succeeded in luring Ubbe away from the Disneys during the resulting dispute, the Disneys were able to buy their way out of their contract with Powers. Roy subsequently oversaw the studio's respective distribution arrangements with Columbia (1930–1932), United Artists (1932–1937), and RKO (1937–1956).

Roy was also instrumental in the Disney studio's foray into merchandising, its thirty-year financing relationship with the Bank of America, its decision to go public in 1940, and the creation of its own distribution company, Buena Vista Distribution Company, in 1953. In addition, Roy negotiated with the three major television networks the sale of Disney's inaugural TV series as a means of financing the construction of Disneyland.

Initially, Roy was Walt's partner in Walt Disney Productions. Once the company went public, Roy was named its executive vice president and business manager. By the following decade, he was chairman of the board. Roy eventually became president and chief executive officer. Walt gave up the position of president—because he "spent too much time signing papers"—in 1960 and became instead "executive producer in charge of all production."

By the time of Walt's death in December 1966, Roy had planned on retiring. He changed his mind, however, in order to lead the company in Walt's absence and, in particular, to oversee the development of Walt's plans to build a second theme park and EPCOT near Orlando, Florida. Roy said in a statement that he and the employees of Walt Disney Productions would "continue to operate Walt Disney's company in the way that he has established and guided it[,]," and he told the senior management of the company that, "We're going to finish this [Florida] park, and we're going to do it just the way Walt wanted it. Don't you ever forget it. I want every one of you to do just exactly what you were going to do when Walt was alive."

In 1969, Roy penned a *Reader's Digest* article about his brother, whom Roy called "a complex man" with whom Roy had his share of battles. "But [Walt]," Roy wrote, "was always quick to shake hands and make up." Roy found that Walt's complexity resulted from his different faces: "To the writers, producers and animators who worked with him, he was a genius who had an uncanny ability to add an extra fillip of imagination to any story or idea. To the millions of people who watched his TV show, he was a warm, kindly personality, bringing fun and pleasure into their homes. To the bankers who financed us, I'm sure he seemed like a wild man, hell-bent for bankruptcy. To me, he was my amazing kid brother, full of impractical dreams that he made come true."

Almost five years after Walt's death, on October 23, 1971, Roy presided, with Lilly and their respective families, over the dedication of Walt Disney World in Lake Buena Vista, Florida. In his comments, Roy recalled, "My brother Walt and I went into business together almost a half-century ago. And he was really, in my opinion, truly a genius—creative, with great determination, singleness of purpose, and drive; and through his entire life he was never pushed off his course or diverted by other things."

Roy then returned to California, to finally begin his retirement, which was to begin with a February 1972 cruise to Australia with Edna. Not long after booking the cruise, Roy and Edna had plans to take some of their grandchildren to the Christmas parade at Disneyland. At the last minute, Roy decided to stay home because he did not feel well, and his son accompanied Edna and the children on their outing. While his family was at Disneyland, Roy collapsed, and he lapsed into a coma shortly after the family returned home. The next day, Monday, December 20, 1971, Roy died of a massive brain hemorrhage. He was seventy-eight years old.

About fifteen years earlier, Walt explained what his older brother meant to him and his success. Walt said, "My father . . . . never understood me. He thought I was the black sheep. This nonsense of drawing pictures! . . . . But my big brother would say, 'Kid, go ahead!' He said, 'Kid, I'm for you.' He encouraged me. When he was away—he was in a veterans hospital for a time—we wrote letters. I could tell him what I was going to do, and he'd write back: 'Go ahead, kid. Good for you, kid.' I was fortunate. I had a big brother and he's still with me. And I still love him. I argue with him. Sometimes I think he's the stubbornest so-and-so I ever met in my life. But I don't know what the hell I'd do without him."

**Ruth Disney** remained in Portland, Oregon, where Flora and Elias Disney lived until Walt and Roy moved their parents to Los Angeles in 1936. Ruth married Theodore Beecher, and they had a son, also named Theodore. Ruth's husband, who had been a sheet metal worker, had difficulty holding a job, and Ruth would turn to Roy for financial assistance. When Walt died in 1966, the prospect of a press frenzy prevented Ruth from traveling to Los Angeles for the funeral, although she attended Roy's funeral five years later. Ruth also outlived the other Disney siblings; Herbert died in 1961 and Ray died in 1989. Ruth died in Portland in 1995 at the age of ninety-two.

**Kathleen Dollard**, after leaving Disney Brothers Studio in March of 1925, lived in Chula Vista in San Diego. She died in New Jersey in 1979, at the age of seventy-two.

**Robert Edmunds** returned to Los Angeles and by 1930 worked in "Cartooning" in "Moving Pictures." Edmunds worked on early *Bosko* cartoons for Harman-Ising and later worked on the *Looney Tunes* series. He was deported in the 1930s after his boss, cartoon producer Leon Schlesinger, discovered that he was a British seaman who had jumped ship. Edmunds died at the U.S. Consulate in London in his native England in 1987. He was eighty-four years old.

**Guy Eyssell** left Kansas City for New York, where he was a manager of Publix theaters in the 1930s. By 1955, Eyssell was the chairman of the board of the New York Music Hall and president of Rockefeller Center, Inc.

**Milton H. Feld** moved to California in 1925 to manage the Metropolitan (later the Paramount) Theatre. He went to New York to co-manage the Publix Theatres, and in 1933 was a co-founder of Monarch Theatres, Inc. By the mid-1930s, Feld was back in California working as a producer and assistant to Darryl F. Zanuck. In 1938, he was hired by Universal, where he was an executive producer at the time of his death in 1947 at the age of fifty-four.

**Harry Forbes** worked as a cameraman and "studio worker," filming many movies in the 1930s while living in Hollywood with his wife Bertha. He died in Los Angeles in 1939 at the age of fifty-two. Forbes was survived by Bertha and their son Jack.

**Allen Freleng** became a motion picture electrician and lived with his brother Friz and their older sister until Allen married his wife Beatrice. He later became a writer and died in California in 1943 at the age of thirty-six.

**Friz Freleng** returned to Kansas City in the fall of 1927 before moving to New York to work on Charlie Mintz's *Krazy Kat* series. He returned to Los Angeles in 1928 and worked under George Winkler's supervision there. He and his younger brother lived with their older sister, Janice, a dry goods saleswoman. In 1931, Freleng joined the animation department at Warner Brothers. By the mid-30s, he lived with Les Clark, who was still at Disney's. Freleng later married a woman named Lilly.

He eventually became a director at Warner Brothers, and spent over thirty years there. In that time, he created such famous Warner characters as Daffy Duck, Tweety Bird, and Yosemite Sam, for whom Freleng admitted serving as the inspiration: "I have the same temperment [*sic*] . . . . I'm small, and I used to have a red mustache." In the early 1960s, he and David DePatie established DePatie-Freleng Enterprises, which produced the Pink Panther and other shorts and TV shows. When he was eighty-four, Freleng gave an interview to the *Kansas City Star* in which he appeared to be at peace with his rocky relationship with Walt, saying, "Walt was a genius, and a genius does what he wants. He doesn't do what *you* want."

Freleng died in Los Angeles in 1995 at the age of ninety. He was survived by his wife, two daughters, and four grandchildren. His Warner Brothers colleague, Chuck Jones, said at the time, "Friz was a great man, who really put Warner Bros. animation together. He was the guiding light who made it all worthwhile."

**Manny Goldstein** spent a total of seventeen years as the treasurer and general manager at Universal. In the mid-1930s, he was the head of distribution for Republic Pictures in New York, and in 1937 was named that studio's general manager. In 1953, Goldstein was named the general production manager of Hal Roach, Jr.'s Lincoln Productions, Inc. Six years later, he joined Columbia "in an executive capacity[.]"

**Marjorie Gossett**'s movie career apparently ended when she was replaced by Lois Hardwick as the lead in the Alice Comedies. By 1930, when she was eleven years old, Marjorie and her mother, Ruth, then twenty-nine, lived with a forty-one-year-old art store designer named Charles Conway. By the mid-1930s, Marjorie worked as a weaver, Ruth worked as a saleswoman, and they lived together a few miles from the Kingswell Avenue studio. In 1950, when she was thirty-one, Marjorie moved to Las Vegas, where she became a photographer and, like Ruth, became the single mother of a daughter. She died in Las Vegas in 2003. She was eighty-four years old.

**Ham Hamilton** remained an animator for the length of his career. His post-Disney jobs included stints with the Winkler company and Walter Lantz (the Oswald series), Harman-Ising (the Bosko series), Leon Schlesinger/Warner Brothers (for directors Friz Freleng and Jack King), and Tex Avery. Hamilton married, and he and his wife Mary had a daughter, Phyllis, and a son, Keith. Hamilton died in Los Angeles in 1951, at the age of fifty-three.

**Irene Hamilton** continued to live with her brother, Ham, and Ham's family after she and Ham left the Walt Disney Studio. Irene also continued to work with Ham; she joined him at the Winkler studio, where she became a cartoonist. Irene eventually married and lived to about the age of eighty-five.

**Esther Hammond** corresponded with Walt almost twenty years after her relatives invested in Laugh-O-gram. She eventually remarried. Esther lived in Monterey, California, at the time of her death in 1950 at the age of fifty-six.

**Fletcher Hammond** moved to Webb City, Missouri, where he worked for his father as the assistant manager of a theater. He died from a skull fracture sustained in a car accident in Springfield, Missouri, in 1933. Hammond was approximately thirty-one years old.

**William F. Hammond**, by 1930, relocated to Webb City, where he managed a theater. He hired his son Fletcher as his assistant manager. Sometime after Fletcher's death in 1933, William moved to Monterey, California, presumably to be with his daughter Esther. She died a few months before he did. Hammond died in Monterey in October 1950 at the age of eighty-eight.

**Lois Hardwick** continued to act in shorts after the Alice Comedies ceased production in 1927. She appeared in a number of 1928–1929 episodes of the Buster Brown series and its spin-off series about Buster's dog, Tige. She also appeared in the film *7th Heaven*, which won several Academy Awards in 1929, including Best Actress for Janet Gaynor, Best Directing for a Dramatic Picture for Frank Borzage, and Best Writing (Adaptation) for Benjamin Glazer. By 1930, Lois' career appears to have ended.

She was by then a high school student living with her family on Sunset Avenue. When she was twenty-five, Lois married Clarence Dodson, twenty-seven, who described himself as a "semi-skilled cement worker and concrete finisher" who served in the Army in World War II. Lois and Clarence later lived in Riverside, California. Lois died in 1978 at the age of sixty-four. Clarence died in Riverside almost twenty years later.

**Fred Harman** returned to the Film Ad company after leaving Kaycee Studios. A year later, he and a partner opened their own short-lived advertising studio, Harman & McConnell. By 1924, Harman worked for Mac Advertising Company, "[b]ut after a whirl at commercial art with printers and engravers in Kansas City," he later wrote, "I was discouraged and the call of the open range found me once more in a Colorado saddle." He communicated with Walt from time to time.

After several years in Colorado and Hollywood, Harman went to New York in 1938 and created the famous *Red Ryder* comic strip that ran until 1962. The 1938 BB gun toy inspired by the *Red Ryder* strip was featured in a 1966 book by Jean Shepherd called *In God We Trust, All Others Pay Cash*, that was made into the 1983 movie classic *A Christmas Story*. In 1968, Harman wrote a biographical article for *True West* magazine, and it included his memories of his years at the Film Ad and Kaycee Studios. He died in 1982 in Phoenix, Arizona, at the age of eighty-three. His son, Fred Harman, III, is the curator of the Fred Harman Art Museum in Pagosa Springs, Colorado. The museum displays, among other things, Fred, Jr.'s oil paintings and *Red Ryder* comic strips.

**Hugh Harman** left Charlie Mintz a year after Harman and the other animators left Walt, when Universal took *Oswald* from Winkler and gave the series to Walter Lantz. Harman "liked [Charlie] very much" but was not fond of George Winkler, whom Harman described as Charlie's "henchman[.]" Said Harman, "George Winkler was the intervening element there [when we worked for Winkler on *Oswald*], and Rudy and I got so fed up with [George] we didn't want to have anything to do with him. We just thought nobody could ever get along with him, he was so petty in so many ways."

In 1929 Harman and Rudy Ising formed their own production company, Harman-Ising, which produced *Bosko the Talk-Ink Kid*, the first cartoon with synchronized dialogue. *Bosko* was distributed by Leon Schlesinger Productions, which eventually became Warner Brothers Cartoons. In 1933 Harman and Ising left Warners, where they produced *Looney Tunes* and created *Merrie Melodies*, and the next year went to MGM, where they produced *Happy Harmonies* and worked (except for an interlude around 1938) until the early 1940s. In 1938, Harman and Ising produced the Silly Symphony cartoon, *Merbabies*, for the Walt Disney Studio.

Harman claimed that Walt and Roy tried to recruit Ising and him to return to the Disney studio at this time. Harman felt that, had he once again become Walt's employee, Walt "would have been very pleasant, been very fair." Harman and Ising won an Academy Award in 1940 for their MGM short *The Milky Way*. Harman survived his older brother Fred by eleven months, dying in 1982 at the age of seventy-nine in Chatsworth, California, after a yearlong illness.

**Walker Harman** worked as a writer for Hugh Harman and Rudy Ising at Harman-Ising. He was also a tap dancer and performer in Los Angeles, and was married by the time he died about a decade after leaving the Walt Disney Studio. Hugh explained, "Walker died, in 1938; he was thirty-two at the time. He died of tuberculosis. He was a rider, and a good jumper. One winter he was jumping, and the horse fell with him, or he fell off the horse. He broke several ribs and had them taped up, then he caught flu that ran into pneumonia, then into TB. He wouldn't pay attention to his health."

**Thurston Harper** returned to work for Walt part-time at the new Hyperion studio eleven months after it opened. Thurston later claimed to have returned to the studio for two years in the mid-1930s, but the studio's records do not support that recollection. He worked for Harman-Ising for a few years in the 1930s, and animated with Ben Clopton and Bill Nolan on the Fleischers' 1939 animated feature, *Gulliver's Travels*.

In the early 1940s, Harper worked at the Fleischer studio in Miami and joined the Navy during World War II. By the late 1960s, he moved to St. Thomas in the Virgin Islands, where he sold advertising and spent time fishing, boating, and scuba diving. His wife died in 1971. Seven years later, Thurston corresponded with the Walt Disney Studios Archives, writing that he was "in extremely good health. [I am a]s strong as a mule and almost as stubborn." He died in Florida in 1987. He was eighty-four years old.

**Rudy Ising** held a number of jobs after first leaving the Walt Disney Studio. He made portraits as an independent photographer, had a mail-order photography finishing business through Kodak, worked at MGM's stills department, got a job with a commercial artist, and produced for a plastic surgeon films on such procedures as "the nose job and the ear job." Ising and his partner, Hugh Harman, later worked at various studios, and they created such series as *Looney Tunes*, *Merrie Melodies*, and *Happy Harmonies*. One of the studios was MGM, where Ising's wife said he "still had the sleeping problem" and where a sleepy bear cartoon character named Barney Bear was, according to Ising, "an imitation of myself, a sleepy bear."

In 1937, on behalf of their own Harman-Ising studio then at MGM, Ising and Harman wired Walt upon the release of *Snow White and the Seven Dwarfs*, "Our pride in the production is scarcely less than yours must be and we are grateful to you for fulfilling an ambition which many of us have long held for our industry."

Two of Rudy's brothers worked as cameramen at Harman-Ising. One, Max Ising, had also worked at Film Ad. Rudy and Hugh won an Academy Award in 1940 for Best Short Subject (Cartoon) for their animated short, *The Milky Way*, which Ising directed. During World War II Rudy became head of the U.S. Army Air Forces animation department. After the war, he focused on TV commercials and government films. He died in Los Angeles in 1992, at the age of eighty-eight.

**Ubbe Iwwerks** remained at the Disney Studio after the 1928 walk-out of Hugh, Ham, and four other animators. He was rewarded with a 20-percent share in Walt and Roy's partnership. Ubbe fully animated *Plane Crazy*, the first Mickey Mouse cartoon, by mid-May, 1928. Besides a number of other Mickey Mouse shorts, Iwwerks directed five of the numerous Silly Symphonies cartoons on which he worked before leaving Walt to start his own studio in 1930.

In something of a replay of the Mintz-engineered defection two years earlier, Iwwerks' departure was choreographed behind Walt's back by a New York city distributor, and his exit hurt Walt deeply. At the time he left the Disney studio in January 1930, Iwwerks was paid for his share of the partnership, which was then worth $2,290. After a ten-year period in which he opened his own studio and launched a series called *Flip the Frog*, Iwwerks returned to the Walt Disney Studio and worked on special processes, which led to a 1960 Academy Award—for designing an advanced optical printer. In 1965 he won a second Academy Award for an advanced traveling matte system. At the time of his death in 1971 at the age of seventy-one, Iwwerks was the director of technical research at Disney, where his sons David and Donald also worked. He was named a Disney Legend in the fields of Animation & Imagineering in 1989.

**Louis Katsis** was still a restaurant cook at the time of his death in Kansas City in 1956 at the age of sixty-eight.

**William E. Kemp**, after serving as the court's trustee for the Laugh-O-gram estate, was appointed to the Kansas Court of Appeals. He was mayor of Kansas City from 1946 to 1955, and died in 1968 at the age of seventy-nine.

**Jack Kloepper** apparently worked at the Beyer Theater at Thompson Avenue and South Street in Excelsior Springs, Missouri, soon after he left Laugh-O-gram in 1923. He claimed that Walt asked him to move to Hollywood with him. "My answer to Walt," Kloepper recalled, "was 'Walt, I'll tell you: you go to Hollywood if you want to. I'll starve to death in Kansas City.'" In 1924, he got a job in sales in Kansas City. By 1930, Kloepper was a motion picture salesman living in Minnesota, apparently without his wife Martha. He eventually worked for United Artists in California, and retired to Atchison, Kansas, in 1970, to, among other things, play a lot of golf. That same year, Kloepper gave a taped interview to the Walt Disney Studios Archives about his time at Laugh-O-gram Films. He died in Kansas in 1985 at the age of eighty-seven.

**Alex Kurfiss** worked as a cartoonist for the *Kansas City Star* and as an artist for a Kansas City advertising company after working at Laugh-O-gram. He lived with his parents in their Kansas City home as of 1930. Kurfiss later studied art at the New York School of Art and in Chicago under noted artist Frederick Mizen. By the late 1940s, he was married and living in Minnesota, where his son died the day of his birth. By 1950, the Kurfisses lived in Blue Springs, Missouri. Kurfiss worked as a commercial artist and his wife Marjorie was a schoolteacher. The couple retired to Marjorie's native Iowa, where he died in 1983 at the age of eighty-four. Kurfiss is listed in *Who Was Who in American Art, 1564–1975, 400 Years of Artists in America*.

**Hazelle A. Linston** worked as a photographer in Los Angeles in the late 1920s.

**John Lott** remained a janitor at the Disney studio for at least a year after the break with Charlie Mintz, and probably into the 1930s. In the early 1940s, he worked at MGM, where he cleaned cels for Hugh and Rudy. Lott married, and lived in Los Angeles until his death in 1970 at the age of eighty-seven.

**Jimmy Lowerre** remained at Film Ad for a few years after Walt's departure. He relocated to Los Angeles, where he worked in the Disney Studio sound department from 1928 until 1957. Lowerre died in 1962 at the age of sixty-eight.

**Red Lyon** left Laugh-O-gram in early 1923 and moved to Los Angeles, where he worked as a Technical Engineer and lived with his brother Wilfred in Inglewood. On Sunday, June 3, 1923, Lyon, his mother, and some friends went for a picnic on a beach by the Palos Verdes hills near Clifton, outside of Redondo Beach. The group included two brothers, Ernest Goodpasture, and his younger brother, Victor, of Huntington Park, and two sisters, Dorothy Klein, eighteen, and Loretta Klein, sixteen, also of Huntington Park. After lunch, the Klein sisters went swimming, even though the beach was not patrolled by lifeguards. The girls became overtaken by the Pacific's strong undertow, and began to scream. Lyon and the Goodpasture brothers ran into the surf to help them, and succeeded in pushing Dorothy and Loretta into the arms of another man who had followed them into the ocean, fully clothed, to assist.

Lyon and the Goodpastures, however, were overcome with exhaustion and could not escape the undertow themselves. The three men were slowly carried out to sea, as Lyon's mother, who had to be restrained from going in after her son, watched in horror. She, the Kleins, and the others on the beach watched Red, Ernest, and Victor float for several hundred feet before disappearing from view. Lifeguards and policemen arrived and a launch was used to search the surf for hours without success.

Victor's body washed ashore two days later. Red's body was found in kelp beds by fishermen almost two weeks later, on Friday, June 15, and Ernest's body was found later that same day near where he went under. Red Lyon was laid to rest at Inglewood Park Cemetery on Saturday, June 16, less than a month after his thirtieth birthday.

**Leslie Mace**, after leaving Laugh-O-gram Films, remarried and moved to St. Louis, where he worked in "talking pictures." He later became a self-employed building consultant. Mace died in Santa Ana, California, in 1977, at the age of seventy-nine.

**James MacLachlan** appears to have stopped working at Film Ad by 1924, although Marjorie MacLachlan remained at the company as a card writer. He died between 1924 and 1930, between the ages of forty-five and fifty-one.

**Mike Marcus** filmed *Steamboat Willie* before he left the Walt Disney Studio on June 30, 1928. Marcus and fellow Mount Holly Hotel resident and ex-Disney staffer Paul Smith no doubt continued to hear about the studio through Les Clark, who also lived at the Mount Holly at the time. Marcus appears to have tried his hand, again, at cartooning in 1928, but also continued to work as a cameraman. In 1929, at the age of twenty-eight, he married a twenty-year-old movie studio commercial artist named Irene. The following year, the Marcuses took in some boarders at their home on North Normandie: Marcus' business partner, twenty-four-year-old Glenn Rogers and his wife of six years, twenty-four-year-old Frances Rogers; and Ardis Warner, a twenty-three-year-old woman from Colorado. By then, Mike and Glenn were movie studio cameramen. Frances, like Irene, was a movie studio commercial artist. Ardis was a typist for a movie critic.

By the late 1930s, the Marcuses appear to have left Los Angeles. According to Ubbe, by the early 1950s, Marcus "was in a penitentiary for life." He died in San Luis Obispo, California, in 1957, when he was fifty-six years old (although the warden of the California Men's Colony jail in San Luis Obispo could not locate records confirming Marcus was an inmate there). Irene died in Los Angeles in 1975 at the age of sixty-six.

**Max Maxwell** worked with Hugh Harman and Rudy Ising after they each left the Walt Disney Studio. Maxwell provided Bosko's voice for Harman-Ising's *Bosko* series for most of the 1930s. In fact, Bosko was named after Maxwell, as Ising recalled: "The name 'Bosko' came from Maxwell; we used to call [Maxwell] Bosko, for what reason, I don't know." He was later an animation production manager at MGM.

On May 23, 1972, fifty years to the day after the State of Missouri issued Laugh-O-gram Films' certificate of incorporation, Maxwell joined Rudy Ising and Walt Pfeiffer as guests at the Disney studio's anniversary commemoration. The studio had two showings (at noon and 12:30 p.m.) in the studio theater of a program of Laugh-O-gram films, including *Puss in Boots, Tommy Tucker's*

*Tooth*, and *Alice's Wonderland*, followed by a luncheon. Max died in Ventura, California, in 1987 at the age of eighty-eight.

**Thomas McCrum** continued to practice dentistry in Kansas City and remained associated with the Deaner Dental Institute. He was also a dentist with the city's Board of Education. McCrum died in 1948 at the age of seventy-one.

**James McRae** continued to work as a realtor at McRae & Abernathy for approximately one year after Walt rented space in that office, until McRae was about seventy-seven years old. He appears to have retired or died a short time later.

**Charlie Mintz** bumped into Walt in New York sometime soon after the sensational premiere of Mickey Mouse in *Steamboat Willie* in late 1928. After the premiere, Walt remained in New York to find a distributor for his new series and saw Mintz in a waiting room at Universal. Walt did not hold a grudge, and greeted Mintz cordially. Mintz lost the Oswald series when Universal gave it a short time later to Walter Lantz, who went on to create Woody Woodpecker.

Mintz and his wife Margaret continued to live in New York with their daughter Katherine and son William until the 1930s. By the middle of that decade, the Mintzes moved to Los Angeles, where the Charles Mintz Studio operated on Santa Monica Boulevard. By 1938, Mintz was president of Screen Gems, Inc., which was located in the same building as the Mintz Studio. Among the cartoons he produced were *Scrappy* and *Color Rhapsodies*. He died in 1940 at the age of fifty at his home in Beverly Hills. At the time of his death, *Variety* called Mintz a "pioneer cartoon producer[.]" Almost seventy years after his death, the Walt Disney Company recognized his role as a real-life Disney antagonist by naming the villain in its Oscar-winning animation feature *Up* "Charles Muntz."

**Baron Missakian** opened his own portrait studio in Kansas City in 1925. He and Nadine Simpson were married two years later. Missakian became an "internationally known portraitist" and photographed Milton Berle, Count Ilya Tolstoy, and Sir Carl Busch. When Walt visited Kansas City in 1931, Missakian made a portrait of him that matched the pose in a portrait he made of Walt at Laugh-O-gram Films nine years earlier.

In 1940, when Missakian was forty-six years old, he suffered a debilitating stroke that left him bedridden and forced him to close his studio. He kept in contact with Walt over the years. Missakian died in 1964 at the age of seventy. After his death, his wife donated two thousand portraits made by Baron to the library at the University of Missouri–Kansas City, and gave the mahogany display table made the year he opened his studio to the Maple Wood Community College in Kansas City, which showcased it in its president's office.

**George Morrell** continued to act on stage and screen, appearing on Broadway and in many westerns. He was married to his wife, Rosalie, for fifty-seven years. Morrell died in Hollywood in 1955, after a long illness. He was eighty-three years old.

**Frank L. Newman** sold his nine Missouri and Wisconsin theaters in 1925. He later moved to the west coast to work for Paramount and Warner Brothers. In 1932, Newman became president of the Seattle-based Evergreen Theatres Corporation. He retired in 1954 and died in Seattle in 1962 at the age of seventy-two.

**Bill Nolan**, after flirting with moving to California to work for the Disneys in early 1928, stayed with the Winkler company. In 1929, Nolan was named the assistant to animator Walter Lantz, to whom Universal gave the *Oswald* series after taking it away from Charlie Mintz. In 1939, Nolan was an animator on the Fleischers' feature, *Gulliver's Travels*, and on the Popeye series in the 1940s. In the 1950s he directed *The Woody Woodpecker Show*. His last series was UI's *Francis* series, for which he was a technical advisor. Nolan died on December 6, 1954, after an operation at the Veterans Hospital in Sawtelle, California. He was sixty years old.

**Walter O'Donnell** continued to act through the 1940s as a "character actor, bit player and extra[.]" He died at the Motion Picture and Television Country Hospital in Woodland Hills, Los Angeles, in 1986, at the age of seventy-five.

**Alexander Pantages** eventually owned thirty vaudeville and movie theaters between the west coast and Alabama, as well as booking offices in Chicago and New York. *Variety* called him "the most colorful and prominent of the old time vaudeville showmen[.]" But the "1929 crash hit him hard[,]" and Pantages "disposed of most of his holdings[.]" He sold his Los Angeles theater to Warner Brothers and a number of other properties to RKO. His 1933 attempt at a "comeback . . . didn't go too far." He then concentrated on his "stable of race horses[.]"

Pantages' later years were marred by two highly publicized scandals. His wife Lois was charged with manslaughter after she hit and killed a pedestrian while driving the family car. Pantages himself was arrested for allegedly assaulting Eunice Pringle, a dancer, in his office at his Los Angeles theater.

Pringle sued Pantages for $1,000. Pantages reportedly spent $1,000,000 to fight the charge but was convicted. He won a second trial, at which he was acquitted. He later settled with Miss Pringle for $3,000. Pantages died of a heart attack in his bed at his Los Angeles home in 1936. He was sixty-five years old. Lois also died from a heart attack five years later, at the age of fifty-seven, after swimming off her son's yacht near Catalina Island. The Pantages' grandson, child actor Tim Considine, starred in the 1959 Disney movie *The Shaggy Dog* and in several *Mickey Mouse Club* serials, including *The Adventures of Spin and Marty* and its sequels.

**Dawn Paris** continued to act, under the stage name of Dawn O'Day, through the 1920s. By 1930, her mother Mimi, who then described herself as a widow, and Dawn O'Day were both movie actresses who roomed with a "boarding house keeper" in Los Angeles. Dawn changed her name again a few years later, after appearing as the title character, Anne Shirley, in a 1934 film version of the book, *Anne of Greene Gables*. Dawn was known thereafter as Anne Shirley, and Mimi was known as Mrs. Mimi Shirley. Anne acted in many movies until her retirement in 1944, seven years after she was nominated for a Best Actress in a Supporting Role Oscar for the Barbara Stanwyck film, *Stella Dallas*. *Los Angeles Times* drama editor Edwin Schallert credited Anne Shirley with "breaking the ice" for other child stars: "[s]he demonstrated that film child prodigies could grow up successfully—a much doubted issue in those days, which has had plenty of proof in subsequent times." She was married to actor John Payne (*Miracle on 34th Street*), producer Adrian Scott (*Murder, My Sweet*), and screenwriter John Lederer. Ann Lederer died on the Fourth of July, 1993, at the age of seventy-four.

**Rudolph Peiser** continued to live at the Elsmere Hotel and operate Peiser's Restaurant until his death in 1927 at the age of forty-nine.

**Lou Pesmen** parted from Bill Rubin about a year or so after they let Walt go from Gray Advertising. By 1921, Pesmen was a partner in another studio named Pesmen & Haner, located at 1331 Oak, about a half-block from the Gray Building. He eventually had his own commercial art studio, The Pesmen Studio, in Kansas City and later in Chicago, where he and his wife and children relocated in the late 1920s. There he did package design work for such clients as Kraft Foods. He visited Walt in Burbank a few decades later. Walt gave him a tour of the studio and had a photograph taken of them with Ubbe Iwwerks. Walt wrote on the photograph, "To Lou Pesmen, My First Boss In The Art World. Sincerely, Walt Disney." Pesmen retired to California in the 1970s. In 1971, Pesmen drafted for the Walt Disney Studios Archives a five-page narrative of his experience with Walt in Kansas City in the early 1920s. Pesmen died in 1987 at the age of ninety-four.

**John Pfeiffer** served as secretary to the leather workers union for over twenty years. He died in Los Angeles, where his son Walter lived and worked for the Walt Disney Studios, in 1953, at the age of eighty-two.

**Walt Pfeiffer** eventually followed Walt Disney to California, where he went to work for the Walt Disney Studios in 1935. Pfeiffer spent his career at Disney, where, in 1937, he co-directed, with storyman Ed Penner and Pinto Colvig (the voice of Goofy), a Mickey Mouse short called *Mickey's Amateurs*. He also held positions in the story department and management. Pfeiffer was honored by the Los Angeles chapter of the Big Brothers Association of America in 1957, and Walt Disney spoke at the awards dinner in Beverly Hills. Pfeiffer retired from the studio in 1972. He died in Los Angeles in 1976 at the age of seventy-five.

**Fred Quimby** became the businessman in charge of MGM's cartoon studio. By his retirement in 1956, he produced such famous series as *Tom and Jerry*, *Barney Bear*, and *Droopy*, and won seven Academy Awards between 1943 and 1952. He died in Santa Monica in 1965. At the time of his death, Quimby was seventy-nine years old.

**Jerry Raggos** moved from Kansas City to Phoenix, Arizona, where, with a loan from Walt of over $1,000, he opened a new restaurant. He died sometime before 1944.

**Albert L. Reeves** in 1936 convened a grand jury that indicted several hundred Kansas City residents who were later convicted of committing voter fraud. This was the first challenge to the corrupt Democratic machine of Kansas City boss Tom Pendergast. Reeves retired from federal bench in 1964, and died in 1971 at ninety-seven years of age.

**Aletha Reynolds** worked as an artist and continued to live with her parents for several years after leaving Laugh-O-gram. She got married in 1936 at the age of thirty-four.

**Bill Rubin** left Lou Pesmen and in 1920 and 1921 worked as a commercial artist out of an office on the eighth floor of the Graphic Arts Building, almost a mile away from the Gray Building. He continued to work for advertising agencies in Kansas City, including the Allen C. Smith Advertising Company, until his death in 1944 at the age of forty-eight. Rubin was survived by his wife and two young daughters.

**Fred Schmeltz** ran his hardware store in Kansas City into his sixties. His wife, Lizzie, became his bookkeeper. The Schmeltzes died within four months of each other in Los Angeles in mid-1955. He was eighty-eight; she was eighty.

**Charles and Nettie Schneider** still lived in their house at 4409 Kingswell Avenue in 1942, when Charles was seventy-eight and Nettie was seventy-seven. During his years in that house, Charles worked as a gardener, and his sons Carl and Lester, who lived with their parents, were, respectively, an electrician and a mechanic. Lester still lived in the house in 1961.

**Leon Sederholm**, as Leon Holmes, made numerous movies in the late 1920s and 1930s. He joined such other child stars as Jackie Coogan and the *Our Gang* cast in "a coterie of tiny stars of the films" chosen by Sid Grauman to serve on the reception committee of a "Screen Kiddies' Premiere" of the Douglas Fairbanks film, *Argentine Nights*, held at Grauman's Chinese Theater at 10 a.m. on Saturday, December 3, 1927. In the late 1920s, Sederholm continued to live on North Hudson Avenue in Los Angeles with his mother Rose and his brothers, Norvin and Robert. In 1930, the family moved to San Rafael in Marin County. By then, twenty-four-year-old Norvin continued to work as a salesman at the Broadway Department Store in downtown Los Angeles. Robert, nineteen, worked as a bank bookkeeper, and Isabel, eighteen, was a department store saleswoman, perhaps working alongside Norvin at Broadway.

By 1933 the family moved back to Hollywood and lived on Hollywood Boulevard about one and one-half miles west of the old Kingswell Avenue studio. That year, Leon, then nineteen, was riding in a car with sixteen-year-old movie actor Frankie Darro when the car skidded in a Sunday rainstorm and hit a lamp post at the intersection of Hollywood Boulevard and Wilton Place, about one block west of Leon's home. Darro was bruised but Leon, who tried to jump from the vehicle, cut his forehead and was taken to Hollywood Receiving Hospital. Within days, Leon sued Darro and Mascot Productions, which owned the car, in Superior Court for damages of over $27,000, claiming that he suffered a skull fracture, among other things. Later, Leon's family lived on Sunset Boulevard.

**Hazel Bounds Sewell** filed for divorce from Glenn Sewell in the late 1920s, and she and Marjorie, then thirteen, moved in with Walt and Lilly at their Lyric

Avenue home. Within a few years, Hazel started dating William H. D. Cottrell, Jr., a native of South Bend, Indiana. Bill Cottrell had done a little dialogue work on the *Krazy Kat* comic strip and went to work at the Disney studio as a cameraman in 1929. He lived on Prospect Avenue, one block south of the old Kingswell studio, with his English-born parents and his older sister. Cottrell was ten years Hazel's junior, and received degrees in English and Journalism from Occidental College. Hazel and Bill were married in 1938, and Hazel left her job as the supervisor of the ink and paint department at about that time. In her resignation letter, Hazel complained that her salary was withheld while she—who ran her department so well that she had saved the company a lot of money, she said—had been out sick. Walt wrote back that he was "greatly shocked by your unwarranted attitude. However, if I were in your place and felt the way you do about the organization where I worked, I would probably do the same thing."

Cottrell became a story man and sequence director on such classic features as *Snow White and the Seven Dwarfs* and *Pinocchio*, and by the 1950s, he was involved in the development of Disneyland, eventually becoming the first president of WED Enterprises, the predecessor entity to Walt Disney Imagineering. Hazel died in 1975 at almost eighty years of age, and her husband retired from the studio seven years later. Cottrell died in 1995 at the age of eighty-nine, one year after he was named a Disney Legend in the fields of Animation & Imagineering.

**Marjorie Sewell**, along with her mother, Hazel, moved in with her Aunt Lilly and Uncle Walt after Hazel's divorce from Glenn Sewell in the late 1920s. Marjorie recalled that Walt was "very good to me . . . . He used to wait for me to come home. He'd be at the top of the stairs when I came in at night, especially if I was late. I was going to boarding school at the time. I'd come in from school on weekends, and he would get annoyed if I had plans for the weekend. 'Why'd you bother to come home? Why'd you bother, if you're not going to be here?' I tell you, I broke the ice for his girls." After the end of her first marriage, Marjorie married Marvin Davis, a 20th Century Fox art director (*Gentlemen Prefer Blondes*, starring Marilyn Monroe), who was hired in 1953 by WED Enterprises, where he helped design Disneyland. He later worked on the development of Walt Disney World, and in the interim was an Emmy-award winning art director for *Walt Disney's Wonderful World of Color* (he worked on such other Disney TV projects as *The Mickey Mouse Club* and *Zorro*) and the art director for such Disney features as *Babes in Toyland* and *Big Red*. Davis retired from the Walt Disney Studios in 1975. In 1994, he was named a Disney legend in the fields of Film & Imagineering. Marvin Davis died in 1998 at the age of eighty-seven. Marjorie Sewell Davis died a year later, at the age of eighty-three.

**Nadine Simpson**, after leaving Laugh-O-gram, worked as a cashier for Metro Pictures and later returned to the Film Exchange, where she was a stenographer. She married Baron Missakian in 1927. By 1930, they lived at 922 E. 30th Street along with Simpson's mother, Josephine, a registered nurse. After Walt's death, Nadine visited Roy and Ubbe at the Walt Disney Studios, and brought with her Walt's Laugh-O-gram director's megaphone, which she had held on to for about forty-five years. In 1970, possibly during the same visit to Burbank, she provided an interview to the Walt Disney Archives about her time at Laugh-O-gram Films. In her later years, Nadine worked as a bookkeeper at Annunciation Church. Nadine died in Kansas City in 1988 at the age of ninety-two.

**Paul Smith** continued to live at the Mount Holly Hotel after leaving the Disney studio for the Mintz venture overseen by George Winkler. Smith later worked for Harman-Ising and Warner Brothers, and then spent twenty years with *Woody Woodpecker* animator Walter Lantz. The veteran animator and cartoon director died in 1980 at the age of seventy-four, and was survived by a wife and two sons.

**Carl Stalling**, while still in Kansas City, provided Walt with the score for 1928's *Steamboat Willie*, the first Mickey Mouse cartoon released to theaters. Stalling later worked at the Disney studio and provided the scores for *The Skeleton Dance* and several other early Mickey Mouse and Silly Symphonies cartoons. He also wrote Mickey's theme song, "Minnie's Yoo Hoo!" By the early 1930s, he left the Disney Studio and worked at other studios, including Ubbe Iwwerks' studio, where Stalling worked on the *Flip the Frog* series. In 1936, Stalling joined Warner Brothers, where he achieved great acclaim as the composer of the *Looney Tunes* series. He retired from Warners in 1958, and died in Hollywood in 1972 at the age of eighty-four.

**Lorey L. Tague** turned to enamel work after leaving Laugh-O-gram. By 1930, he left Kansas City and settled in Herrington, Kansas, where he worked as a radio electronics technician. He died in Manhattan, Kansas, in 1984 at the age of eighty-eight. His wife Frances died in 1981. Two decades before his death, as Lowry Tague, he published his memoirs, in which he said that his work at Laugh-O-gram was "fun, excitement, adventure[,]" although the memoirs do not otherwise dwell on his work for Walt.

**Phil Tannura** later worked as a photographer and went on to become a veteran movie (*The Babe Ruth Story*) and TV (*The Jack Benny Program*) cinematographer. After his retirement he lived in Beverly Hills. Tannura died in 1973 at the age of seventy-six.

**Mary Tebb** left the Disney Studios in June 1929, and went back to school. Within a year, she lived with her parents in Aberdeen, Washington. Her father Thomas was from England and managed a lumber agency. Her mother Jane was from Wisconsin. Mary had a younger brother and sister. By the 1940s, Mary returned to Los Angeles and became an artist for Leon Schlesinger Productions, which by then produced Bugs Bunny and Daffy Duck cartoons. In 1945, she returned to the Disney Studios as an inker and painter, working on such classic animated Disney shorts as 1954's *The Social Lion,* and becoming head of the studio's color model department. She retired from the studio in 1973, when she was seventy-two years old. She died on Bainbridge Island, Washington, twenty years later.

**Ruthie Tompson** stopped acting after appearing in the Alice Comedies, although her sister, Dorothy W. Tompson, acted in movies as Dorothy Wade. (Dorothy "went on to be a starlet . . . and did several pictures," said Ruthie, including *An American in Paris*, the 1951 classic that won the Best Picture Oscar. Dorothy appeared in *Paris* as a ballet dancer). After attending Hollywood High School, Ruthie worked at Dubrock's Riding Academy, where she got reacquainted with polo players Walt and Roy Disney in the mid-1930s. Walt offered her a job as an inker and painter, and in 1935, at the age of twenty-four, she went to work at the Walt Disney Studio on Hyperion, where she worked on Walt's upcoming release, *Snow White and the Seven Dwarfs*. Ruthie received numerous promotions over the years, and in 1952 was one of the first three women admitted to the Hollywood camera union. She remained at the studio for nearly forty years, working on almost all animated features from the 1940s through the mid-1970s. She retired in 1975. The Walt Disney Company named her a Disney Legend in the field of Animation in 2000. As of this writing, Ruthie, one hundred years old, lives at the Motion Picture and Television Country House and Hospital in Woodland Hills, Los Angeles.

**Otto Walliman** went back to being a baker after Laugh-O-gram failed. Otto died in Kansas City in 1935 at the age of fifty-nine. His wife Dorothy died a year later.

**George Winkler** eventually married while in Los Angeles, and settled there. He continued to work as a cartoonist and studio manager, including as manager of Screen Gems after his brother-in-law, Charles Mintz, and sister, Margaret Winkler Mintz, moved to Hollywood in the mid-1930s. Despite being ousted from the Oswald series by the Winkler company, Walt later wrote a letter of recommendation for George Winkler. Winkler left the Screen Gems studio after Charlie's death. He lost his first wife to cancer. Winkler's second wife, Esther, was the daughter of a wealthy marine salvage operator, and after a brief stint as head of inking and painting at the Schlesinger studio, Winkler joined his in-laws' North Hollywood marine salvage company. He died in 1995 at the age of ninety-three.

**Margaret Winkler** retired from her distribution company around 1924, and raised her children, Katherine and William Mintz. In 1989, seventy years after the creation of Felix the Cat, Margaret was visited in her upstate New York nursing home by John Canemaker, a noted animator and animation historian. According to Canemaker, Margaret had been given a Felix toy by her daughter and son-in-law, but by then did not recognize the character, nor the name of Pat Sullivan or even that of her husband, Charlie Mintz, who died almost fifty years earlier. Margaret died on June 21, 1990, at the age of ninety-five.

**Edmund J. Wolf** remained at the Linwood State Bank after investing in Laugh-O-gram, and still worked at a bank in Kansas City as of 1930. He died in Kansas in 1955.

**Lillian Worth** continued to live and act in Los Angeles, where she died in 1981 at the age of seventy-four.

## His Series

Some of the **Newman Laugh-O-Grams** made by Walt during his "home experimenting" in early 1921 still exist.

**Lafflets** made by Walt at Kaycee Studios and Laugh-O-gram Films have not survived.

The seven **Laugh-O-grams Fairy Tales** made at Kaycee Studios and Laugh-O-gram films (as well as *Tommy Tucker's Tooth* and *Alice's Wonderland*) still exist.

**The Alice Comedies** were reissued shortly after the advent of sound. Some of the 1925 titles, which encompassed the last few Virginia Davis shorts, the single Dawn Paris short, and the first several Margie Gay shorts, were reissued by the Raytone company after it added music and sound effects.

Forty of the fifty Alice Comedies produced in California from 1923 to 1927 survive, including: all twelve reels from the first season of Alice, starring

Virginia Davis and produced on Kingswell Avenue; all eighteen reels from season two, all starring Margie Gay except for two starring Virginia Davis and one starring Dawn Paris, all of which were made on Kingswell Avenue; and nine of the twenty-six season three reels, all produced on Hyperion Avenue. Six of Margie Gay's sixteen Hyperion reels survive, and three of Lois Hardwick's ten reels survive.

**Oswald the Lucky Rabbit** was produced by Charlie Mintz after he took the series over from Walt in early 1928. Universal later gave the series to Walter Lantz, the creator of Woody Woodpecker, who produced the series into the 1930s. Oswald remained a comic book character into the 1960s. Thirteen of the twenty-six Oswalds produced by Walt Disney at the Hyperion Avenue studio survive.

In 2006, seventy-eight years after Walt lost the series to Mintz, the Walt Disney Studios regained the rights to Oswald. That year, an ESPN sports network commentator named Al Michaels wanted to follow his on-screen partner, John Madden, to NBC to host *Sunday Night Football*. By then, ESPN was owned by The Walt Disney Company, and NBC was owned by NBC Universal. ESPN offered to let Michaels out of his contract if NBC agreed to several non-cash terms, including the broadcast rights to the Ryder Cup golf tournament, highlight footage from the 2008 Summer Olympics, a weekly promotion for ESPN during *Sunday Night Football*—and the rights to Oswald the Lucky Rabbit.

NBC agreed, and on February 9, 2006, it was announced that Oswald was returning to the Walt Disney Studios. The deal was reportedly instigated by Disney chief executive officer Robert Iger, of whom Walt's daughter said, "When Bob was named CEO [of The Walt Disney Company], he told me he wanted to bring Oswald back to Disney, and I appreciate that he is a man of his word." Iger explained that "[a]s the forerunner to Mickey Mouse and an important part of Walt Disney's creative legacy, the fun and mischievous Oswald is back where he belongs."

# Acknowledgments

*Walt before Mickey* would not have been possible without the guidance, advice, and friendship of Michael Barrier, Didier Ghez, Howard Green, Diane Disney Miller, and Dave Smith. You each have my unending thanks and gratitude.

I am also appreciative to the following individuals who generously provided me with their time, insights, and encouragement: Ted Cauger; Steven Clark; Robert S. Disney, III; David Gerstein; Katherine and Richard Greene; Jim Hardwick; Fred Harman, III; Marie Cowles Heinbaugh; Sonny Jaben; J. B. Kaufman; David Lesjak; Kay Malins; Leonard Maltin; the late Virginia Davis McGhee; Tim O'Day; Don Peri; Sandra Pesmen; Ruthie Tompson; and Dr. Tim Tytle.

I thank my research assistant, Boo Susanin, and my friends at The Walt Disney Company Archives, The Walt Disney Family Museum, the Motion Picture & Television Reading Room of the Library of Congress, the New York Public Library, the Museum of Modern Art in New York, the Kansas City Public Library, and the National Film Information Service at the Margaret Herrick Library, Fairbanks Center for Motion Picture Study, Academy of Motion Picture Arts and Sciences.

A special thank you goes to Margaret Adamic and her assistant, Max Hof, of Disney Publishing Worldwide. Margaret, thank you for all you did to make possible the inclusion in this book of photographs owned by The Walt Disney Company.

Heartfelt thanks go to Walter Biggins, Shane Gong, Anne Stascavage, and Steve Yates at the University Press of Mississippi, and to copy editor Johnny Lowe.

Finally, my deepest thanks go to my beloved wife Barbara; our adored children, Jack, Annabel, and Boo; and Jeter, the world's best dog. I love you all.

# Notes

## Introduction

xi **During Thanksgiving week** *Walt Disney: An American Original*, Bob Thomas, Disney Editions, New York, 1994 edition, 351–52.

xi **executives visited him** One of "Walt's Boys," Harry Tytle, Airtight Seals Allied Productions, Royal Oak, 1997.

xi **his writers prepared** *Walt Disney: The Triumph of the American Imagination*, Neal Gabler, Alfred A. Knopf, New York, 2006, 627 (citing memorandum from Spec McClure to Tommie Wilck, December 7, 1966, Walt Disney Archives).

xi **a secretary bring** Gabler, 628 (citing interview of Tommie Wilck by Bob Thomas, Walt Disney Archives).

xi **On Monday, November 21** Thomas (1994 ed.), 351–52.

xi **the animation building** "The Death of Walt Disney," Milton Gray, *APAtoons*, May–June 2001.

xi **a new script** Thomas (1994 ed.), 351.

xi **driven to nearby; screened a rough** Gabler, 628 (citing *Walt Disney*, Richard Hubler, unpublished, 838).

xii **admitted to St. Joseph's** "Disney Undergoes Surgery on Lung," *Los Angeles Times*, November 23, 1966, 1.

xii **X-ray (administered prior** "Growing Up Disney," *People*, December 21, 1998, 56.

xii **tumor** "Walt Disney, 65, Dies on Coast; Founded an Empire on a Mouse," the *New York Times*, December 16, 1966, 1.

xii **his left lung** "Disney Gets Clean Bill From Doctors," *Daily Variety*, November 23, 1966, 15.

xii **Surgeons removed part** "Disney Undergoes Surgery . . ."

xii **informed Walt's family** "Growing Up Disney."

xii **tumor was cancerous** *Building A Company: Roy O. Disney And The Creation Of An Entertainment Empire*, Bob Thomas, Hyperion, New York, 1998, Thomas (1998), 295.

xii **smoked since his** Gabler, 626.

xii **six months to** "Growing Up Disney."

## Prologue

3 **"I was 18; "first job was; "started working with** "Mickey Mouse—Inspiration from Mouse in K.C. studio," Lowell Lawrance, *Kansas City Journal-Post*, September 8, 1935.

3 **seventeen years old** Thomas (1994 ed.), 24.

3    **had returned to** *Inside the Dream: The Personal Story of Walt Disney*, Katherine and
      Richard Greene, Disney Editions, New York, 2001, 20.

3    **Friday, October 10** Walt left Marseille, France, on the SS *Canada* on Thursday,
      September 4, 1919, and arrived in New York on Friday, October 10. Ancestry.com,
      *New York Passenger Lists, 1820–1957.*

3    **after working as** The Greenes (2001), 20.

3    **"truly a Missourian** *Walt Disney's Missouri*, Brian Burnes, Robert W. Butler, and Dan
      Viets, Kansas City Star Books, Kansas City, 2002, vii.

3    **from the ages** *The Animated Man: A Life of Walt Disney,* Michael Barrier, University
      of California Press, Berkeley, 2007, 17, 20–21. *The Story of Walt Disney*, Diane Disney
      Miller, as told to Pete Martin, Henry Holt and Company, New York, 1956, 19. The
      material in this book was given to Pete Martin by Walt. See email from Diane
      Disney Miller to T. Susanin, January 19, 2010. In her introduction to an edition
      of this book reissued by Disney Editions in 2005 to commemorate the fiftieth
      anniversary of Disneyland, Mrs. Miller wrote, "I must announce that I did not write
      this book. . . .[T]he book was wholly written by Mr. Martin[.]"

3    **"[W]as I going** "Father Goose," *Time*, December 27, 1954, electronic version.

3    **"decided on art** "Walt Disney's Success Laid to Ability to Think as Child Does,"
      Garrett D. Byrnes, the *Evening Bulletin, Providence*, December 27, 1935, 24.

3    **After being turned** Thomas (1998), 39.

3    **twenty-six** Thomas (1998), 13. Roy was born on June 24, 1893, and was eight and one-
      half years older than Walt.

3    **a Navy veteran** Thomas (1998), 35, 38.

3    **was a clerk** *1919 Kansas City, Missouri City Directory*, Gate City Directory Company,
      Kansas City, 1919, 979.

3    **Bank in downtown** Thomas (1998), 39.

3    **The bank, a; was located towards** Burnes, Butler, and Viets, 14, 73.

3    **"I have two** Miller, 59; Gabler, 44 (citing interview of Walt Disney by Pete Martin,
      Reel 5, 43–44).

3    **Louis A. Pesmen** Pesmen did not have a middle name, but used the middle initial "A"
      because he thought LAP made a nice monogram. Email from Sandra Pesmen to T.
      Susanin, May 16, 2008.

3    **twenty-seven, was born** Draft card of Louis A. Pesmen, Ancestry.com, *World War I
      Draft Registration Cards, 1917–1918.*

3    **came to the United** Email from Sonny Jaben to T. Susanin, April 9, 2008.

3    **His family settled** Draft card of Louis Pesmen.

3    **where he returned; Like his father** Email from Sonny Jaben to T. Susanin, April 9,
      2008.

3    **worked elsewhere in; Pesmen had light** Draft card of Louis Pesmen.

3    **"a man of** Email from Sonny Jaben to T. Susanin, April 9, 2008.

3    **"meticulously groomed** Email from Sandra Pesmen to T. Susanin, April 14, 2008.

4    **married for several** Louis Pesmen and Reba Polansky Application for License to
      Marry, June 3, 1919, Ancestry.com, *Missouri Marriage Records, 1805–2002.*

4    **was a partner; "Pesmen-Rubin Commercial** untitled article by Louis A. Pesmen,
      1971. According to animation scholar Michael Barrier, this article was written in 1971
      "at the invitation of David R. Smith of the Walt Disney Archives[.]" Barrier (2007
      book), 334, note 65. Neal Gabler states that this article was written on August 11, 1971.
      See Gabler, 652.

4    **the only source; Pesmen-Rubin appears** Pesmen writes that the studio was called the Pesmen-Rubin Commercial Art Studio (Pesmen, 1), but that name does not appear in the Kansas City 1919 and 1920 city directories. Disney recalled that he worked for Gray (Lawrance) and his Gray Advertising colleague Ub Iwerks (who then spelled his name Ubbe Iwwerks) wrote that he worked for the "Pessman [*sic*] & Rubin Gray Advertising Agency." Barrier (2007 book) 334, note 68 (citing 1943 Disney employment form completed by Iwerks).

4    **two-story** Gabler, 44 (citing Disney interview by Martin, Reel 5, 43–44).

4    **Gray Building** Gray Advertising Company advertisement, the *Kansas City Star*, October 8, 1922, 13A.

4    **14th and Oak Streets** Gray advertisement, the *Kansas City Star*, October 8, 1922, 13A; Pesmen, 1.

4    **taught evening classes** Pesmen, 1.

4    **twenty-four-year-old Bill; his wife, Edith** Draft card of William Rubin, Ancestry.com, *World War I Draft Registration Cards, 1917–1918*; 1920 federal census, Kansas City, January 6, 1920, Sheet 5A, Ancestry.com, *1920 United States Federal Census*.

4    **lived two blocks** 1919 Kansas City city directory, 1782 (Rubins lived at 2321 E. 28th Street); *1920 Kansas City, Missouri City Directory*, Gate City Directory Company, Kansas City, 1920, 1719 (Pesmens lived at 2511 E. 28th Street).

4    **Reba Pesmen** Louis Pesmen and Reba Polansky Application for License to Marry, June 3, 1919.

4    **was of medium** Draft card of William Rubin

4    **Russian-born insurance solicitor** 1900 federal census, Kansas City, June 5, 1900, Sheet 5, Ancestry.com, *1900 United States Federal Census*.

4    **self-employed commercial artist** Draft card of William Rubin.

4    **such Gray clients** Pesmen, 1–2; interview of Sandra Pesmen by T. Susanin, December 12, 2006.

4    **"quiet, polite young; "[w]henever an artist; Rubin liked the** Pesmen, 1.

4    **"all these corny** Barrier (2007 book), 24 (citing Walt Disney interview by Pete Martin, May or June, 1956).

4    **"good quality" drawings; He and Rubin** Pesmen, 1.

4    **"worked at this; "had to go** Barrier (2007 book), 24 (citing Martin interview of Walt Disney, 1956).

4    **concluded, "He's good** Pesmen, 1.

4    **"thought I was** *The Man Behind the Magic: The Story of Walt Disney*, Katherine and Richard Greene, Viking, New York, 1998 edition, 32.

4    **Rubin offered him** Gabler, 45 (citing Martin interview of Walt Disney, Reel 5, 43–44).

4    **"'That'll do fine** Pesmen, 1.

4    **half that salary** Thomas (1994 ed.), 55.

4    **pay was "magnificent"** Lawrance.

4    **"could have kissed** Gabler, 45 (citing Martin interview of Walt Disney, Reel 5, 45).

4    **"[m]ost of the** Lawrance.

4–5  **consisted of pencilling** Byrnes, 24.

5    **Walt also created** Miller, 60.

5    **"About that time** Lawrance.

5    **Iwwerks, eighteen** *The Hand Behind The Mouse*, Leslie Iwerks, John Kenworthy, Disney Editions, New York, 2001, 2. Iwwerks was born on March 24, 1901.

5    **started at Gray's** Thomas (1994 ed.), 56; Iwerks, 4.

5    **left high school; Ubbe returned to** Iwerks, 2.

5    **According to Ubbe's; third wife of** Iwerks, 2, 4; 1920 federal census, Kansas City,
     January 8, 1920, Sheet 7A.

5    **Eert Ubben Iwwerks** Iwerks, 1–2; 1920 federal census, Kansas City, January 8, 1920,
     Sheet 7A.

5    **left Laura for** Iwwerks, 3.

5    **house on Landis; a studio photographer** 1920 federal census, Kansas City, January 8,
     1920, Sheet 7A; 1920 Kansas City city directory, 1313.

5    **"a fantastic lettering** Pesmen, 2.

5    **paid Ubbe $60** Miller, 61.

5    **Ubbe recalled that** Iwerks, 4.

5    **the ninth grade; alternating between signing** "Art Work of Walt Disney in School
     Here," Dorothy Storck, *Chicago's American*, April 27, 1967, 52.

5    **"rough pencil sketches; "[f]ew of my** Lawrance.

5–6  **Carey Salt Company; "sensitive to constructive; "all right with** Pesmen, 1.

6    **Among Lou Pesmen's** Pesmen, 2.

6    **Newman, twenty-nine** Frank Newman obituary, *Variety*, July 11, 1962, reprinted in
     *Variety Obituaries, Volume 5: 1957–1963*, Garland Publishing, Inc., New York, 1988.

6    **several Kansas City** Burnes, Butler, and Viets, 127; Thomas (1994 ed.), 59.

6    **Newman Theatre, located** Burnes, Butler, and Viets, 127.

6    **"The Dominant Theater** Newman Theatre advertisement, the *Kansas City Star*,
     March 5, 1922, 10D.

6    **opened in June; $400,000 and featured** Burnes, Butler, and Viets, 127, 129.

6    **Pesmen designed the** Pesmen, 2.

6    **a stage proscenium; Above the title** Burnes, Butler, and Viets, 75.

6    **the elephant that; "go ahead with; Walt asked if; "No, just one; Walt's "familiar grin;
     Walt not only; "[n]o apologies were** Pesmen, 2.

6    **November 23, 1919; over two weeks** Newman Theatre advertisement, the *Kansas City
     Star*, November 23, 1919, 21C (this ad states that the film was initially going to play
     for "One Week Only").

6    **"I was asked** "The Hollywood Scene," Lowell E. Redelings, *Hollywood Citizen-News*,
     February 18, 1957. The film was based on the 1902 play, *The Admirable Crichton* by
     J. M. Barrie, the author of *Peter Pan*.

6    **"all I had** Thomas (1994 ed.), 55.

6    **"until early in** Byrnes, 24.

6    **By some accounts** See, for example, Miller, 60.

6    **The Pesmen family** Email from Sandra Pesmen to T. Susanin, December 5, 2006.

7    **"When you go; "But in a** Burnes, Butler, and Viets, 75.

7    **"tricks of the** Miller, 60.

7    **"That's what I** Barrier (2007 book), 24 (citing Martin interview of Walt Disney, 1956).

7    **"To tide me** Lawrance.

7    **Walt contemplated opening** "Ub Iwerks, 1901–1971," David R. Smith, *Funnyworld*,
     Spring 1972, 33.

7    **"feeling well qualified** Lawrance.

7    **he still thought** Smith (1972 article), 33.

7    **"fate was against** "How Silly Symphonies and Mickey Mouse Hit the Up Grade,"
     Florabel Muir, *New York Sunday News*, December 1, 1929, reprinted in *Walt Disney*

*Conversations*, edited by Kathy Merlock Jackson, University Press of Mississippi, Jackson, 2006, 3–4.

7 **census enumerator** 1920 federal census, Kansas City, January 7, 1920, Sheet 5A.

7 **was "out of** Lawrance.

7 **"I've got an** Miller, 61.

7 **"couldn't quite fathom** Barrier (2007 book), 24 (citing Martin interview of Walt Disney, 1956).

7 **"a little commercial** Lawrance.

7 **"sounded like an optical** Barrier (2007 book), 25 (citing Martin interview of Walt Disney, 1956).

7 **"Please send me; "Your father and; "[I]t's my money; His parents forwarded; spent the money** Miller, 62.

8 **The secretary of** 1920 Kansas City city directory, 846.

8 **thirty-year-old** 1900 federal census, Buchanan, Missouri, June 13, 1900, Sheet 19.

8 **Alvin Buell** Draft card of Alvin Buell Carder, Ancestry.com, *World War I Draft Registration Cards, 1917–1918*.

8 **Carder Martin Publishing; Both the National** 1920 Kansas City city directory, 1642, 1782.

8 **Mutual Building, located** 1920 Kansas City city directory, 1636.

8 **Carder's parents** Death certificate of Joseph Carder, February 3, 1937, Missouri State Archives, www.sos.mo.gov, *Missouri Death Certificates, 1910–1957*; 1900 federal census, Buchanan, June 13, 1900, Sheet 19.

8 **lived at 3026 Bellefontaine** 1920 Kansas City city directory, 846.

8 **since 1914** Barrier (2007 book), 17 (citing deed of trust from the Scherrers to the Disneys dated September 4, 1914).

8 **Joe Carder had; wife and six** 1900 federal census, Buchanan, June 13, 1900; 1910 federal census, Kansas City, April 15, 1910, Sheet 4A, Ancestry.com, *1910 United States Federal Census*.

8 **Kansas City in 1907** Death certificate of Joseph Carder (moved to Kansas City in 1907).

8 **sometime after 1910; no longer lived** 1910 federal census, Kansas City, April 15, 1910 (Sheet 4A) (showing the Carders, without Alvin, live on Garfield).

8 **tall, medium-built; his own printing; Carder Menu Services** Draft card of Alvin Buell Carder.

8 **and lived with** 1920 federal census, Kansas City, January 7, 1920, Sheet 5B.

8 **Walt's initial overture; when Walt offered** Gabler, 47 (citing *Autobiography*, Walt Disney, unpublished, 1934); Miller, 62.

8 **complete with toilet** Burnes, Butler, and Viets, 76.

8 **"managed to pick** Lawrance.

8 **marketing and cartooning** *Disney: The First 100 Years*, Dave Smith and Steve Clark, Disney Editions, New York, 1999, 11–12.

8 **called on local** Gabler, 47 (citing *Autobiography*, Walt Disney, unpublished, 1934).

8 **"The firm that; "You should have** "He Gave Us Mickey Mouse," Jack Jamison, *Liberty*, January 14, 1933.

8 **"early project[s] was** Iwwerks, 5.

8 **"school chum** Lawrance.

8 **three houses away** 1910 federal census, Kansas City, April 19, 1910, Sheet 5B.

8 **Walter's had moved; a harness maker** 1900 federal census, Chicago, June 6, 1900, Sheet 7.

9 **the General Secretary** 1919 Kansas City city directory, 1683; 1920 Kansas City city directory, 1724.

9 **German-born wife, Clara; two daughters who** 1920 federal census, Kansas City, January 9, 1920, Sheet 12B.

9 **"was always welcome; "second mother" to** *The Magic Kingdom Walt Disney and the American Way of Life*, Steven Watts, Houghton Mifflin Company, New York, 1997, 14 (citing interview of Walt Pfeiffer by Bob Thomas, April 26, 1973, 11, 21).

9 **"felt so happy** Interview of Diane Disney Miller by Richard Hubler, June 11, 1968, reprinted in *Walt's People: Talking Disney with the Artists who Knew Him, Volume 6*, edited by Didier Ghez, Xlibris Corporation, 2008, 176.

9 **"I had started** "An Oregonian in Disneyland," Roy Wolfe, the *Sunday Oregonian Magazine*, July 8, 1951, 6.

9 **"had stage ambitions; "got up a** Lawrance.

9 **"wowed the kids** Wolfe, 6.

9 **"[Pfeiffer's] father," said; "The Two Walts; local amateur theater** Lawrance.

9 **impersonation of Charlie** Burnes, Butler, and Viets, vii.

9 **"won several prizes** Lawrence.

9 **"got the hook** Wolfe, 6.

9 **Pfeiffers had moved** 1920 federal census, Kansas City, January 9, 1920, Sheet 12B.

9 **Pfeiffer, then forty-nine** 1900 federal census, Chicago, June 6, 1900, Sheet 7.

9 **still the General** 1920 Kansas City city directory, 1724.

9 **used his union; Walt and Ubbe** Smith (1972 article), 33.

9 **which featured the** Smith and Clark, 12.

9 **"The first month** Lawrance.

9 **Railway Exchange Building** Burnes, Butler, and Viets, 76.

9 **7th and Walnut Avenues; eight floors housed** 1920 Kansas City city directory, 570–71.

9 **"help wanted" ad** Kansas City Slide Company advertisements, the *Kansas City Star*, January 29, 1920, 15; January 30, 1920, 23; January 31, 1920, 8.

10 **"I started, actually** Interview of Walt Disney by Fletcher Markle, Canadian Broadcast Corporation, September 25, 1963, reprinted in *Walt Disney Conversations*, 89.

10 **"It was with** "Walt Disney Tells Us What Makes Him Happy," S. J. Woolf, the *New York Times*, July 10, 1938, 18 (electronic version).

10 **"help wanted" ad; "Artist, Cartoon and Wash; The ad ran** Kansas City Slide Company advertisements, the *Kansas City Star*, January 29, 1920, 15; January 30, 1920, 23; January 31, 1920, 8.

10 **the "second month** Lawrance.

10 **Company's president** 1920 Kansas City city directory, 861. The 1922 city directory also states Cauger's title as "president" (*1922 Kansas City, Missouri City Directory*, Gate City Directory Company, Kansas City, 1922, 937), but the 1923 city directory states his title as "manager." *1923 Kansas City, Missouri City Directory*, Gate City Directory Company, Kansas City, 1923, 910.

10 **Arthur Vern** Burnes, Butler, and Viets, 87.

10 **his cartooning needs** Miller, 64.

10 **"[i]n some manner; "nearly floored me** Lawrance.

10 **"I knew I** Woolf, 18.

10    **Walt accepted the** Miller, 64.

10    **Ubbe's granddaughter wrote** Iwwerks, 6.

10    **"turned what there** Lawrance.

10    **"Slides and Animated; 1015–1017 Central** 1919 Kansas City city directory, 1336; 1920 Kansas City city directory, 1362.

10    **forty-one-year-old** Death certificate of Arthur V. Cauger, October 27, 1945, Missouri State Archives, www.sos.mo.gov, *Missouri Death Certificates, 1910–1957.*

10    **twenty employees and** Gabler, 48-49 (citing Martin interview of Walt Disney, Reel 5, 52-53 and Disc 5 CD).

10    **theater exhibitor in** "Kansas City's Own 'Daddy' of Ad Films Is Honored by His Hollywood 'Alumni,'" *Boxoffice*, February 3, 1945, 59.

10–11  **"would get the local; "got so much** Burnes, Butler, and Viets, 88.

11    **In 1910, Cauger** "Kansas City's Own 'Daddy' . . . ," 59; Arthur V. Cauger obituary, *Variety*, November 7, 1945, reprinted in *Variety Obituaries, Volume 3: 1939–1947*, Garland Publishing, Inc., New York, 1988.

11    **opened the Slide** "Kansas City's Own 'Daddy' . . . ," 59.

11    **on Grand Avenue; A few years later** Burnes, Butler, and Viets, 4, 94.

11    **bought a house** 1920 federal census, Kansas City, January 1920, Sheet 10B.

11    **artists drew theater; that were photographed** Burnes, Butler, and Viets, 4.

11    **"Of course," said** Markle, *Walt Disney Conversations*, 89.

11    **The cut-out figures** Interview of Hugh Harman by Michael Barrier, December 3, 1973, 7.

11    **They were pinned; then the joints** "New Tracks in Old Trails," Fred Harman, *True West*, October 1968, 10.

11    **photographed the action; I'd start with** Miller, 67-68.

11    **"the few customers** Gabler, 49 (citing Martin interview of Walt Disney, 1956, Reel 5, 54).

11–12  **"[t]wo months [after** Lawrance.

12    **Ubbe, however, recalled** Barrier (2007 book), 25 (citing Iwerks' 1943 Disney employment form, which states that Iwerks started at the Slide Company in March of 1920).

12    **Walt noted that** Watts, 53 (citing Martin interview of Walt Disney, Reel 5, 54).

12    **its office moved** 1920 Kansas City city directory, 1362.

12    **city's hospital district** Burnes, Butler, and Viets, 14, 94.

12    **"I got a** Gabler, 49 (citing letter from Walt Disney to Mack, May 12, 1920).

12    **clothier, a furniture** Harman, 10.

12    **roof dealer, and** Markle, *Walt Disney Conversations*, 90; Thomas (1994 ed.), 58.

12    **"Our salesman stands; "Don't kill your** Harman, 10.

12    **"a little stiff"** Barrier (2007 book), 27 (citing Martin interview of Walt Disney, 1956).

12    **"[Y]ou had to** Markle, *Walt Disney Conversations*, 90.

12    **hat company ad; Cauger liked the** Miller, 67.

12    **a thrift company** Thomas (1994 ed.), 58.

12    **man running hard** Miller, 70. Miller mistakenly writes that this ad was created for Laugh-O-gram Films, Inc.

12    **"You can't drift** Thomas (1994 ed.), 58.

12    **George E.** George E. Lowerre entry, January 30, 1962, Ancestry.com, *California Death Index, 1940–1997.*

12    **"Jimmy" Lowerre** Thomas (1994 ed.), 58.

12  **a twenty-six-year-old Kansas** 1920 federal census, Kansas City, January 5, 1920, Sheet 4B; 1920 Kansas City city directory, 1474.

12  **Jimmy let Walt** Thomas (1994 ed.), 57.

12  **William McAtee Lyon** Email from Dave Smith to T. Susanin, February 25, 2008. Lyon was apparently named after his uncle, William McAtee, who lived with the Lyons in Chicago when William was a teenager. 1910 federal census, Chicago, April 21, 1910, Sheet 5B.

12  **known as "Red** Interview of Rudolf Ising by J. B. Kaufman, August 14, 1988, reprinted in *Walt's People: Talking Disney with the Artists who Knew Him, Volume 1*, edited by Didier Ghez, Xlibris Corporation, 2005, 21.

12  **signed his letters** Email from Dave Smith to T. Susanin, February 25, 2008.

12  **also twenty-six and** 1900 federal census, Ashton, Illinois, June 5, 1900, Sheet 4; 1910 federal census, Chicago, April 21, 1910, Sheet 5B.

12  **Red's father was** 1900 federal census, Ashton, Illinois, June 5, 1900, Sheet 4.

12  **publishing house proofreader** 1910 federal census, Chicago, April 21, 1910.

12  **Red lived with** 1920 federal census, Moline, Illinois, January 5, 1920, Sheet 5B.

13  **impressed Walt with** Email from Michael Barrier to T. Susanin, March 19, 2008.

13  **Cauger changed the** 1921 Kansas City city directory, 1480. While the company's new name appeared in the 1921 city directory, the exact date of the name change is not known.

13  **nineteen-year-old** Fred Harman, Jr. entry, January 1982, Ancestry.com, *Social Security Death Index*.

13  **Fred C.** 1921 Kansas City city directory, 1311.

13  **Harman, Jr.** 1922 Kansas City city directory, 1292; 1910 federal census, Pagosa Springs, Colorado, April 2, 1910, Sheet 4B.

13  **Show Card and Title** Notes of Fred Harman, Jr. in margin of Film Ad photograph, August 24, 1970 (provided to T. Susanin by Fred Harman, III).

13  **clerk at a** 1920 Kansas City city directory, 1206.

13  **"busty frontier town; "Missouri farm boy** Harman, 7.

13  **"heap of self** Harman, 6.

13  **"Long winter nights** Harman, 8.

13  **"All of us** Hugh Harman, Interview of Hugh Harman and Rudolf Ising by Michael Barrier, October 31, 1976, 103.

13  **"Someone sent a; "The Harmans moved** Harman, 8.

13  **City directories and** 1919 Kansas City city directory, 1186; 1920 Kansas City city directory, 1206 (collection); 1910 federal census, Pagosa Springs, April 2, 1910, Sheet 4B; 1920 federal census, Kansas City, January 1920, Sheet 10B (law office adjustor).

13  **Missouri Home Guard** Harman, 8.

13  **spent summers working; "go up to; was "mighty impressed; "find that warm** Harman, 9–10.

13  **A photograph from** *Walt in Wonderland: The Silent Films of Walt Disney*, Russell Merritt and J. B. Kaufman, Le Giornate del Cinema Muto, Pordenone, Italy, 1993 edition (distributed by The Johns Hopkins University Press, Baltimore), 36.

13  **James Edward** Draft card of James MacLachlan, Ancestry.com, *World War I Draft Registration Cards, 1917–1918*.

13  **the "Art Boss** Notes of Fred Harman, Jr., August 24, 1970.

14   **Marjorie, who was** 1920 federal census, Kansas City, January 2, 1920, Sheet 1A
     (Marjorie was sixteen in 1920); 1920 Kansas City city directory, 1526; 1921 Kansas
     City city directory, 1666; 1922 Kansas City city directory, 1622 (all indicating
     that Marjorie was an artist); *1924 Kansas City, Missouri City Directory*, Gate City
     Directory Company, Kansas City, 1924, 1537 (indicating that Marjorie was a card
     writer).

14   **MacLachlan, a forty-one-year-old "artist" in the; A tall Canada** 1920 federal census,
     Kansas City, January 2, 1920, Sheet 1A.

14   **medium-sized frame; MacLachlan had lost; at least 1917** Draft card of James
     MacLachlan.

14   **"was kind of; "a little too; "felt the boss** Barrier (2007 book), 27 (citing Martin
     interview of Walt Disney, 1956).

14   **raise to forty; Walt did, too** Harman, 10.

14   **The young artists** Burnes, Butler, and Viets, 77.

14   **Walt was supposedly; During this period** Thomas (1994 ed.), 59.

14   **A picture of Walt** Burnes, Butler, and Viets, 104.

14   **"doubled in brass** Barrier (2007 book), 27 (citing Martin interview of Walt Disney,
     1956).

14   **began appearing in** Thomas (1994 ed.), 58.

14   **Once, when an; Walt played a** Miller, 66.

14   **Walt eventually wrote** Gabler, 51 (citing Martin interview of Walt Disney, Reel 5,
     56–57).

14   **"would plan things** Barrier (2007 book), 27 (citing Martin interview of Walt Disney,
     1956).

14   **Like Walt, Ubbe** Smith (1972 article), 33.

14–15 **According to his granddaughter; "Tinkering with the; They spent their** Iwwerks,
     8–9.

15   **Kansas City Public Library; "Now, it was; "I gained my first** Barrier (2007 book),
     26 (citing Martin interview of Walt Disney, 1956; letter from Walt Disney to Irene
     Gentry, August 17, 1937).

15   **"there was only** "The Man of the Land Disney," Don Alpert, *Los Angeles Times*,
     "Calendar" Section, April 30, 1961, 5.

15   **"any book that** Burnes, Butler, and Viets, 125.

15   **Ubbe showed Walt** Gabler, 56 (citing Martin interview of Disney, Reel 5, 56).

15   **Public Library had** Burnes, Butler, and Viets, 77.

15   **book consists of** *Muybridge's Complete Human and Animal Locomotion: All 781 Plates
     from the 1887 "Animal Locomotion" by Eadweard Muybridge, Volumes I—III*, Dover
     Publications, Inc., New York, 1979.

15   **the Muybridge sequences; "get the phases; "the mechanics of** Barrier (2007 book),
     27 (citing Martin interview of Walt Disney, 1956).

15   **"The trick of** Alpert, 5.

15   **He and Ubbe** Gabler, 56 (citing Ub Iwerks, KCKN Disney Transcription Spot, March
     29, 1945).

15   **pressed a former** Gabler, 56 (citing *Walt Disney*, Hubler, 105-06).

15   **"[W]e started doing** Alpert, 5.

15   **"would bend an** Miller, 66.

15    "[n]ew tricks and; "[Film Ad staffers] hadn't Barrier (2007 book), 27 (citing Martin interview of Walt Disney, 1956).

15    "I didn't invent "The Amazing Secret of Walt Disney," Don Eddy, *American Magazine*, August 1955, 113.

16    Walt and Ubbe made Thomas (1998), 42.

16    "We made a; "He just didn't Barrier (2007 book), 29 (citing Martin interview of Walt Disney, 1956).

16    mahogany box camera Miller, 67; Gabler, 51 (citing Martin interview of Walt Disney, Reel 5, 64).

16    "He kept saying Barrier (2007 book), 27 (citing Martin interview of Walt Disney, 1956).

16    "Walt wanted to "Even at 50 Years of Age, A Mouse Named Mickey Hasn't Lost His Appeal," Faye A. Silas, the *Kansas City Times*, November 11, 1978, 8B.

16    "[M]y boss," summed Woolf, 18.

16    In early 1921 Walt worked on his first cartoon for about a month ("One of the Great Geniuses!" Richard H. Syring, *Silver Screen*, November 1932, 48), and it premiered at the Newman Theatre on March 20, 1921. See Newman Theatre advertisement, the *Kansas City Star*, March 20, 1921, 2B. Thus, Walt may have begun experimenting with his own cartoons in early 1921.

16    "[m]y home experimenting Lawrance.

16    using the garage "Up to Date in Kansas City," David R. Smith, *Funnyworld*, Fall 1978, 23.

16    "for income Barrier (2007 book), 28 (citing interview of Roy O. Disney by Richard Hubler, June 18, 1968).

16    Walt told an Syring, 48.

16    small, cement-block structure Burnes, Butler, and Viets, vii.

16    $5 a month Syring, 48.

16    With Roy's help Thomas (1994 ed.), 59.

16    built a stand Miller, 68–69.

16    "set up a cartoon Barrier (2007 book), 28 (citing Hubler interview of Roy Disney, 1968).

16    "He'd be out Interview of Ruth Disney by Dave Smith, November 4, 1974, reprinted in *Walt's People: Talking Disney with the Artists who Knew Him, Volume 8*, edited by Didier Ghez, Xlibris Corporation, 2009, 34.

16    "[T]hat was Walt Gabler, 60 (citing interview of Roy O. Disney by Richard Hubler, June 18, 1968).

16–17    "wanted to experiment Barrier (2007 book), 28 (citing Martin interview of Walt Disney, 1956).

17    own logo, which; It showed a; Tying together his Merritt and Kaufman, 33; Burnes, Butler, and Viets, 106.

17    "I had some ideas; "One was to "Showman of the World Speaks," *Motion Picture Exhibitor*, October 19, 1966, 1.

17    By February 1921; "the first shake-up; Six officers, including; "It's for the; "We want new; "forerunners of a "Shake-Up In Police Jobs," the *Kansas City Star*, February 6, 1921, 1.

17    twenty-three-second cartoon *The Legendary Laugh-O-grams Fairy Tales*, DVD, Inkwell Images, 2006.

17   **"It wasn't really** Miller, 69.
17   **One of Walt's; "There was a; Walt animated a; "[B]y the time; "growing into an** Pesmen, 3.
18   **The crime cartoon; The fashion cartoon; The last of; This sequence is** *The Legendary Laugh-O-grams Fairy Tales.*
18   **a month to finish** Syring, 48.
18   ***Local Happenings*** "Mickey Mouse Meet Your Maker," Sidney Skolsky, *Hearst International-Cosmopolitan*, February 1934, 171.
18   **"led to the** Lawrence.
18   **animated solely by** Merritt and Kaufman, 38.
18–19 **"laughed long and** Pesmen, 3.
19   **"named [his film** Syring, 48.
19   **A surviving collection** *The Legendary Laugh-O-grams Fairy Tales.*
19   **(which may have** Disney scholars Michael Barrier, J. B. Kaufman and Russell Merritt posit that the surviving version of this film could be a sample reel that Walt made to show other potential Kansas City or Los Angeles clients like the *Kansas City Post* or Alexander Pantages, respectively. Email from Michael Barrier to T. Susanin, April 7, 2009 (citing Barrier [2007 book], 28 [which in turn cites Merritt and Kaufman 125]). Former Disney Company archivist Dave Smith felt this collection was made by a film historian or by the Disney film library "just as a fun thing to do and show to Walt." Email from Michael Barrier to T. Susanin, June 27, 2010.
19   **"went down to** Syring, 48.
19   **manager of Newman's** 1921 Kansas City city directory, 1154.
19   **10th and Main** Newman's Royal Theatre advertisement, the *Kansas City Star*, November 23, 1919, 21C.
19   **also managed the** 1919 Kansas City city directory, 1615.
19   **12th and Main** Newman Theatre advertisement, the *Kansas City Star*, November 23, 1919, 21C.
19   **"Of course," wrote** Gabler, 57 (citing letter from Walt Disney to Frank Newman, June 21, 1933).
19   **"The fellow who** Barrier (2007 book), 29 (citing Martin interview of Walt Disney, 1956).
19   **"I like it** Thomas (1994 ed.), 59.
19   **"sold the film** Lawrance.
19   **I was sitting** Eddy, 113.
20   **"Frank Newman, who** "Showman of the World Speaks," 1. According to a 1919 edition of *Newman Theatres Magazine*, Newman owned four theatres in Kansas City: The Newman, The Royal, The Regent, and the Twelfth Street Theatre. *Newman Theatres Magazine*, Volume One, Number Sixteen, 1920, 2.
20   **"[a] digest of** *Newman Theatres Magazine*, Volume One, Number 16, 11.
20   ***News and Views*; Sunday, March 20; "most delightful entertainment; "a Peppy Play;** *Mamma's Affair* ran A "Special Added; In the News** Newman Theatre advertisement, the *Kansas City Star*, March 20, 1921, 2B.
20   **"The film created; he was asked** Lawrance.
20–21 **Feld asked him** Miller, 71.
21   **He also had** Thomas (1994 ed.), 59–60.
21   **When Feld wanted** Miller, 71.

21   **"catch [Newman treasurer** "Showman of the World Speaks," 1. According to the
     *Newman Theatres Magazine,* Eyssell was the Assistant Manager of Newman's
     company. *Newman Theatres Magazine,* Volume One, Number 16, 1920, 10.
21   **"But," said Walt; "[Newman] was paying** Barrier (2007 book), 29 (citing Martin
     interview of Walt Disney, 1956).
21   **"I got to** Miller, 72; Gabler, 58 (citing Martin interview of Disney, Reel 5, 66–67).
21   **recognized and complimented** Miller, 72.
21   **"was pleased with** Silas, 8B.
21   **Film Ad employees** Thomas (1994 ed.), 60.
21   **as potential clients** Miller, 72.
21   **"[t]he big showman** Syring, 48.

# Kaycee Studios

22   **fall of 1921** Gabler 59 (citing *Autobiography,* Walt Disney).
22   **and colleague Fred** "Hugh Harman," Bob Clampett, *Cartoonist Profiles,* June 1983, 22.
22   **"this little shop"** Barrier (2007 book), 29 (citing Martin interview of Walt Disney, 1956).
22   **a streetcar barn** Barrier interview of Harman, December 3, 1973, 4.
22   **30th and Holmes** Hugh Harman, Interview of Hugh Harman and Rudolf Ising by
     Michael Barrier, October 29, 1976, 8.
22   **Harman-Disney Studio** Barrier interview of Harman, December 3, 1973, 4.
22   **spent their evenings** Miller, 72.
22   **Vern Cauger, claimed** Gabler, 59 (citing interview of A. V. Cauger, March 29, 1945).
22   **"secretly"** Harman, 10.
22   **"little studio" above; "shook as if** Barrier interview of Harman, December 3, 1973, 4.
22   **With savings from** Barrier (2007 book), 29 (citing Martin interview of Walt Disney,
     1956).
22   **and Fred purchased** Harman, 10.
22   **for $300** Gabler, 59 (citing *Autobiography,* Walt Disney).
22   **"for long-range money** Harman, 10.
22   **their plan was** Interview of Fred Harman, III, by T. Susanin, December 8, 2006.
22   **"were moonlighting [from** Barrier interview of Harman, December 3, 1973, 2.
22   *The Little Artist Hollywood Cartoons: American Animation in Its Golden Age,* Michael
     Barrier, Oxford University Press, New York, 1999, 36.
22   **"would come [to** Barrier interview of Harman, December 3, 1973, 2.
22–23 **"work all night; "months and months;"know when [Walt; (although when they;**
     **"an artist, a** Barrier interview of Harman, December 3, 1973, 3.
23   **local daily newspaper** Affidavit of Publication of J. Mora Boyle, Director of
     Advertising, the *Kansas City Journal-Post,* November 22, 1923 (stating that the
     *Journal* was the newspaper's morning edition; the *Post* was its evening edition; and
     the *Journal-Post* was the Sunday edition). This affidavit is from Laugh-O-gram Films
     bankruptcy case file, *In the Matter of Laugh O Gram Films, Inc.,* U.S. District Court
     for the Western Division of the Western District of Missouri, Case No. 4457.
23   *Journal Screen Review* Gabler, 56.
23   **shooting a girl** Gabler, 58-59 (citing films shown to him by Kaye Malins of the Walt
     Disney Hometown Museum in Marceline, Missouri. See Gabler, 655).

23  **Kaycee Studios** Kaufman interview of Ising, *Walt's People, Volume 1*, 20.

23  **local nickname for** For example, see "The Throng Fades Away," the *Kansas City Star*, November 3, 1921, 1.

23  **one such effort** *Walt: The Man Behind The Myth*, DVD, The Walt Disney Family Foundation, 2001.

23  **involving Walt's niece; "Walt was experimenting** *Remembering Walt: Favorite Memories of Walt Disney*, Amy Boothe Green and Howard E. Green, Disney Editions, New York, 1999, 6.

23  **This film shows; Another film shows; Other versions of** *Walt: The Man Behind The Myth*.

23  **(Walt's parents had** Barrier, 27–28.

24  **Other footage using; filmed a ten-second** *Walt: The Man Behind The Myth*.

24  **By the time; second-floor office** Barrier interview of Harman, December 3, 1973, 11.

24  **the Standard Phonograph** Standard Phonograph Co. entry, the *Kansas City Telephone Book*, Kansas City, 1921, 147.

24  **(Kaycee may have** Hugh recalled that Walt and Fred were in two studio locations before moving to Troost Avenue, one in the car barn building, and another at 30th and Holmes. Hugh Harman, Barrier interview of Harman and Ising, October 29, 1976, 13. In that same interview, however, Hugh stated that the car barn was at 30th and Holmes. Barrier interview of Harman and Ising, October 29, 1976, 8.

24  **"was just bare** Barrier interview of Harman, December 3, 1973, 11.

24  **In a variation** Gabler, 58 (citing Hometown Museum films).

24  **five or so other** Interview of Ted Cauger by T. Susanin, January 5, 2007.

24  **used Model T** Harman, 10.

24  **"very hard, traveling** Harman, 11.

24  **"had a lot of; Roy felt that** Barrier (2007 book), 31 (citing Hubler interview of Roy O. Disney, 1968).

24  **Cauger's son confirms** Interview of Ted Cauger by T. Susanin, January 5, 2007.

24  **Walt and Fred failed; "Our rent was** Harman, 11.

24–25  **Before they lost; In** *Mill*, **drawings; The man Walt** Hugh Harman and Rudy Ising, Barrier interview of Harman and Ising, October 29, 1976, 2–3. Hugh believed that *The Old Mill* was filmed about a year after Kaycee Studio disbanded, but Rudy Ising remembered that the film was made while Kaycee was still in existence. Hugh's recollection of driving Fred and Walt's Ford to Atherton seems to corroborate Rudy's account.

25  **Pathé News, the; Pathé agreed to; "We could clean** Harman, 10.

25  **The convention began** "Honor Guests At Station," the *Kansas City Star*, October 28, 1921, 1; "Gen. Jacques, First Guest," the *Kansas City Star*, October 29, 1921, 1.

25  **"[t]housands of persons** "Hail The Guests!" the *Kansas City Star*, October 30, 1921, 1.

25  **Walt and Fred had** Harman, 11.

25  **"stop [the camera** Thomas (1994 ed.), 63.

25  **on Sunday afternoon; "fifty contesting and visiting** "Fliers In The Air Today," the *Kansas City Star* , October 30, 1921, 8A.

25  **"crawled through the; On Sunday they; Walt and Fred; "with puttees and bill; "convinced Walt that; As a result; "took several hundred** Harman, 11.

25  **"Fred sat in** Miller, 77–78.

25  **"safely back in** Harman, 11.

25   **The flying circus** "A Condensed Program Of Legion Week," the *Kansas City Star*, October 30, 1921, 1.

26   **"to those who** "Flame Alight!" the *Kansas City Star*, November 1, 1921, 1.

26   **A few hours** "Parade To Thousands," the *Kansas City Star*, November 1, 1921, 1.

26   **The father of** Thomas (1994 ed.), 63.

26   **Walt and Fred** Miller, 78.

26   **probably to Chicago** Kaufman interview of Ising, *Walt's People, Volume 1*, 27.

26   **"turned out to be** Harman, 11.

26   **"whirling brightness which** Miller, 78.

26   **"Our hopes for** Harman, 11.

26   **The convention ended** "The Throng Fades Away," 1.

26   **Hugh Harman suggested** Barrier interview of Harman, December 3, 1973, 9. See also Hugh Harman, Barrier interview of Harman and Ising, October 29, 1976, 7.

26   **"Walt had great** Hugh Harman, Barrier interview of Harman and Ising, October 29, 1976, 7.

26   **"Fred told [Walt** Barrier interview of Harman, December 3, 1973, 9.

26   **"had no malice** Barrier interview of Harman, December 3, 1973, 11.

26   **Fred, however, stated** Harman, 11.

26   **Fred then focused** 1922 Kansas City city directory, 1292.

26   **continued to film** Kaufman interview of Ising, *Walt's People, Volume 1*, 25.

26   **the project consumed; "[f]or six months** Lawrance.

27   **with Red Lyon; "Pathé News, for** Kaufman interview of Ising, *Walt's People, Volume 1*, 25.

27   **When a studio; He was asked; If Pathé did** Miller, 76-77.

27   **placed an advertisement** Kaycee Studios "Education" advertisement, the *Kansas City Star*, February 5, 1922, 3B.

27   **solution was to; "motion picture cartooning; the "Education" section; "CARTOONISTS. Art Students** Kaycee Studios advertisement, the *Kansas City Star*, February 5, 1922, 3B.

27   **more traditional ad; On Wednesday, March 8** Kaycee Studios advertisement, the *Kansas City Times*, March 8, 1922, 12. (Kaycee is mistakenly referred to as K.C. in this ad).

27   **the morning edition** For example, see above the banner on the *Kansas City Times*, January 29, 1917, 1, where the *Times* is described as "The Morning Kansas City Star."

27   **CARTOONIST wanted for** Kaycee advertisement, the *Kansas City Times*, March 8, 1922, 12. It is possible that the newspaper misspelled Disney's and the studio's names because Disney or a colleague phoned the ad in to the paper. See, for example, "How to Phone Your Want Ad," the *Kansas City Times*, December 3, 1921, 10.

27   **eighteen-year-old; Rudolph Carl** 1910 federal census, Kansas City, April 15, 1910, Sheet 1B; Rudolf Ising entry, July 13, 1992, Ancestry.com, *Social Security Death Index* and *California Death Index, 1940–1997*.

27   **Kansas City native** Silas, 8B.

27   **one of many; widowed father** 1910 federal census, Kansas City, April 15, 1910, Sheet 1B.

27   **German-born** 1910 federal census, Kansas City, April 15, 1910, Sheet 1B; death certificate of Henry A. Ising, September 16, 1936, Missouri State Archives, www.sos.mo.gov, *Missouri Death Certificates, 1910-1957*.

27  **street laborer; United States in 1890** 1910 federal census, Kansas City, April 15, 1910, Sheet 1B.

27  **"I came from** Rudy Ising, Barrier interview of Harman and Ising, October 31, 1976, 105.

27  **Rudy's father, Henry** 1910 federal census, Kansas City, April 15, 1910, Sheet 1B.

27  **After trying ranching** Rudy Ising, Barrier interview of Harman and Ising, October 31, 1976, 104.

27  **By the time** Rudy Ising, Barrier interview of Harman and Ising, October 31, 1976, 100; see also 1919 Kansas City city directory, 1286; 1920 Kansas City city directory, 1312.

27–28  **"Largest Exclusive Wholesale; "live men that** E. H. Roberts Portrait Company advertisement, the *Kansas City Star*, December 19, 1921, 7B.

28  **was a printer** 1919 Kansas City city directory, 1286.

28  **he was promoted** 1920 Kansas City city directory, 1312.

28  **one of his older** 1910 federal census, Kansas City, April 15, 1910, Sheet 1B; 1920 federal census, Kansas City, January 24, 1920, Sheet 10A; 1920 Kansas City city directory, 1312.

28  **"I had signed** Rudy Ising, Barrier interview of Harman and Ising, October 31, 1976, 100. Landon refers to the Landon School of Illustrating and Cartooning.

28  **"read an ad; "no pay, for** Kaufman interview of Ising, *Walt's People, Volume 1*, 22–23.

28  **"I was intrigued** Silas, 8B.

28  **"wanted to learn** Kaufman interview of Ising, *Walt's People, Volume 1*, 23.

28  **At some point** 1923 Kansas City city directory, 1699 (the first entry for the new restaurant appears in the 1923 city directory, so it must not have been open by the time the 1922 city directory was printed).

28  **by the time** Kaufman interview of Ising, *Walt's People, Volume 1*, 22–23 ("[It was] before Laugh-O-grams . . . . He [ ] called [his studio] the Kay-Cee Studio then. . . . [T]his was up above a restaurant[.]"); Kansas City 1923 city directory, 1699.

28  **owned by** 1923 Kansas City city directory, 1699.

28  **"a very nice** Barrier interview of Harman, December 3, 1973, 11.

28  **Peiser, forty-three, was** Death certificate of Rudolph Peiser, June 19, 1927, Missouri State Archives, www.sos.mo.gov, *Missouri Death Certificates, 1910–1957*.

28  **hailed from Independence** 1910 federal census, Independence, Missouri, April 1910, Sheet 11A.

28  **Kansas City in 1914** Death certificate of Rudolph Peiser (moved to Kansas City in 1914).

28  **By 1922, Peiser** 1922 Kansas City city directory, 1814.

28  **the Old Dutch Inn** 1922 Kansas City city directory, 572.

28  **three buildings away** 1922 Kansas City city directory, 1814.

28  **the Elsmere Hotel** 1922 Kansas City city directory, 1814. The Elsmere was located at 1105 Linwood Boulevard. 1922 Kansas City city directory, 1116; 1923 Kansas City city directory, 1073.

28  **Fred Harman also** 1922 Kansas City city directory, 1292.

28  **Rudy did not** Kaufman interview of Ising, *Walt's People, Volume 1*, 23.

28  **"[t]he only guys** Kaufman interview of Ising, *Walt's People, Volume 1*, 20-21.

28  **Walt told a** "Now Mickey Mouse Enters Art's Temple," Douglas W. Churchill, the *New York Times*, June 3, 1934, 12.

28  **also said elsewhere** Thomas (1994 ed.), 61.

28    **"I put an ad** Barrier (2007 book), 29 (citing Martin interview of Walt Disney, 1956).

28    **"I can't pay** Miller, 72.

28–29  **"two partitioned offices** Kaufman interview of Ising, *Walt's People, Volume 1*, 23.

29    **"weren't even plywood** Rudy Ising, Barrier interview of Harman and Ising, October 29, 1976, 15.

29    **"you went up** Rudy Ising, Barrier interview of Harman and Ising, October 29, 1976, 4.

29    **"was about 50** Rudy Ising, Barrier interview of Harman and Ising, October 29, 1976, 15.

29    **inker and painter** Interview of Rudolf Ising by Michael Barrier, June 2, 1971, 1.

29    **"would go to; he found Red** Kaufman interview of Ising, *Walt's People, Volume 1*, 21.

29    **"was there long** Kaufman interview of Ising, *Walt's People, Volume 1*, 25.

29    **"three or four months; "mostly it was** Kaufman interview of Ising, *Walt's People, Volume 1*, 21.

29    **"had to do** Kaufman interview of Ising, *Walt's People, Volume 1*, 23.

29    **"kind of was; According to Rudy; "If there were** Kaufman interview of Ising, *Walt's People, Volume 1*, 28–29.

29    **"I was in** Barrier interview of Harman, December 3, 1973, 2.

29    **"imbued with the** Hugh Harman, Barrier interview of Harman and Ising, October 31, 1976, 104.

29    **"quite a large; "tiny, really tiny** Hugh Harman, Barrier interview of Harman and Ising, October 29, 1976, 15.

29    **"Walt didn't know** Kaufman interview of Ising, *Walt's People, Volume 1*, 23.

29    **That was before** Kaufman interview of Ising, *Walt's People, Volume 1*, 25.

30    **three-hundred-foot shorts that** Smith (1978 article), 23.

30    **"joke reel about** Kaufman interview of Ising, *Walt's People, Volume 1*, 37.

30    **"They were more; He and Walt; "to have horse** Kaufman interview of Ising, *Walt's People, Volume 1*, 21

30    **"that when the; "when the short; was a photograph** Kaufman interview of Ising, *Walt's People, Volume 1*, 27–28.

30    **completed in the** If Walt began working on *Little Red Riding Hood* in November of 1921, the six-month period in which he animated it (see Lawrance) would have ended around April of 1922.

30    **six-minute, seventeen-second; In the Kaycee** *The Legendary Laugh-O-grams Fairy Tales.*

31    **Walt promoted Rudy** Kaufman interview of Ising, *Walt's People, Volume 1*, 25, 36.

31    **"did the lab; felt he was** Rudy Ising, Barrier interview of Harman and Ising, October 29, 1976, 45.

31    **"ever animated on; "There was a; "remember[cd] that scene; "got a feeling** Kaufman interview of Ising, *Walt's People, Volume 1*, 25, 36.

31    **was probably completed** Laugh-O-gram Films, Inc., Articles of Association, May 18, 1922 Articles of Association, Article IV.

31    **appear as two; "modernized version of; a prologue for; The plot centers** *The Legendary Laugh-O-grams Fairy Tales.*

32    **"wrote a couple** Kaufman interview of Ising, *Walt's People, Volume 1*, 22.

32    **Walt's parents had** Email from Dave Smith to T. Susanin, July 23, 2010.

32    **a rooming house; He had fallen** Kaufman interview of Ising, *Walt's People, Volume 1*, 22.

32   **He also had** Kaufman interview of Ising, *Walt's People, Volume 1*, 24.

32   **an often-repeated** See, for example, Barrier interview of Ising, June 2, 1971, 5–6.

32   **When the process** Kaufman interview of Ising, *Walt's People, Volume 1*, 23.

32   **at Peiser's** Rudy Ising, Barrier interview of Harman and Ising, October 29, 1976, 4.

32   **"No, I don't; "Well, I'll be; After the man; The process server; "No, he hasn't; "just as a friend; Walt Pfeiffer and Walt** Kaufman interview of Ising, *Walt's People, Volume 1*, 23–24.

32   **"saved up about** Kaufman interview of Ising, *Walt's People, Volume 1*, 22.

32   **Walt concluded that** Churchill, 12.

32   **United Film Ad Service** 1922 Kansas City city directory, 2165.

# Laugh-O-gram Films, Inc.

34   **leave Film Ad** Smith (1978 article), 23.

34   **"[d]uring the next** "Showman Of The World Speaks, " 1.

34   **named Laugh-O-gram Films** Articles of Association, Article I.

34   **"Some time after** Syring, 48.

34   **"When I finished** Byrnes, 24.

34   **"[w]e managed to** Lawrance.

34   **"local merchants" whom** Barrier interview of Harman, December 3, 1973, 11.

34–35   **The corporate documents; Walt pooled $7,752; Most of that amount; Walt's biggest assets; the two fairy tales; Walt chose to; He valued the; (which he listed; The additional $2,052** Articles of Association, Article III.

35   **"got these people** Barrier interview of Ising, June 2, 1971, 2.

35   **seventy shares of** Articles of Association, Article IV.

35   **who turned twenty-nine** 1900 federal census, Ashton, Illinois, June 5, 1900, Sheet 4.

35   **left that venture** Kaufman interview of Ising, *Walt's People, Volume 1*, 25.

35   **out-of-the-home photographer** 1920 federal census, Moline, Illinois, January 5, 1920, Sheet 5B.

35   **boast to Walt** Barrier interview of Harman, December 3, 1973, 9.

35   **as its "cinematographer** 1922 Kansas City city directory, 1579.

35   **"Technical Engineer** Smith (1978 article), 24.

35   **Red held thirty** Articles of Association, Article IV.

35   **lived two blocks** Dr. Cowles lived at 1524 Grand Avenue by 1910 and until about 1920. 1910 federal census, Kansas City, April 15, 1910, Sheet 8A; 1920 Kansas City directory, 926.

35   **William Fletcher Hammond, fifty** 1900 federal census, Flora, Kansas, June 11, 1900, Sheet 6; William Fletcher Hammond entry, October 9, 1950, Ancestry.com, *California Death Index, 1940-1997*.

35   **widowed** 1910 federal census, Flora, Kansas, April 1, 1910, Sheet 2A; 1930 federal census, Webb City, Missouri, April 4, 1930, Sheet 4B, Ancestry.com, *1930 United States Federal Census*.

35   **druggist** 1895 state census, Flora, Kansas, March 1, 1895, Ancestry.com, *Kansas State Census Collection, 1855-1925*; 1900 federal census, Flora, Kansas, June 11, 1900, Sheet 6; 1910 federal census, Flora, Kansas, April 1, 1910, Sheet 2A.

35   **from Kansas** 1895 state census, Flora Kansas, March 1, 1895.

35 **few years before 1910** 1905 state census, Flora, Kansas, March 1, 1905, Ancestry. com, *Kansas State Census Collection, 1855–1925* (Maggie Hammond is still alive); 1910 federal census, Flora, Kansas, April 1, 1910, Sheet 2A (William Hammond is a widower).

35 **have been thirty-five** 1905 state census, Flora, Kansas, March 1, 1905 (Maggie is 30 years old).

35 **Initially, William remained; work in "retail** 1910 federal census, Flora, Kansas, April 1, 1910, Sheet 2A.

35 **then twenty-four** 1900 federal census, Flora, Kansas, January 11, 1900 (stating that Esther was born in October 1893).

35 **was married there** Leslie B. Mace and Esther I. Hammond Application for License to Marry, July 18, 1916, Ancestry.com, *Missouri Marriage Records, 1805–2002.*

35 **a few years later** 1921 Kansas City directory, 1301 (William lives in Kansas City); 1920 Kansas City directory, 1196 (Fletcher lives in Kansas City).

35 **By 1921, the** 1921 Kansas City directory, 1301.

35 **two younger brothers** 1875 state census, Parker, Kansas, March 1, 1875, Page 10, Ancestry.com, *Kansas State Census Collection, 1855–1925.*

35 **two Kansas City; One, eventually called Hammond; The other, Hammond** 1920 Kansas City directory, 1196; 1922 Kansas City directory, 1282.

35–36 **At various times** 1921 Kansas City directory, 1300.

36 **railroad contractors in** 1910 federal census, Springfield City, Missouri, April 25, 1910; 1920 federal census, Kansas City, January 7, 1920, Sheet 7B (Lycurgus Hammond); 1920 federal census, Kansas City, January 8, 1920, Sheet 6A (John R. Hammond).

36 **as a bookkeeper** 1922 Kansas City directory, 1282.

36 **forty shares of** Articles of Association, Article IV.

36 **was about twenty or twenty-one** Death certificate of Fletcher Hammond, August 18, 1933, Missouri State Archives, www.sos.mo.gov, *Missouri Death Certificates, 1910–1957* (indicating he was born about 1901); 1905 state census, Flora, Kansas, March 1, 1905 (indicating he was born about 1902).

36 **"I suppose it** The Greenes (1998 ed.), 38.

36 **at 2816 Bales; was a clerk** 1922 Kansas City directory, 1282.

36 **ten shares of** Articles of Association, Article IV.

36 **for two years** 1920 Kansas City directory, 1196.

36 **fifty-year-old bank teller** 1920 federal census, Kansas City, January 6 and 7, 1920, Sheet 6B.

36 **employed by the** 1922 Kansas City directory, 2274.

36 **natives of Pennsylvania; fifteen-year-old son** 1920 federal census, Kansas City, January 6 and 7, 1920, Sheet, 6B.

36 **Troost Avenue Bank** 1920 Kansas City directory, 2152; 1921 Kansas City directory, 2355.

36 **Wolf held four** Articles of Association, Article IV.

36 **at $15,36, although; Three hundred shares of stock** Articles of Association, Article III.

36 **other investors included** Email from Dave Smith to T. Susanin, April 2, 2008.

36 **Board of Directors** Articles of Association, Article V.

36 **was incorporated on; signed by Walt; recorded by the Jackson** Articles of Association, I, III–IV. In the Articles, the company's name is listed as "Laugh O Gram

Films, Inc.," without the hyphens and lowercase "g" that subsequently appeared in the typical spelling of "Laugh-O-gram Films, Inc."

36 **issued on May 20** Laugh-O-gram Films, Inc. Articles of Association Certificate, May 20, 1922.

36 **State of Missouri issued** State of Missouri, Certificate of Incorporation, Laugh-O-gram Films, Inc., May 23, 1922.

36 **Suite 218** 1922 Kansas City directory, 1443.

36 **1127 East 31st Street** Smith (1978 article), 24 (photograph of "Red" Lyon's business card).

36 **The McConahy Building was; 31st Street and Forest** 1922 Kansas City directory, 1590.

36–37 **main shopping districts** The Greenes (1998 ed.), 38.

37 **South Central Business** Schedules Of The Bankruptcy Filed By Petitioning Creditors, November 13, 1923, 2 (establishing that Laugh-O-gram was a member of the South Central Business Association).

37 **south of the city's; 10th Ward residential** Burnes, Butler, and Viets, 14, 94.

37 **Suite 206, a photography** 1922 Kansas City directory, 544, 1537.

37 **laundry service and** Smith (1978 article), 24.

37 **Forest Inn Café** Gabler, 71 (citing Martin interview of Disney, Reel 6 and 7, 4).

37 **"Exclusive Agents** L. J. Baer advertisement, the *Kansas City Star*, April 16, 1922, 15B.

37 **thirty-seven, a Kansas City** Death certificate of Lawrence J. Baer, February 6, 1937, Missouri State Archives, www.sos.mo.gov, *Missouri Death Certificates, 1910–1957*.

37 **son of a German** Death certificate of Lawrence J. Baer; 1920 federal census, Kansas City, January 16, 1920, Sheet 13A.

37 **Baer operated L. J. Baer; "Real Estate Managers; Grand Avenue Temple** 1922 Kansas City directory, 753.

37 **"modern 2-story; "[s]uitable [for] doctors** L. J. Baer advertisement, the *Kansas City Star*, April 16, 1922, 15B.

37 **Baer ran another; and then another; "want[ed] druggist, restaurant; "[s]everal fine offices** L. J. Baer advertisements, the *Kansas City Star*, April 26, 1922, 2; April 27, 1922, 22; April 28, 1922, 28; April 30, 15B.

37 **In early May; "gents' furnishings** L. J. Baer advertisement, the *Kansas City Star*, May 4, 1922, 22; May 5, 1922, 32.

37 **May 7 ad; on May 11; "Each room has** L. J. Baer advertisement, the *Kansas City Star,* May 7, 1922, 13B; May 11, 1922, 26.

37 **"will make low** L. J. Baer advertisement, the *Kansas City Star*, May 16, 1922, 20.

37 **"few fine offices** L. J. Baer advertisement, the *Kansas City Star*, May 21, 1922, 13B.

37 **"Four fine light** L. J. Baer advertisement, the *Kansas City Star*, May 28, 1922, 14B.

38 **title was "artist** 1922 Kansas City directory, 1400.

38 **CARTOONISTS—Animators** Laugh-O-gram advertisement, the *Kansas City Star*, May 28, 1922, 4B; Laugh-O-gram advertisement, the *Kansas City Star*, May 29, 1922, 13.

38 **several** "Cartoon history stars KC artists," by Brian Burnes, the *Kansas City Star*, February 22, 1990, 3D.

38 **(Hugh and Rudy; three rooms located** Hugh Harman and Rudy Ising, Barrier interview of Harman and Ising, October 29, 1976, 14.

38 **northwest corner of** Merritt and Kaufman (book), 41; Burnes, Butler, and Viets, 2.

38    **with four windows** Interview of Nadine Missakian by Dave Smith, August 12, 1970, reprinted in *Walt's People: Talking Disney with the Artists who Knew Him, Volume 5*, edited by Didier Ghez, Xlibris Corporation, 2007, 23.

38    **two rooms** Harman and Rudy Ising, Barrier interview of Harman and Ising, October 29, 1976, 14.

38    **across the hall; the south side** Smith interview of Missakian, *Walt's People, Volume 5*, 25–26.

38    **"laboratory and camera** Hugh Harman, Barrier interview of Harman and Ising, October 29, 1976, 14.

38    **the north side** Smith interview of Missakian, *Walt's People, Volume 5*, 25–26.

38    **"a lobby and** Hugh Harman, Barrier interview of Harman and Ising, October 29, 1976, 14.

38    **subdivided with a** Smith interview of Missakian, *Walt's People, Volume 5*, 25.

38    **A bathroom** Burnes, Butler and Viets, 2–3.

38    **twenty-four-year-old** Draft card of Leslie Bryan Mace, Ancestry.com, *World War I Draft Registration Cards, 1917–1918*.

38    **salesman** 1920 federal census, Sweetwater, Texas, February 7, 1920, Sheet 16A.

38    **sales manager** "Laugh-O-Gram Cartoons Announced," *Motion Picture News*, June 17, 1922, 3257. This might be the first time the company's name is spelled with hyphens.

38    **Missouri native** 1920 federal census, Sweetwater, Texas, February 7, 1920, Sheet 16A.

38    **the Vitagraph Company** Draft card of Leslie Bryan Mace.

38    **on Monday, May 29; $84 per month** Assignment of Laugh-O-gram Contract by Leslie B. Mace to Dr. J. V. Cowles, October 16, 1922 (attached to M. L. Cowles' Laugh-O-gram bankruptcy claim filed on July 21, 1924).

38    **married in Kansas City** Mace-Hammond Application for License to Marry, July 18, 1916, *Missouri Marriage Records 1805–2002*.

38    **Esther was twenty-four** 1900 federal census, Flora, Kansas, January 11, 1900 (stating that Esther was born in October 1893).

38    **marriage license application** Mace-Hammond Application for License to Marry, July 18, 1916 (stating that Esther was twenty).

38    **to Sweetwater, Texas** 1920 federal census, Sweetwater, Texas, February 7, 1920, Sheet 16A.

38    **Esther Mace returned; Esther apparently declared** 1921 Kansas City directory, 1664.

38    **other separated women** For example, Josephine Simpson, the mother of Laugh-O-gram employee Nadine Simpson, was similarly listed as a widow even though the man to whom she was married had not died. In 1894, Josie Simpson, a Missouri native, married thirty-year-old Henry Simpson, a Scottish farmer, when she was eighteen. By 1900, the Simpsons lived in Bowling Green, Missouri, and had a six-year-old son, Edward, and a four-year-old daughter, Nadine, the future Laugh-O-gram employee. See *United States Federal Census, 1900*, Ancestry.com, 1900 federal census, Bowling Green, Missouri, June 19, 1900. By 1920, Josie and Henry's marriage fell apart. Nadine, now twenty-four and a bookkeeper with a film company, lived with her mother Josephine, who was working as a nurse in Kansas City. See 1920 federal census, Kansas City, January 23, 1920, Sheet 6B. Edward, now twenty-six and employed by a railroad, lived with his father, Henry, in Harrisonville City, Missouri. Living with Henry and Edward was Henry's second wife, Tenie; Tenie's son, fourteen-year-old Clarence Green; and Henry's and Tenie's

five-year-old son, Eugene. See 1920 federal census, Grand River, Missouri, January 19, 1920, Sheet 9B. Despite the fact that Henry was alive and remarried, Josephine listed herself as a widow in 1920. See 1920 federal census, Kansas City, January 23, 1920, Sheet 6B.

38  **back in Kansas** 1922 Kansas City directory, 1621.

38  **visit Kaycee Studios** Barrier (2007 book), 30 (citing his interview of Hugh Harman, 1973); "The Careers of Hugh Harman and Rudolf Ising," Mike Barrier, *Millimeter*, February 1976, 46 (Hugh Harman first met Walt Disney when Disney animated with Fred Harman).

38  **"came right in** Kaufman interview of Ising, *Walt's People, Volume 1*, 29.

38  **Hugh was eighteen** Hugh Harman entry, November 22, 1982, Ancestry.com, *Social Security Death Index* and *California Death Index* (establishing that Hugh was born on August 31, 1903).

39  **born and raised** 1910 federal census, Pagosa Springs, Colorado, April 2, 1910, Sheet 4B; Hugh Harman, Barrier interview of Harman and Ising, October 31, 1976, 101.

39  **had an interest** Harman, 8.

39  **was eleven years; A short time** Hugh Harman, Barrier interview of Harman and Ising, October 31, 1976, 102, 104.

39  **Hugh did some** Burnes, 3D.

39  **drawings for a** Hugh Harman, Barrier interview of Harman and Ising, October 31, 1976, 103.

39  **"Hugh thought about** Email from Fred Harman, III, to T. Susanin, December 14, 2006.

39  **Hugh joined the; "I'd hoped to** Barrier interview of Harman, December 3, 1973, 8.

39  **"just out of; "despaired of a; from Fred** Barrier interview of Harman, December 3, 1973, 11.

39  **"Fred wasn't with** Hugh Harman, Barrier interview of Harman and Ising, October 31, 1976, 102.

39  **"With that," Hugh** Barrier interview of Harman, December 3, 1973, 11.

39  **"looked rather glamorous** Barrier interview of Harman, December 3, 1973, 12.

39  **"it wasn't hard** Barrier interview of Harman, December 3, 1973, 11.

39  **"had an appointment** Kaufman interview of Ising, *Walt's People, Volume 1*, 29–30.

39  **the salary of** Silas, 8B.

39  **Lorey L. Tague** Kaufman interview of Ising, *Walt's People, Volume 1*, 29.

39  **Lorey, twenty-five** Lorey Tague obituary, *Manhattan Mercury*, December 17, 1984, A2; Lorey Tague entry, December 1984, Ancestry.com, *Social Security Death Index*.

39  **born in Rhode Island; World War I** Tague obituary, *Manhattan Mercury*.

39  **When he saw** *Divine Frequency*, Lowry Tague, Exposition Press, New York, 1962, 83.

39  **married for almost; eighteen-year-old wife** Lorey L. Tague and Frances C. McCune Application for License to Marry, February 19, 1921, Ancestry.com, *Missouri Marriage Records 1805–2002*.

39  **their infant, Pearl** Tague 84.

39  **Harry Tague** 1923 Kansas City directory, 1963.

39  **Maxwell, nineteen, an Arkansan** 1920 federal census, Hico, Arkansas, January 23, 1920, 22B.

39  **"and thought to** "Original Disney cartoon gang remembers Laugh-O-Grams," Michael Harris, the *Burbank Daily Review*, May 25, 1972.

39    **in Hico, Arkansas** 1920 federal census, Hico, Arkansas, January 23, 1920, Sheet 22B.

39–40  **"had done the** Harris.

40    **"Kansas City State** Kaufman interview of Ising, *Walt's People, Volume 1*, 29. Rudy may
        be referring to the Junior College of Kansas City, which prior to 1919 was known as
        the Kansas City Polytechnic Institute and is now comprised of the five Metropolitan
        Community Colleges of Kansas City. See www.mcckc.edu. Click on "Explore MCC"
        on tool bar, then click on "Our History: A Proud Past."

40    **I was going to** Merritt and Kaufman, 44 (citing interview of Carman Maxwell by Milt
        Gray and Michael Barrier, 1977).

40    **$10 per week** Harris.

40    **Twenty-one-year-old** 1910 Kansas City, April 4, 1910; Alex Kurfiss entry, December
        1983, Ancestry.com, *Social Security Death Index*.

40    **commercial artist Alexander** 1921 Kansas City directory, 1541.

40    **from Kansas City** Alex W. Kurfiss obituary, *Sioux City Journal*, December 1983.

40    **son of an architect** 1920 federal census, Kansas City, January 6, 1920, Sheet 3A.

40    **Kansas City Art** Alex W. Kurfiss obituary, *Sioux City Journal*.

40    **draftsman, commercial artist** 1919 Kansas City directory, 1385; 1920 Kansas City
        directory, 1414; 1921 Kansas City directory, 1541.

40    **"a successful commercial artist** Kaufman interview of Ising, *Walt's People, Volume 1*, 35.

40    **A baker named Otto** 1920 Kansas City directory, 2073.

40    **born in Switzerland** Draft card of Otto Walliman, Ancestry.com, *World War I Draft
        Registration Cards, 1917–1918*.

40    **turn of the century** Death certificate of Otto Walliman, June 3, 1935, Missouri State
        Archives, www.sos.mo.gov, *Missouri Death Certificates, 1910–1957*.

40    **Schulze Baking Company** Draft card of Otto Walliman draft card.

40    **He was still** 1922 Kansas City directory, 2193.

40    **At forty-six, he** Draft card of Otto Walliman.

40    **only married animator** See, for example, Gabler, 67.

40    **Otto was married** Death certificate of Otto Walliman.

40    **studio's "Scenario Editor** Burnes, Butler, and Viets, 105.

40    **attended Westport High; school's 1921 yearbook; drawing pays tribute** Burnes,
        Butler and Viets, 133.

41    **"Jack"** Adolph Kloepper obituary, *Atchison Daily Globe*, March 3, 1985.

41    **Kloepper, twenty-five** Draft card of Adolph Kloepper, Ancestry.com, *World War I
        Draft Registration Cards, 1917–1918*.

41    **business manager** Smith (1978 article), 24. See also 1923 Kansas City directory, 1413
        (listing Kloepper as manager of Laugh-O-gram).

41    **was from Lancaster; veteran of World** Kloepper obituary, *Atchison Daily Globe*.

41    **clerk at Ridenour-Baker** Draft card of Adolph Kloepper; 1919 Kansas City directory,
        1372.

41    **at the YMCA** 1919 Kansas City directory, 1372.

41    **"lodger" at a; traveling salesman** 1920 federal census, Kansas City, January 7-9, 1920,
        Sheet 15A; 1920 federal census, Lancaster, Kansas, November 10, 1920, Sheet 3B.

41    **Duplex Printing Machine; 3112 Troost Avenue** 1921 Kansas City directory, 1526.

41    **He married twenty-two-year-old** Adolph H. Kloepper and Martha L. Hudson
        Application for License to Marry, June 27, 1922, Ancestry.com, *Missouri Marriage
        Records, 1805–2002*.

41   **$50 per week** Smith (1978 article), 24.

41   **purchase from Schroer; "General Machine Works; The purchase was** Schroer Brothers Machine Works invoice dated October 15, 1924 (attached as Exhibit A to its Laugh-O-gram bankruptcy claim filed on October 29, 1924). The Schroer Brothers receipt refers to the company as "Laugh O Gram Films," spelling the name the same way it was spelled in the incorporation papers (i.e., without hyphens and with a lower case "g").

41   **ad in the *Motion*; Laugh-O-Gram Cartoons Announced** "Laugh-O-Gram Cartoons Announced," *Motion Picture News*, June 17, 1922,

41   **The following week** Merritt and Kaufman, 41.

41–42   **The transaction came; "Walt decided that** Kaufman interview of Ising, *Walt's People, Volume 1*, 23–24.

42   **Red and Jack** Chas. M. Stebbins Picture Supply Company invoice dated September 1922 (attached to its Laugh-O-gram bankruptcy claim dated November 30, 1923).

42   **"After we incorporated** Kaufman interview of Ising, *Walt's People, Volume 1*, 27, 31.

42   **two more purchases** Schroer Brothers invoice, October 15, 1924.

42   **five purchases, starting; The first four; Together these orders; Laugh-O-gram's fifth July** Schutte Lumber invoice, October 6, 1924.

42   **staff was allowed** Barrier interview of Harman, December 3, 1973, 14.

42   **"a Series of; "All That The** Laugh-O-gram Films advertisement, *Motion Picture News*, July 15, 1922, 291.

42   **"We had made** Kaufman interview of Ising, *Walt's People, Volume 1*, 23–24.

42   **incorporation papers** Articles of Association, Article III.

43   **In the Laugh-O-gram** From a private collection; identified by David Gerstein.

43   **According to Rudy; The first time** Kaufman interview of Ising, *Walt's People, Volume 1*, 47–48.

43   **Hugh believed that; "We had a; "Otto . . . . could paint** Barrier interview of Harman, December 3, 1973, 33.

44   **look for a distributor** "Plan Distribution of Laugh-O-Gram," *Motion Picture News*, August 26, 1922, 1055.

44   **of his return** Leslie quit Laugh-O-gram by mid-October, so if the parade did not take place before he left for New York in mid-August, it must have occurred after he returned to Kansas City in the second half or September and before Leslie quit in mid-October. See Mace assignment to Cowles, October 16, 1922.

44   **participated in a; Walt, Leslie, and** Smith (1978 article), 27.

44   **a car affixed** Merritt and Kaufman, 44.

44   **the Isis Theatre** Isis Theatre advertisement, the *Kansas City Star*, November 23, 1919, 21C.

44   ***Topics—News*** Isis Theatre advertisement, the *Kansas City Star*, July 25, 1922, 15.

44   ***Screen Snapshots*** Isis Theatre advertisement, the *Kansas City Star*, July 26, 1922, 10.

44   ***Home Made Movies*** Isis Theatre advertisement, the *Kansas City Star*, October 9, 1922, 13.

44   **Accompanying him was** "Plan Distribution of Laugh-O-Gram," 1055.

44   **physician** Draft card of John V. Cowles.

44   **Laugh-O-gram Films' Treasurer** "Plan Distribution of Laugh-O-Gram," 1055.

44   **late forties or** Depending on the document, Cowles was forty-five, forty-nine, fifty-one, or fifty-four in 1922. See 1930 federal census, Kansas City, April 4, 1930, Sheet

4A (indicating he was forty-five in 1922); draft card of John V. Cowles, Ancestry. com, *World War I Draft Registration Cards, 1917–1918* (indicating he was forty-nine in 1922); 1900 federal census 1900 federal census, Argentine, Kansas, June 19, 1900, Sheet 10 (indicating he would have been fifty-one in 1922); and 1910 federal census, Kansas City, April 15, 1910, Sheet 8A (indicating he would have been fifty-four in 1922).

44 **was a Kansas** John V. Cowles obituary, the *Kansas City Times,* June 12, 1943, 54.

44 **the Spanish-America war** 1930 federal census, Kansas City, April 4, 1930, Sheet 4A.

44 **Kansas City Homeopathic College** Cowles obituary, the *Kansas City Times.*

44 **Main Street Bank** Smith interview of Missakian, *Walt's People, Volume 5,* 24.

44 **lived at 300** 1922 Kansas City directory, 1003.

44 **of sixteen years** 1910 federal census, Kansas City, April 15, 1910, Sheet 8A.

44 **Minnie Lee** "Disneyland designer dies at 83," the *Burbank Leader,* October 17, 2001, electronic version.

44 **early to mid-thirties** 1920 federal census, Kansas City, January 10, 1920, Sheet 8A (indicating that Minnie Cowles was thirty-three years old in 1922); 1910 federal census, Kansas City, April 15, 1910, Sheet 8A (indicating that she was thirty-five years old in 1922).

44 **his second wife** 1900 federal census, Argentine, Kansas, June 19, 1900, Sheet 10 (indicating that J. V. Cowles, a twenty-nine-year-old physician born in Kansas in 1871 to a father from Indiana and a mother from Kentucky, was in his fourth year of marriage to Fannie, a twenty-five-year-old physician who came to the United States as a teenager in 1889. This census information about Dr. Cowles is corroborated, with the exception of information about age, by the information about him contained in his World War I draft card, the 1910 federal census, and the 1930 federal census).

44 **three young children** 1920 federal census, Kansas City, January 10, 1920, Sheet 8A.

44–45 **Plan Distribution of** "Plan Distribution of Laugh-O-Gram," *Motion Picture News,* August 26, 1922, 1055.

45 **intended to exclude** Articles of Association, Article III.

45 **Alex's printed signature** Burnes, Butler and Viets, 85.

45 **likely Alex** Hugh said that he forgot the artist's name, that it was "Art something-or-other[.]" Later in life, Hugh knew or recalled the Laugh-O-gram artists, including Walt, Rudy, Red, Max, and Otto, except for Alex and Lorey. He was probably thinking of Alex when he referred to "Art."

45 **"could never get** Barrier interview of Harman, December 3, 1973, 50.

45 *Goldie Locks and* *Goldie Locks* must have been completed by early October, 1922, since the cartoon that succeeded it, *Puss in Boots,* was nearly finished by that time. See, for example, Gabler, 68; Smith (1978 article), 25 (both citing Red Lyon's letter to his mother dated October 7, 1922, in which he writes that the fifth cartoon was almost finished).

45 **In *Goldie Locks*** *Goldie Locks* was identified by David Gerstein and Cole Johnson.

45 **"there was never** Kaufman interview of Ising, *Walt's People, Volume 1,* 52.

45 **The logo** Merritt and Kaufman, (book), 38–39.

45–46 **A photograph from; The poster copy** Burnes, Butler, and Viets, 102–03.

46 **which operated out** Schedules Of The Bankruptcy Filed By Petitioning Creditors, November 13, 1923, 2.

46  **Walt and the** Gabler, 66 (citing interview of Walt Pfeiffer by Bob Thomas, April 26, 1973).

46  **Walt became friends** Barrier interview of Ising, June 2, 1971, 39.

46  **Rudy dated at** Smith interview of Missakian, *Walt's People, Volume 5*, 23.

46  **twenty-six-year-old Nadine** 1900 federal census, Bowling Green, Missouri, June 19, 1920, Sheet 6.

46  **the Film Exchange; Nadine arranged to** Kaufman interview of Ising, *Walt's People, Volume 1*, 55–57.

46  **Select Pictures Corporation** 1919 Kansas City directory, 1857.

46  **L. J. Selznick Enterprises** 1920 Kansas City directory, 1902.

46  **Phoenix Film Corporation** 1921 Kansas City directory, 2083.

46  **stenographer at George** 1922 Kansas City directory, 2017.

46  **Densmore Hotel** 1919 Kansas City directory, 1857; 1920 Kansas City directory, 1902; 1921 Kansas City directory, 2083.

46  **apparently after a** Marriage Record of Harry B. Houf and Nadine Simpson, October 4, 1920, Ancestry.com, *Missouri Marriage Records, 1805–2002*.

46  **local car salesman** 1920 federal census, Kansas City, January 9, 1920, Sheet 8B.

46  **her mother** 1922 Kansas City directory, 2017.

46–47  **had worked before; [s]ometimes Nadine would** Kaufman interview of Ising, *Walt's People, Volume 1*, 55–56.

47  **first of eight; The hardware supplies** Franz Wurm Hardware & Paint Company invoice dated January 13, 1924 (attached to its Laugh-O-gram bankruptcy claim dated February 23, 1924).

47  **The company also** Alexander Printing Company invoice, November 1923 (attached to its Laugh-O-gram bankruptcy claim dated November 28, 1923).

47  **two thousand business cards** Inter Collegiate Press Proof of Debt, November 24, 1923 (attached to its Laugh-O-gram bankruptcy claim dated December 14, 1923).

47  **Records from the** *Kansas City Journal* and the *Kansas City Post* invoice, undated (attached to the *Kansas City Journal-Post* Laugh-O-gram bankruptcy claim dated November 24, 1923).

47  **(the morning daily** Affidavit of Publication of J. Mora Boyle, Directory of Advertising, the *Kansas City Journal-Post*, November 22, 1923.

47  **SCENARIO writer for** Laugh-O-gram Films advertisement, the *Kansas City Post*, September 1, 1922, 12.

47  **for a male; stated "Girls wanted** Smith (1978 article), 24.

47–48  **Motion Picture News, Inc.** Motion Picture News, Inc. invoice, undated (attached as Exhibit A to its Laugh-O-gram bankruptcy claim filed February 18, 1924).

48  **the McAlpine Hotel; "bills were amounting** Gabler, 65 (citing Kloepper Transcription of Tape, October 1970).

48  **"spent all the money** Smith interview of Missakian, *Walt's People, Volume 5*, 24.

48  **"nobody was interested** Kaufman interview of Ising, *Walt's People, Volume 1*, 24.

48  **Walt ordered Leslie** Smith (1978 article), 25.

48  **Before Leslie departed** Memorial of Agreement between the Trustee for Laugh-O-gram and Pictorial Club, Inc., January 24, 1924.

48  **"[W]e finally sold** Lawrance.

48  **"sold this [series** Smith interview of Missakian, *Walt's People, Volume 5*, 24.

48  **deal with Pictorial** Statement of Increase of Capital Stock of Laugh-O-gram Films, Inc., dated March 17, 1923 and executed June 2, 1923, 1.

48    **Pictorial agreed to; The contract called** Trustee-Pictorial Memorial of Agreement, January 24, 1924.

48    **"always full of; "We used to** Harris.

48    **"completely enthused with** Silas, 8B.

48    **"used to sit** Kaufman interview of Ising, *Walt's People, Volume 1*, 36.

48    **"we'd start drawing** Kaufman interview of Ising, *Walt's People, Volume 1*, 37.

48    **"easy to invent; main references** Barrier interview of Harman, December 3, 1973, 14.

48    **"We started an art; "Walt thought that** Kaufman interview of Ising, *Walt's People, Volume 1*, 55.

49    **"We were all under; "We sure had** Harris.

49    **"happy spirit that** Gabler, 67 (citing letter from Jack Kloepper to Dave Smith, October 27, 1970).

49    **Walt Pfeiffer said** Gabler, 67 (citing Thomas interview of Pfeiffer, 1973).

49    **In one, taken** Smith (1978 article), 25; Harris.

49    **[F]or publicity shots** Kaufman interview of Ising, *Walt's People, Volume 1*, 26.

49    **"I remember [that** Harris.

49    **"to Union Station** Kaufman interview of Ising, *Walt's People, Volume 1*, 26.

49    **Swope Park, one** Smith (1978 article), 25.

49    **called Buzzard's Roost** Burnes, Butler, and Viets, 105.

49    **"Hugh Harman and** Barrier (2007 book), 34 (citing letter from Carman Maxwell to Bob Thomas, August 20, 1973).

49    **Swope Park photograph; The same group** Smith (1978 article), 28–29.

49    **Film clips survive** *Walt: The Man Behind The Myth.*

50    **"the king. He** Kaufman interview of Ising, *Walt's People, Volume 1*, 36.

50    **The action in** *The Legendary Laugh-O-grams Fairy Tales.*

50    **"It will take** Gabler, 68; Smith (1978 article), 25 (both citing letter from Red Lyon to his mother, October 7, 1922).

50–51  **"I am going** Gabler, 68.

51    **"Walt and I** Kaufman interview of Ising, *Walt's People, Volume 1*, 25.

51    **a "real challenge** Harris.

51    **"turning out some** Gabler, 68 (citing letter from Red Lyon to his mother, October 16, 1922).

51    **"company is worse** The Greenes (1998 ed.), 40; Smith (1978 article) 25 (both citing letter from Red Lyon to his mother, October 16, 1922).

51    **Leslie Mace quit; On October 16** Mace assignment to Cowles, October 16, 1922.

51    **amount of $511.84; Dr. Cowles, in turn** M. L. Cowles Proof of Debt dated July 3, 1924 (attached to her Laugh-O-gram bankruptcy claim dated July 21, 1924).

51    **Dr. Cowles later transferred** Mace assignment to Cowles, October 16, 1922.

51    **"by Doctor's side** Interview of Marie Cowles Heinbaugh by T. Susanin, May 30, 2008.

51–52  **"Recording The Baby's; "regular business of; "'Red Lyon,' cinematographer; "crank[] furiously for; "such momentous occasions; "projector service; "In the future; "properly convinced; "[G]ad," the article; "say the fateful** "Recording The Baby's Life In Films," the *Kansas City Star*, October 29, 1922, 3D.

52    **"[H]e had an; "[I]n fact he** Kaufman interview of Ising, *Walt's People, Volume 1*, 23.

52    **"Walt always wanted** Barrier interview of Ising, June 2, 1971, 7.

52    **"wore puttees like** Barrier interview of Ising, June 2, 1971, 45–46.

52    **Suite 206 of** 1922 Kansas City directory, 554, 1537.

52   **to Suite 210** 1923 Kansas City directory, 616, 1454

52   **Photographers Lydia E. Morris** 1921 Kansas City directory, 1572; 1922 Kansas City directory, 1537.

52   **portrait photographers** Silas, 8B.

52   **twenty-eight-year-old** Draft card of Siroon Missakian, Ancestry.com, *World War I Draft Registration Cards, 1917–1918.*

52   **"Baron"** Baron Missakian obituary, the *Kansas City Times*, July 8, 1964.

52   **of Armenian descent; States in 1914** 1920 federal census, Providence, Rhode Island, January 16, 1920, Sheet 19B.

52   **City the year** "Photographer's Table a Gift to College," Virginia Stollings, undated newspaper article, *The Baron Missakian Collection*, Department of Special Collections, Miller Nichols Library, University of Missouri—Kansas City. This article probably appeared in 1976, since Missakian's wife is listed as eighty years old in the article, and she was reported to be ninety-two years old when she died twelve years later in 1988. Nadine Missakian obituary, the *Kansas City Times*, December 14, 1988, E6.

52   **apprentice to the** Baron Missakian obituary, the *Kansas City Times*.

52   **boys' choir in** Baron Missakian obituary, the *Kansas City Times*; Stollings.

52   **quit performing once** Stollings.

52   **World War I; sang for Liberty** Baron Missakian obituary, the *Kansas City Times*.

52–53   **between 1917 and** Draft card of Siroon Missakian draft card; 1920 federal census, Providence, Rhode Island, January 16, 1920, Sheet 19B; "More About Some of the Speakers You Will See and Hear at Chicago," Charles Abel, *The Professional Photographer*, August 5, 1937, 60.

53   **"because he wanted** Stollings.

53   **lion statue in** Box #5, *The Baron Missakian Collection*.

53   **interior portrait of; In that photograph** Burnes, Butler, and Viets, ii.

53   **from Alexander Printing** Alexander Printing invoice, November 1923.

53   **eleven deliveries of** Franz Wurm invoice, January 13, 1924.

53   **two hundred sheets of cels** E. I. du Pont de Nemours & Company invoice dated November 30, 1923 (attached to its Laugh-O-gram bankruptcy claim dated December 18, 1923).

53   **Kansas City Paper** Kansas City Paper House invoice dated October 1923 and Proof of Claim dated November 22, 1923 (attached to its Laugh-O-gram bankruptcy claim dated November 22, 1923).

53   **on Saturday, November 4; "perform work, labor** Creditor's Petition of Ubbe Iwwerks, October 4, 1923.

53   **By 1922, when** 1922 Kansas City directory, 1401.

53   **Ubbe was hesitant; "Had it not been; "The news of** Iwwerks, 15–16.

53   **"was really a** Kaufman interview of Ising, *Walt's People, Volume 1*, 29.

54   **On November 11** Proof of Claim of Nadine Simpson, October 2, 1924 (attached to her Laugh-O-gram bankruptcy claim dated October 4, 1924).

54   **"[s]tenographer-bookkeeper; "very nice," and; "Walt's drawing board; "Mr. Kloepper [who** Smith interview of Missakian, *Walt's People, Volume 5*, 25.

54   **On November 19** Proof of Debt of Aletha Reynolds, February 25, 1924 (attached to her Laugh-O-gram bankruptcy claim dated February 26, 1924).

54   **twenty-year-old Aletha** 1920 federal census, Kansas City, January 1920, Sheet 7B.

54  **$12 per week** Burnes, Butler, and Viets, 116.

54  **Aletha was raised** 1910 federal census, Kansas City, April 18, 1910, Sheet 5A.

54  **lived with her** 1922 Kansas City directory, 1892; 1920 federal census, Kansas City, January 1920, Sheet 7B.

54  **still in school** 1921 Kansas City directory, 1951.

54  **"general artwork** Reynolds Proof of Debt, February 25, 1924.

54  **reel called *Jack*** Memorandum of Agreement between Laugh-O-gram Films, Inc., Trustee Joseph M. Jones and Pictorial Clubs, Inc., of New York, January 24, 1924, 2, 5.

54  **apparently included** *Jack, the Giant Killer* was identified by David Gerstein. The synopsis comes from Gerstein's copy of a review published in *The Educational Screen*, Volume III, Number 3, March 1924, pages 118, 124.

54  **The story begins** *Legendary Laugh-O-grams Fairy Tales.*

54  **A final gag** From a private collection; identified by David Gerstein.

54  **some familiar Laugh-O-gram** *The Legendary Laugh-O-grams Fairy Tales.*

55  **Dr. Cowles lent** M. L. Cowles, Proof of Debt, July 3, 1924.

55  **Walt executed a; Walt signed the; Dr. Cowles endorsed** Note from Laugh-O-gram to John Cowles dated November 30, 1922 (attached to M. L. Cowles' Laugh-O-gram bankruptcy claim dated July 21, 1924).

55  **"down to the last** Harris.

55  **Thomas B. McCrum, forty-six** 1930 federal census, Kansas City, April 12, 1930, Sheet 21A.

55  **dentist with the** 1922 Kansas City directory, 1594.

55–56  **asked Walt to produce; Dr. McCrum offered to; [O]ne night the** Miller, 79–80.

56  **Rudy went with; "talked to the** Kaufman interview of Ising, *Walt's People, Volume 1*, 30–31.

56  **Benton faculty members** Smith (1978 article), 30.

56  **The story focused** *The Legendary Laugh-O-grams Fairy Tales.*

56  **"quite a few** Kaufman interview of Ising, *Walt's People, Volume 1*, 30.

56  **Walt ultimately selected; even though "[t]here** Smith (1978 article), 30.

56  **For a few weeks** Merritt and Kaufman, 47.

56  **shot the still** Kaufman interview of Ising, *Walt's People, Volume 1*, 55.

56  **another Benton alumnus** Lawrance.

56  **filmed the live-action** Burnes, Butler, and Viets, 107.

56  **Because classes were; "[e]verything went smoothly** Smith (1978 article), 30.

56  **I don't recall** Merritt and Kaufman, 47.

56  **educational film with** *The Legendary Laugh-O-grams Fairy Tales.*

57  **"two men; "gave me a** Smith (1978 article), 30.

57  **made about $50** Gabler, 69 (citing Martin interview of Walt Disney, 1956).

57  **On Thursday, January 4; A hearing was** Summons of the Justice of the Peace, Kaw Township, Jackson County, *E. M. McConahy v. Laugh-O-Gram Films*, January 4, 1923.

57  **Walt stopped paying** Laugh-O-gram Statement of Account for Walter J. Pfeiffer, June 30, 1923 (attached to Pfeiffer's Laugh-O-gram bankruptcy claim dated March 17, 1924).

57  **By the middle** Proof of Debt of Lorey Tague dated December 12, 1923 (attached to his Laugh-O-gram bankruptcy claim dated December 24, 1923).

57  **Bills that Walt** Franz Wurm invoice, January 13, 1924; du Pont invoice, November 30, 1923; Exhibitors Trade Review Company invoice, January 1, 1923, (attached to its Laugh-O-gram bankruptcy claim dated February 18, 1924).

57   **On Friday, January 26** File cover, *E. M. McConahy v. Laugh-O-gram Films* (attached to M. L. Cowles' Laugh-O-gram bankruptcy claim dated July 21, 1924).

57   **does not appear** McConahy is not listed individually in the 1920 through 1924 Kansas City directories.

57   **Mrs. M. F. Wood** Burnes, Butler, and Viets, 2–3.

58   **Mrs. Paul G. Brauer** 1922 Kansas City directory, 616.

58   **Walt turned to; "special instance** Proof of Debt of M. L. Cowles dated July 3, 1924 (attached to M. L. Cowles' Laugh-O-gram bankruptcy claim dated July 21, 1924).

58   **"The Doctor" and** Interview of Marie Cowles Heinbaugh by T. Susanin, May 29, 2008.

58   **Rudy never remembered** Barrier interview of Ising, June 2, 1971, 4.

58   **"Walt live[] with** Green and Green, 6.

58   **(He also lived in** Burnes, Butler, and Viets, 85; 1923 Kansas City directory, 1028.

58   **"showed more tenacity** Miller, 76.

58   **"Things were really; "We didn't ever** Harris.

58   **One day, when** Smith (1978 article), 26.

58   **When [Walt's] restaurant** Miller, 80.

59   **probably the blackest** Burnes, Butler, and Viets, 109.

59   **managed the restaurant** Barrier interview of Harman, December 3, 1973, 19.

59   **"a very nice** Smith interview of Missakian, *Walt's People, Volume 5*, 26.

59   **"I said, 'Why** Silas, 8B.

59   **"the boys; "down there at** Smith interview of Missakian, *Walt's People, Volume 5*, 26.

59   **"was the world's** Barrier interview of Harman, December 3, 1973, 19.

59   **This is [at]** Smith interview of Missakian, *Walt's People, Volume 5*, 23–24.

59   **"drive and ambition** Gabler, 68 (citing Missakian notes).

59   **"always a very; "never heard him** "She Liked Disney as Her Boss," Rosalind K. Young, the *Kansas City Times*, December 20, 1966, 5A.

59   **"met Baron through; "They were both; "Baron used to** Stollings.

59   **Roy's girlfriend, Edna** "I Live with a Genius," Mrs. Walt Disney as told to Isabella Taves, *McCall's*, February 1953, 104.

60   **Edna was born; She grew up** Introduction to interview of Edna Disney by Richard Hubler dated June 11, 1968, *Walt's People, Volume 6*, 161.

60   **3025 Agnes Street; Edna lived with; Edna was a; Edward was a** 1921 Kansas City city directory, 1189; 1922 Kansas City directory, 1176; 1923 Kansas City city directory, 1127.

60   **Edna and Roy** Introduction to Hubler interview of Edna Disney, *Walt's People, Volume 6*, 161; Thomas (1998), 333.

60   **Mitch used to** Smith interview of Ruth Disney, *Walt's People, Volume 8*, 27.

60   **"My brother brought** Introduction to Hubler interview of Edna Disney, *Walt's People, Volume 6*, 161.

60   **"going together; "stopped at the; "wanted a quarter; "a very cute; "Roy was always** Hubler interview of Edna Disney, *Walt's People, Volume 6*, 162.

60   **going to marry** Introduction to Hubler interview of Edna Disney, *Walt's People, Volume 6*, 161.

60   **condition in hospitals** Introduction to Hubler interview of Edna Disney, *Walt's People, Volume 6*, 161; Thomas (1998), 40–41; Miller, 84–85.

60   **"Walt used to** Green and Green, 8.

60   **"Kid, I have; Walt later said** Miller, 79.

60   **"soon after making** Byrnes, 24.

60 "**Immediately after the** Lawrance.

60–61 "**worthless,**" "**[t]hen Dr. Cowles** Smith interview of Missakian, *Walt's People, Volume 5*, 24.

61 **paid a $13.50 phone** Kansas City Telephone Company cashier's stub dated February 27, 1923 (attached to M. L. Cowles' Laugh-O-gram bankruptcy claim dated July 21, 1924).

61 **John Fredrick** John Fredrick Schmeltz entry, August 7, 1955, Ancestry.com, *California Death Index, 1940–1997*; 1923 Kansas City directory, 1833 (J. Fred)

61 **Schmeltz, fifty-five; Kansan and the; his wife Lizzie** 1900 federal census, Kansas City, June 7, 1900, Sheet 13B.

61 **By 1919 he; 2410 East 15th Street** 1919 Kansas City directory, 1809.

61 "**appealed to [Schmeltz** Analysis Of Fact And Application To Law filed by Petitioner Fred Schmeltz, undated, 1.

61 **check to Briggs; number of loans; invest almost $2,500** Schmeltz's Analysis Of Fact And Application To Law, 2.

61 "**unwilling**" **to advance** Schmaltz's Analysis Of Fact And Application To Law, 1.

61 **On February 13** Schmeltz's Analysis Of Fact And Application To Law, 2.

61 **The $506.76 mortgage** Chattel Mortgage from Laugh-O-gram to Fred Schmeltz dated February 13, 1923 (attached as Exhibit B to Certification of Referee to Judge dated January 9, 1926).

61 **The accompanying note** from Laugh-O-gram to Fred Schmeltz (attached as Exhibit C to Referee Certification dated January 9, 1926).

61 **Walt approved this** Referee Certification dated January 9, 1926, 1.

61 **Walt stopped drawing** Byrnes, 24.

61 "**animated cartoons and; as February 10** Gabler, 70 (citing letter from Paul Cromelin to Laugh-O-gram, February 10, 1923; letter from Laugh-O-gram to Paul Cromelin, March 28, 1923).

61 **Universal and Commercial** Gabler, 70 (citing letter from H. A. Boushey to Jack Kloepper, April 4, 1923; letter from Commercial Traders Cinema Corporation to Laugh-O-gram, May 12, 1923).

61 **reworking of some** Merritt and Kaufman, 46.

62 "**editorial work in** Reynolds Proof of Debt, February 25, 1924.

62 **including** *Golf in* Smith (1978 article), 31.

62 *Descha's Tryst With* Merritt and Kaufman, 126.

62 "**a cat and** Barrier interview of Ising, June 2, 1971, 3.

62 **sometimes using matchstick** Kaufman interview of Ising, *Walt's People, Volume 1*, 37.

62 "**Ub[be] was in; [Ubbe] went in;** "**a character with** Kaufman interview of Ising, *Walt's People, Volume 1*, 37–38.

62 "**You will note;** "**[W]ithin a very** Smith (1978 article), 31.

62 **While Universal and** Gabler, 70 (citing letter from H. A. Boushey to Jack Kloepper, April 4, 1923; letter from Commercial Traders Cinema Corporation to Laugh-O-gram, May 12, 1923).

63 "**waived by the; The purpose of; At the meeting; The proposal to** Statement of Increase of Capital Stock, 1.

63 **As a result** Statement of Increase of Capital Stock, 2.

63 **The resulting** "**Statement; Elsewhere, the Statement** of Increase of Capital Stock, 1.

63 "**crack the market** Gable, 70 (citing Martin interview of Disney, Disc 5, CD).

63    **Four-year-old Virginia** Merritt and Kaufman, 49.

63    **Mr. and Mrs. Thomas** Burnes, Butler, and Viets, 113.

63    **traveling furniture salesman** Interview of Virginia Davis McGhee by John Province, 1992, *Hogan's Alley*, www.cagle.com/hogan/interviews/davis/home.asp.

63    **"would be gone** Province interview of McGhee, *Hogan's Alley*.

63    **[M]y mother took** Interview of Virginia Davis McGhee by Russell Merritt and J. B. Kaufman, June 5, 1991, reprinted in *Walt's People: Talking Disney with the Artists who Knew Him, Volume 4*, edited by Didier Ghez, Xlibris Corporation, 2007, 17–18.

63    **Georgia Brown Dramatic** The Georgia Brown Dramatic School was located at 2312 Troost Avenue, across the street from Peiser's Old Dutch Inn delicatessen. 1922 Kansas City directory, 572.

63    **"long curls and** Province interview of McGhee, *Hogan's Alley*.

63    **"they used to** Merritt and Kaufman interview of McGhee, *Walt's People, Volume 4*, 18.

63    **Warneker's Bread** Province interview of McGhee, *Hogan's Alley*.

63–64 **"just a picture; Walt saw one; "called my mother** Merritt and Kaufman interview of McGhee, *Walt's People, Volume 4*, 18.

64    **"already had this** Burnes, Butler, and Viets, 113.

64    **"explained to my** Province interview of McGhee, *Hogan's Alley*.

64    **"liked [Walt] a** Burnes, Butler, and Viets, 112.

64    **"'Sure, we'll shoot** Merritt and Kaufman interview of McGhee, *Walt's People, Volume 4*, 18.

64    **offered Virginia five; signed on Thursday** Merritt and Kaufman 49.

64    **Aletha Reynolds quit; still owed $200** Reynolds Proof of Debt, February 25, 1924.

64    **"still unable to** Intervening Petition of Fred Schmeltz, August 15, 1924, 1.

64    **Schmeltz wrote Laugh-O-gram** Schmeltz Intervening Petition, 2; Schmeltz's Analysis Of Fact And Application To Law, 2.

64    **Walt owed Max** Laugh-O-gram Statement of Account for Carman Maxwell, June 30, 1923 (attached as Exhibit C to his Laugh-O-gram bankruptcy claim dated February 25, 1924).

64    **(both Hugh and** Hugh Harman and Rudy Ising, Barrier interview of Harman and Ising, October 29, 1976, 1.

64    **at the Davises'** Province interview of McGhee, *Hogan's Alley*.

64    **In the studio scenes** *Walt Disney Treasures—Disney Rarities, Celebrated Shorts: 1920s-1960s*, DVD, Buena Vista Home Entertainment, 2005.

64    **who wore her** Merritt and Kaufman interview of McGhee, *Walt's People, Volume 4*, 17.

64    **The bedroom scene** Merritt and Kaufman interview of McGhee, *Walt's People, Volume 4*, 18.

64    **Davis's sister, Louise** Interview of Virginia Davis McGhee by T. Susanin, March 7, 2009.

64    **"'do this' and** Merritt and Kaufman interview of McGhee, *Walt's People, Volume 4*, 19.

64    **"We built the** Rudy Ising, Barrier interview of Harman and Ising, October 29, 1976, 61.

64    **"were nothing more** Barrier interview of Harman, December 3, 1973, 15.

64    **"telling stories. All** Burnes, Butler, and Viets, 113.

64–65 **Walt dispensed with; "'Look frightened,' or** Province interview of McGhee, *Hogan's Alley*.

65    **"Did you ever; "That's where I** Burnes, Butler, and Viets, 112.

65    **Walt could no** Smith interview of Missakian, *Walt's People, Volume 5*, 26.

65 **"landlady kicked him** Young, 5A.

65 **sofa chair** Miller, 78.

65 **his drawing room** Smith interview of Missakian, *Walt's People, Volume 5*, 26.

65 **"slept there for** Gabler, 71 (citing Kloepper tape).

65 **Once a week** Miller, 78.

65 **located west of** Burnes, Butler, and Viets, 14, 94.

65 **He would walk** Miller, 78.

65 **Stalling, a local** "An Interview With Carl Stalling," Mike Barrier, *Funnyworld*, Spring 1971, 21.

65 **a "Song-O-Reel** Merritt and Kaufman, 48.

65 **Stalling, thirty-one, was** Introduction to interview of Carl Stalling by Michael Barrier and Milton Gray, June 4, 1969, November 25, 1969, *Walt's People, Volume 6*, 15.

65 **Kansas City Conservatory; the early 1920s** Burnes, Butler and Viets, 130.

65 **31st Street and Troost** Isis Theatre advertisement, The *Kansas City Star*, November 23, 1919, 21C.

65 **"played the organ** Barrier (1971 article), 21.

65 **The organ that; its newspaper ads** Isis Theatre advertisement, the *Kansas City Star*, February 26, 1922, 8D.

65 **"Walt was making** Barrier (1971 article), 21.

65 **"because a couple** Rudy Ising, Barrier interview of Harman and Ising, October 31, 1976, 101.

65 **"[t]he words would** Barrier (1971 article), 21.

65 **a 1922 song by** Smith (1978 article), 33.

65 **the Coon-Sanders** Burnes, Butler, and Viets, 107.

65 **agreement with *Martha's*** Smith (1978 article), 33.

66 **[A] quaint old-fashioned** Iwerks, 22.

66 **According to Rudy** Kaufman interview of Ising, *Walt's People, Volume 1*, 38.

66 **"Walt was going** Barrier interview of Ising, June 2, 1971, 4.

66 **"shot it; "built the sets** Kaufman interview of Ising, *Walt's People, Volume 1*, 38.

66 **Nadine remembered** Smith interview of Missakian, *Walt's People, Volume 5*, 23.

66 **A photograph from** Merritt and Kaufman, 48.

66 **"Kansas City locations; "old Watts Mill** Smith (1978 article), 33.

66 **"where Walt and** Smith interview of Missakian, *Walt's People, Volume 5*, 23.

66 **from the on-location** Burnes, Butler, and Viets, 108.

66 **shot by Baron** *The Baron Missakian Collection*.

66 **(Red Lyon has** See, for example, Merritt and Kaufman, 48.

66 **This photograph shows** Burnes, Butler, and Viets, 108.

66 **owed $75.50, quit** Simpson Proof of Claim, October 2, 1924.

66 **"[u]ntil they folded** Smith interview of Missakian, *Walt's People, Volume 5*, 25.

66 **Ubbe, who had** Creditor's Petition of Ubbe Iwwerks, October 4, 1923, 2.

66 **returned to his** Iwerks, 24.

66 **"quit . . . just for** Barrier interview of Harman, December 3, 1973, 25.

66 **On Monday, May 14** Letter from Walt Disney to M. J. Winkler, May 14, 1923, reprinted in Smith (1978 article), 33.

66 **New York distributor** Merritt and Kaufman, 50.

67 **We have just** Letter from Walt Disney to M. J. Winkler, May 14, 1923, reprinted in Smith (1978 article), 33.

67  **Walt sent the** Gabler, 70 (citing letter from Walt Disney to Paul Cromelin, May 16, 1923).

67  **"I shall, indeed; "If it is** Letter from M. J. Winkler to Mr. Walter E. Disney, May 16, 1923.

67  **Walt owed Rudy** Laugh-O-gram Statement of Account for Rudolph C. Ising, undated but prepared on or after June 23, 1923 (attached to his Laugh-O-gram bankruptcy claim dated February 25, 1924).

67  **owed Clifford J. Collingsworth** Schmeltz's Intervening Petition, 2.

67  **Great Northern Loan** 1922 Kansas City directory, 977.

67  **Liberty Home Builders** 1923 Kansas City directory, 947.

67–68  **Collingsworth locked Walt; Collingsworth went so; Walt turned to; "officers and officials[]; Walt acquiesced, but; on Saturday, May 19** Schmeltz's Intervening Petition, 2–3.

68  **(With the funds** Ising Statement of Account; Maxwell Statement of Account.

68  **Collingsworth then allowed** Schmeltz's Intervening Petition, 3-4.

68  **"to move during** Harris.

68  **Schmeltz also guaranteed; lease that Walt; On Thursday, May 24** Schmeltz's Intervening Petition, 3–4.

68  **Rudy helped move** Rudy Ising, Barrier interview of Harman and Ising, October 29, 1976, 5.

68  **On Tuesday, May 29; It also authorized; The meeting was** Schmeltz's Intervening Petition, 4; Brief of Trustee On Claim Of Fred Schmeltz, undated, 3.

68  **By Saturday, June 2; "Walter E. Disney; executed a note; The loan, plus; The mortgage gave; Walt also, and** Chattel Mortgage from Laugh-O-gram to Fred Schmeltz dated June 2, 1923 (attached as Exhibit D to Certification of Referee to Judge dated January 9, 1926); Note from Laugh-O-gram to Fred Schmeltz (attached as Exhibit C to Referee Certification); Assignment of Contract, June 1923 (attached as Exhibit E to Referee Certification).

68–69  **"with the authority; secure the re-payment** Assignment of Contract, June 1923 (attached as Exhibit E to Referee Certification).

69  **Hamilton, who lived** 1923 Kansas City directory, 1221.

69  **"service and [a]** Balthasher Electric Company Proof of Debt dated December 21, 1923 (attached to its Laugh-O-gram bankruptcy claim dated December 22, 1923).

69  **Hugh recalled that** Clampett, 22.

69  **"taking turns with** Barrier (2007 book), 36 (citing letter from Max Maxwell to Bob Thomas, August 20, 1973).

69  **On June 18, Walt; Owing to the** Notes from the [Disney] Archives' folders of Disney correspondence with the Winklers and Charles Mintz," Michael Barrier, June 1994 ("Winkler correspondence" folder) (citing letter to Margaret Winkler, June 18, 1923); Burnes, Butler, and Viets, 111.

69  **Walt sent a** Gabler, 71 (citing letter from Walt Disney to Paul Cromelin, June 18, 1923).

69  **Margaret wrote back** June 1994 Barrier Notes ("Winkler correspondence" folder) (citing letter from M. J. Winkler to Walt Disney, June 25, 1923).

69  **on Friday, June 22** Statement of Increase of Capital Stock, 2.

69  **"I tried my** Lawrance.

70  **"is completed yet** June 1994 Barrier Notes ("Winkler Film Corp." file) (citing letter from M. J. Winkler to Walt Disney, June 23, 1923).

70  **[during] those lean** Smith (1978 article), 33.
70  **The day after** Ising Statement of Account.
70  **"[o]ur ideas were** Silas, 8B.
70  **Walt owed Rudy** Statement of Account.
70  **on Saturday, June 30; Laugh-O-gram still owed** Maxwell Statement of Account; Pfeiffer Statement of Account.
70  **Max received his** Maxwell Statement of Account.
70  **In one of his; decided to approach; "I spent a** Lawrance.
70  **"almost all by** Clampett, 22.
70  **"spoiled" him by** Barrier interview of Harman, December 3, 1973, 12–13.
70  **Rudy, however, recalled** Rudy Ising, Barrier interview of Harman and Ising, October 29, 1976, 1–2.
70  **had to reshoot** Rudy Ising, Barrier interview of Harman and Ising, October 29, 1976, 1; Smith (1978 article) 33.
70  **"It nearly killed** Barrier interview of Harman, December 3, 1973, 16.
70  *Alice's Wonderland* **ran** *Walt Disney Treasures—Disney Rarities, Celebrated Shorts: 1920s–1960s,* DVD, Buena Vista Home Video, 2005. As Michael Barrier points out, however, "Specifying the duration of silent films is tricky, since there was no standard speed." Email from Michael Barrier to T. Susanin, June 27, 2010.
72  **By Friday, July 6; he sued the; a Kaw Township; When the constable; "in the absence** Transcript of Judgment, *Adolph H. Kloepper v. Laugh-O-gram,* July 26, 1923.
72  **Schmeltz paid Rudolph** Analysis Of Fact And Application To Law, 2.
72  **"that deal fell; "That seemed to** Lawrance.
72  **"really disconsolate . . . just** Barrier interview of Harman, December 3, 1973, 12.
72  **"I've got to; "felt he shouldn't** Barrier interview of Harman, December 3, 1973, 16.
73  **mail order course** Barrier (2007 book), 35. Rudy showed Michael Barrier a newspaper advertisement and a flier for the Animated Cartoon Studios, which listed Walt as the general manager and Rudy as the education director. Walt and Rudy claimed that customers would make "large earnings" and "remuneration" that would "amaze" them.
73  **"was seriously considering** Barrier (2007 book), 38 (citing letter from Rudy Ising to Michael Barrier, December 20, 1979).
73  **"I finally came** "Showman of the World Speaks," 1.
73  **Walt would have** Thomas (1998), 43.
73  **"Kid I think** Thomas (1994 ed.), 66.
73  **Roy suggested that** Merritt and Kaufman, 50.
73  **who also encouraged** Gabler, 72 (citing Martin interview of Walt Disney, Disc 6, CD); Thomas (1998), 43.
73  **"My only hope** "Showman of the World Speaks," 1.
73  **"finally turned my** Muir, *Walt Disney Conversations,* 4.
73  **"take my chances** "M. Mouse a Local Boy," the *Kansas City Star,* February 13, 1942, 6.
73  **late July 1923** Miller, 81.
73  **spent the two** Byrnes, 24.
73–74  **"antiquated; from the *Martha*** "The Amazing Story of Walt Disney," Jack Alexander, *The Saturday Evening Post,* October 31, 1953, 80.
74  **asked to try** Miller, 80–81.
74  **Walt claimed that** Alexander, 80.

74   **for $10 or; his first customers** Miller, 81.
74   **Dr. and Mrs. Leland Viley** Silas, 8B.
74   **two hundred feet of; other jobs followed** Miller, 81.
74   **"movie fan" for; "This," he recalled** Byrnes, 24.
74   **California and $40** Miller, 81.
74   **On Friday, July 20** Schmeltz's Analysis Of Fact And Application To Law, 2.
74   **for "operating expenses"** Schmeltz Intervening Petition, 4.
74   **At 11:30 a.m. on** *Kloepper v. Laugh-O-gram* Transcript of Judgment.
74   **Schmeltz wrote a** Schmeltz's Analysis Of Fact And Application To Law, 2.
74   **"the studio as** Kaufman interview of Ising, *Walt's People, Volume 1*, 59.
74   **"put in a** Hugh Harman, Barrier interview of Harman and Ising, October 29, 1976, 10.
74   **"went there to** Rudy Ising, Barrier interview of Harman and Ising, October 29, 1976, 10.
74   **"packed all my** "Showman of the World Speaks," 1.
74   **"with that wonderful** "Showman of the World Speaks," 1.
74   **dinner with Edna** Thomas (1998), 43.
74   **Herbert's mother-in-law** Gabler, 73 (citing letter from William Rast to Walt Disney, January 9, 1959; letter from William Rast to Donn Tatum, September 18, 1979).
74   **California Limited train** Miller, 81.
74   **first-class ticket; an upper berth** Miller, 82.
74   **"big day, the** Gabler, 74–75 (citing Martin interview of Disney, Reels 6 and 7, p. 8).
74   **"just free and** The Greenes (1998 ed.), 41.
75   **hot day** Alexander, 80.
75   **August of 1923** Alexander, 80; Byrnes, 24.
75   **told his daughter** Butler and Viets, vii.
75   **"Walt always said** Harris.

# Disney Brothers Studio

79   **"I met [Walt]** Roy Disney, "Unforgettable Walt Disney," *Reader's Digest*, February 1969, 214–15.
79   **"I landed in** Byrnes, 24. See also interview of Walt Disney by Tony Thomas, *Voices for the Hollywood Past*, reprinted in *Walt Disney Conversations*, 62 ("I came to Hollywood[ ] . . . in August, 1923[.]"); Lillian Disney and Taves, 106 ("He landed there [in Hollywood] in August, 1923, a few months before he was twenty two.").
79   **may not have** The Greenes (1998 ed.), 41.
79   **"The pull toward** "The Magic Worlds of Walt Disney," Robert De Roos, *National Geographic*, August 1963, 173.
79   **With 58 motion** "Statistical Facts About Los Angeles," Morris M. Rathburn, *Los Angeles City Directory*, The Los Angeles Directory Company, Los Angeles, 1923, 1, 6.
79   **suffered from tuberculosis** Smith and Clark, 15; interview of Roy Disney by Richard Hubler, June 18, 1968, *Walt's People, Volume 6*, 150–51.
79   **west of the city** *The Disney Studio Story*, Richard Hollis and Brian Sibley, Crown, New York, 1988, 12.
79   **Walt moved in** Miller, 83.
79   **Samuel** Smith interview of Ruth Disney, *Walt's People, Volume 8*, footnote at 51.

79 **"my brother, . . . took** Syring, 48.

79 **Robert lived in; He dabbled in** *Los Angeles City Directory*, The Los Angeles Directory Company, Los Angeles, 1924, 821; "Mr. & Mrs. Disney," *Ladies' Home Journal*, March 1941, 146.

79 **he was sixty-two** The Greenes (1998 ed.), 42.

79 **4406 Kingswell Avenue** 1924 Los Angeles city directory, 821.

79 **his second wife; thirty-year-old Charlotte** 1930 federal census, Los Angeles, April 8, 1930, Sheet 22B, Ancestry.com, *1930 United States Federal Census*. Robert was first married on June 4, 1988, when he was twenty-eight years of age. His first wife, Margaret L. Rogers, died while traveling in Denver, where she caught pneumonia. It appears that, as a widower, Robert was interested in both Charlotte and Charlotte's mother, but it was Charlotte that he married on June 4, 1921, the thirty-third anniversary of his marriage to Margaret. At the time of his second wedding, Robert was fifty-two; Charlotte was twenty-nine. See 1930 federal census, Los Angeles, April 8, 1930, Sheet 22B; Smith interview of Ruth Disney, *Walt's People, Volume 8*, 20–21 and footnote 3 at 51.

79 **Ann** Charlotte Ann Disney entry, January 31, 1979, Ancestry.com, *California Death Index, 1940–1997*.

79 **Hussey** Smith interview of Ruth Disney, *Walt's People, Volume 8*, footnote 3 at 51.

79 **five months pregnant** Robert S. Disney, Jr., entry, June 24, 1996, Ancestry.com, *Social Security Death Index*.

79 **their son, Robert, Jr.** 1930 federal census, Los Angeles, April 8, 1930, Sheet 22B.

79 **German shepherd, Peggy** Merritt and Kaufman, 57, 128; Thomas (1994 ed.), 73.

79 **Charlotte is recalled** Email from Diane Disney Miller to T. Susanin, May 17, 2009.

79 **"a little bit** Interview of Robert S. Disney, III by T. Susanin, June 5, 2009.

79–80 **"[n]othing remarkable" and** Email from Diane Disney Miller to T. Susanin, May 30, 2009.

80 **"very loving, gracious** Interview of Robert Disney, III, by T. Susanin, June 5, 2009.

80 **"meant well" but** Miller, 89.

80 **"demanded a lot; Our first argument** Miller, 87–88.

80 **Walt paid Robert** Miller, 83.

80 **"[t]he government did** The Greenes (2001), 30.

80 **Roy did not; "No, I'm too** Thomas (1994 ed.), 70.

80 **"When I got** The Greenes (1998 ed.), 42.

80 **"fed up with** Barrier (2007 book), 39 (citing Martin interview of Walt Disney, 1961).

80 **"What I wanted** "The Wide World of Walt Disney," *Newsweek*, December 31, 1962, 49–50.

80 **"ambition at that; "[a]nything. [I wanted** Barrier (2007 book), 39 (citing Martin interview of Walt Disney, 1961).

80 **"learn . . . the picture** Thomas, *Conversations*, 62–63.

80 **During his first** Gabler, 77 (citing Martin interview of Walt Disney, Reels 6 and 7, 17).

80 **"Walter Disney, representing** Miller, 84.

81 **"one of the big** Gabler, 77 (citing Martin interview of Walt Disney, Reels 6 and 7, 17).

81 **Walt would arrive** Miller, 84.

81 **His efforts to; red Pacific Electric** Thomas (1994 ed.), 69–70.

81 **Walt's cousin, Alice** Gabler, 77 (citing interview of Alice Disney Allen by Dave Smith dated October 5, 1972).

81 **Charlie Chaplin's studio** Thomas (1994 ed.), 69.

81 **on La Brea Avenue** 1923 Los Angeles city directory, 3611.

81 **Metro Goldwyn Mayer and Paramount** Gabler, 77 (citing Martin interview of Walt Disney, Disc 6).

81 **"I got a; Walt said that** Thomas (1994 ed.), 70–71.

81 **"went [to the** Greenes (2001), 28.

81 **He was selected** Thomas (1994 ed.), 71.

81 **"Well," Walt said** The Greenes (2001 ed.), 28.

81 **"I kept saying; "'Why don't you** Hubler interview of Roy Disney, November 17, 1967, *Walt's People, Volume 6*, 152; Barrier (2007 book), 39–40 (citing same interview).

81 **through August and** De Roos, 173.

81 **"I didn't figure** "Showman of the World Speaks," 1.

81 **"went from one** The Greenes (2001), 28.

81 **"I tried to** Thomas, *Walt Disney Conversations*, 62–63.

81 **"With the print** Lawrance.

81 **Walt also pitched** Gabler, 78 (citing Hubler, *Walt Disney*, 132).

81 **drew in January** Gabler, 45–46 (citing Inventory of Moore Collection, Ruth Beecher Folder, Walt Disney Archives).

81–82 **Heeding distributors' advice** Byrnes, 24; Lawrance; Alexander, 80.

82 **On Saturday, August 25; Dear Miss Winkler; In the past; The first picture** Letter from Walt Disney to Miss M. J. Winkler, August 25, 1923.

83 **Margaret was twenty-eight; She, her parents; Her father, Leopold** 1910 federal census, New York, April 19, 1910, Sheet 7A, Ancestry.com, *1910 United States Federal Census*.

83 **In 1915, when; Harry Warner** *Felix: The Twisted Tale of the World's Most Famous Cat*, John Canemaker, Pantheon Books, New York, 1991, 60.

83 **Warner Brothers'** Gifford, 102; *Reel Women: Pioneers of the Cinema, 1896 to the Present*, Ally Acker, Continuum, New York, 1991, 331.

83 **"I was secretary** *Before Mickey: The Animated Film, 1898–1928*, Donald Crafton, The University of Chicago Press, Chicago, 1993, 206 (citing *Moving Picture World*, March 10, 1924).

83 **Warner respected and; serving as Warner's** Canemaker (1991), 60.

83 **1921, Pat Sullivan** Canemaker (1991), 59–60.

83 **the producer-director** Gifford, 104

83 **approached Harry Warner** Canemaker (1991), 59–60.

83 **When Margaret expressed; Warner also thought** Canemaker (1991), 60.

83 **throughout her career** Canemaker (1991), 60 (citing letter from George Winkler to John Canemaker, December 3, 1989).

83 **December 1921** Canemaker (1991), 60.

83 **in January 1922** Gifford 105.

83 **state's rights basis** Email from Michael Barrier to T. Susanin, June 27, 2010.

83 **in either late 1921** Gifford, 86.

83 **or in 1922** Gifford, 86; Canemaker (1991), 60.

83 **Margaret announced in** Canemaker (1991), 60.

83 **simply, "M. J. Winkler** Letterhead on letter from Margaret J. Winkler to Walter E. Disney, May 16, 1923.

83 **she had become** Canemaker (1991), 60.

83    **"I had . . . years** Crafton, 206 (citing *Moving Picture World*, March 10, 1924).

83    **the middle initial** Canemaker (1991), 60.

83    **"the great live-wire** Crafton 307 (citing *Moving Picture World*, March 4, 1922; April 1, 1922; April 8, 1922).

83–84  **was worried about; option to renew** Canemaker (1991), 80.

84    **Fleischer was forming** Barrier (2007 book), 40. Fleischer's Red Seal Corporation began distributing *Out of the Inkwell* on January 1, 1924. Gifford, 86.

84    **Margaret wrote Sullivan; a contract dispute** Canemaker (1991), 80.

84    **On August 30; Sullivan wrote to; As a result** Canemaker (1991), 82–83.

84    **on Friday, September 7** Letter from M. J. Winkler to Mr. Walt. Disney, September 7, 1923.

84–85  **Dear Mr. Disney; It is necessary** Letter from M. J. Winkler to Walt. Disney, September 7, 1923.

85    **sent the reel** Hubler interview of Roy Disney, November 17, 1967, *Walt's People, Volume 6*, 150; Gabler, 78 (citing same interview).

85    **"told me to go** Byrnes, 24.

85    **"awaited developments** Lawrance.

85    **Lloyd's Film Storage** Miller, 87.

85    **sometime after her** Gabler, 80. Margaret asked, in a letter dated September 7, 1923, to see the film, and she wired Walt on October 15, 1923, that she had seen it.

85    **"I just couldn't** The Greenes (2001), 28.

85    **"Things looked pretty; "I was flat** Lawrance.

85    **"I couldn't get** DeRoos, 173.

85    **"shortage of directorial; "decided to give** Miller, 85.

85    **"[t]hings didn't look** Byrnes, 24.

85    **"[b]efore I knew** The Greenes (2001), 28.

85    **garage behind 4406** Miller, 85; The Greenes (2001), 29.

85    **"old dilapidated" used** Lawrance; Miller, 91.

85    **John W. Peterson** 1923 Los Angeles city directory, 2443.

85    **forty-four** 1930 federal census, South Pasadena, April 4 and 5, 1930, Sheet 3B, Ancestry.com, *1930 United States Federal Census*.

85    **was the proprietor** 1923 Los Angeles city directory, 258.

85    **California Camera Hospital** 1923 Los Angeles city directory, 755, 2443.

85    **nearly a decade** *Los Angeles City Directory*, The Los Angeles Directory Company, Los Angeles, 1915, 2336.

85    **Suite 321 of the** 1923 Los Angeles city directory, 755.

85    **"Shutter Repairs" and; "Equipped with Precision** 1923 Los Angeles city directory, 258.

85    **a camera stand** Miller, 85.

85    **Alexander Pantages, who** 1923 Los Angeles city directory, 2333.

85    **Pantages, forty-six** 1920 federal census, Los Angeles, January 21, 1920, Sheet 4A, Ancestry.com, *1920 United States Federal Census*.

85    **from Greece in** 1930 federal census, Los Angeles, April 7, 1930, Sheet 15A, Ancestry.com, *1930 United States Federal Census*.

85    **As a young; Five years later** "Pantages, Vet Vaudeville Showman, Dies at 65; Had a Colorful Career," Joe Bigelow, *Variety*, February 19, 1936, reprinted in *Variety Obituaries, Volume 2: 1929–1938*, Garland Publishing, Inc., New York, 1988.

85    **Lois Mendenhall, a** Lois M. Pantages obituary, July 23, 1941, *Variety Obituaries, Volume 3.*
85    **By 1915, Pantages** 1915 Los Angeles city directory, 1581.
85    **Carl J. Walker** 1915 Los Angeles city directory, 1581, 2059.
85–86  **an office building** 1915 Los Angeles city directory, 1581.
86    **The businesses in** 1915 Los Angeles city directory, 340, 945, 1111, 2370–71, 1432.
86    **In the fall** 1923 Los Angeles city directory, 2388.
86    **Pantages, Lois, their** 1920 federal census, Los Angeles, January 21, 1920, Sheet 4A.
86    **North Vermont Avenue; Room 211** 1923 Los Angeles city directory, 2388.
86    **"Finally I managed; "special little joke** Lawrance.
86    **"the name of** Byrnes, 24.
86    **"turn[ing] out a;** Byrnes, 24.
86    **was not convinced** Miller, 86.
86    **"He was interested** Byrnes, 24.
86    **"I think you** Miller, 86.
86    **"I set about** Byrnes, 24.
86    **"my little stick; The characters told; The settings were; "The best way** Miller, 86.
86    **on Monday, October 8** "Disney Before Burbank: The Kingswell and Hyperion Studios," David R. Smith, *Funnyworld,* Summer, 1979, 33; Merritt and Kaufman, 53.
86    **McRae & Abernathy** 1924 Los Angeles city directory, 369, 2651.
86    **James A. McRae** 1923 Los Angeles city directory, 2051.
86    **seventy-six, was born** 1920 federal census, Los Angeles, January 16, 1920, Sheet 5A, Ancestry.com, *1920 United States Federal Census.*
86    **Claude C. Abernathy** 1923 Los Angeles city directory, 380.
86    **forty-four** Claude C. Abernathy entry, October 15, 1970, Ancestry.com, *Social Security Death Index.*
86    **former insurance agent** 1920 federal census, Los Angeles, June 5, 1920, Sheet 7A, Ancestry.com, *1920 United States Federal Census*; 1915 Los Angeles city directory, 283; 1923 Los Angeles city directory, 380.
86    **from Ohio** 1920 federal census, Los Angeles, June 5, 1920, Sheet 7A.
86    **lived less than** 1923 Los Angeles city directory, 380.
86    **almost a decade** 1915 Los Angeles city directory, 283.
86    **Abernathy was married** 1920 federal census, Los Angeles, June 5, 1920, Sheet 7A.
86    **"rented the back** Lawrance.
86    **double that amount** Smith (1979 article), 33; Merritt and Kaufman, 53; Thomas (1994 ed.), 73.
86    **Walt found the** Miller, 89.
86    **who ran the** Letter from Thurston Harper to Dave Smith, October 20, 1973.
86    **"swing a cat; Abernathy laughed at** Miller, 89.
86    **Walt borrowed $75** Gabler, 82 (citing Studio Accounting Books, 1923–1930).
87    **"[w]hile I was** Lawrance.
87    **BELIEVE SERIES CAN; WILL PAY FIFTEEN** Thomas (1994 ed.), 72 (citing telegram from Margaret Winkler to Walt Disney, October 15, 1923).
87    **Margaret offered Walt** Email from Dave Smith to T. Susanin, June 5, 2009; Gabler, 80 (citing telegram from Margaret Winkler to Walt Disney, October 15, 1923).
87    **Walt was to** Email from Dave Smith to T. Susanin, June 5, 2009.
87    **"Alice must be** June 1994 Barrier Notes ("Winkler Film Corp." file) (citing telegram from M. J. Winkler to Walt Disney, October 15, 1923).

87   **he immediately wired** Email from Dave Smith to T. Susanin, June 5, 2009.

87   **"I was surprised** *Walt Disney: Famous Quotes,* edited by Dave Smith, Walt Disney
     Theme Parks and Resorts, Lake Buena Vista, 1994, 3.

87   **after wiring Margaret** Email from Dave Smith to T. Susanin, June 5, 2009.

87   **took a bus** Thomas (1994 ed.), 72.

87   **"[t]ypical porch type** Hubler interview of Roy Disney, June 18, 1968, *Walt's People,*
     *Volume 6* , 151; Gabler, 80–81 (citing same interview). See also Barrier (2007), 41
     (citing Hubler interview of Roy Disney, November 17, 1967); Thomas (1998), 44
     (quoting same interview).

87   **"found his way** Thomas (1998), 44.

87–88  **"We're in! It's; He wondered whether** Miller, 87.

88   **could marry Edna** Thomas (1998), 47.

88   **"I talked . . . Roy** DeRoos, 173.

88   **"always had been** Lawrance.

88   **They agreed to** "Mickey Mouse's Financial Career," Arthur Mann, *Harper's Magazine,*
     May, 1934, 715.

88   **"So," said Roy** Thomas (1998), 44.

88   **"I dropped the** Byrnes, 24.

88   **signing and mailing** June 1994 Barrier Notes ("Winkler Film Corp." file) (citing
     telegram from M. J. Winkler to Walt Disney, October 16, 1923).

88   **looked for financing** Thomas (1994 ed.), 72; Miller, 87–88.

88   **asked their original** Letter from Walt Disney to Mrs. Margaret Davis, October 16,
     1923.

88   **hired the first** "Walt Disney Productions: Chronological List of Personnel—October,
     1923–April, 1930," David R. Smith, April 28, 1978, 1. This two-page list was prepared
     by David R. Smith, former Chief Archivist, The Walt Disney Company, from Roy's
     accounting books and other Disney company records, such as personnel records.
     Email from Dave Smith to T. Susanin, May 18, 2009.

88   **Margaret prepared and** Email from Dave Smith to T. Susanin, June 5, 2009; Gabler,
     80 (citing letter from Margaret Winkler to Walt Disney, October 16, 1923).

88   **outright sale contract** Mann, 715.

88   **that required delivery** Gabler, 80 (citing letter from Margaret Winkler to Walt Disney,
     October 16, 1923). Barrier says it was due on January 1. See Barrier (2007 book), 41.

88   **She also asked** Gabler, 80 (citing letter from Margaret Winkler to Walt Disney,
     October 16, 1923).

88   **Margaret wired Walt; (the contract's delivery** Email from Dave Smith to T. Susanin,
     June 5, 2009.

88   **Margaret also gave; "Inquire of Harry** June 1994 Barrier Notes ("Winkler Film
     Corp." file) (citing telegram from M. J. Winkler to Walt Disney, dated October 16,
     1923).

88   **Roy applied for** Thomas (1994 ed.), 72.

88   **to Uncle Robert; heard that Walt** Miller, 87–88.

88   **witness the signing** Gabler, 80 (citing letter from Walt Disney to Margaret Winkler,
     October 24, 1923).

88–89  **wrote to Margaret; I have at** Letter from Walt Disney to Mrs. Margaret Davis,
     October 16, 1923.

89   **Walt offered Virginia** Merritt and Kaufman, 55.

89   **"My mother was** The Greenes (2001), 29.

89 **Just after he; she planned on** Gabler, 81 (citing letter from Mrs. T. J. Davis to Walt Disney, August 16, 1923).

89 **Disney Brothers Studio** Barrier (2007 book), 42.

89 **Miss Kathleen G. Dollard** *Los Angeles City Directory*, The Los Angeles Directory Company, Los Angeles, 1925, 757.

89 **sixteen-year-old** Kathleen Dollard entry, 1979, Ancestry.com, *Social Security Death Index*.

89 **lived about two** 1925 Los Angeles city directory, 757.

89 **was hired that** Smith (1978 list), 1; Dave Smith email to T. Susanin, May 18, 2009; Miller, 94.

89 **"established the first** "Showman of the World," 1.

89 **"I'll make the** Greenes (1991), 44.

89–90 **"short history of; I would also** June 1994 Barrier Notes ("Winkler Film Corp." file) (citing letter from M. J. Winkler to Walt Disney, October 17, 1923).

90 **"I am now** June 1994 Barrier Notes ("Winkler Film Corp." file) (citing letter from Walt Disney to M. J. Walker, October 24, 1923).

90 **That Saturday, Walt; Walt offered Virginia; He also offered; "low salary at** Gabler, 81 (citing letter from Walt Disney to Mrs. T. J. Davis, October 20, 1923).

90 **"responsibility and standing** June 1994 Barrier Notes ("Winkler Film Corp." file) (citing letter from Walt Disney to Harry M. Warner, October 21, 1923).

90 **Miss M. J. Winkler** June 1994 Barrier Notes ("Winkler Film Corp." file) (citing letter from H. M. Warner to Walt Disney, October 23, 1923).

90 **the financial report** Merritt and Kaufman, 55.

90 **"[t]he first of** Letter from Walt Disney to M. J. Winkler, October 24, 1923.

90–91 **In my last** Letter from Walt Disney to Mrs. Margaret Davis, October 24, 1923.

91 **the last weekend** Gabler, 82. According to Gabler, Margaret Davis wired her acceptance of Walt's offer on October 28, 1923.

91 **"Walt found a** Green and Green, 9.

91 **"There were two** Province interview of McGhee, *Hogan's Alley*; see also Merritt and Kaufman interview of McGhee, *Walt's People, Volume 4*, 20.

91 **Virginia later suggested** Interview of Virginia Davis McGhee by T. Susanin, March 7, 2009.

91 **would last for** Miller, 92.

91 **"to have the** June 1994 Barrier Notes ("Winkler Film Corp."" file) (citing letter from M. J. Winkler to Walt Disney, November 7, 1923).

91 **California by train; "went into real** Merritt and Kaufman, 63-64; Merritt and Kaufman interview of McGhee, *Walt's People, Volume 4*, 20–21.

91 **Within a year** 1925 Los Angeles city directory, 727.

91 **J. M. Overell** 1924 Los Angeles city directory, 1746, 2545.

91 **"The Mecca For** 1924 Los Angeles city directory, 395.

91 **"Homes Furnished Complete** 1924 Los Angeles city directory, 202.

91 **began and ended; The live-action scenes; The animated portion** *Disney Cartoons of the 1920's: Alice Comedies, Vol. 1*, DVD, Tom's Vintage Film, 2005.

91 **"they look so; "everybody loves animals** "Walt Disney," Paul Hollister, the *Atlantic Monthly*, December 1940, 690.

91 **Uncle Robert's house** *Disney Cartoons of the 1920's: Alice Comedies, Vol. 1*, DVD, Tom's Vintage Film, 2005.

92 **in Santa Monica; Virginia's parents and** Merritt and Kaufman, 54–55.

92   "I'd never seen; "That was a The Greenes (2001), 29.

92   **German shepherd, Peggy; The dog appeared** *Disney Cartoons of the 1920's: Alice Comedies, Vol. 1*, DVD, Tom's Vintage Film, 2005.

92   **"a family enterprise; "very informal. We** Province interview of McGhee, *Hogan's Alley.*

92   **Walt wrote and** Merritt and Kaufman, 56, 127. See also Miller, 92 (Walt did all the animation).

92   **"did all the** Thomas, *Walt Disney Conversations*, 63.

92   **The film required** "The Only Unpaid Movie Star," Harry Carr, *The American Magazine*, March, 1931, 57.

92   **One source claimed; dry goods cartons** Byrnes, 24.

92   **"swiped from an** "Growing Pains," Walt Disney, *Journal of the Society of Motion Picture Engineers*, January–June 1941, 106.

92   **"rigged up a; "and a little** Lawrance.

92   **"Walt did all** Roy Disney, 215.

92   **"In order to** Miller, 91.

92   **Uncle Robert finally** Gabler, 82 (citing Studio Accounting Books, 1923–1930); Thomas (1998), 48; Roy Disney, 215; Lawrance.

92   **Roy recorded this; Ledger #1 shows** Thomas (1998), 48.

92   **the first installment; The second installment** Gabler 82 (citing Studio Accounting Books, 1923–1930).

92   **expenses Roy recorded** Thomas (1998), 48-49; see also The Greenes (2001), 30.

93   **"Costumes and Properties** 1923 Los Angeles city directory, 3204.

93   **The studio also** Thomas (1998), 48.

93   **a daily newspaper** 1923 Los Angeles city directory, 1960.

93   **a $200 camera** The Greenes (2001), 30.

93   **the Disney brothers** Gabler, 83. Gabler cites "Voice of Broadway," by Louis Sobol, *New York Journal-American*, February 5, 1938, as his source for information about the Disneys' moves, but this article does not mention the Disneys at all. However, there were three Olive Hill apartments near the Kingswell studio where Walt and Roy might have lived in late 1923: Olive Hill Court was a half-mile southwest of the studio, on North Edgemont Street (1923 Los Angeles city directory, 2344); Olive Hill Apartments was two blocks south of the studio, on Hollywood Boulevard (1924 Los Angeles city directory, 1730); and another Olive Hill Court was located on North Vermont Avenue, a half-block north of Kingswell (1925 Los Angeles city directory, 1498).

93   **an apartment complex** 1924 Los Angeles city directory, 1370.

93   **Roy's physical condition** Miller, 91.

93   **"we got an; "used to go** Barrier (2007 book), 43 (citing interview of Roy Disney by Richard Hubler, February 20, 1968); Thomas (1998), 50.

93   **"as soon as** Lawrance.

93   **Winkler got married; Charles B. Mintz** Canemaker (1991), 80.

93   **thirty-three, was born** 1910 federal census, New York, April 16, 1910, Sheet 4B, Ancestry.com, *1910 United States Federal Census.*

93   **Charlie first met** Canemaker (1991), 80.

93   **Within two years** Draft card of Charles B. Mintz dated June 5, 1917, Ancestry.com, *World War I Draft Registration Cards, 1917–1918.*

93   **a jewelry store** 1920 federal census, New York, January 4, 1920, Sheet 5A, Ancestry. com, *1920 United States Federal Census*.

93   **(a second brother** 1910 federal census, New York, April 16, 1910, Sheet 4B.

93   **Charlie became a; handled marketing and** Canemaker (1991), 82.

93   **"grim-faced man** *Talking Animals and Other People*, Shamus Culhane, St. Martin's Press, New York, 1986, 25.

93   **Margaret's brother, George** Canemaker (1991), 82.

93   **Margaret and Charlie** Canemaker (1991), 80.

93   **That month, they** Canemaker (1991), 82.

93   **a cheaper room** Gabler, 83 (again, erroneously citing Sobol); see also "A Kid From Chicago, With Ham & Plenty of Mustard," Phil Santora, *Daily News*, September 30, 1964, 42.

93   **They moved into** Thomas (1994 ed.), 75.

93   **"just a single** Barrier (2007 book), 43 (citing Hubler interview of Roy Disney, February 20, 1968); Thomas (1998), 50.

94   **owned by Charles** Barrier (2007 book), 43 (citing Hubler interview of Roy Disney, February 20, 1968).

94   **Charles (fifty-nine) and** 1900 federal census, June 11, 1900, Plymouth, Iowa, Sheet 5B, Ancestry.com, *1900 United States Federal Census*.

94   **married in their** 1930 federal census, April 11, 1930, Los Angeles, Sheet 23A, Ancestry. com, *1930 United States Federal Census*.

94   **with their five** 1900 federal census, Plymouth, Iowa, June 11, 1900, Sheet 5B.

94   **By the time; Their youngest child** 1920 federal census, January 5, 1920, Le Mars, Iowa, Sheet 3B, Ancestry.com, *1920 United States Federal Census*.

94   **Within three years** 1923 Los Angeles city directory, 2719.

94   **cooked and ate** Byrnes, 24.

94   **"Later," Walt recalled** Lawrance. See also Carr, 57; "Mickey-Mouse Maker," Gilbert Seldes, *The New Yorker*, December 19, 1931, 24.

94   **"inexpensive** Santora, 42.

94   **"dreary** "Mickey Mouse's Father," *McCall's*, August 1932, 28.

94   **"there was many** "Father Goose."

94   **the Garden Cafeteria** 1923 Los Angeles city directory, 1290; 1924 Los Angeles city directory, 997, 1559; 1925 Los Angeles city directory, 1358, 2259; *Los Angeles City Directory*, The Los Angeles Directory Company, Los Angeles, 1928, 1459 (1710 North Vermont Avenue).

94   **George F. S. Marsh** 1925 Los Angeles city directory, 1357 (1711 North Vermont Avenue).

94   **the Ivey Cafeteria** 1925 Los Angeles city directory, 921, 1105, 2258 (1754 North Vermont Avenue).

94   **for ice cream** See, generally, *Walt Disney's Nine Old Men & the Art of Animation*, John Canemaker, Disney Editions, New York, 2001, 9 (citing letter from Les Clark to John Canemaker, July 1973).

94   **The Chocolate Den** 1925 Los Angeles city directory, 621, 632, 1211, 2121 (1716 North Vermont Avenue).

94   **A. L. Farris** 1924 Los Angeles city directory, 919, 2504; 1925 Los Angeles city directory, 826; *Los Angeles City Directory*, The Los Angeles Directory Company, Los Angeles, 1926, 848, 2215 (1728 North Vermont Avenue).

94   **hired their second; Ann began work** Smith (1978 list), 1.

94    **They wanted to** Merritt and Kaufman, 53, 55.

94    **4589 Hollywood Boulevard; cost ten dollars** Smith (1979 article), 33; see also Thomas (1994 ed.), 73 (lot at intersection of Hollywood Boulevard and Rodney Drive); Thomas (1998) 47 (lot on Hollywood Boulevard). Kathy Merlock Jackson and Merritt and Kaufman write that Walt and Roy rented the vacant lot in January. See Kathy Merlock Jackson, *Walt Disney: A Bio-Bibliography*, Greenwood Press, Westport, 1993, 8–9; Merritt and Kaufman, 57. Specifically, Jackson writes that the Disneys rented the empty lot at 4589 Hollywood Boulevard in January for $10 a month.

94    **The company records; cigars for their; tools** Gabler, 83 (citing Check Stub no. 1, Studio Accounting Books, 1923–1930).

94    **lumber likely used; curtain that might** The Greenes (2001), 30.

94    **"We'd film in** Iwerks, 31 (quoting from interview of Virginia Davis McGhee by Leslie Iwerks, 1998; see Iwerks, 236). See also Miller, 90.

94–95 **"Walt was always** Green and Green, 10.

95    **"lead me into** Province interview of McGhee, *Hogan's Alley*.

95    **He gave Roy; also borrowed $200** Gabler, 82–83 (citing Studio Accounting Books, 1923–1930); Thomas (1998), 48–49).

95    **Roy told Walt** Miller, 91–92.

95    **"few hundred dollars** Barrier (2007 book), 41 (citing Hubler interview of Roy Disney, June 18, 1968). See also Thomas (1994 ed.), 72 (Roy loaned the studio $200); Lawrance; see Carr, 56; Seldes, 24; "Mickey Mouse, And How He Grew," Irving Wallace, *Collier's*, April 9, 1949, 35 (Roy loaned the studio $250).

95    **parents helped by** The Greenes (1998 ed.), 44.

95    ***Alice's Day At*** Merritt and Kaufman, 127.

95    **it's original due** Email from Dave Smith to T. Susanin, June 5, 2009. Smith explains that when Margaret telegraphed her offer to Walt on October 15, she required that the first reel be delivered by December 15. When Walt wired his acceptance of her offer that same day, he stated that he could deliver the first reel by January 1. The next day, Margaret wired her approval of the January 1st delivery date, but when she mailed the signed contracts that same day, she listed the delivery date as January 2.

95    **Walt subsequently negotiated** Email from Dave Smith to T. Susanin, June 5, 2009 (citing telegram from Walt Disney to Margaret Winkler, October 15, 1923).

95    **"producing one series** "Showman of the World," 1.

95    **the same team** Merritt and Kaufman, 128. Ann Loomis started work at Disney Brothers Studio on December 8, 1923. Smith (1978 list), 1.

95    **four subsequent reels** This young actor appears to have co-starred in *Alice's Spooky Adventure, Alice's Wild West Show, Alice and the Dog Catcher* and *Alice Stage Struck*. *Disney Cartoons of the 1920's: Alice Comedies, Vol. 1*, DVD, Tom's Vintage Film, 2005 (*Spooky Adventure* and *Dog Catcher*); *Walt Disney Treasures—Disney Rarities, Celebrated Shorts: 1920s–1960s*, DVD, Buena Vista Home Video, 2005 (*Wild West Show*); *Disney's Alice Comedies, Volume 2*, DVD, Tom's Vintage Film, 2005 (*Stage Struck*).

95    **December 19; In the ad; the ad worked** Canemaker (1991), 83.

95    **Wednesday, December 26** Gabler, 84 (citing letter from Margaret Winkler to Walt Disney, December 26, 1923).

95    **In the wire** Barrier (1999 book), 580, note 103 (citing telegram from Margaret Winkler to Walt Disney, December 26, 1923).

96    **"DAY AT SEA** Thomas (1994 ed.), 73 (citing telegram from Margaret Winkler to Walt Disney, December 26, 1923).

96    **"All our films** Merritt and Kaufman, 57 (citing telegram from Margaret Winkler to Walt Disney, December 26, 1923).

96    **"We believe [*Day*** Merritt and Kaufman, 127 (citing telegram or letter from Margaret Winkler to Walt Disney, December 26, 1923).

96    **While Alice's Day** June 1994 Barrier Notes ("Winkler Film Corp." file) (citing letter from M. J. Winkler to Walt Disney, December 26, 1923).

96    **"[B]y Christmas we** Hubler interview of Roy Disney, November 17, 1967, *Walt's People, Volume 6*, 151; Barrier (2007 book), 41 (citing same interview).

96    **"[t]hought we were** Barrier (2007) book, 41 (citing Hubler interview of Roy Disney, November 17, 1967)

96    **The brothers had** Miller, 90; Seldes, 24.

96    **each ordered meat** Carr, 57.

96    **We agree with; "[a] customer wanted** June 1994 Barrier Notes ("Winkler Film Corp.") (citing letter from M. J. Winkler to Walt Disney, January 9, 1924).

96    **"the very lowest** June 1994 Barrier Notes ("Winkler Film Corp." (citing letter from M. J. Winkler to Walt Disney, January 10, 1924).

96    **Margaret made her** Gabler, 82 (citing Studio Accounting Books, 1923–1930).

96    **repaid their Uncle** Thomas (1998), 48.

96    **although they subsequently** Thomas (1994 ed.), 78.

97    **"[t]he first [Alice** Miller, 91.

97    **Sometime that week** See Thomas (1998), 51 (citing interview of Lillian Disney Truyens by Bob Thomas, April 19, 1973) (establishing that Lillian started work right after interviewing at the studio); Smith (1978 list), 1 (Lillian started work on Monday, January 14, 1924).

97    **asked Kathleen Dollard** Miller, 94.

97    **Hazel Bounds Sewell, twenty-six** 1920 federal census, January 2, 1920, Lapwai Precinct, Idaho, Sheet 1B, Ancestry.com, *1920 United States Federal Census*.

97    **one of ten** Interview of Diane Disney Miller by Richard Hubler, June 11, 1968, *Walt's People, Volume 6*, 173.

97    **raised on the** Introduction to interview of Lillian Disney by Richard Hubler, April 16, 1968, *Walt's People, Volume 6*, 140.

97    **her father Willard; Hazel's mother, Jeannette; The Bounds family; They were poor** Hubler interview of Diane Disney Miller, *Walt's People, Volume 6*, 173; email from Diane Disney Miller to T. Susanin, May 16, 2009.

97    **At the age** 1920 federal census, Lapwai Precinct, Idaho, January 2, 1920, Sheet 1B; 1930 federal census, April 16, 1930, Los Angeles, Sheet 16B, Ancestry.com, *1930 United States Federal Census*.

97    **The couple lived** 1920 federal census, Lapwai Precinct, Idaho, January 2, 1920, Sheet 1B.

97    **After eight years; on North Vermont** 1924 Los Angeles city directory, 2013.

97    **In late December** Gabler, 92–93 (citing Thomas interview of Lillian Disney Truyens, April 19, 1973).

97 **twenty-four-year-old sister; the youngest of** Introduction to Hubler interview of Lillian Disney, *Walt's People, Volume 6*, 140.

97 **She was born** Email from Diane Disney Miller to T. Susanin, May 16, 2009.

97 **"I was a** Lillian Disney and Taves, 103.

97 **had attended business** Miller, 95.

97 **"[t]o live with** Hubler interview of Lillian Disney, *Walt's People, Volume 6*, 141.

97 **"got a job** Lillian Disney and Taves, 103.

97 **"said [the Disneys** Thomas (1998), 51 (citing Thomas interview of Lillian Disney Truyens, April 19, 1973).

97 **"tiny office" in** Thomas (1998), 51 (citing Thomas interview of Lillian Disney Truyens, April 19, 1973).

97 **"little studio" at** Hubler interview of Lillian Disney, *Walt's People, Volume 6*, 141.

97 **"[t]hat's when I** Thomas (1998), 51 (citing interview of Lillian by Bob Thomas, 1973).

97 **"He didn't even** Barrier (book 2007), 43 (citing interview of Lillian Disney by Pete Martin, May or June 1956).

97 **"was wearing a** Thomas (1998), 51 (citing Thomas interview of Lillian Disney Truyens, April 19, 1973).

97 **"I have a** Miller, 94; email from Diane Disney Miller to T. Susanin, January 19, 2010.

97 **Lillian interviewed for** Thomas (1998), 51 (citing Thomas interview of Lillian Disney Truyens, April 19, 1973).

97 **"got the job** Lillian Disney and Taves, 103.

97 **"to work for** Introduction to Hubler interview of Lillian Disney, *Walt's People, Volume 6*, 141.

97–98 **"I went to** Thomas (1998), 51 (citing Thomas interview of Lillian Disney Truyens, April 19, 1973).

98 **Monday, January 14** Smith (1978 list), 1.

98 **joined her for** The Greenes (1998 ed.), 45.

98 **The courtship between** Email from Diane Disney Miller to T. Susanin, May 17, 2009.

98 **"We used to; "He used to** Hubler interview of Lillian Disney, April 16, 1968, *Walt's People, Volume 6*, 141; Barrier (2007), 44 (citing same interview).

98 **Ford "runabout"** Thomas (1998), 51 (citing Thomas interview of Lillian Disney, 1973).

98 **"Ford roadster [had]** Hubler interview of Lillian Disney, *Walt's People, Volume 6*, 141.

98 **"When he started** Green and Green, 11.

98 **"He took the; "[a] wonderful man** Hubler interview of Lillian Disney, *Walt's People, Volume 6*, 141.

98 **"a good listener** Miller, 97.

98 **"He was always; "His work," she; "Did he ever; "If he didn't; "When he got** Hubler interview of Lillian Disney, *Walt's People, Volume 6*, 141–42.

98 **"One night he** Green and Green, 11.

98 **Lilly said he; "Roy and Walt** Thomas (1998), 51 (citing interview of Lillian Disney by Bob Thomas, 1973).

98 **The brothers agreed** Miller, 95.

98 **Walt bought a** Thomas (1998), 51 (citing interview of Lillian Disney by Bob Thomas, 1973).

98 **Roy's cost $35.00** Miller, 95.

98 **"always got the** Hubler interview of Lillian Disney, *Walt's People, Volume 6*, 141–42.

98   "When he came Thomas (1998), 51 (citing interview of Lillian Disney by Bob Thomas, 1973).

98   "stood up and Green and Green, 11.

98   One night, Walt; "Suddenly," Lilly said; "was customary in Miller, 94–95.

98–99 On Monday, January 21; "I sincerely believe; "I wish to June 1994 Barrier Notes ("Winkler correspondence" folder) (citing letter from Walt Disney to M. J. Winkler, January 21, 1924).

99   offer to purchase June 1994 Barrier Notes ("Winkler Film Corp." file) (citing telegram from M. J. Winkler to Walt Disney, January 18, 1924).

99   "I believe your June 1994 Barrier Notes ("Winkler correspondence" folder) (citing letter from Walt Disney to M. J. Winkler, January 21, 1924).

99   "such an extremely; "as an emergency Letter from M. J. Winkler to Mr. Walt Disney, January 31, 1924.

99   has been thrown; "had quite a; "did not file; Walt suggested that Letter from Walt Disney to Miss M. J. Winkler, February 26, 1924.

99   "Alice in Wonderland June 1994 Barrier Notes ("Winkler Film Corp." file) (citing telegram from Joseph M. Jones to Walt Disney, January 26, 1924).

99   completed by January 21 June 1994 Barrier Notes ("Winkler correspondence" folder) (citing letter from Walt Disney to M. J. Winkler, January 21, 1924).

99   "Virginia Davis, 5-year old "Starred in Cartoons," Los Angeles Times, February 3, 1924.

99   "great improvement on; "lack of humor; "see what you Letter from M. J. Winkler to Mr. Walt. Disney, January 31, 1924.

100  The live-action sequences Disney Cartoons of the 1920's: Alice Comedies, Vol. 1, DVD, Tom's Vintage Film, 2005.

100  by using neighborhood; Even when he Miller 90.

100  ten-year-old Leon 1920 federal census, January 12, 1920, San Francisco, Sheet 6B, Ancestry.com, 1920 United States Federal Census.

100  lived on North 1925 Los Angeles city directory, 1726.

100  was born in 1920 federal census, January 12, 1920, San Francisco, Sheet 6B; Leon A. Sederholm entry, November 26, 1913, California Birth Index, 1905–1995, Ancestry. com.

100  Alfred Sederhulden, thirty-eight; Leon's mother, Rose; The Sederhuldens lived 1910 federal census, San Francisco, April 29, 1910, Sheet 9A, Ancestry.com, 1910 United States Federal Census; 1920 federal census, January 5, 1920, San Francisco, Sheet 3B, Ancestry.com, 1920 United States Federal Census; 1920 federal census, January 12, 1920, San Francisco, Sheet 6B.

100  Leon was the 1920 federal census, January 12, 1920, San Francisco, Sheet 6B; 1920 federal census, January 12, 1920, San Francisco, Sheet 7B, Ancestry.com, 1920 United States Federal Census.

100  Alf 1925 Los Angeles city directory, 1726; 1926 Los Angeles city directory, 1800.

100  died a few years 1920 federal census, January 5, 1920, San Francisco, Sheet 3B.

100  "inmates" in the 1920 federal census, January 12, 1920, San Francisco, Sheets 6B–7B.

100  Rose got a 1920 federal census, January 5, 1920, San Francisco, Sheet 3B.

100  By the time; Norvin, then eighteen 1925 Los Angeles city directory, 1726.

100  Walter D. 1920 federal census, January 9, 1920, Los Angeles, Sheet 11B, Ancestry.com, 1920 United States Federal Census.

100   "**Spec**" Merritt and Kaufman, 57.

100–101   **thirteen, was the; Walter's mother, like; Several years before** 1920 federal census, January 9, 1920, Los Angeles, Sheet 11B.

101   **thirteen-year-old Ruth S.; Ruth's father was** 1930 federal census, April 14, 1930, Los Angeles, Sheet 19A.

101   **By 1924 the; The Roberts family** 1924 Los Angeles city directory, 1911.

101   "**a neighbor down** Interview of Ruthie Tompson by Didier Ghez, December 21, 2007, 1.

101   **I met Walt** Iwerks, 32 (quoting from interview of Ruthie Tompson by Leslie Iwerks, 1993. See Iwerks, 238).

101   **According to Ruthie** Email from Ruthie Tompson to T. Susanin, November 29, 2009; see also Ghez interview of Tompson, 1-2.

101   **Dorothy, twelve** 1930 federal census, April 14, 1930, Los Angeles, Sheet 19A.

101   **Other local children** Emails from Ruthie Tompson to T. Susanin, November 29, 2009 and December 9, 2009. Ruthie is not certain about which neighborhood children appeared in the Alice Comedies due to her "hazy memory[.]" See also Ghez interview of Tompson, 2 ("In fact one of the other children that was among the players [in the Alice series] .... was Phillips, Frank Phillips.").

101   **Carl Grade, a** 1923 Los Angeles city directory, 1370; 1924 Los Angeles city Directory, 1051.

101   "**hills where we** Email from Ruthie Tompson to T. Susanin, December 9, 2009.

101   **on nearby Talmadge** 1923 Los Angeles city directory, 3117; 1924 Los Angeles city directory, 2264.

101   "**It was such** Iwerks, 31 (quoting from interview of Ruthie Tompson by Leslie Iwerks, 1993. See Iwerks, 238).

101   "**played with the** Merritt and Kaufman interview of McGhee, *Walt's People, Volume 4*, 27.

101   "**We'd have our** Province interview of McGhee, *Hogan's Alley.*

101–2   "**I hated her!** Merritt and Kaufman, 56 (quoting from Merritt and Kaufman interview of Ruthie Tompson. See Merritt and Kaufman, 11).

102   "**he and Roy** Province interview of McGhee, *Hogan's Alley.*

102   "**tight distribution deadlines** Green and Green, 10.

102   **played by Joe** Merritt and Kaufman, 60 (photograph), 133 (Merritt and Kaufman state that Allen appeared in *Alice and the Dog Catcher* rather than *Alice's Spooky Adventure*, but a viewing of each short shows that this is an error).

102   **thirty-six-year-old** Joe Allen obituary, *Variety*, February 9, 1955, reprinted in *Variety Obituaries, Volume 4: 1948–1956*, Garland Publishing, Inc., New York, 1988.

102   "**photo player**" 1924 Los Angeles city directory, 389.

102   **whose brother, David** 1923 Los Angeles city directory, 406; *Los Angeles City Directory*, The Los Angeles Directory Company, Los Angeles, 1927, 347; Joe Allen obituary, *Variety Obituaries, Volume 4.*

102   **on Hollywood Boulevard** 1923 Los Angeles city directory, 406; 1924 Los Angeles city directory, 388.

102   **The baseball scene** *Disney Cartoons of the 1920's: Alice Comedies, Vol. 1*, DVD, Tom's Vintage Film, 2005.

102   **The prison scene; Jeff Davis visited** Merritt and Kaufman, 59.

102   **In February** Smith (1978 list), 1.

102   *Spooky Adventure* **was** Merritt and Kaufman, 128.

102　**$15 a week** Notes from the [Walt Disney Archives'] earning account book labeled on its cover "General Expense Account 1925–1926–1927 By Roy O. Disney," Michael Barrier, February 1997 (citing "Salary Account" pages, March 1, 1924 through December 20, 1924).

102　**"Ham"** Letter from Walt Disney to Roy Disney, March 2, 1928, 10:30 p.m.

102　**twenty-five** 1910 federal census, Edgely, North Dakota, April 22, 1910, 1B, Ancestry.com, *1910 United States Federal Census.*

102　**helped Walt animate** Merritt and Kaufman, 128.

102　**Ham was born** 1910 federal census, April 22, 1910, Edgely, North Dakota, Sheet 1B; 1920 federal census, January 2, 1920, Grand Forks, North Dakota, Sheet 11A, *1920 United States Federal Census.*

102　**The family later** 1910 federal census, April 22, 1910, Edgely, North Dakota, Sheet 1B.

102　**Ham still lived** 1920 federal census, January 2, 1920, Grand Forks, North Dakota, Sheet 11A.

102　**He started at** Smith (1978 list), 1.

102　**On February 22; studio shipped** *Spooky* Letter from Walt Disney to Miss M. J. Winkler, February 26, 1924.

102　**fog and clouds** Merritt and Kaufman, 57.

102–3　**"I am trying; By the time** Letter from Walt Disney to Miss M. J. Winkler, February 26, 1924.

103　*Alice's Wild West* Merritt and Kaufman, 128.

103　**This reel featured; a western show** *Walt Disney Treasures—Disney Rarities, Celebrated Shorts: 1920s—1960s,* DVD, Buena Vista Home Video, 2005.

103　**"because I was** Merritt and Kaufman interview of McGhee, *Walt's People, Volume 4,* 19.

103　**Tubby O'Brien; group of bullies; Marjorie, appears as; The closing live-action; In the background** *Disney Treasures—Disney Rarities, Celebrated Shorts: 1920s–1960s,* DVD, Buena Vista Home Video, 2005.

103　**On Sunday, February 24; at 4649 Kingswell** Smith (1979 article), 33; Barrier (2007 book), 42. Two days later, Walt wrote Margaret that, "My address is now 4649 Kingswell instead of 4406 Kingswell, Hollywood." Letter from Walt Disney to Miss M. J. Winkler, February 26, 1924.

103　**"in a little** Clampett, 18.

103　**Disneys also rented** Merritt and Kaufman, 57.

103　**converted into an; The studio rent** Thomas (1994 ed.), 73.

103　**the garage rent** Smith (1979 article), 33.

103　**man named Gulstrand** Letter from Thurston Harper to Dave Smith, October 20, 1973.

103　**Hans E. Gulstrand** 1923 Los Angeles city directory, 1416.

103　**brothers named Gulstrand; Harold N. Gulstrand; The Gulstrands were; Harold's younger brother; He was two** 1930 federal census, Los Angeles, April 9, 1930, Page 18A, Ancestry.com, *1930 United States Federal Census; Los Angeles City Directory,* The Los Angeles Directory Company, Los Angeles, 1929, 1015.

104　**On Saturday, March 1** Merritt and Kaufman, 127.

104　**"novel idea. . . very** Smith and Clark, 17.

104　**allow me to** Letter from M. J. Winkler to Mr. Walt Disney, March 4, 1924.

104　**earlier that month** Canemaker (1991), 83–84.

104　**Margaret asked Walt; she edited out; Margaret added that; "sure that it** Letter from M. J. Winkler to Mr. Walt Disney, March 4, 1924.

104   **on Tuesday, April 1** Merritt and Kaufman, 128.

104   **"more criticism on** June 1994 Barrier Notes ("Winkler Film Corp." file) (citing letter from Walt Disney to M. J. Winkler, March 28, 1924).

104–5  **"a very good; "there will be; Her editors even; "it an excellent; "improve a little; "wherever possible" in; "I am happy** Letter from M. J. Winkler to Walt Disney, April 7, 1924.

105   *Fishy Story*'s **opening; She gets Peggy; Alice's unsuspecting mother** *Disney Cartoons of the 1920's: Alice Comedies, Vol. 1*, DVD, Tom's Vintage Film, 2005.

105   **As Alice's mother** *Disney Cartoons of the 1920's: Alice Comedies, Vol. 1*, DVD, Tom's Vintage Film, 2005.

105   **one of forty** Rathburn, 1923 Los Angeles city directory, 7.

105   **"for not having; "So we used** Redelings.

105   **The crew on** Merritt and Kaufman, 133.

105   **April and May** Letter from Walt Disney to M. J. Walker, May 9, 1924.

105   **poster advertising the** *Disney Cartoons of the 1920's: Alice Comedies, Vol. 1*, DVD, Tom's Vintage Film, 2005.

105–6  **production was halted** "Five Counties Freed Of Ban," *Los Angeles Times*, May 3, 1924, 3; "Voting Will Not Suffer By Quarantine," *Los Angeles Times*, May 3, 1924, 3.

106   **"almost half through; "quarantine had slackened** Letter from Walt Disney to M. J. Winkler, May 9, 1924.

106   **last Alice Comedy** Merritt and Kaufman, 133.

106   **takes a bow; Walt and Ham; In one scene** *Disney Cartoons of the 1920's: Alice Comedies, Vol. 1*, DVD, Tom's Vintage Film, 2005.

106   **1852 North Vermont** 1923 Los Angeles city directory, 844, 252.

106   **A production still** Merritt and Kaufman, 134–35.

106   **A. B. Strode Co.** 1924 Los Angeles city directory, 2147, 2655.

106   **rented Bell and** Merritt and Kaufman, 65.

106   **thirty-six-year-old Harry W.** 1930 federal census, April 15, 1930, Los Angeles, Sheet 20B, Ancestry.com, *1930 United States Federal Census*.

106   **from Ohio with** 1930 federal census, April 15, 1930, Los Angeles, Sheet 20B.

106   **had filmed movies** Merritt and Kaufman, 65.

106   **through George Winkler** June 1994 Barrier Notes ("Winkler Film Corp." file) (citing letter from Walt Disney to Charles Mintz, August 15, 1924). Walt referred, in this letter to Mintz, to "Harry Forbes, George Winkler's camera man[.]"

106   **two subsequent Alice** Merritt and Kaufman, 133–34. Forbes also filmed, between June and August of 1924, *Alice the Peacemaker* and *Alice Gets in Dutch*.

106   **on May 1** Merritt and Kaufman, 128.

106   **On "Walt Disney, the** Thomas (1994 ed.), 76 (citing *Motion Picture News* review of *Alice's Wild West Show*).

106   **In this reel** *Of Mice and Magic*, Leonard Maltin, McGraw-Hill Book Co., New York, 1980, 32 (citing *Moving Picture World*, May 10, 1924).

106–7  **Pat Sullivan and; Their trial had** Canemaker (1991), 83–84.

107   **Earlier in the** Smith (1972 article), 33; Merritt and Kaufman, 63.

107   **he was ready** Letter from Walt Disney to Ubbe Iwwerks, June 1, 1924.

107   **"Trying to do** Lawrance.

107   **"heard from [Walt** Barrier interview of Harman, December 3, 1973, 20.

107   **On Friday, May 9** Letter from Walt Disney to M. J. Winkler, May 9, 1924.

107   **Hugh, Rudy, and** Barrier (2007 book), 46; Merritt and Kaufman, 72.

107   **"I had a** Barrier interview of Ising, June 2, 1971, 3.

107   **"then Hugh, Max** Kaufman interview of Ising, *Walt's People, Volume 1*, 40.

107   **"The boys in** Letter from Walt Disney to M. J. Winkler, May 9, 1924.

107   **"come out, right** Barrier interview of Ising, June 2, 1971, 8.

107   **"advanced technically" but** Barrier interview of Harman, December 3, 1973, 20.

107–8  **on Sunday, June 1; Dear Friend Ubbe** Letter from Walt Disney to Ubbe Iwwerks, June 1, 1924.

108   **Margaret Winkler arrived** Iwerks, 28–29.

108   **least a week** Smith (1972 article), 33–34.

109   **Received your letter** from Walt Disney to Ubbe Iwwerks, June 10, 1924.

109   **worked on *Alice*; no longer animating** Merritt and Kaufman, 133.

109   **"I was able** Thomas, *Walt Disney Conversations*, 63.

109–10  **"Walt was never** Thomas (1998), 49.

110   **twenty-two-year-old Mike Marcus** 1920 federal census, Minneapolis, January 5, 1920, Sheet 3A, Ancestry.com, *1920 United States Federal Census*; Michael J. Marcus entry, January 20, 1957, Ancestry.com, *California Death Index, 1940–1997*; Smith (1978 list), 1.

110   **"never could master** Miller, 91.

110   **Marcus was born** 1920 federal census, Minneapolis, January 5, 1920, Sheet 3A; 1930 federal census, April 2, 1930, Los Angeles, Sheet 1A, Ancestry.com, *1930 United States Federal Census*.

110   **Mike lived with; His father was** 1920 federal census, Minneapolis, January 5, 1920, Sheet 3A.

110   **and eventually lived** 1925 Los Angeles city directory, 1352.

110   ***Alice the Peacemaker*** *Disney Cartoons of the 1920's: Alice Comedies, Vol. 1*, DVD, Tom's Vintage Film, 2005.

110   **"They only did** Province interview of McGhee, *Hogan's Alley*.

110   **the cat who** *Disney Cartoons of the 1920's: Alice Comedies, Vol. 1*, DVD, Tom's Vintage Film, 2005.

110   **was named Mike** Merritt and Kaufman, 133.

110   **The live-action; In one scene; In another, it** *Disney Cartoons of the 1920's: Alice Comedies, Vol. 1*, DVD, Tom's Vintage Film, 2005.

110–11  **Fourth of July; "In Hollywood a** "Actors Mix With Cartoons," *Los Angeles Times*, July 6, 1924, B31.

111   **leave until July** Smith (1972 article), 34.

111   **Ubbe and his** Gabler, 85 (citing letter from Walt Disney to Thomas B. McCrum, August 4, 1924).

111   **During the trip** Iwerks, 29.

111   **The drive took** Smith (1972 article), 34.

111   **rented a house** Iwerks, 30.

111   **4334 Russell Avenue** 1925 Los Angeles city directory, 1106.

111   **Ubbe began work** Smith (1978 list), 1.

111   **salary of $40** Thomas (1994 ed.), 75; Thomas (1998), 49.

111   **posters, titles, and lobby** Smith (1972 article), 34; Smith (1979 article), 34.

111   **Ham, who got** February 1997 Barrier General Expense Account Notes (citing "Salary Account" pages, March 1, 1924 through December 20, 1924).

111   **around the time; production in August** Merritt and Kaufman, 133–34.

111 *Dutch* **was the** Merritt and Kaufman, 133–34.

111 **Mrs. Hunt** Merritt and Kaufman, 134.

111 **Spec O'Donnell and** *Disney Cartoons of the 1920's: Alice Comedies, Vol. 1*, DVD, Tom's Vintage Film, 2005.

111 **"I know one** Merritt and Kaufman, 66 (quoting from Merritt's and Kaufman's interview of Marjorie Sewell Davis. See Merritt and Kaufman, 11).

112 **"borrowed my mother's** Province interview of McGhee, *Hogan's Alley*.

112 **"Well, he didn't** Merritt and Kaufman interview of McGhee, *Walt's People, Volume 4*, 25–26.

112 **"Ubbe has been** Iwerks, 30.

112 **On August 7; "progressed quite a; "our people will** June 1994 Barrier Notes ("Winkler Film Corp." file) (citing letter from Charles Mintz to Walt Disney, August 7, 1924).

112 **Charlie dispatched his** Barrier (2007 book), 49.

112 **"fix up this** June 1994 Barrier Notes ("Winkler Film Corp." file) (citing letter from Charles Mintz to Walt Disney, August 7, 1924).

112 **George, twenty-two** 1910 federal census, New York, April 19, 1910, Sheet, 7A, Ancestry.com, *1910 United States Federal Census*.

112 **born in Hungary** 1930 federal census, Los Angeles, April 8, 1930, Sheet 19A, Ancestry.com, *1930 United States Federal Census*.

112 **who seemed nervous** Rudy Ising, Barrier interview of Harman and Ising, October 29, 1976, 55.

112 **and suffered from** "From the *Film Daily Year Book* for 1927," Michael Barrier, September 20, 2009, www.MichaelBarrier.com.

112 **"hatchet man** Culhane, 24.

112 **was knowledgeable about** Merritt and Kaufman, 68.

112 **Brothers Studio $45.54** February 1997 Barrier Notes (citing "Current Production Account" pages).

112 **"took a lot** "A Visit with Walt Disney," Lee Edson, *Thinking*, May 1959, reprinted in *Walt Disney Conversations*, 73.

112 **"It was a fight; "Then, said Walt** Barrier (2007 book), 42 (citing Martin interview of Walt Disney, 1956).

112 **promissory note in** Gabler, 89 (citing Ledger, 1924–1927; Studio Accounting Books, 1923–1930).

112 **"in a very** June 1994 Barrier Notes ("Winkler Film Corp." file) (citing letter from Walt Disney to Charles Mintz, August 15, 1924).

112 **from Dr. McCrum** Gabler, 99 (citing letter from Walt Disney to Thomas B. McCrum, August 20, 1924).

113 **We need money** Thomas (1994 ed.), 75–76 (citing letter from Walt Disney to Charles Mintz, August 29, 1924).

113 **"girl stand out; "good, if not** Gabler, 86.

113 **"When I first** Green and Green, 10.

113 **"Roy would tell** Barrier (2007 book), 45 (citing interview of Lillian Disney by Pete Martin, May or June 1956).

113 **Walt asked Charlie** June 1994 Barrier Notes ("Winkler Film Corp." file) (citing letter from Charles Mintz to Walt Disney, September 4, 1924).

113–14 **"very much satisfied; "doing a wise; "[t]his may not; I might say** Letter from C. B.
   Mintz to Mr. Walt Disney, October 6, 1924.

114 **"to wait, let** Letter from George Winkler to Mr. Walt Disney, November 13, 1924.

114 **"I hope you; "so well liked; "unanimous" opinion; "one radical fault; "is always very**
   Letter from C. B. Mintz to Mr. Walt Disney, October 24, 1924.

114 **underway in October; to assist Ubbe** Merritt and Kaufman, 136.

114 **Carl Thurston Harper, Jr.** Carl Thurston Harper entry, March 25, 1987, Ancestry.com,
   *Florida Death Index, 1877–1998.*

114 **general practice lawyer** 1920 federal census, Madisonville, Texas, February 2, 1920,
   Sheet 15A, Ancestry.com, *1920 United States Federal Census.*

114 **Both Thurston's father** 1920 federal census, Madisonville, Texas, February 2, 1920,
   Sheet 15A; draft card of Carl Thurston Harper.

114 **age of seventeen** 1920 federal census, Madisonville, Texas, February 3, 1920, Sheet 15B,
   Ancestry.com, *1920 United States Federal Census.*

114 **"a big, almost** Kaufman interview of Ising, *Walt's People, Volume 1*, 48.

114 **"a very wonderful; "a clash of** Letter from Thurston Harper to Dave Smith, October
   20, 1973.

114 **"a multi-talented person** Letter from Thurston Harper to Dave Smith, March 23, 1978.

114–15 **"taciturn and retiring; "always acted as; "I didn't hate** Letter from Thurston
   Harper to Dave Smith, October 20, 1973.

115 **ceded to Charlie's** Merritt and Kaufman, 66, 128.

115 **Walt removed part** Merritt and Kaufman, 128

115 **"Mr. Mintz; "In fact," Walt; George Winkler would; "[a]fter George cuts; If we had;
   We have talked** Letter from Walt Disney to Charles Mintz, November 3, 1924.

115–16 **"about doing away; "we can bring; "stand back of** Letter from George Winkler to
   Mr. Walt Disney, November 13, 1924.

116 **"I was not very** Thomas (1998), 51.

116 **"[t]hey tried to use** Barrier (2007 book), 42 (citing "1986 interview posted on the Walt
   Disney Family Museum site in 2001").

116 **"He was fun** Green and Green, 11.

116 **"went Hollywood** Eddy, 113.

116 **bought a used** Thomas (1994 ed.), 77.

116 **"ostentatious"** Eddy, 113.

116 **dark gray** Thomas (1994 ed.), 77.

116 **Moon roadster** Gabler, 92 (citing Hubler interview of Lillian Disney, April 16, 1968;
   Hubler, *Disney*, 760).

116 **He adored the** The Greenes (1998 ed.), 47.

116 **hood ornament; "We used to** The Greenes (2001), 35.

116 **prepared for the** Iwerks, 32 (citing Crafton).

116 **Ubbe also reworked** Smith (1979), 34; Merritt and Kaufman, 66.

116 **"converted the hand** Letter from Thurston Harper to Dave Smith, March 23, 1978.

116 **improved the exposure** Merritt and Kaufman, 66.

116 **"many" Saturday appearances** Merritt and Kaufman interview of McGhee, *Walt's
   People, Volume 4*, 21.

116 **"[I]t would be Little; "[I]t would be mainly** Merritt and Kaufman interview of
   McGhee, *Walt's People, Volume 4*, 22–23.

116  **She would appear** Province interview of McGhee, *Hogan's Alley*.
116  **"I didn't care** Merritt and Kaufman interview of McGhee, *Walt's People, Volume 4*, 26.
117  **Dear Mr. Mintz; "We would appreciate** Letter from Walt Disney to Charles Mintz, December 2, 1924.
117  **"animals afford a** Letter from Walt Disney to Charles Mintz dated December 2, 1924.
117  **George got Charlie** Merritt and Kaufman, 68.
117  **"We have gone** June 1994 Barrier Notes ("Winkler Film Corp." file) (citing letter from Charles Mintz to Walt Disney, December 8, 1924).
117  **George left New** June 1994 Barrier Notes ("Winkler Film Corp." file) (citing telegram from Charles Mintz to Walt Disney, December 11, 1924).
117  **The Disney Brothers** Email from Dave Smith to T. Susanin, October 14, 2008; letter from Thurston Harper to Dave Smith, March 1978.
117  **He estimated that; The diagram shows** The Greenes (2001), 30.
117  **The inside of** Smith (1979 article), 32.
117  **A hallway inside** Smith (1979 article), 33.
117  **A three-foot high; The Pathé camera** Smith (1979 article), 34.
117  **run by Mike** Letter from Thurston Harper to Dave Smith, March 1978.
117  **center of the** Smith (1979 article), 33.
117  **sink and unused** Smith (1979 article), 34.
117  **To the right** Smith (1979 article), 33.
117  **Roy's desk** Smith (1979 article), 33-34.
117  **(which held the; inkers and painters; sat to the** Smith (1979 article), 34.
117–18  **"The chairs were** Letter from Thurston Harper to Dave Smith dated March 1978.
118  **"punch holes in; "had two levels; "set up his** Letter from Thurston Harper to Dave Smith dated March 23, 1978.
118  **Along the right** Smith (1979 article), 34.
118  **The first of** Letter from Thurston Harper to Dave Smith dated March 23, 1978; Smith (1979 article), 33–34.
118  **The rest of** Smith (1979 article), 34.
118  **In the back** Smith (1979 article), 33.
118  **It was accessible; "inexpensive and utilitarian** Smith (1979 article), 34.
118  **That month, Charlie** Thomas (1994 ed.), 76.
118  **Walt and Charlie** Merritt and Kaufman, 70.
118  **paying themselves a; Prior to that** Gabler, 89 (citing Ledger, 1924–1927; Studio Accounting Books, 1923–1930).
118  **"At that time** Lillian Disney and Taves, 104.
118  **permitted staff members** Barrier (2007 book), 45 (citing "General Expense Account 1925–1926–1927 by Roy O. Disney").
118  **"The artist's work** Thomas (1994 ed.), 76 (citing *Kinematographic Weekly* review of *Alice and the Three Bears*).
118  *Alice Cans the* Merritt and Kaufman, 136.
118  **"Each one of** Thomas (1994 ed.), 76 (citing *The Moving Picture World* review of *Alice Cans the Cannibals*).
118  *Alice Gets Stung*; **new live-action cameraman** Merritt and Kaufman, 136.
118  **last Alice Comedy** Merritt and Kaufman, 136; J. B. Kaufman, "Wonderland Revisited," *Griffithiana*, No. 65, 1999, 141.

118   **of George Winkler** Gabler, 90 (citing letter from Walt Disney to George Winkler, September 29, 1924).

118   **secretary-treasurer of; (Margaret was still** *New York City Directory*, R. L. Polk & Company, Inc., New York, 1925, 2397.

119   **Philip Tannura as** Merritt and Kaufman, 136.

119   **twenty-seven, was born; The Tannuras had** 1910 federal census, April 19, 1910, New York, Sheet 5A, Ancestry.com, *1910 United States Federal Census*; Philip Tannura entry, December 7, 1973, Ancestry.com, *Social Security Death Index* and *California Death Index, 1940–1997*.

119   **as Walt redid; had Ubbe, Ham** Merritt and Kaufman, 127–28.

119   **pay Virginia for** Merritt and Kaufman, 70.

119   **"The reason my** Merritt and Kaufman interview of McGhee, *Walt's People, Volume 4*, 39–40, note 18 (citing Virginia Davis interview by John Province, 1992).

119   **"once or twice** Province interview of McGhee, *Hogan's Alley*.

119   **Walt and Roy** Merritt and Kaufman, 70.

119   **"They wanted me** Merritt and Kaufman interview of McGhee, *Walt's People, Volume 4*, 39–40, note 18 (citing Virginia Davis interview by John Province, 1992).

119   **"My mother said** Merritt and Kaufman, 70 (quoting from Merritt and Kaufman interview of Alice Davis McGhee. See Merritt and Kaufman, 11).

119   **did not socialize** Merritt and Kaufman interview of McGhee, *Walt's People, Volume 4*, 25–26.

119   **Jeff Davis was** In 1925, Jeff Davis was forty-one and Margaret Davis was thirty-five. See 1920 federal census, Kansas City, Missouri, January 22, 1920, 7B, Ancestry.com, *1920 United States Federal Census*.

119   **"nothing in common** Merritt and Kaufman interview of McGhee, *Walt's People, Volume 4*, 25.

119   **"always loved him** Merritt and Kaufman interview of McGhee, *Walt's People, Volume 4*, 26.

119   **"It was Mintz** Province interview of McGhee, *Hogan's Alley*.

119   **"having money problems** Province interview of McGhee, *Hogan's Alley*.

120   **"were mostly upset** Province interview of McGhee, *Hogan's Alley*.

120   **a letter written** Gabler, 97 (citing letter from Jeff and Margaret Davis to Walt Disney, January 7, 1925).

120   **gave Ubbe a** Smith (1972 article), 34.

120   **This meant that; Ham also got** February 1997 Barrier Notes (citing "Salary Account— Straight Payroll" pages, December 1924 through December 1926).

120   **By February, when** Merritt and Kaufman, 137.

120   **five and one-half-year old** Marjorie T. Gossett entry, January 6, 2003, Ancestry.com, *Social Security Death Index*.

120   **Margie Gay** Merritt and Kaufman, 71.

120   **Marjorie Teresa Gossett** Marjorie T. Gossett obituary, *Las Vegas Review Journal*, January 8, 2003.

120   **summer of 1919** Marjorie T. Gossett entry, January 6, 2003, Ancestry.com, *Social Security Death Index*.

120   **eighteen-year-old Ruth** 1930 federal census, April 8, 1930, Los Angeles, Sheet 5A, Ancestry.com, *1930 United States Federal Census*.

120 **by then worked** 1920 federal census, January 4, 1920, Muskogee, Oklahoma, Sheet 4A, Ancestry.com, *1920 United States Federal Census.*

120 **been widowed by** 1930 federal census, April 8, 1930, Los Angeles, Sheet 5A.

120 **and divorced from** 1920 federal census, January 4, 1920, Muskogee, Oklahoma, Sheet 4A; 1920 federal census, January 4, 1920, Muskogee, Oklahoma, Sheet 4A.

120 **from Missouri** 1920 federal census, January 8, 1920, Muskogee, Oklahoma, Sheet 8B, *1920 United States Federal Census.*

120 **and Oklahoma** 1930 federal census, April 8, 1930, Los Angeles, Sheet 5A.

120 **Ruth boarded the** 1920 federal census, January 8, 1920, Muskogee, Oklahoma, Sheet 8B; 1920 federal census, January 4, 1920, Muskogee, Oklahoma, Sheet 4A.

120 **Mrs. Ruth Gay** 1925 Los Angeles city directory, 898.

120 **"You have'nt [*sic*]** Gabler, 90 (citing letter from Walt Disney to Hugh Harman, February 27, 1925).

120 **"things that can; "After you see** Gabler, 90 (citing letter from Walt Disney to Rudy Ising, March 30, 1925).

120–21 **Photographs that Walt** Merritt and Kaufman, 85.

121 **"We are engaging** Letter from Thurston Harper to Dave Smith, October 20, 1973.

121 **"big date[s]" that** Thomas (1998), 51 (citing Thomas interview of Lillian Disney Truyens, April 19, 1973).

121 **"downtown"** Hubler interview of Lillian Disney, *Walt's People, Volume 6*, 142.

121 **"go see No** Thomas (1998), 51 (citing Thomas interview of Lillian Disney Truyens, April 19, 1973).

121 **Walt loved the** Email from Diane Disney Miller T. Susanin, May 17, 2009.

121 **The musical "sensation[']s; March 9 premiere** "Music Play Has Opening Tomorrow," *Los Angeles Times*, March 8, 1925, 22.

121 **Fourth of July** "'No, No, Nanette' to Leave Mason Saturday, July 4," *Los Angeles Times*, June 4, 1925, A9.

121 **"written with a; make it to Broadway** "Music Play Has . . . ," March 8, 1925, 22.

121 **played in San Francisco** "'No, No, Nanette' . . . ," June 4, 1925, A9.

121 **New York cast** "Music Play Has . . . ," March 8, 1925, 22.

121 **two expansive opening** "Music Play Has . . . ," March 8, 1925, 22; "Rehearsals of Gay Musical Show, 'No, No, Nanette,' Reflect Brilliant Array of Talent," Grace Kingsley, *Los Angeles Times*, March 8, 1925, D19.

121 **theater attendance record** "'No, No, Nanette' . . . ," June 4, 1925, A9.

121 **In March, the** Merritt and Kaufman, 137.

121 **a Moscow hen; as Julius** *Disney Treasures—Disney Rarities, Celebrated Shorts: 1920s—1960s*, DVD, Buena Vista Home Video, 2005.

121 **with Dawn Paris** Merritt and Kaufman, 70.

121 **five-year-old Dawn** 1930 federal census, Los Angeles, April 12, 1930, Sheet 13B, Ancestry.com, *1930 United States Federal Census.*

121 **stage name, "Dawn; worked in movies** Merritt and Kaufman, 70.

121 **Dawn Evelyeen Paris** "Anne Shirley; Actress Starred in Childhood and as an Adult," *Los Angeles Times*, July 7, 1993, A12.

121 **born in New York** 1930 federal census, Los Angeles, April 12, 1930, Sheet 13B.

121 **in 1919** Anne Lederer entry, July 4, 1993, Ancestry.com, *Social Security Death Index.*

121 **forty-six-year-old Henry Paris** 1920 federal census, January 8, 1920, New York, Sheet 4A, Ancestry.com, *1920 United States Federal Census.*

121   **He, too, was** 1910 federal census, April 18, 1910, New York, Sheet 7B, Ancestry.com, *1910 United States Federal Census.*

121   **Mimi came to; By the time** 1920 federal census, January 8, 1920, New York, Sheet 4A.

121   **Dawn was photographed** "Anne Shirley; Actress Starred . . ."

122   **became a "photoplayer** 1924 Los Angeles city directory, 1724.

122   **It is possible** 1925 Los Angeles city directory, 1524.

122   **The terms the** Merritt and Kaufman, 70.

122   **after a month** Merritt and Kaufman, 137.

122   **"Sometimes there was** Merritt and Kaufman, 70 (quoting from Merritt and Kaufman interview of Anne Shirley Lederer. See Merritt and Kaufman, 11, 70).

122   **month of March** Canemaker (1991), 92.

122   **renewed tension between** Canemaker (1991), 94.

122   **from May 1924** Canemaker (1991), 84.

122   **to May 1925; With two months** Canemaker (1991), 92.

122   **The lawyer, over; Charlie declined; he and Margaret** Canemaker (1991), 94.

122   **"since January 2** Merritt and Kaufman, 55–56 (photograph of Copyright Registration of the Alice Comedy trademark, as published in *Official Gazette*, May 19, 1924, 562).

122   **was still $15** February 1997 Barrier Notes (citing "Personal Salary Account pages through fall, 1925).

122   **One night, after** Hubler interview of Roy Disney, February 20, 1968, *Walt's People, Volume 6*, 153; Gabler, 92 (citing same interview and interview of Mrs. Edna Disney by Richard Hubler, August 20, 1968).

122   **"It came to** Thomas (1998), 50.

122   **"When Roy told** Miller, 96.

122–23   **"left Walt alone; "apparently he didn't** Barrier (2007 book), 43 (citing Hubler interview of Roy Disney, February 20, 1968).

123   **"teased Walt that** Lillian Disney and Taves, 104.

123   **"said he married; "Walt always used** Green and Green, 11.

123   **should not marry** Miller, 96.

123   **"Which do you** Miller, 98.

123   **Edna, thirty-five** 1910 federal census, Kansas City, Missouri, April 26, 1910, Sheet 10A, Ancestry.com, *1910 United States Federal Census.*

123   **and her mother; arrived in Los Angeles** Gabler, 92 (citing Hubler interview of Roy Disney, February 20, 1968; Hubler interview of Edna Disney, August 20, 1968); Thomas (1998), 50; introduction to Hubler interview of Edna Disney, *Walt's People, Volume 6*, 161.

123   **The following day** Gabler, 91 (citing letter from Rudy Ising to Walt Disney, April 8, 1925).

123   **"a complex for** Gabler, 91 (citing interview of Roy Disney by Richard Hubler, June 18, 1968).

123   **"Ub[be] . . . , the Harman** Hubler interview of Lillian Disney dated April 16, 1968, *Walt's People, Volume 6*, 143; Barrier (2007 book), 44 (citing same interview).

123   **"was already working** Hubler interview of Edna Disney, *Walt's People, Volume 6*, 162.

123   **"Roy and I; honeymooned at the** Thomas (1998), 50.

123   *Alice Loses Out*; **That month, *Alice*** Merritt and Kaufman, 137–38.

123   **live-action bookend** *Disney's Alice Comedies, Volume 2*, DVD, Tom's Vintage Film, 2005.

123–24  **Marjorie Sewell, who** Merritt and Kaufman, 138.

124  **"I thought she** Merritt and Kaufman, 71–72 (quoting from Merritt and Kaufman interview of Marjorie Sewell Davis. See Merritt and Kaufman, 11).

124  **"[i]n all honesty; "[T]he girls who** Province interview of McGhee, *Hogan's Alley.*

124  **Appearing with Marjorie** *Disney's Alice Comedies, Volume 2,* DVD, Tom's Vintage Film, 2005.

124  **Kathleen Dollard, left** Smith (1978 list), 1.

124  **after extensive negotiations** Gabler, 90.

124  **"Rudy and I** Barrier interview of Harman, December 3, 1973, 21. See also "Hugh Harman (1903–1982)," Will Friedwald with Jerry Beck and Mark Kausler, *Graffiti,* Spring 1984, 3.

124  **Inker and painter** Smith (1978 list), 1.

124  **In May, perhaps** February 1997 Barrier Notes (citing "Salary Account—Straight Payroll" pages, December, 1924 through December, 1926).

124  **Lillian, probably because** Barrier (2007 book), 45 (citing "General Expense Account 1925–1926–1927 by Roy O. Disney").

124  **"I quit work; Afterwards, she only** Lillian Disney and Taves, 104.

124  **"Walt didn't like** Gabler, 95 (citing Hubler interview of Lillian Disney, April 16, 1968).

124  **Ham's sister Irene** Smith (1978 list), 1.

124  **as a painter** Interview of Rudolf Ising by Michael Barrier, November 30, 1973, 30.

124  **At nineteen, she** 1910 federal census, Edgely, North Dakota, April 22, 1910, Sheet 1B.

124  **She lived with** 1925 Los Angeles city directory, 979.

124  **Studio records show** Smith (1978 list), 1.

124  **twenty-two** Thomas (1998), 234.

124  **started as an** Smith (1978 list), 1.

124  **but Ruth denied** Smith interview of Ruth Disney, *Walt's People, Volume 8,* 37.

124  **"We came out** Clampett, 18.

124  **on Monday, June 22** Barrier (2007 book), 46.

124–25  **immediately upon their** Barrier interview of Ising, June 2, 1971, 8.

125  *Alice's Tin Pony* Merritt and Kaufman, 138–39.

125  **Hugh was hired** Smith (1978 list).

125  **as an inker** Barrier interview of Ising, November 30, 1973, 30.

125  **lived with Uncle** Barrier interview of Ising, June 2, 1971, 7.

125  **"I was able** Thomas, *Walt Disney Conversations,* 63.

125  **"Nothing [was different** Kaufman interview of Ising, *Walt's People, Volume 1,* 40–41.

125  **"same group," Disney** Merritt and Kaufman, 72 (quoting from Merritt and Kaufman interview of Rudy Ising. See Merritt and Kaufman, 11).

125  **"I did assistant** Merritt and Kaufman, 72 (quoting from Merritt and Kaufman interview of Rudy Ising. See Merritt and Kaufman, 11).

125  **A few days** Merritt and Kaufman, 72.

125  **became a cartoonist** 1925 Los Angeles city directory, 1352.

125  **the Pathé camera** Kaufman interview of Ising, *Walt's People, Volume 1,* 44.

125  **rented Bell and** Merritt and Kaufman, 65.

125  **paid Hugh $45; Walker Harman earned; As a result** February 1997 Barrier Notes (citing "Salary Account—Straight Payroll" pages, December 1924 through December 1926).

125   **the day before** February 1997 Barrier Notes (citing "Salary Account—Straight Payroll" pages, December 1924 through December 1926).

125   **Roy's salary remained** Thomas (1998), 49.

125   **Walt was now** February 1997 Barrier Notes (citing "Salary Account—Straight Payroll" pages, December 1924 through December 1926).

125   **on Monday, July 6** Smith (1979 article), 34.

125   **vacant** Merritt and Kaufman, 76; email from Dave Smith to T. Susanin, August 25, 2008.

125   **2719 Hyperion** 1927 Los Angeles city directory, 732.

125   **south of Griffith Park** *The Art of Walt Disney: from Mickey Mouse to the Magic Kingdom*, Christopher Finch, Harry N. Abrams, Inc., New York (1995 ed.), 31.

125   **Silver Lake region** Smith and Clark, 22.

125   **near the fabled** Thomas (1998), 52.

125   **The brothers planned** Merritt and Kaufman, 76.

125   **60-by-40-foot lot** Thomas (1998), 52.

126   **Sometime that week** Gabler, 95 (citing Ledger, 1924–1927; Studio Accounting Books, 1923–1930, July 13, 1925 entry; letter from Walt Disney to Carl Stalling, September 16, 1925).

126   **On Monday, July 13** The Greenes (1998 ed.), 48; Miller, 98.

126   **wore lavender** The Greenes (1998 ed.), 48; The Greenes (2001), 36.

126   **"very fascinated and** Hubler interview of Diane Disney Miller, *Walt's People, Volume 6*, 176.

126   **The couple honeymooned** Gabler, 95 (citing letter from Walt Disney to Carl Stalling, September 16, 1925).

126   **In Walt's absence** Merritt and Kaufman, 139.

126   **which used scenes; *Chops the Suey*** *Alice in Cartoon Land by Walt Disney*, DVD, VCI Entertainment, 2007.

126   **The photograph of** Merritt and Kaufman, 139.

126   **Paul L. Ries** 1923 Los Angeles city directory, 2588, 3646; 1924 Los Angeles city directory, 1900; 1925 Los Angeles city directory, 1635; 1926 Los Angeles city directory, 1702; 1927 Los Angeles city directory, 1667; 1928 Los Angeles city directory, 1772; 1929 Los Angeles Los Angeles city directory, 1812).

126   **Their office was** 1925 Los Angeles city directory, 1635.

126   **the Rieses worked** Email from J. B. Kaufman to T. Susanin, March 5, 2009.

126   **Another special effect** *Alice in Cartoon Land by Walt Disney*, DVD, VCI Entertainment, 2007.

126   **numerous other Alice** See, for example, *Disney Cartoons of the 1920's: Alice Comedies, Vol. 1*, DVD, Tom's Vintage Film, 2005 (*Alice's Day At Sea*); *Disney's Alice Comedies, Volume 2*, DVD, Tom's Vintage Film, 2005 (*Alice Cans the Cannibals*; *Alice the Toreador*).

126   **"was a very** Barrier interview of Harman, December 3, 1973, 36.

126   **New York Supreme Court** Canemaker (1991), 95.

126   **The Mintzes argued** Canemaker (1991), 94.

126   **In late July; On August 3** Canemaker (1991), 94–95.

126   **after visiting Walt's** Gabler, 95 (citing letter from Walt Disney to Carl Stalling, September 16, 1925).

126 **they had looked** Barrier (2007 book), 45 (citing Martin interview of Walt Disney, May or June 1956).

127 **settled into an** Gabler, 99 (citing Thomas interview of Lillian Disney Truyens, April 19, 1973).

127 **the Ray Apartment** 1925 Los Angeles city directory, 1608; 1926 Los Angeles city directory, 1673.

127 **at 4639 Melbourne Avenue** 1926 Los Angeles city directory, 770. The Disney Archives lists the address as 4637 Melbourne Avenue. See Barrier (2007 book), 45 (citing email from Dave Smith to Michael Barrier, April 24, 2006).

127 **Walt still lived** 1925 Los Angeles city directory, 753.

127 **with the Schneiders** 1925 Los Angeles city directory, 1710.

127 **Lilly still lived** 1925 Los Angeles city directory, 522.

127 **with Hazel Sewell** 1925 Los Angeles city directory, 1733.

127 **one-room honeymoon** The Greenes (1998 ed.), 49.

127 **small kitchenette apartment** Miller, 99; see also Hollis and Sibley, 13 (rent was $40 a month).

127 **"so unhappy because; "I was used** Gabler, 99–100 (citing Thomas interview of Lillian Disney Truyens, April 19, 1973).

127 **the Schneiders' house** 1925 Los Angeles city directory, 753.

127 **apartment on Melbourne; 4535 Melbourne** 1926 Los Angeles city directory, 770.

127 **"On Melbourne [is** Hubler interview of Edna Disney, *Walt's People, Volume 6*, 162.

127 **"was sincere, high-minded; "was a handsome** *My Life in 'toons: From Flatbush to Bedrock in Under a Century*, Joseph Barbera, Turner Publishing, Inc., 1994, 72.

127 **"drawled and spoke** Barbera, 71.

127 **found them "amiable** *A Cast of Friends*, Bill Hanna with Tom Ito, Da Capo Press, www.dacapopress.com, 1996, 19.

127 **their good-humored, optimistic** Hanna, 20.

127 **"study in contrasts; "the artist of** Hanna, 21.

127 **"leisurely warm and** Hanna, 56.

127 **"very quiet and** Hanna, 21.

127 **"drawing was very** Barrier interview of Harman, December 3, 1973, 41.

127 **"was always interested** Hugh Harman, Barrier interview of Harman and Ising, October 29, 1976, 50.

127–28 **"couldn't draw very; "fine, sketchy lines** Barrier interview of Ising, November 30, 1973, 32.

128 **expert on motion** Rudy Ising, Barrier interview of Harman and Ising, October 31, 1976, 87.

128 **"was able to; "He'd have made; "was really a** Barrier interview of Ising, November 30, 1973, 32.

128 **"Ubbe was never** Barrier interview of Harman, December 3, 1973, 42.

128 **"Alice was shot; Walt would direct** Kaufman interview of Ising, *Walt's People, Volume 1*, 42.

128 **"was the one** Kaufman interview of Ising, *Walt's People, Volume 1*, 47.

128 **"He was always** Barrier interview of Ising, June 2, 1971, 45.

128 **[W]e would sit** Kaufman interview of Ising, *Walt's People, Volume 1*, 50–51.

128–29 **"general story meeting** Barrier interview of Harman, December 3, 1973, 5.

129 **"An idea would** The Greenes (1998 ed.), 49.

129 "**very, very little** Barrier interview of Harman, December 3, 1973, 46.

129 "**We got so** Rudy Ising, Barrier interview of Harman and Ising, October 31, 1976, 73.

129 "**outside.... [on] a; "doing the camera** Rudy Ising, Barrier interview of Harman and Ising, October 29, 1976, 14.

129 "**We think that** Barrier (1999 book), 42 (citing letter from Rudy Ising to Ray Friedman, August 7, 1925).

129 **first two years; Rudy's brother, Louis** 1926 Los Angeles city directory, 1147.

129 **Ubbe also lived** 1925 Los Angeles city directory, 1106.

129 "**You saw them** Kaufman interview of Ising, *Walt's People, Volume 1*, 46.

129 "**when [Walt] first** Barrier interview of Ising, June 2, 1971, 44.

129 [**W]e used to** Kaufman interview of Ising, *Walt's People, Volume 1*, 41–42.

130 "**used to play** Kaufman interview of Ising, *Walt's People, Volume 1*, 48.

130 "[**w]hen we first** Barrier interview of Harman, December 3, 1973, 41.

130 "**picture shows** Hubler interview of Edna Disney, *Walt's People, Volume 6*, 162.

130 "[**W]e would do** Barrier interview of Harman, December 3, 1973, 41.

130 "**I've just got** The Greenes (1998 ed.), 49.

130 "**We'd go out** Barrier (2007 book), 45 (citing Martin interview of Lillian Disney, May or June 1956).

130 **Lilly would sleep** The Greenes (1998 ed.), 49.

130 "**When we were** Barrier (2007 book), 45 (citing Martin interview of Lillian Disney, May or June 1956).

130 "[**Energetic?] Oh, yes** Hubler interview of Edna Disney, *Walt's People, Volume 6*, 162.

130 "**Once, soon after** Lillian Disney and Taves, 104.

130–31 **fell behind in; he informed Charlie** Merritt and Kaufman, 78.

131 **he and Roy; Ham and Rudy** February 1997 Barrier Notes (citing "Salary Account—Straight Payroll" pages, December 1924 through December 1926).

131 **offered a bonus** Merritt and Kaufman, 78.

131 **wrote to Carl** Gabler, 99 (citing letter from Walt Disney to Carl Stalling, September 16, 1925).

131 *Alice in the Jungle*; **using live-action footage** Merritt and Kaufman, 66, 140.

131 **Margaret Davis (still** Gabler, 97 (citing letter from Charles Mintz to Mrs. Margaret J. Davis, October 1, 1925).

131–32 "**further holding up; Don't you think** Letter from C. B. Mintz to Mr. Walt Disney, September 26, 1925.

132 **via registered mail** Letter from C. B. Mintz to Mr. Walt Disney, October 6, 1925.

132 **First, let me** Letter from Walt Disney to Mr. C. B. Mintz, October 2, 1925.

132 **On October 6, 1925; "would not have; He catalogued for** Letter from C. B. Mintz to Mr. Walt Disney, October 6, 1925.

132 **Margaret Winkler had** Letter from M. J. Winkler to Mr. Walt Disney, March 4, 1924 (*Spooky Adventure*); Letter from M. J. Winkler to Walt Disney, April 7, 1924 (*Wild West Show*).

132 **Charlie himself praised** Letter from Charles Mintz to Walt Disney, August 7, 1924 (*Peacemaker*).

132 *Gets in Dutch* Letter from C. B. Mintz to Mr. Walt Disney, October 6, 1924 (*Gets in Dutch*).

132–33  "had any of; Haven't you a; "an absolute total; "would eventually be; "should whole-heartedly be; "man enough so Letter from C. B. Mintz to Mr. Walt Disney, October 6, 1924.

133  Our contract calls Letter from Walt Disney to Mr. C. B. Mintz, October 15, 1925.

133  "Walt resented the Barrier interview of Harman, December 3, 1973, 27.

133  he ripped up Barrier interview of Ising, November 30, 1973, 27.

133–34  One time [Thurston Kaufman interview of Ising, *Walt's People, Volume 1*, 48–49.

134  a part-time janitor Barrier (2007 book), 46; Smith (1979 article), 34; Letter from Thurston Harper to Dave Smith, March 1978.

134  "The sink was Letter from Thurston Harper to Dave Smith, March 1978.

134  John R. Lott 1929 Los Angeles city directory, 1393; John Lott entry, October, 1970, Ancestry.com, *Social Security Death Index*.

134  forty-two 1930 federal census, April 11, 1930, Los Angeles, Sheet 5A, Ancestry.com, *1930 United States Federal Census*.

134  started work at Smith (1978 list), 1.

134  He was born 1930 federal census, April 11, 1930, Los Angeles, Sheet 5A.

134  had already been 1924 Los Angeles city directory, 1464; 1925 Los Angeles city directory, 1279.

134  We are striving June 1994 Barrier Notes ("Winkler Film Corp." file) (citing letter from Walt Disney to Charles Mintz, November 6, 1925).

134  Charlie responded by; Charlie revealed that Gabler, 96 (citing telegram from Charles Mintz to Walt Disney, November 11, 1925).

134–35  a new contract; Charlie even invited; ("I will pay; make new arrangements June 1994 Barrier Notes ("Winkler Film Corp." file) (citing telegram from Charles Mintz to Walt Disney, November 11, 1925).

135  "rests entirely with; "a great distance; "[i]ndependent [cartoon] market; "[My] negotiations [with; Charlie's new national; "get together on; "work along with; "would have about; ("$900.00 payable on; "before making a Letter from C. B. Mintz to Mr. Walt Disney, November 17, 1925.

135  "indeed happy at; "that we admit; "Mrs. Mintz and; Charlie was aware Letter From C. B. Mintz to Mr. Walt Disney, November 24, 1925.

136  "the intermediary; he Barrier interview of Harman, December 3, 1973, 26.

136  Charlie therefore offered; "should be the; Charlie explained that; Charlie calculated that Letter from C. B. Mintz to Mr. Walt Disney, November 24, 1925.

136  continued into December June 1994 Barrier Notes ("Winkler Film Corp." file) (citing telegrams from Charles Mintz to Walt Disney, November 24 and December 7 and 15, 1925).

136  *Alice's Little Parade* Merritt and Kaufman, 141.

136  the last reel Merritt and Kaufman, 141.

136  by year's end Merritt and Kaufman, 72.

136  "If you think Thomas (1994 ed.), 80 (citing letter from Charles Mintz to Walt Disney, undated).

136  That Christmas, Walt; "At Christmas time Clampett, 18.

136–37  By year's end; "a hopeless task; "get together; Walt's counter offer; "positively not work; Charlie offered Walt; "very, very quickly; Charlie was through; "a doubt in; "must keep paying Letter from C. B. Mintz to Walt. Disney, December 31, 1925.

137   **in Tijuana; Walt drove part** Gabler, 100 (citing letter from Rudy Ising to Nadine Missakian, January 22, 1926).

137   **George Winkler sent; Once profits reached; "six like series; The next day; "have embodied in; "toys, novelties, newspaper** Letter from Walt Disney to Mr. George Winkler, January 9, 1926.

137   **MY OFFER IS** June 1994 Barrier Notes ("Winkler Film Corp." file) (citing telegram from Walt Disney to Charles Mintz, January 17, 1926); Thomas (1994 ed.), 80.

137   **on Monday, February 8** June 1994 Barrier Notes ("Winkler Film Corp." file) (citing telegram from Walt Disney to Charles Mintz, February 8, 1926).

137   **Under the terms; The first thirteen; The price was** Merritt and Kaufman, 78.

138   **Tuesday, February 9** Email from Dave Smith to T. Susanin, June 5, 2009.

138   **between Friday, February 12** Michael Barrier's research of weather reports in the *New York Times* showed that "rain fell in L.A. five straight days" on those dates. Email from Michael Barrier to T. Susanin, June 30, 2010.

138   **"rainy day in** Barrier (1999 book), 43 (citing letter from Rudy Ising to Max Maxwell, February 28, 1926; Barrier (2007 book), 49 (citing same letter).

138   **"in February . . . [that** Clampett, 18.

138   **"rented an old** Barrier interview of Harman, December 3, 1973, 49.

138   **"We hauled all** Barrier interview of Harman, December 3, 1973, 48.

138   **"I guess we; "were glad to** Barrier interview of Harman, December 3, 1973, 49.

# Walt Disney Studio

139   **In mid-February** Barrier (1999 book), 43 (citing letter from Rudy Ising to Max Maxwell, February 28, 1926; Barrier (2007 book), 49 (citing same letter).

139   **eastern border of** *Disney Animation: The Illusion of Life*, Frank Thomas & Ollie Johnston, Abbeville Press, New York, 1981, 141.

139   **"was mainly a; "very much used** Interviews of Ben Sharpsteen by Don Peri, 1974–1977, reprinted in *Working with Walt: Interviews with Disney Artists*, Don Peri, University Press of Mississippi, Jackson, 2008, 4.

139   **"a quiet little** "Animated Cartoon Pictures Speak Universal Languages; Secrets of How These Fantastic Comedies of the Screen Are Produced," Alice Ames Winter, *The Motion Picture Monthly*, January 1931, 7.

139   **"hardly noticed on** Thomas & Johnston, 141.

139   **at 2719 Hyperion** Smith (1979 article), 35.

139   **"little green and** Gabler, 98 (citing *Autobiography*, Walt Disney, 1939, third installment, 5).

139   **"little square building** Interview of Wilfred Jackson by Frank Thomas and Ollie Johnston May 18, 1978, reprinted in *Walt's People: Talking Disney with the Artists who Knew Him, Volume 7*, edited by Didier Ghez, Xlibris Corporation, 2008, 27.

139   **stucco** Thomas (1994 ed.), 80.

139   **1600 square feet** Smith (1979 article), 37; Gabler 98 (citing interview of Ben Sharpsteen by Don Peri, February 6, 1974, 3); Thomas & Johnston, 141.

139   **"wasn't much bigger** Clampett, 18.

139   **60-by-40-foot** Thomas (1994 ed.), 80.

139 **Griffith Park Boulevard** Black, 61.

139 **a main intersection** Peri interview of Sharpsteen, Peri, 4.

139 **The first property** Peri interview of Sharpsteen, Peri, 4; see also interview of Ben Sharpsteen by Don Peri, October 21, 1974, reprinted in *Walt's People: Talking Disney with the Artists who Knew Him, Volume 3,* edited by Didier Ghez, Xlibris Corporation, 2006, 19.

139 **2701 Hyperion** *Los Angeles City Directory,* The Los Angeles Directory Company, Los Angeles, 1936, 2567.

139 **pipe organ factory** Thomas & Johnston, 141; Gabler, 98; Peri interview of Sharpsteen, *Walt's People, Volume 3,* 19.

139 **2711 Hyperion** 1929 Los Angeles city directory, 1282.

139 **The third property; 2719 Hyperion** 1927 Los Angeles city directory, 732; Peri interview of Sharpsteen, *Walt's People, Volume 3,* 19.

139 **vacant lot** Thomas & Johnston, 141.

139 **"Walt's little shed** Thomas and Johnston interview of Jackson, *Walt's People, Volume 7,* 27.

140 **provided privacy** Thomas & Johnston, 141

140 **had a stage** Thomas and Johnston interview of Jackson, *Walt's People, Volume 7,* 27.

140 **staff of nine** Smith (1978 list), 1.

140 **On Tuesday, February 20; It was another** Email from Dave Smith to T. Susanin, June 5, 2009.

140 **the front door** Smith (1979 article), 36.

140 **Walt's office was** Black, 61.

140 **Roy's office; the camera room where; The dark room** Smith (1979 article), 36.

140 **"loafing room** Barrier (2007 book), 49 (citing letter from Rudy Ising to his family members, April 13, 1926).

140 **Between Walt's office** Smith (1979 article), 36.

140 **tables used by; "long table for** Smith (1979 article), 35.

140 **between Roy's office; Against the center** Smith (1979 article), 36.

140 **Behind the studio** Thomas and Johnston interview of Wilfred Jackson, *Walt's People, Volume 7,* 27.

140 **"big 2 x 4 structure** Rudy Ising, Barrier interview of Harman and Ising, October 29, 1976, 15.

140 **"was a platform** Hugh Harman, Barrier interview of Harman and Ising, October 29, 197, 15.

140 **"We had to** Rudy Ising, Barrier interview of Harman and Ising, October 29, 1976, 15.

140 **"Roy reasoned that** Thomas (1994 ed.), 80.

140 **"was my idea** Thomas (1998), 53; Kinney 198. Roy Disney told Dave Smith that "it was his [Roy's] idea to name the studio after Walt because the public could better identify with a single individual." See Gabler, footnote at 664. Also, "David Smith, Disney archivist, says that Roy O. Disney once told him that it was *his* decision to change the studio name because of Walt's dominant creative role." Watts, 459 n. 4.

140 **Roy's son, however; Roy's son claimed** Watts, 44 (citing interview of Roy E. Disney by Steven Watts, December 27, 1993).

141 **always kind of** Interview of Roy Edward Disney by Charles Solomon, July 20, 1998, reprinted *Walt's People: Talking Disney with the Artists who Knew Him, Volume 8,* edited by Didier Ghez, Xlibris Corporation, 2009, 365.

141   Hugh also recalled; "When we came; "between Walt and Clampett, 18.

141   "One evening when *Walt Disney and Assorted Other Characters: An Unauthorized Account of the Early Years at Disney's,* Jack Kinney, Harmony Books, New York, 1988, 198.

141   The Disneys moved Gabler, 100 (citing Thomas interview of Lillian Disney Truyens, April 19, 1973).

141   fall of 1926 *1926 Los Angeles White Pages,* Southern California Telephone Company, Los Angeles, September, 1926.

141   1307 North Commonwealth 1927 Los Angeles city directory, 732.

141   furniture had gotten Barrier (1999), 49 (citing letter from Rudy Ising to Max Maxwell, February 28, 1926).

141   "the plaster was Barrier interview of Harman, December 3, 1973, 48–49.

141   "just like drawing Barrier interview of Harman, December 3, 1973, 48.

141   *Alice's Monkey Business* Merritt and Kaufman, 142.

142   "'Alice's Mysterious Mystery; "concede that I; The Alice Comedies; "special efforts Letter from C. B. Mintz to Mr. Walt Disney, February 13, 1926.

142   "found several things Letter from Walt Disney to Charles Mintz, March 1, 1926.

142   I received your June 1994 Barrier Notes ("Winkler Film Corp." file) (citing letter from Charles Mintz to Walt Disney, March 9, 1926).

142   The Mintzes retained June 1994 Barrier Notes ("Winkler correspondence folder") (citing letter from Asher Blum to M. J. Winkler, March 16, 1926).

142   "Statement Of Facts" Undated "Statement Of Facts" forwarded by the M. J. Winkler company to Asher Blum on March 15, 1926. See June 1994 Barrier Notes ("Winkler correspondence folder") (citing letter Asher Blum to M. J. Winkler, March 16, 1926), making clear that one of the Mintzes sent the "Statement Of Facts" to Blum for analysis on March 15.

143   trustee successfully demanded; allowed Pictorial to Memorandum of Agreement between Laugh-O-gram Films, Inc., Trustee Joseph M. Jones and Pictorial Clubs, Inc., of New York, January 24, 1924, 2, 5.

143   Mintzes became aware; merely "employed" by; "While we were "Statement Of Facts," 1–2.

143   "Mr. Disney has June 1994 Barrier Notes ("Winkler correspondence" folder) (citing Asher Blum letter to M. J. Winkler, March 16, 1926).

143   On Sunday, March 21; He arrived in June 1994 Barrier Notes ("Winkler Film Corp" file) (citing letter from Charles Mintz to Walt Disney, March 9, 1926).

143–44  Qualifying the contract; Charlie, by then June 1994 Barrier Notes ("Winkler correspondence" folder) (citing letter from Walt Disney to Winkler Film Corp., March 30, 1926).

144   Winkler Pictures, Incorporated Letter from C. B. Mintz to Mr. Walt Disney, May 7, 1926.

144   You asked me June 1994 Barrier Notes ("Winkler Film Corp." file) (citing letter from Charles Mintz to Walt Disney, May 20, 1926).

144   I want to thank June 1994 Barrier Notes ("Winkler Film Corp." file) (citing letter from Walt Disney to Charles Mintz, June 15, 1926).

144   series of photographs See, for example, Finch, 31; Merritt and Kaufman, 77. Michael Barrier writes that such photographs were probably taken as publicity shots, but that Rudy Ising told Barrier in 1979 that there was "[n]o particular reason for the taking

of these [types of] photos that I can think of. Walt did like to have photos taken of himself and his staff every so often." "A Day in the Life: Disney, February 1927," Michael Barrier, March 6, 2008, www.MichaelBarrier.com.

145 **"finally dried out** Barrier interview of Harman, December 3, 1973, 50–51.

145 **formal photograph in** Finch, 28.

145 **"write me in** June 1994 Barrier Notes ("Winkler Film Corp." file) (citing letter from Walt Disney to Charles Mintz, June 22, 1926).

145 **studio still showing** Merritt and Kaufman, 77.

145 **"We were always** Rudy Ising, Barrier interview of Harman and Ising, October 29, 1976, 51.

145 **On Sunday, August 1; "will leave Walt** Gabler, 101 (citing Harman and Ising letter to C. G. Maxwell, August 1, 1926).

145 **In August Walt; *Clara Cleans Her*; Ubbe did the** Merritt and Kaufman, 145–46.

145 **the cast included** *Disney's Laugh-O-Grams*, DVD, Cartoons On Film, 2005.

145 **August also saw** Barrier (2007 book), 49 (citing email from Dave Smith to Michael Barrier, October 31, 2005).

145 **Two months earlier** Gabler, 104 (citing General Expenses Account, 1925, 1926, 1927).

145 **Los Feliz** Barrier (2007 book), 49.

145–46 **"In '26, we** Thomas (1998), 54.

146 **Pacific Ready-Cut** Barrier (2007 book), 49 (citing Hubler interview of Roy Disney, June 18, 1968).

146 **The houses each; "exorbitant** Miller, 99.

146 **terms of Charlie's** Letter from C. B. Mintz to Walt Disney, November 17, 1925.

146 **Joe Kennedy** Crafton, 161.

146 **on Monday, September 6** Merritt and Kaufman, 141–42.

146 **Not long after** Bob started at the studio on September 13, 1926. Smith (1978 list), 1.

146 **twenty-two-year-old Robert Edmunds** Merritt and Kaufman, 146.

146 **British seaman** Hugh Harman, Barrier interview of Harman and Ising, October 29, 1976, 63.

146 **Bob had sometimes; "virtually lived with** Hugh Harman, Barrier interview of Harman and Ising, October 29, 1976, 64.

146 **Bob's first reel** Merritt and Kaufman, 146.

146 **"was the first** Hugh Harman, Barrier interview of Harman and Ising, October 29, 1976, 62–63.

146 **Bob left the** Smith (1978 list), 1.

146 **"went up north** Hugh Harman, Barrier interview of Harman and Ising, October 29, 1976, 63.

146 **Walt closed his; Unbeknownst to Walt** Barrier (2007), 53.

146 **"We made one** Kaufman interview of Ising, *Walt's People, Volume 1*, 32.

146 **Walt gave Ubbe** Smith (1972 article), 34.

146 **Walt still had** February 1997 Barrier Notes (citing "Salary Account—Straight Payroll" pages, December 1924 through December 1926).

146 **Paul Smith** Smith (1978 list), 1.

146 **twenty** Paul J. Smith obituary, November 1, 1980, reprinted in *Variety Obituaries, Volume 9: 1980–1983*, Garland Publishing, Inc., New York, 198

146 **assistant** Barrier interview of Ising, November 30, 1973, 27.

146 **short time later** Paul started at the studio on December 8, 1926. Smith (1978 list), 1.

146  **for $18 a** February 1997 Barrier Notes (citing "Salary Account—Straight Payroll" pages, December 1924 through December 1926).

147  **"Walt Disney just lived** Barrier (2007 book), 52 (citing interview of Paul Smith by Milton Gray, March 22, 1978).

147  **"pretty good" animator; "He wasn't a** Hugh Harman, Barrier interview of Harman and Ising, October 29, 1976, 44.

147  **"Mrs. Mintz, the** Letter from C. B. Mintz to Mr. Walt Disney, December 6, 1926.

147  **Throughout the year** Gabler, 99 (citing General Expense Account, 1925, 1926, 1927).

147  **between $1,800 and** Miller, 99.

147  **Two days after** Merritt and Kaufman, 145.

147  **in very tight** June 1994 Barrier Notes ("Winkler Film Corp." file) (citing letter from Walt Disney to Charles Mintz, December 27, 1926.

147  **Ham Hamilton left** Smith (1978 list), 1.

147  *Circus Story* **(eventually** Merritt and Kaufman, 147.

147  **Supervisor of Production** "From the *Film Daily Year Book* for 1927," Michael Barrier, September 20, 2009, www.MichaelBarrier.com.

147  **decided to replace** Gabler, 101.

147  **veteran child actor** Iwerks, 39.

147  **Lois Eleanor Hardwick, twelve** Lois Dodson entries, November 1978, Ancestry. com, *Social Security Death Index*, and November 30, 1978, *California Death Index, 1940–1997.*

147  **the daughter of; as a laborer** 1920 federal census, Rowland, California, January 30, 1920, Sheet 4A, Ancestry.com, *1920 United States Federal Census* (William was born in Mississippi); 1930 federal census, West Covina, California, April, 1930, Sheet 2A, Ancestry.com, *1930 United States Federal Census* (William was born in Tennessee).

147  **grammar school janitor** 1930 federal census, West Covina, California, April, 1930, Sheet 2A.

147  **older brother, Frederick** 1920 federal census, Rowland, California, January 30, 1920, Sheet 4A.

147  **E. 57th Street** 1926 Los Angeles city directory, 1025.

147  **still the President** "From the *Film Daily Year Book* for 1927," Michael Barrier, September 20, 2009, www.MichaelBarrier.com.

148  **In regard to** Letter from Walt Disney to C. B. Mintz, January 26, 1927.

148  **. . . I certainly did; "might just be** Letter from C. B. Mintz to Mr. Walt Disney, January 31, 1927.

148  **"Lois Hardwick[ ] . . . . was** Province interview of McGhee, *Hogan's Alley.*

148  **Early in 1927; Walt's house was** Barrier (2007 book), 49 (citing Hubler interview of Roy Disney, 1968).

148  **"Each one," Lilly** Hubler interview of Lillian Disney, *Walt's People, Volume 6*, 145.

148  **Walt said that** Miller, 99.

148  **"One of our** Hubler interview of Lillian Disney, *Walt's People, Volume 6*, 143.

148  **Unless they had** Thomas (1998), 53–54.

148–49  **Lilly's mother moved** Gabler, 105.

149  **"Walt was so** The Greenes (2001), 36.

149  **On Friday, January 5; Ubbe's friend, Santa; courtship included weekend; Ubbe was away** Iwerks, 43–44; Gabler 101.

149  **On Monday, January 15** Barrier (2007 book), 54.

149 **"I got [Friz** Hugh Harman, Barrier interview of Harman and Ising, October 29, 1976, 47–48.

149 **"everybody [at the; "this little red-headed** Barrier (2007 book), 54 (citing interview of C. G. Maxwell by Milton Gray, April 6, 1977).

149 **twenty-two** Introduction to interview of Friz Freleng by J. B. Kaufman, January 8, 1991 and July 20, 1991, reprinted *Walt's People: Talking Disney with the Artists who Knew Him, Volume 2,* edited by Didier Ghez, Xlibris Corporation, 2006, 15.

149 **was a year** Barrier (2007 book), 54.

149 **Well, when I** "Interview with Fritz Freleng," Reg Hartt, *Griffithiana,* December 1988, 33.

149 **Friz sat next; "'Well, you can't** Kaufman interview of Freleng, *Walt's People, Volume 2,* 16–17.

149 **Hugh mentioned Friz** Iwerks, 44.

149 **"I'd told Walt** Barrier interview of Harman, December 3, 1973, 52.

149 **"Hugh recommended that** Burnes, 1D.

149 **"different offers"** Kaufman interview of Freleng, *Walt's People, Volume 2,* 16.

149 **"I told Walt** Kaufman interview of Freleng, *Walt's People, Volume 2,* 17.

150 **"Walt was one; "[b]eing the first** Burnes, 1D.

150 **"Walt met me** Interview of Friz Freleng, *Walt's People, Volume 2,* 17; see also Burnes, 3D.

150 **not long after** "A Day in the Life: Disney, February 1927," Michael Barrier, March 6, 2008, www.MichaelBarrier.com. Barrier concludes that, based on the dates of employment of those seen in this series of photographs, the pictures were taken between Saturday, February 5, and Thursday, February 10, 1927. With regard to the formal look of these photographs, Rudy told Barrier that Walt "might have thought that being dressed in suits instead of the well known shot [from 1926] of us all in golf pants would be more dignified."

150 **Friz joined his** Merritt and Kaufman, 84; "A Day in the Life: Disney, February 1927," Michael Barrier, March 6, 2008, www.MichaelBarrier.com.

150 **Paul Smith and** "A Day in the Life: Disney, February 1927," Michael Barrier, March 6, 2008, www.MichaelBarrier.com.

150 **assistant** Barrier interview of Ising, November 30, 1973, 27.

150 **animator Norman** Smith (1978 list), 1.

150 **twenty-three** "Norman Blackburn; Producer and Advertising Executive," *Los Angeles Times,* February 27, 1990, A24.

150 **"Everybody is wearing; "I didn't think** Burnes, 1D.

150 **"We have a secret** Barrier (2007 book), 53 (citing letter from Rudy Ising to Adele Ising, January 29, 1927).

150 **"quite confident of** Barrier (1999), 45 (citing letter from Hugh Harman and Rudy Ising to Max Maxwell, January 9, 1927).

150 **On Wednesday, February 23** Smith (1978 list), 1.

150 **few days before** Finch, 33. Les recalled that he "graduated from high school on a Thursday and I went to work [at the studio] on a Monday[,]" but his actual start date, gleaned from Disney Archives records, fell on a Wednesday.

150 **Leslie James Clark; The family lived** Canemaker (2001), 9–10.

150 **Les passed the** Interview of Les Clark by Frank Thomas and Ollie Johnston, September 18, 1978, reprinted in *Walt's People: Talking Disney with the Artists who Knew Him, Volume 8,* edited by Didier Ghez, Xlibris Corporation, 2009, 55.

150 **"working a part-time** Finch, 33.

150 **It was during** Interview of Les Clark by Don Peri, August 13, 1978, reprinted in *Working with Walt: Interviews with Disney Artists*, Don Peri, University Press of Mississippi, Jackson, 2008, 120–21; Canemaker (2001), 9 (citing letter from Les Clark to John Canemaker, July 1973).

151 **"a malt shop** Peri interview of Clark, Peri, 120.

151 **"used to come over** Finch, 33.

151 **"used to come in** Peri interview of Clark, Peri, 120.

151 **praised the lettering** Canemaker (2001), 9 (citing letter from Les Clark to Frank Thomas and Ollie Johnston, September 14, 1978).

151 **ice cream and confectioners** 1924 Los Angeles city directory, 2504; 1925 Los Angeles city directory, 826; 1926 Los Angeles city directory, 848, 3325. (By 1926, Farris moved his shop two doors north, to the corner of N. Vermont and Kingswell).

151 **Albert Lawson; one block north** 1924 Los Angeles city directory, 919; 1927 Los Angeles city directory, 809.

151 **By early 1927; "While I was** Finch, 33.

151 **on Saturday, February 19** Peri interview of Clark, Peri, 120. Les says that he met with Walt on the Saturday before he started work, and Les started at the studio on February 23, 1927. Smith (1978 list), 1.

151 **"told him I** Finch, 33.

151 **"swift, deft; "might just be** Canemaker (2001); 9 (citing letter from Les Clark to Michael Barrier, December 1, 1973).

151 **"invited me to** Finch, 33.

151 **The other was** Smith (1978), 1.

151 **twenty-one** Ben Clopton entry, November, 1987, Ancestry.com, *Social Security Death Index*.

151 **"You see . . . the** Kaufman interview of Ising, *Walt's People, Volume 1*, 45.

151 **"had some very** Hugh Harman, Barrier interview of Harman and Ising, October 29, 1976, 49.

151 **"Ben developed this** Barrier interview of Harman, December 3, 1973, 41.

151 **He commuted to** Kaufman interview of Freleng, *Walt's People, Volume 2*, 17.

151 **I rented a room** Kaufman interview of Freleng, *Walt's People, Volume 2*, 17–18.

152 **Well, Hugh Harman** Kaufman interview of Freleng, *Walt's People, Volume 2*, 21.

152 **"I'd become very** Barrier (2007), 54 (citing interview of Friz Freleng by Joe Adamson, University of California, Los Angeles, Department of Theater Arts, for "An Oral History of the Motion Picture in America," 1968–69).

152 **"made mistakes and** Barrier (1999 book), 46 (citing tape recorded letter from Friz Freleng to Michael Barrier, circa July 1976).

152 **"I don't think** Barrier (2007), 54 (citing Adamson interview of Freleng).

152 **Rudy left** Friedwald, 3; Barrier (2007 book), 46; Gabler, 101 (citing Barrier [1999], 45).

152 **(although Rudy later** According to Michael Barrier, "Rudy was explicit about being fired, but also explicit about its being a friendly, almost casual parting—no animosity." Barrier confirms that Rudy was "very much a night owl[,]" and Barrier struggled to keep awake during their late night interviews. Email from Michael Barrier to T. Susanin, June 26, 2009.

152 **How did I** Kaufman interview of Ising, *Walt's People, Volume 1*, 52–53.

152 **"I don't blame** Barrier interview of Harman, December 3, 1973, 24.

153 **[u]p to the** Letter from Walt Disney to C. B. Mintz, February 26, 1927.

153 **"later pictures; "[a]t that time** Letter from C. B. Mintz to Mr. Walt Disney, March 3, 1927.

153 **Charlie, concluding a** "'U' Will Release Animated Cartoon Comedies," *Motion Picture News*, March 25, 1927, 1052.

153 **Robert** *1925 New York City City Directory*, R. L. Polk & Company, Inc., New York, 1925, 2281.

153 **H. Cochrane, the vice** "'U' Will Release Animated Cartoon Comedies," *Motion Picture News*, March 25, 1927, 1052.

153 **boss, Carl Laemmle** Thomas (1994 ed.), 83.

153 **president of Universal** 1925 New York City city directory, 2281.

153 **he wanted a** Thomas (1994 ed.), 83.

153 **"Universal Film Company** Mann, 715.

153 **Margaret Winkler thought** Thomas (1994 ed.), 83.

153 **"Winklers talked to** Rudy Ising, Barrier interview of Harman and Ising, October 29, 1976, 20.

153 **Walt had pictures** Letter from Walt Disney to C. B. Mintz, January 26, 1927.

153 **"national organization** Letter from C. B. Mintz to Mr. Walt Disney, January 31, 1927.

153 **"So," according to** Rudy Ising, Barrier interview of Harman and Ising, October 29, 1976, 20.

153 **"just sat down** Barrier interview of Harman, December 3, 1973, 39.

153 **"several rough pencil** Letter from Walt Disney to C. B. Mintz, January 26, 1927.

153–54 **I received the** Letter from C. B. Mintz to Mr. Walt Disney, January 31, 1927.

154 **Universal liked the; Only then did** Thomas (1998), 55; see also Thomas (1994 ed.), 83.

154 **a committee at** Email from Diane Disney Miller to T. Susanin, January 19, 2010.

154 **Charlie arrived in** "'U' Will Release Animated Cartoon Comedies," *Motion Picture News*, March 25, 1927, 1052.

154 **met with Walt** Gabler, 102.

154 **Charlie agreed to** "'U' Will Release Animated Cartoon Comedies," *Motion Picture News*, March 25, 1927, 1052; Barrier (2007 book), 51 (citing "General Expense Account 1925–1926–1927 by Roy O. Disney").

154 **On Saturday, March 12; "U" to Release** "'U' to Release 'Oswald,'" *Moving Picture World*, March 12, 1927.

154 **George Winkler was** "The Big Bad Wolf," *Fortune*, November 1934, 146.

154 **Universal Announces Release** Crafton, 209 (citing "Universal Announces Release of 'Oscar [sic] the Rabbit' Cartoons," *Moving Picture World*, March 12, 1927). The March 12, 1927, issue of *Moving Picture World*, however, is cited immediately above, and does not include the article to which Crafton cites. Perhaps Crafton meant to cite to a different trade journal.

154 **had designed Oswald** Merritt and Kaufman, 86.

154–55 **It was announced** Barrier interview of Harman, December 3, 1973, 38. See also Hugh Harman, Barrier interview of Harman and Ising, October 29, 1976, 19–20.

155 **"[i]t was decided** Hugh Harman, Barrier interview of Harman and Ising, October 29, 1976, 20.

155 **By late March** Merritt and Kaufman (book), 149–50.

155 **"safely [to] find** June 1994 Barrier Notes ("Winkler Film Corp." file) (citing telegram from Charles Mintz to Walt Disney, March 28, 1927).

155   **I guess I; he addressed it** June 1994 Barrier Notes ("Winkler Film Corp." file) (citing letter from Charles Mintz to Walt Disney, April 1, 1927).

155   **On Saturday, April 2; That same day** Smith (1978 list), 1.

155   **"in steps from** Smith (1972 article), 34.

155   **The first Oswald** Merritt and Kaufman, 86.

155   **"The theme of** Barrier interview of Harman, December 3, 1973, 37.

155–56  **Oswald arrived today** Night letter from Charles Mintz to Walt Disney, April 15, 1927.

156   **(1) Approximately 100** Thomas (1994 ed.), 83.

156   **Sometimes there are** Iwerks, 44–45.

156   **He has no** Thomas (1994 ed.), 83.

156   **(5) Why is Oswald** Iwerks, 45.

156   **[s]orry [that] we** June 1994 Barrier Notes ("Winkler Film Corp." file) (citing telegram from Charles Mintz to Walt Disney, April 15, 1927).

156   **As he worked** Merritt and Kaufman, 150.

156   **"neat and trim;"younger character, peppy** Thomas (1994 ed.), 83.

156   **"shown in the;"peculiarly ... OSWALD** Gabler 102–03 (citing letter from Walt Disney to Charles Mintz, April 27, 1927).

156   **"[B]y the time** Thomas (1994 ed.), 83.

156   **"poorest pictures have** Gabler, 103 (citing letter from Walt Disney to Charles Mintz, April 27, 1927).

157   **"man of experience** Gabler, 104 (citing letter from Walt Disney to Charles Mintz, April 27, 1927).

157   **"We [animators] had** Barrier interview of Harman, December 3, 1973, 40.

157   **1917 Harold Lloyd** Iwerks, 45.

157   **eagerly anticipated by** Merritt and Kaufman, 87.

157   **In this short** *Walt Disney Treasures—The Adventures of Oswald the Lucky Rabbit,* DVD, Buena Vista Home Entertainment, 2007.

157   **Well, Walt would** Kaufman interview of Freleng, *Walt's People, Volume 2,* 22.

157   **Hugh helped animate; "Walt," said Hugh** Barrier interview of Harman, December 3, 1973, 38.

157   **"thought of the** Barrier interview of Harman, December 3, 1973, 37.

157–58  **"It was a; when the rabbit** Kaufman interview of Freleng, *Walt's People, Volume 2,* 24–25.

158   **from** *Alice's Picnic* Merritt and Kaufman, 148.

158   **"Mrs. Julius** Merritt and Kaufman, 81 (citing *Alice's Picnic* copyright application script summary).

158   **I remember one** Kaufman interview of Freleng, *Walt's People, Volume 2,* 23.

158   **shipped** *Trolley Troubles* Merritt and Kaufman, 150.

158–59  **This picture is** Thomas (1994 ed.), 84 (citing letter from Walt Disney to Charles Mintz dated after receipt by Mintz of the second Oswald cartoon).

159   **Ham Hamilton returned; sister, Irene, left** Smith (1978 list), 1.

159   **"very best of** Kaufman interview of Freleng, *Walt's People, Volume 2,* 18.

159   **Maxwell, who moved** Smith (1978), 1.

159   **Twenty-one-year old** 1930 federal census, Los Angeles, April 8, 1930, Page 7B, Ancestry.com, *1930 United States Federal Census.*

159   **animator Ray Abrams** Smith (1978 list), 1.

159   "started as beginners Hugh Harman, Barrier interview of Harman and Ising, October 29, 1976, 39.

159   "the period when Barrier (2007 book), 52 (citing letter from Max Maxwell to Bob Thomas dated August 20, 1973).

159   "We'd all be Barrier (2007 book), 52 (citing interview of Paul Smith by Milton Gray dated March 22, 1978).

159   *Universal Weekly* featured Gabler, 103 (citing *Universal Weekly* inside cover, May 28, 1927).

159   Something NEW from *Universal Weekly* inside cover, May 28, 1927.

159–60  five-cent candy bar; "F. F. Vincent; "The Vogan Candy; The extensive advertising; "The bar immediately; "his face as "Universal's Oswald Cartoon Comedies Backed by Chocolate Bar Tie-Up," *Universal Weekly*, August 20, 1927, 32, reprinted in Merritt and Kaufman, 112.

160   Philadelphia Badge Company Thomas (1994 ed.), 85.

160   discontent over *Poor* Gabler, 102.

160   it premiered at Merritt and Kaufman, 150; Iwerks, 45; Crafton, 209–10.

160   at the Roxy Crafton, 209–10.

160   "As conductor on Thomas (1994 ed.), 84 (citing *The Film Daily* review of *Trolley Troubles*).

160   "good for a C. S. Sewell, editor, "Timely Reviews of Short Subjects," *Moving Picture World*, August 13, 1927, 470.

160   If the first "Opinion of Current Productions," Chester J. Smith, *Motion Picture News*, August 19, 1927, 526.

160   *Alice in the Big* Merritt and Kaufman, 150.

160   "she was terrible Carr, 57.

160   Walt lost money Gabler, 99 (citing General Expense Account, 1925, 1926, 1927).

160   "The Alice cartoons Roy Disney, 215.

160   One unit was Merritt and Kaufman, 98, 152–53.

161   twenty-year-old Allen 1920 federal census, Kansas City, January 3, 1920, Page 2A, Ancestry.com, *1930 United States Federal Census*; Allen E. Freleng entry, March 17, 1943, Ancestry.com, *Social Security Death Index*.

161   Freleng, was hired Smith (1978 list, 1).

161   led the other Merritt and Kaufman, 98, 152–53.

161   A new animator Smith (1978 list), 1.

161   twenty John W. Cannon entry, December 6, 1946, Ancestry.com, *California Death Index, 1940–1997*.

161   Walt now offered Merritt and Kaufman, 98.

161   Story meetings were; A one-page synopsis Barrier interview of Harman, December 3, 1973, 36.

161   "[u]nless you were Gabler, 100 (citing CD ROM), *Walt Disney: An Intimate History of the Man and His Magic*, CD-ROM, Pantheon Productions, 1998.

161   Hugh claimed that Barrier interview of Harman, December 3, 1973, 21.

161   Walker Harman left Smith (1978 list), 1.

161   "[e]verybody was conspiring Crafton, 208 (citing his interview of Friz Freleng, 1979).

161   telling him I Barrier (2007 book), 54 (citing tape-recorded letter from Friz Freleng to Michael Barrier, circa July 1976).

161 **"even though Rudy** Hugh Harman, Barrier interview of Harman and Ising, October 29, 197, 16.

161 **"asked Rudy to** Barrier interview of Harman, December 3, 1973, 24.

161 **"den of strife** Barrier (1999 book), 67 (citing letter from Rudy Ising to Thurston Harper, circa mid-1927).

161 **"a lot to** Barrier (1999 book), 47 (citing letter from Rudy Ising to Bruno (last name unknown), June 29, 1927).

161 **Charlie Mintz had** Barrier interview of Harman, December 3, 1973, 27 (Hugh says this took place in mid-1928, but this happened in mid-1927); Gabler, 106.

161 **who would go** Miller, 100.

162 **approach Hugh about** Barrier interview of Harman, December 3, 1973, 27.

162 **"made telephone calls; "at various places** Barrier (2007 book), 55 (citing interview of Paul Smith by Milton Gray, March 22, 1978).

162 **"I was interested** Hugh Harman, Barrier interview of Harman and Ising, October 29, 1976, 19.

162 **"told me frankly; "asked me if; "didn't want to undercut** Barrier interview of Harman, December 3, 1973, 27.

162 **"to engage in; "Winklers have made** Barrier (2007 book), 54–55 (citing letter from Rudy Ising to Ray Friedman, August 27, 1927).

162 **he quit the** Barrier (2007 book), 54.

162 **The previous day; As Friz rode; The next day Friz collected his** Watts, 45 (citing Adamson [1968 and 1969], 5–6).

162 **"Walt and I; "I couldn't take** Burnes, 3D.

162–63 **"Walt was just** Kaufman interview of Freleng, *Walt's People, Volume 2*, 19.

163 **"was the best** Hugh Harman, Barrier interview of Harman and Ising, October 29, 1976, 44.

163 **"Walt was very** Hugh Harman, Barrier interview of Harman and Ising, October 29, 1976, 48.

163 **"We used to; "almost every other; Finally, Friz would** Barrier interview of Harman, December 3, 1973, 53.

163 **"I used to be** Watts, 46 (citing Martin/Miller interview, Reel 11, 5–6).

163 **Two weeks after** Merritt and Kaufman, 152.

163 **In this reel** *Walt Disney Treasures—The Adventures of Oswald the Lucky Rabbit*, DVD, Buena Vista Home Entertainment, 2007.

163 **eventually named Fanny** Merritt and Kaufman, 88. Fanny was replaced with a cat girlfriend in several 1928 Oswald shorts, including *Rival Romeos*, *Bright Lights*, *Ozzie of the Mounted*, *Oh What A Knight*, and *Sky Scrappers*. *Walt Disney Treasures—The Adventures of Oswald the Lucky Rabbit*, DVD, Buena Vista Home Entertainment, 2007.

163 **"lives up to** C. S. Sewell, editor, "Timely Reviews of Short Subjects," *Moving Picture World*, September 10, 1927, 116.

163 **The next three** Merritt and Kaufman, 152.

163 **In *Mechanical Cow*** *Walt Disney Treasures—The Adventures of Oswald the Lucky Rabbit*, DVD, Buena Vista Home Entertainment, 2007.

163 **"has a wild** Sewell (August 13, 1927).

163 **Hugh recalled that; "figured out a** Hugh Harman, Barrier interview of Harman and Ising, October 29, 1976, 20–21.

163 **"hero in action** Sewell (August 13, 1927); see also *Walt Disney Treasures—The Adventures of Oswald the Lucky Rabbit*, DVD, Buena Vista Home Entertainment, 2007.

163 **"chock full of** Thomas (1994 ed.), 84 (citing *Motion Picture News* review of *Poor Papa*).

163 **Oswald is a** *Walt Disney Treasures—The Adventures of Oswald the Lucky Rabbit*, DVD, Buena Vista Home Entertainment, 2007.

164 **"In addition to** Thomas (1994 ed.), 84–85 (citing *Moving Picture World*).

164 **"Oswald looks like** Thomas (1998), 55–56 (citing *The Film Daily* review).

164 **"larger and larger** Miller, 100.

164 **brothers purchased ten; They also invested** Gabler, 104 (citing General Expenses Account, 1925–1926–1927).

164 **Ubbe invested his; and bought a** Iwerks, 48–49.

164 **Roy hired inkers** Smith (1978 list), 1.

164 **a former maid** 1928 Los Angeles city directory, 462 (the 1928 city directory likely used 1927 address and job information).

164 **twenty-six-year-old Mary Tebb** Mary Tebb entry, March 16, 1993, Ancestry.com, *Social Security Death Index*.

164 **cousin, Ruby Bounds** Smith (1978 list), 1.

164 **Rudy wrote to; "at present working** Barrier (2007 book), 55 (citing letter from Rudy Ising to Friz Freleng, November 15, 1927).

164 **The November Oswald** *Walt Disney Treasures—The Adventures of Oswald the Lucky Rabbit*, DVD, Buena Vista Home Entertainment, 2007; Merritt and Kaufman, 153.

164 **The December reels** Merritt and Kaufman, 153–54.

164 **"accomplished the astounding** Merritt and Kaufman, 87.

164 **"enabled the [Disney** Carr, 57.

164 **had grown to** Smith (1978 list), 1. But see Gabler, 104 (citing *Autobiography*, Walt Disney, 1934), suggesting that there were twenty-two employees at this time; Gabler, footnote at 666 (citing Studio Accounting Books, 1923–1930), suggesting there were sixteen employees then.

164–65 **Walt's weekly salary; brothers cleared $500** Gabler, 104 (citing General Expenses Account, 1925–1926–1927).

165 **prepared to ship** *Ozzie of the Mounted* was shipped in late January, 1928. Merritt and Kaufman, 157.

165 **George Winkler continued** Barrier (1976 article), 46–47.

165 **Ubbe suspected George's** Iwerks, 50.

165 **"fortnightly" visits to** Thomas (1994 ed.), 85.

165 **Ubbe told Walt** Gabler, 106 (citing interview of Ub Iwerks, circa 1956, Walt Disney Archives).

165 **called them "renegades** Barrier (1999 book), 48 (citing "typewritten notes based on unrecorded interview with Iwerks" from the Walt Disney Archives. Barrier believes that the interview of Iwerks was done by Bob Thomas in the 1950s. See Barrier [1999 book], 581, note 131).

165 **on Thursday, February 2** "Extends Winkler Contract for Additional Three Years," *The Film Daily*, February 16, 1928, 1.

165 **"one of the best** Gabler, 106 (citing *The Film Daily*, February 16, 1928).

165 **"Our plans to** Barrier (2007 book), 55 (citing letter from Rudy Ising to Friz Freleng, February 10, 1928).

165 **brothers talked and** Thomas (1998), 56.

165 **Walt told a reporter** Lawrance.

165 **"At the end** Byrnes, 24.

166 **The [Oswald] series** Walt Disney (1941 article), 107.

166 **While he intended** Gabler, 106.

166 **"couldn't break even; "was paying them; "I went along** Lillian Disney and Taves, 104.

166 **Walt left for** "Notes from the [Disney] Archives' file of Walt Disney's 1928 correspondence from New York," Michael Barrier, June 1994 and February 1997 (citing Walt Disney night letter wired to Roy Disney February 21, 1928 and received same date) (Walt wanted to "find how things stand [with Fox and MGM] before seeing Charlie[.]"); letter from Walt Disney to Roy Disney dated February 28, 1928, 2. Barrier explains that a night letter is a type of telegram that is "put into the mail at the point of delivery, as opposed to delivering it to the recipient by messenger. In other words, Walt could send Roy a night letter by Western Union on Monday and Roy would receive the telegram in the mail on Tuesday." Email from Michael Barrier to T. Susanin, July 1, 2009.

166 **Walt and Lilly; They checked into** Walt Disney letter to Roy Disney, February 28, 1928, 1.

166 **120 West 45th Street** Hotel Knickerbocker entry, *Manhattan and The Bronx Telephone Directory, Winter Issue—1928-28*, New York Telephone Company, New York, 1927.

166 **Walt did not; "find how things** June 1994 and February 1997 Barrier Notes (citing Walt Disney night letter wired to Roy Disney February 21, 1928 and received same date).

166 **Walt first went** Walt Disney letter to Roy Disney, February 28, 1928, 1.

166 **John W. Alicoate** John W. Alicoate entry, *Manhattan and The Bronx Telephone Directory, Winter Issue—1927-28*.

166 **publisher of the Film** "Commentary: *Walt Disney's* Errors and Ambiguities," Michael Barrier, www.michaelbarrier.com/Commentary/Gabler/GablerErrata.htm.

166 **"The Newspaper of** *The Film Daily*, February 16, 1928, 1.

166 **at 1650 Broadway** *The Film Daily* entry, *Manhattan and The Bronx Telephone Directory, Winter Issue—1927-28*.

166 **thirty-eight** "John Alicoate Dead," the *New York Times*, June 22, 1960, 35.

166 **manager and secretary; in the army** "Commentary: *Walt Disney's . . .*"

166 **law school at Georgetown; He became the; He wrote screenplays** "John Alicoate Dead."

167 **by 1926, he** "Commentary: *Walt Disney's . . .*"

167 **letter introducing him** "Commentary: *Walt Disney's . . .*" (citing Martin interviews of Walt Disney, 1956).

167 **Jack was not; "a dandy fellow; "not get too** Walt Disney letter to Roy Disney, February 28, 1928, 1.

167 **"Alicoate said that** Walt Disney letter to Roy Disney, February 28, 1928, 2.

167 **Jack told Walt; Jack said that** Walt Disney letter to Roy Disney, February 28, 1928, 1.

167 **Jack thought that** Walt Disney letter to Roy Disney, February 28, 1928, 1–2.

167 **"heads" of MGM** Walt Disney letter to Roy Disney, February 28, 1928, 1. *Manhattan and The Bronx Telephone Directory, Winter Issue—1927-28*.

167 **Salesman** Email from Michael Barrier to T. Susanin, June 27, 2010.

167 **Frederick C.** Fred C. Quimby entry, *Manhattan and The Bronx Telephone Directory, Winter Issue—1927–28;* "Frederick Clinton Quimby Funeral Announcements," *Los Angeles Times,* September 19, 1965, E10.

167 **forty-two** "Rites Set for Film Cartoonist Fred Quimby," *Los Angeles Times,* September 20, 1965, B9.

167 **agreed to see** Walt Disney letter to Roy Disney, February 28, 1928, 1.

167 **a long one** Walt Disney letter to Roy Disney, February 28, 1928, 2.

167 **was "very cold** Walt Disney letter to Roy Disney, February 28, 1928, 1.

167 **"Wednesday was a** Walt Disney letter to Roy Disney, February 28, 1928, 2.

167 **"a dandy day** Walt Disney letter to Roy Disney, February 28, 1928, 1.

167 **"like a hick** Walt Disney letter to Roy Disney, February 28, 1928, 2.

167 **one half-block north** Metro Goldwyn Picture Corp. entry, *Manhattan and The Bronx Telephone Directory, Winter Issue—1927–28.*

167 **"not a bad; Nor was Fred; of "the Boys; Fred asked Walt; Walt left MGM; Walt then went** Walt Disney letter to Roy Disney, February 28, 1928, 2.

167 **Room 660** See, for example, letter from Walt Disney to Miss M. J. Winkler, August 25, 1923.

167 **220 West 42nd Street** M. J. Winkler entry, *Manhattan and The Bronx Telephone Directory, Winter Issue—1927–28.*

168 **"very nice" and; "talk business" at** Walt Disney letter to Roy Disney, February 28, 1928, 2.

168 **which was cold** Walt Disney letter to Roy Disney, February 28, 1928, 1

168 **and the Mintzes** Walt Disney letter to Roy Disney, February 28, 1928, 2.

168 **44th and Broadway** Hotel Astor entry, *Manhattan and The Bronx Telephone Directory, Winter Issue—1927–28.*

168 **During lunch, the** Walt Disney letter to Roy Disney, February 28, 1928, 2. The Mintzes lived at 600 West 161st Street. Chas. B. Mintz entry, *Manhattan and The Bronx Telephone Directory, Winter Issue—1927–28.*

168 **Red Kahn, editor; "Red" accidentally dropped** Walt Disney letter to Roy Disney, February 28, 1928, 2.

168 **As the Disneys; On Saturday morning; "so short a; Walt then phoned** Walt Disney letter to Roy Disney, February 28, 1928, 3.

168 **That same day** Smith (1978 list); letter from Walt Disney to Roy Disney, March 2, 1928, 10:30 p.m., 1.

168 **"the 'go by** Letter from Walt Disney to Roy Disney, March 2, 1928, 10:30 p.m., 1.

168 **"very cold and; "homesick ever since** Walt Disney letter to Roy Disney, February 28, 1928, 1.

168 **(Walt had given** Hubler interview of Lillian Disney, *Walt's People, Volume 6,* 143. Almost three decades later, this gift—and its packaging—inspired a scene in Walt's 1955 animated feature, *Lady and the Tramp.* The Greenes (2001), 97.

168 **New York debut** Merritt and Kaufman, 154.

168 **53rd and Broadway** Colony Theatre entry, *Manhattan and The Bronx Telephone Directory, Winter Issue—1927–28.*

168 *The Leopard Lady* Merritt and Kaufman, 154.

169 **"THE SAME OLD** Walt Disney letter to Roy Disney, February 28, 1923, 3

169 **Walt began the** Miller, 100.

169  **"more <u>credit</u> [for; If the Disneys; "the way he** Walt Disney letter to Roy Disney, February 28, 1923, 3

169  **"percentage deal" and; "please be patient** June 1994 and February 1997 Barrier Notes (citing Walt Disney night letter wired to Roy Disney February 28, 1928 and received same date).

169  **Walt also followed** Walt Disney letter to Roy Disney, February 28, 1928, 2–3.

169  **Walt thought about; "Hell no," Jack; It was a; "that's what talks; He told Walt** Walt Disney letter to Roy Disney, February 28, 1928, 3.

169  **That night, Walt** Walt Disney letter to Roy Disney, February 28, 1928, 1.

169  **well-reviewed film** "The Screen: Lorelei Lee and Dorothy," Mordaunt Hall, the *New York Times*, January 16, 1928, 24; "The Blonde's Victory: Lorelei Lee Comes to the Screen With Her Pert Friend Dorothy," Mordaunt Hall, the *New York Times*, January 22, 1928, 111.

169  *Blondes* **had opened** Hall (January 16, 1928), 24.

169  **alternating Loew's theaters** Loew's Lexington Theater advertisement, the *New York Times*, February 25, 1928, 16; "This Week's Photoplays," the *New York Times*, February 26, 1928, 111.

169  **when he and Lilly** Walt Disney letter to Roy Disney, February 28, 1928, 1, 3.

169–70  **"definitely turned me; "hang onto Charlie; "have our entire** Walt Disney letter to Roy Disney, February 28, 1928, 3.

170  **"definitely found out** Walt Disney letter to Roy Disney, March 2, 1928, 10:30 p.m., 2.

170  **56th Street and 10th Avenue** Fox Film Corporation entry, *Manhattan and The Bronx Telephone Directory, Winter Issue—1927–28.*

170  **also turned him; Walt went back** Walt Disney letter to Roy Disney, March 2, 1928, 10:30 p.m., 2.

170  **"has sure been** Walt Disney letter to Roy Disney, March 2, 1928, 10:30 p.m., 1.

170  **"bluff Charlie" because; That night, Walt; "the gang" under; Walt wired Roy** Walt Disney letter to Roy Disney, March 2, 1928, 10:30 p.m., 2.

170  **"Break with Charlie; "ironclad" staff contracts; "protection without responsibility; "absolute secrecy [is]** "Additional notes from the [Disney] Archives' file of Walt Disney's 1928 correspondence from New York," Michael Barrier, February 1997 (citing Walt Disney night letter wired to Roy Disney February 29, 1928, and received March 1, 1928).

170  **The next day, Lilly** Walt Disney letter to Roy Disney, March 2, 1928, 10:30 p.m., 1.

170  **thirty-four** William C. Nolan obituary, December 15, 1954, *Variety Obituaries, Volume 4.*

170  **producer of Winkler** "From the *Film Daily Year Book* for 1927," Michael Barrier, September 20, 2009, www.MichaelBarrier.com.

170  **"take charge" of; Charlie had even; Nolan said that; "it is sure; "glad to see; Nolan had no; "get plenty of** Walt Disney letter to Roy Disney, March 2, 1928, 10:30 p.m. 1.

170–71  **"pulled bluff" on; Walt told Charlie; "was very nice; He told Walt; "offered to compromise; Walt, wanting to; He offered to; Charlie could not; Then it was; "quit fooling around; "Ah! [G]o on; "very friendly terms** Walt Disney letter to Roy Disney, March 2, 1928, 10:30 p.m., 2.

171  **the "present crew** February 1997 Barrier Additional Notes (citing the second of two Walt Disney night letters wired to Roy Disney March 1, 1928, and received March 2, 1928).

171    "boys sign contracts; "know [the] reason; complain to Universal; "sending another wire** February 1997 Barrier Additional Notes (citing the first of two Walt Disney night letters wired to Roy Disney March 1, 1928, and received March 2, 1928).

171    **The second night; It also let; "[I]unched with Bill; "necessary [that] I** February 1997 Barrier Additional Notes (citing the second of two Walt Disney night letters wired to Roy Disney March 1, 1928, and received March 2, 1928).

171    **Ubbe signed a** Smith (1972 article), 34.

171    **Les Clark stayed** Smith (1978 list), 1; Canemaker (2001), 12; Peri interview of Clark, Peri, 121.

171    **"I was approached** Peri interview of Clark, Peri, 121. Clark forgot about Johnny Cannon.

172    **"let it ride; If Charlie didn't; "Well—don't worry; Jack called** Walt Disney letter to Roy Disney, March 2, 1928, 10:30 p.m., 3.

172    **Emmanuel H. Goldstein** 1925 New York City city directory, 2281.

172    **the treasurer of** 1925 New York City city directory, 2281; "Scouts Rumor Of Deal For Universal Films," the *New York Times*, August 4, 1927, 25; "Prize-Fight Film Inquiry," the *New York Times*, September 9, 1927, 15.

172    **send Walt right** Walt Disney letter to Roy Disney, March 2, 1928, 10:30 p.m., 3.

172    **57th Street and Fifth Avenue** Universal Pictures Corp. entry, *Manhattan and The Bronx Telephone Directory, Winter Issue—1927–28*.

172    **"some big bugs** Walt Disney letter to Roy Disney, March 2, 1928, 10:30 p.m., 3.

172    **"from his office** Walt Disney letter to Roy Disney, March 2, 1928, 10:30 p.m., 3.

172    **could have been** 1925 New York City city directory, 2281.

172    **Robert H. Cochrane, forty-nine** "R. H. Cochrane, Led Universal Pictures," the *New York Times*, June 2, 1973, 34.

172    **Philip D. "P.D. Cochrane, fifty-one** "P. D. Cochrane, 71, Film Pioneer, Dies," the *New York Times*, August 10, 1958, 92.

172    **co-founded Universal Pictures; Robert and P. D. were** "R. H. Cochrane, Led . . . ;" "P. D. Cochrane, 71, . . ."

172    **the city editor** "R. H. Cochrane, Led . . ."

172    **In 1904, the; One of the; The store's manager** "P. D. Cochrane, 71, . . ."

172    **In 1906, Robert** "R. H. Cochrane, Led . . ."

172    **three Chicago movie; The two Cochranes; By 1912 the; Together, Laemmle and** "P. D. Cochrane, 71, . . ."

172    **"big boy was; "advice and got** Walt Disney letter to Roy Disney, March 2, 1928, 10:30 p.m., 4.

172–73   **The unnamed Universal; "they want good; "were tickled at; "call [Walt] in** Walt Disney letter to Roy Disney, March 2, 1928, 10:30 p.m., 3.

173    **They offered to; They told Walt** Walt Disney letter to Roy Disney, March 2, 1928, 10:30, p.m., 3–4.

173    **"work like hell** Walt Disney letter to Roy Disney, March 2, 1928, 10:30 p.m., 4.

173    **Roy sent two; In one of** Walt Disney letter to Roy Disney, March 2, 1928, 10:30 p.m., 1.

173    **According to Hugh** Barrier interview of Harman, December 3, 1973, 29.

173    **Hugh, Ham, Paul** Smith (1978 list), 1.

173    **"ma[d]e it clear** Barrier (1976 article), 47.

173    **"means only one** Walt Disney letter to Roy Disney, March 2, 1928, 10:30 p.m., 1.

173    **"That hurt!** Walt Disney (1941 article), 107.

173 **wrote at 10:30** Walt Disney letter to Roy Disney, March 2, 1928, 10:30 p.m., 1.

173–74 **"I feel very; "will find them; "I hate to; Walt hoped that; "the same Oswalds;** **"unless I make; He wrote that** Walt Disney letter to Roy Disney, March 2, 1928, 10:30 p.m., 4.

174 **Walt was worried** Miller, 101.

174 **Walt called Charlie; "quite a talk; "very anxious" to; "he and Ubb[e]; "could get some** Walt Disney letter to Roy Disney, March 5, 1928, 10:00 p.m.

174 **That night Walt; "Charlie [was] trying** February 1997 Barrier Additional Notes (citing Walt Disney night letter wired to Roy Disney March 4, 1928, and received March 5, 1928).

174 **down with colds; a noon meeting; "per Universal[']s instructions; "insisted on taking** Walt Disney letter to Roy Disney, March 5, 1928, 10 p.m.

174 **Charlie offered Walt** Walt Disney letter to Roy Disney, March 5, 1928, 10 p.m.

174 **"But that's impossible; "We couldn't make** *Disney's Art of Animation: From Mickey Mouse to Beauty and the Beast*, Bob Thomas, Hyperion, New York, 1991, 11.

174 **"[T]here was no** *The Disney Treasures*, Robert Tieman, Disney Editions, New York, 2003, 7.

174 **"tried every way** Walt Disney letter to Roy Disney, March 5, 1928, 10 p.m.

174 **"Either you come; protect himself from** Thomas (1994 ed.), 86–87.

174 **"If they'll do** Miller, 103.

174 **"left [Charlie] with; Walt then went; Walt phoned Manny; "mentioned [to Manny; "immediately went into** Walt Disney letter to Roy Disney, March 5, 1928, 10 p.m.

175 **"that [Charlie] owned; "he was out** Lillian Disney and Taves, 104.

175 **that the bottom** Miller, 101.

175 **"because he would** Lillian Disney and Taves, 104.

175 **"[k]eep up your; "regards to all** Walt Disney letter to Roy Disney, March 5, 1928, 10 p.m.

175 **"stuck around close; "waited all day** Walt Disney letter to Roy Disney, March 7, 1928, 1.

175 **with Bill Nolan** Walt Disney letter to Roy Disney, March 7, 1928, 2.

175 **"[b]est cartoons he** Walt Disney letter to Roy Disney, March 7, 1928, 3.

175 **they had lunch** Walt Disney letter to Roy Disney, March 7, 1928, 2.

175 **"with open eyes** Walt Disney letter to Roy Disney, March 7, 1928, 2–3.

175 **agreed on a salary** Walt Disney letter to Roy Disney, March 7, 1928, 3.

175 **Walt wanted the** Walt Disney letter to Roy Disney, March 7, 1928, 4.

175 **whose $120 weekly** Email from Dave Smith to T. Susanin, July 20, 2009.

175 **$150 weekly package** Walt Disney letter to Roy Disney, March 7, 1928, 3.

175 **talked about a; "a dandy fit** Walt Disney letter to Roy Disney, March 7, 1928, 4.

175 **Just as he; Specifically, Nolan repeated** Walt Disney letter to Roy Disney, March 7, 1928, 3. As Walt's letter makes clear, the animator's name was David Hand.

175 **almost two years** Smith (1978 list), 2.

175 **at 5 p.m.** Walt Disney letter to Roy Disney, March 7, 1928, 1–2.

175 **"I am sorry; ("you know how; "take advantage of; "insist that Charlie** Walt Disney letter to Roy Disney, March 7, 1928, 2.

176 **"feeling fine except** Walt Disney letter to Roy Disney, March 7, 1928, 4.

176 **"still hanging around; "WILL FIGHT IT; "fight to the** Walt Disney letter to Roy Disney, March 7, 1928, 1.

176 **"Well it looks; "rush thing[s] any** Walt Disney letter to Roy Disney, March 9, 1928.

176 **"so absorbed in** Walt Disney letter to Roy Disney, March 5, 1928, 10 p.m.

176 **"pull as many; "helpless to make; That weekend, the** Walt Disney letter to Roy Disney, March 9, 1928.

176 **and was located** 1925 New York City city directory, 2241.

176 **"out-and out cutthroat business; "putting a knife** Watts, 44 (citing Martin/Miller interview, Reel 11, 3; Reel 5, 47; Reel 2, 36).

176 **On the evening** June 1994 and February 1997 Barrier Notes (citing Walt Disney night letter wired to Roy Disney February 28, 1928, and received same date).

176 **"LEAVING TONIGHT STOPPING; "DON'T WORRY[,] he** Telegram from Walt Disney wired to Roy Disney, March 13, 1928 (reproduced at Thomas (1991), 11); email from Dave Smith to T. Susanin, June 30, 2009 (citing same).

176 **"Roy was running** Byrnes, 24.

176 **"[e]ven my husband's** Lillian Disney and Taves, 104.

176 **"I was scared** Lillian Disney and Taves, 104.

176–77 **"Let's get the** Miller, 101.

177 **"took Oswald, [and]** Byrnes, 24.

177 **staff who remained; (Mike Marcus left** Smith (1978 list), 1.

177 **("I never liked** "Walt Disney: A Portrait of the Artist," Gerald Nachman, *New York Post*, October 10, 1965, 45.

177 **"raging lion" on; "He had gambled** Eddy, 113.

# Epilogue

179 **with the assistance** Merritt and Kaufman, 159. The new animator was Wilfred Jackson. Peri, 62–65.

179 *Plane Crazy* **was** Barrier (2007 book), 57 (citing "General Expense Account 1925–1926–1927" entry dated May 15, 1928).

179 **providing Mickey's voice;** *Willie* **premiered at** *Disney A to Z: The Official Encyclopedia*, Dave Smith, Disney Editions, New York, 2006 edition, 633.

179 **Special Academy Award** Smith (2006 ed.), 3.

179 **One 1932 entry** Smith (2006 ed.), 173.

179 **every year but** Smith (2006 ed.), 3–4.

179 **highest grossing feature** Smith (2006 ed.), 618.

179 **won Walt another** Smith (2006 ed.), 4.

180 **was diagnosed with** Barrier (2007 book), 315.

180 **postoperative cobalt treatments** Thomas (1998) 297.

180 **"there is no; resume a full** "Disney Gets Clean . . . ;" Barrier (2007 book), 215.

180 **spending Thanksgiving with; in Palm Springs** Gabler, 628–29.

180 **On Wednesday, November 30** Thomas (1994 ed.), 353; "Disney in Hospital for Checkup After Surgery," *Los Angeles Times*, December 7, 1966, 1; "Death Comes in Hospital Near Burbank Studio," Harry Trimborn, *Los Angeles Times*, December 16, 1966, 1.

180 **taken directly back** Green and Green, 197.

180 **daily hospital visit** Thomas (1998), 297.

180 **"Walt lay on; "drove himself right** "Disney's Brother Has Plans for Future," Bob Thomas, *Arkansas Democrat*, January 9, 1967, 7.

180 **acute circulatory collapse** Trimborn, 1.

180    **A private service** "Services for Walt Disney Held as He Asked—for Family Only," *Los Angeles Times*, December 17, 1966, 1.

180    **ashes** Barrier (2007 book), 317.

180    **were interred** Gabler, 33 (citing his interview of Diane Disney Miller; Forest Lawn Brochure, Disney, Walt Death Folder, Walt Disney Archives).

180    **Disney family asked** "Walt Disney, 65, Dies . . . ;" "Services for Walt Disney . . ."

181    **over nine hundred awards** Trimborn, 3.

181    **Presidential Freedom Medal** "Walt Disney, 65, Dies . . ."

181    **Harvard and Yale** "Walt Disney: Images of Innocence," *Time*, December 23, 1966.

181    **thirty-two Academy Awards** Smith (2006 ed.), 3.

181    **"able to build** Markle interview, *Walt Disney Conversations*, 102.

181    **had four thousand employees** Trimborn, 1.

181    **"$100-million-a-year entertainment empire** "Walt Disney, 65, Dies . . ."

181    **"If I had** Markle interview, *Walt Disney Conversations*, 102.

181    **The Peiser building** See *Mandelbaum v. City of Kansas City*, Missouri Court of Appeals, Western District, No. WD 55596, April 13, 1999.

181    **was still in existence; left the studio** Kaufman interview of Ising, *Walt's People, Volume 1*, 59.

181    **including Raggos** Gabler, 74 (citing Walt Disney letter to Jerry Raggos, March 4, 1935).

181    **could be paid** Miller at 80; "Showman of the World Speaks," 1.

181    **on Tuesday, August 7** Schmeltz's Analysis Of Fact And Application To Law, 7.

181    **For Rudy Ising; By the end; "Hugh, Maxwell and I** Kaufman interview of Ising, *Walt's People, Volume 1*, 59.

182    **"In September 1923** Smith (1978 article), 33–34; See Schmeltz's Intervening Petition, 5–6.

182    **on Thursday, October 4; Ubbe claimed that** Creditor's Petition of Ubbe Iwwerks.

182    **"[b]ack in Kansas City** Byrnes, 24.

182    **although his claim** "Showman of the World Speaks," 1.

182    **collectively, about $10,500** Referee Elmer Powell's List of Debts, January 25, 1927.

182    **On Tuesday, October 16; studio's "final wake; The "wake" was** Smith interview of Missakian, *Walt's People, Volume 5*, 24.

182    **Dr. Cowles offered to** Smith (1978 article), 33.

182    **Two days later** Application to Be Made Joint Petitioning Creditors, October 18, 1923.

182    **declared Laugh-O-gram** Order of Judge Albert L. Reeves, October 30, 1923.

182    **the liquidation trustee** Order Appointing a Temporary Receiver Herein, October 30, 1923.

182    **interviewed Dr. Cowles** Order of Referee in Bankruptcy Elmer Powell, December 11, 1923.

182    **made a demand** Application for Expenses and Report of Attorneys for the Trustee, February 21, 1924, 1.

182    **When Pictorial ignored** Attorneys Application for Expenses, 2–3, 8, 14.

182    **Pictorial paid less** Report of the Trustee, His Application for Reimbursement of Expenses Incurred by Him, And His Claim for Compensation, May 21, 1925, 3.

182    **In May of 1925; the court accepted** Order Accepting Resignation of Trustee, May 19, 1925; Order and Record of Cases Recommended for Settlement, July 15, 1925.

182    **Jones was replaced** Order Appointing Receiver In An Emergency, May 25, 1925.

182   **One of Kemp's first** Schmeltz's Intervening Petition; Brief of Trustee On Claim of Fred Schmeltz.

182   **The court rejected** Order Denying Intervention of Fred Schmeltz, August 27, 1925.

182   **Schmeltz appealed the** Petition for Review, September 5, 1925.

182–83 **agreed that Schmeltz's; In particular, Reeves** Order, January 27, 1926.

183   **Another of Kemp's first** Application of Trustee for Authority to Employ Counsel to Go Immediately to New York City, August 5, 1925; Order, August 5, 1925.

183   **Pictorial resumed payments** Report of William E. Kemp, Trustee, April 26, 1926.

183   **By mid-August** Order, August 19, 1926; Kemp Report, April 26, 1926; Supplemental Report of Trustee and Application for Dividend, January 13, 1927.

183   **Kemp produced a** Notice to Creditors, June 26, 1926; List of Debts, July 7, 1926; Order Regarding Dividends, July 9, 1926.

183   **A supplemental dividend** Supplemental Report of Trustee and Application for Dividends, January 13, 1927; Order Regarding Dividends, January 25, 1927.

183   **in the end** Smith (1978 article), 34.

183   **Kemp issued his final** Final Report of Trustee, August 23, 1927.

183   **the court's final** Order Closing the Estate, December 28, 1927.

183   **Suite 218 were; The LeMorris** 1924 Kansas City city directory.

183   **In 1993, a nonprofit** "A groundbreaking for Walt: KC group rebuilding Disney's Laugh-O-Gram studio," Robert W. Butler, the *Kansas City Star*, April 10, 2001, E1.

183   **but Claude Abernathy** 1925 Los Angeles city directory, 375, 2243; 1926 Los Angeles city directory, 365, 2360.

184   **fabric weaver Kathy** 1929 Los Angeles city directory, 1106.

184   **Colonial Upholstering Shop** 1936 Los Angeles city directory, 425, 2671.

184   **health food markets** 1938 Los Angeles city directory, 783, 2461 (B. L. Getman's health food store); *Los Angeles City Directory*, The Los Angeles Directory Company, Los Angeles, 1939, 1832, 2475; *Los Angeles City Directory*, The Los Angeles Directory Company, Los Angeles, 1942, 2111 (Anna Sargent's health food store).

184   **a hardware store** 1936 Los Angeles city directory, 2571, 2576 (Frank A. Goyette's hardware store).

184   **housed different bakeries** 1938 Los Angeles city directory, 774, 2407 (Mrs. Jane M. Geary's bakery); 1939 Los Angeles city directory, 277, 2419; 1942 Los Angeles city directory, 305, 2683 (Edward T. Boeshar's bakery).

184   **most of the feature *Pinocchio*; parts of the feature *Fantasia*** Email from Dave Smith to T. Susanin, August 19, 2009.

184   **Additions to the; In 1930, the; A large two-story** Smith (1979 article), 36.

184   **the Disneys purchased** Thomas & Johnston, 141.

184   **J. W. Klein Organ** 1929 Los Angeles city directory, 2515.

184   **pipe organ company** 1929 Los Angeles city directory, 1282.

184   **This building eventually** Smith (1979 article), 37.

184   **In 1934, as** Smith (1979 article), 37–38.

184   **moved the company** Smith (1978 list), 1; Smith (1979 article), 32.

184   **the forty-four-acre site** Smith (2006 ed.), 718.

184   **The move took; although some employees** Smith (1979 article), 38.

185   **only four made** Smith (1978 list), 1. There were five other colleagues from the pre-Mickey Mouse era who worked with Walt again later: Carl Stalling (joined the Walt Disney Studio in October 1928), Jimmy Lowerre (joined the studio in November 1928), Walt Pfeiffer and Ruthie Tompson (both rejoined Walt in 1935), and Ubbe

Iwwerks (rejoined in 1940). Smith (1978 list), 1 (Stalling, Lowerre, Iwwerks); Smith (2006 ed.), 529 (Pfeiffer); email from Dave Smith to T. Susanin, March 5, 2009 (Tompson).

185 **several Hyperion buildings; the Hyperion Bungalow; The nearby Burbank studio; The Burbank Shorts; the current Sound** Email from Dave Smith to T. Susanin, August 18, 2009.

185 **they sold the** "Manufacturers Buy Old Disney Studios," *Los Angeles Times*, May 11, 1941.

185 **by 1956 located; 2727 Hyperion Avenue** *Los Angeles Street Address Directory*, The Pacific Telephone And Telegraph Company, Los Angeles, May 8, 1956, 386.

185 **as of 1960** *Los Angeles Street Address Directory*. Los Angeles: The Pacific Telephone And Telegraph Company, March 29, 1960, 405.

185 **Shell Oil station** 1939 Los Angeles city directory, 1894; May 1956 Los Angeles street address directory, 386; March 1960 Los Angeles city directory, 405.

185 **late 1950s and** May, 1956 Los Angeles street address directory, 386; March, 1960 Los Angeles city directory, 405.

185 **a partnership between** Smith (2006 ed.), 717.

185 **short time, Ubbe** Smith (1972 article), 34.

185 **Studios incorporated as** Smith (2006 ed.), 717.

185 **went public in** Thomas (1998), 139–40.

185 **In 1986, the** Smith (2006 ed.), 717.

185 **approximately 150,185 people** "Companies at a glance," *USA Today*, September 1, 2009, 2B.

185 **revenues of over** The Walt Disney Company Annual Report 2008, Financial Highlights, 1.

185–186 **"leading diversified international** "Company Overview," The Walt Disney Company, http://corporate.disney.go.com/corporate/overview.html.

186 **Claude Abernathy continued** 1925 Los Angeles city directory, 375, 2243; 1926 Los Angeles city directory, 365, 2360.

186 **Abernathy later became** 1930 federal census, Los Angeles, April 28, 1930, Sheet 14B, Ancestry.com, *1930 United States Federal Census*.

186 **He died in; He was ninety-two** Claude Abernathy entry, October 15, 1970, Ancestry.com, *Social Security Death Index*.

186 **Ray Abrams worked** 1929 Los Angeles city directory, 309.

186 **Abrams died in** Ray Abrams entry, June, 1981, Ancestry.com, *Social Security Death Index* and *California Death Index, 1940–1997*.

186 **Jack Alicoate became** "Commentary: *Walt Disney's* Errors . . ."

186 **co-published the *Film*; Alicoate died in; He was seventy** "John Alicoate Dead."

186 **married, remained in** 1938 Los Angeles city directory, 118; 1939 Los Angeles city directory, 118; 1942 Los Angeles city directory, 124.

186 **Allen died in; He had been** Joe Allen obituary, *Variety Obituaries, Volume 4*.

186 **sixty-eight-year-old brother** Dave Allen obituary, January 12, 1955, *Variety Obituaries, Volume 4*.

186 **By 1925, Dave** "Dave Allen Once Hired 5186 Extras," Fred W. Fox, *Los Angeles Mirror*, March 20, 1954, 5–6.

186 **"handle[d] the employment** Dave Allen obituary, *Variety Obituaries, Volume 4*.

186 **almost a decade** 1927 Los Angeles city directory, 347; 1928 Los Angeles city directory, 621; 1929 Los Angeles city directory, 326.

186  **known as Central** "Dave Allen Of Casting Bureau Is Accused," clipping from
      unidentified newspaper dated May 17, 1934, from the National Film Information
      Service, Margaret Herrick Library, Fairbanks Center for Motion Picture Study,
      Academy of Motion Picture Arts and Sciences.

186  **1934 sex scandal** "Star Witness to Testify In Dave Allen Trial," *Los Angeles Evening
      Herald Express*, July 12, 1934, 1; "Morals Retrial of Dave Allen to Await High Court
      Decision," *The Citizen*, October 3, 1935.

186  **The scandal cost** "Trial of Ex-Casting Bureau Head Dropped," *Daily News*, December
      3, 1935, 1, 8; "Dave Allen's Costly Victory," *Variety*, December 4, 1935; "Dave Allen
      Loses His Mate," *Examiner*, October 20, 1936.

186  **eventually joined Columbia** "Dave Allen Once Hired . . ."

186  **He died the** Dave Allen obituary, *Variety Obituaries, Volume 4*.

186  **Lawrence Baer remained** Death certificate of Lawrence Baer, February 6, 1937,
      Missouri State Archives, www.sos.mo.gov, *Missouri Death Certificates, 1910–1957*.

186  **Esther Benson stayed** Smith (1978 list), 1.

186  **By 1936, Esther** 1936 Los Angeles city directory, 216.

186  **she still lived** 1938 Los Angeles city directory, 235.

187  **a newspaper cartoonist** 1930 federal census, Los Angeles, April 15, 1930, Sheet 14A,
      Ancestry.com, *1930 United States Federal Census*.

187  **and a writer** 1938 Los Angeles city directory, 261; 1939 Los Angeles city directory, 263.

187  **By the 1940s** Obituary of Norman Blackburn's mother, November 18, 1942, *Variety
      Obituaries, Volume 3*.

187  **an NBC program; He helped create; Blackburn died in; He was eighty-six** "Norman
      Blackburn; Producer and Advertising Executive," *Los Angeles Times*, February 27,
      1990, A24.

187  **left the studio** Smith (1978 list), 1.

187  **Disney family heard** Email from Diane Disney Miller to T. Susanin, May 30, 2009.

187  **Johnny Cannon was** Smith (1978 list), 1.

187  **He and his** 1936 Los Angeles city directory, 350.

187  **Cannon died in** John W. Cannon entry, December 6, 1946, Ancestry.com, *California
      Death Index, 1940–1997*.

187  **at Forest Lawn** Johnny Cannon funeral announcement, *Los Angeles Times*, December
      10, 1946, 8.

187  **Al Carder and his; where he owned** 1930 federal census, Evanston, Illinois, April 8, 1930.

187  **Joe Carder continued** Death certificate of Joseph Carder.

187  **Cauger finally sold** Interview of Ted Cauger by T. Susanin, June 20, 2008.

187  **By the 1940s** Arthur V. Cauger obituary, *Variety Obituaries, Volume 3*.

187  **kept in touch** For example, see Gabler, 49 (citing A. V. Cauger letter to Disney,
      September 11, 1942), 62 (Disney letter to Mel Cauger, August 16, 1946), 407 (Disney
      letter to Nina Cauger, June 25, 1942).

187  **February 1942** "M. Mouse A Local . . .".

187  **Nearly three years; In attendance besides** "Kansas City's Own 'Daddy' . . . ," 59; Smith
      (1978 article) 34.

187  **Cauger died nine; He was sixty-seven** Death certificate of Arthur Cauger, October
      27, 1945, Missouri State Archives, www.sos.mo.gov, *Missouri Death Certificates,
      1910–1957*.

187 **"pioneer animated film** Arthur Cauger obituary, *Variety Obituaries, Volume 3.*

187 **since they, like Clark** 1928 Los Angeles city directory, 646, 1451, 1555, 1941; 1929 Los Angeles city directory, 1754.

188 **(Clark lived with** 1936 Los Angeles city directory, 400.

188 **Clark was an** Canemaker (2001), 13–14.

188 **Clark animated on** Canemaker (2001), 18–19, 21.

188 **Prior to becoming** Canemaker (2001), 25–28.

188 **the earliest hire** Canemaker (2001), 7, 9.

188 **the others were** Canemaker (2001), vii, 2.

188 **Clark's father eventually** Canemaker (2001), 10.

188 **Two of his** Introduction to interview of Royal "Mickey" Clark by Jim Korkis and Didier Ghez, August 2008, private collection.

188 **Clark retired from** Smith (1978 list), 1.

188 **"temporary** Canemaker (2001), 9 (citing letter from Les Clark to Michael Barrier, December 1, 1973).

188 **When he retired** "Les Clark, Animator Of Mickey Mouse, Snow White," *Los Angeles Times*, September 17, 1979, B18.

188 **He died in** Canemaker (2001), 28.

188 **Ten years after** Smith (2006 ed.), 179. The Disney Legends award was first presented in 1987, and it is The Walt Disney Company's honor for individuals who have made significant contributions to the company. Smith (2006 ed.), 178.

188 **Ben Clopton worked** 1929 Los Angeles city directory, 638.

188 **Clopton married and** 1938 Los Angeles city directory, 450; 1939 Los Angeles city directory, 456.

188 **relocated to Helena** Ben Clopton entry, November, 1987, Ancestry.com, *Social Security Death Index.*

188 **P. D. Cochrane commuted; He worked to; As a result; By the time; He died at** "P. D Cochrane, 81. . ."

189 **Robert H. Cochrane remained; At that time; He also served; Cochrane died in; He was 94** "R. H. Cochrane, Led . . ."

189 **John Cowles, Jr.** "Disneyland designer dies . . . "

189 **a barn** Disney "Walt's Barb," Carolwood Pacific Historical Society website, www. Carol-wood.com/WaltsBarn.

189 **died in 2001** "Disneyland designer dies . . ."

189 **Dr. John V. Cowles, Sr.** 1930 federal census, Kansas City, April 4, 1930, Sheet 4A.

189 **and maintained sporadic; At times, Walt** Diane Disney Miller email to T. Susanin, May 21, 2008; interview of Marie Cowles Heinbaugh by T. Susanin, May 30, 2008.

189 **died of leukemia** Interview of Marie Cowles Heinbaugh by T. Susanin, May 29, 2008; John Cowles obituary, the *Kansas City Times.*

189 **Minnie Cowles, according** Gabler, 116 (citing his interview with John Cowles, Jr.).

189 **Upon Dr. Cowles' death; She remarried and** Interview of Marie Cowles Heinbaugh by T. Susanin, May 29, 2008.

189 **Jeff died around** Merritt and Kaufman interview of McGhee, *Walt's People, Volume 4*, 26.

189 **Margaret predeceased him** Interview of Virginia Davis McGhee by T. Susanin, March 7, 2009.

189 **Virginia Davis returned to** Merritt and Kaufman interview of McGhee, *Walt's People, Volume 4*, 32–33; "Walt Disney Star Virginia Davis dies," Associated Press, the *Hollywood Reporter*, August 17, 2009.

189 **In 3 on** Merritt and Kaufman, 70–71; Merritt and Kaufman interview of McGhee, *Walt's People, Volume 4*, 30.

189 **Anne Shirley was** "Anne Shirley; Actress Starred . . ."; 1936 Los Angeles city directory, 1656; *Los Angeles City Directory*, The Los Angeles Directory Company, Los Angeles, 1938, 1881.

190 **was married** Interview of Virginia Davis McGhee by T. Susanin, March 7, 2009.

190 **two adopted daughters** Interview of Virginia Davis McGhee by T. Susanin, March 7, 2009.

190 **In 1998 Virginia** Smith (2006 ed.), 179.

190 **She died in** "Walt Disney Star Virginia . . ."

190 **Edna Francis Disney** Thomas (1998), 339, 344.

190 **Her brother Mitch** Thomas (1998), 333.

190 **Roy's best friend** Email from Diane Disney Miller to T. Susanin, May 17, 2009.

190 **moved to California** Thomas (1998), 333.

190 **Edna remained in; She frequently visited** Thomas (1998), 342.

190 **Roy E. Disney** Thomas (1998), 79.

190 **"[s]he drove [her** Thomas (1998), 342.

190 **In December 1984; She was visited** Thomas (1998), 343.

190 **On December 18; Edna predicted, "I** Thomas (1998), 343–44.

190 **Edna died on** Thomas (1998), 344.

190 **Edna was named** Smith (2006 ed.), 179.

190 **"violent reaction" and** Lillian Disney and Taves, 104.

190 **Walt quietly suggested; "I said it** Eddy, 113.

190 **Disneys' two daughters** Miller, 146.

190 **"Walt said I** Green and Green, 19.

190 **"Severest Critic; "I tried to** Lillian Disney and Taves, 40.

191 **"Lilly was the** Thomas (1998), 51–52.

191 **traveled to Marceline; She was accompanied** Burnes, Butler and Viets, 178–79.

191 **the White House** "Lillian Disney Dies at 98," Myrna Oliver, Diane Haithman, *Los Angeles Times*, December 18, 1997, A1.

191 **In October 1971** Thomas (1998), 331–32.

191 **In 1973 she; Specifically, Lillian presided** Smith and Clark, 117.

191 **Lillian's philanthropic works** Introduction to Hubler interview of Lillian Disney, *Walt's People, Volume 6*, 140.

191 **"I have always; In 1993, Lillian; "We shared a** Oliver and Haithman, A1.

191 **real estate man** "Disney Heirs' Stock May Be King," Ellen Farley, *Los Angeles Times*, April 1, 1984, E1, E8.

191 **from 1969 until** Introduction to Hubler interview of Lillian Disney, *Walt's People, Volume 6*, 140.

191 **death in 1981** "Disney Heirs' Stock . . ."

191 **Lillian suffered a; She died the** Introduction to Hubler interview of Lillian Disney, *Walt's People, Volume 6*, 140.

191 **She was survived** "Disney Heirs' Stock . . ."

191    **Lilly was named** Smith (2006 ed.), 179.

192    **were featured in; "[f]air-haired and blue-eyed; "is the possessor; "Child Marvel At;
       "the old nick** "Child Marvel At Memory," *Los Angeles Times*, December 31, 1927, A9.

192    **"Right now [Robert; by that Christmas** Thomas (1998), 90–91.

192    **In the 1930s** 1939 Los Angeles city directory, 594. Email from Dave Smith to T.
       Susanin, July 23, 2010.

192    **Robert died in** Robert S. Disney obituary, August 5, 1953, *Variety Obituaries, Volume 4*.

192    **Charlotte stayed at** May 1956 Los Angeles street address directory, 412; March 1960
       Los Angeles street address directory, 434; email from Dave Smith to T. Susanin, July
       23, 2010.

192    **Around that time** Email from Robert S. Disney, III, to T. Susanin, July 1, 2009.

192    **Charlotte died a; She was eighty-seven** Charlotte Disney entry, January 31, 1979,
       Ancestry.com, *Social Security Death Index*.

192    **died in Merced** Robert S. Disney, Jr., entry, June 24, 1996, Ancestry.com, *Social Security
       Death Index*.

192    **death in 1971** Roy Disney obituary, *Variety Obituaries, Volume 7*.

192–93  **To offset the** Thomas (1998), 64.

193    **In 1929, Roy; While Powers succeeded** Thomas (1998), 64–66.

193    **Columbia (1930–1932)** Thomas (1998), 66; Smith (2006 ed.), 134.

193    **United Artists (1932–1937)** Thomas (1998), 73; Smith (2006 ed.), 704.

193    **RKO (1937–1956)** Thomas (1998), 105; Smith (2006 ed.), 575.

193    **foray into merchandising; Bank of America** Thomas (1998), 67.

193    **public in 1940** Thomas (1998), 139–40.

193    **Buena Vista Distribution** Thomas (1998), 176–77.

193    **inaugural TV series** Thomas (1998), 183–85.

193    **executive vice president** Thomas (1998), 140.

193    **chairman of the board** Thomas (1998), 5.

193    **president and chief** Roy Disney obituary, *Variety Obituary, Volume 7*.

193    **"spent too much; "executive producer in** "After First Shock of Disney's Demise
       Spotlight Shifts to Brother & Staff," *Variety*, December 21, 1966, reprinted in *Variety
       Obituaries, Volume 6: 1964–66*, Garland Publishing, Inc., New York, 1988.

193    **planned on retiring; He changed his** Thomas (1998), 313.

193    **"continue to operate; "We're going to** Thomas (1998), 300.

193    **"a complex man** Roy Disney, 213.

193    **share of battles; "But [Walt]," Roy** Roy Disney, 216.

193    **"To the writers** Roy Disney, 213–14.

194    **Roy presided, with; "My brother Walt** Thomas (1998), 331.

194    **Roy then returned** Thomas (1998), 332–33.

194    **Not long after; Roy decided to; Roy collapsed, and** Thomas (1998), 338–39.

194    **Roy died of; He was seventy-eight** Roy Disney obituary, *Variety Obituaries, Volume 7*.

194    **"My father . . . . never** Thomas (1998), 4–5.

194    **Ruth Disney remained** Thomas (1998), 234.

194    **Los Angeles in 1936** "Gas Fumes Kill Disney's Mother," *Los Angeles Times*, November
       27, 1938, 1.

194    **Ruth married Theodore; Ruth's husband, who** Thomas (1998), 234.

194    **When Walt died** Gabler, 633 (citing his interview of Diane Disney Miller).

194 **she attended Roy's** Thomas (1998), 340.

194 **Herbert died in** Thomas (1998), 234.

194 **Ray died in** Thomas (1998), 236.

194 **Ruth died in** Thomas (1998), 234.

194 **lived in Chula; She died in** Kathleen Dollard entry, June, 1979, Ancestry.com, *Social Security Death Index.*

195 **Robert Edmunds returned** 1927 Los Angeles city directory, 771.

195 **by 1930 worked** 1930 federal census, Los Angeles, April 2 and 3, 1930, Sheet 2A, Ancestry.com, *1930 United States Federal Census.*

195 **Edmunds worked on** Rudy Ising, Barrier interview of Harman and Ising, October 29, 1976, 62.

195 **He was deported** Hugh Harman and Rudy Ising, Barrier interview of Harman and Ising, October 29, 1976, 63.

195 **Edmunds died at; He was eighty-four** Robert C. Edmunds entry, 1987, Ancestry.com, *Social Security Death Index.*

195 **manager of Publix** Obituary of father of Gus Eyssell, September 27, 1932, *Variety Obituaries, Volume 2.*

195 **By 1955, Eyssell** Obituary of mother of Gus Eyssell, September 15, 1955, *Variety Obituaries, Volume 4.*

195 **Milton H. Feld moved; He went to; By the mid-1930s; In 1938, he** Milton Feld obituary, September 10, 1947, *Variety Obituaries, Volume 3.*

195 **cameraman and "studio; living in Hollywood** 1926 Los Angeles city directory, 881; 1928 Los Angeles city directory, 894; 1936 Los Angeles city directory, 646; 1939 Los Angeles city directory, 729; 1930 federal census, Los Angeles, April 15, 1930, Sheet 20B, Ancestry.com, *1930 United States Federal Census.*

195 **He died in** Harry Forbes obituary, August 23, 1939, *Variety Obituaries, Volume 3.*

195 **Forbes was survived** Harry Forbes obituary, *Los Angeles Times*, August 20, 1939, A16.

195 **Allen Freleng became; lived with his** 1930 federal census, Los Angeles, April 9, 1930, Sheet 19A, Ancestry.com, *1930 United States Federal Census.*

195 **Allen married his** 1936 Los Angeles city directory, 665.

195 **He later became** 1938 Los Angeles city directory, 739.

195 **and died in** Allen E. Freleng entry, March 17, 1943, Ancestry.com, *Social Security Death Index.*

195 **Friz Freleng returned** Kaufman interview of Freleng, *Walt's People, Volume 2*, 19; Barrier (2007 book), 55 (citing letter from Rudy Ising to Friz Freleng, November 15, 1927).

195 **moving to New York; He returned to** Burnes, Butler and Viets, 136.

195 **He and his** 1930 federal census, Los Angeles, April 9, 1930, Sheet 19A.

195 **In 1931, Freleng** Burnes, Butler and Viets, 136.

195 **By the mid-30s** 1936 Los Angeles city directory, 665.

195 **Freleng later married** 1939 Los Angeles city directory, 751; 1942 Los Angeles city directory, 851.

195 **He eventually became; In that time** Burnes, Butler and Viets, 136.

195–96 **"I have the; In the early** "Animator Friz Freleng Dies at 89 Hollywood," *Los Angeles Times*, May 27, 1995, B1.

196 **"Walt was a** Burnes, Butler and Viets, 136.

196   **Freleng died in** Isadore P. Freleng entry, May 26, 1995, Ancestry.com, *Social Security Death Index* and *California Death Index, 1940–1997*.

196   **at the age; He was survived; "Friz was a** "Animator Friz Freleng . . ."

196   **Manny Goldstein spent** "Dexter Will Star in '12 to the Moon,'" *Los Angles Times*, April 14, 1959, 23.

196   **In the mid-1930s** *The Shocking Miss Pilgrim: A Writer in Early Hollywood*, Frederica Sagor Maas, The University Press of Kentucky, Lexington, 1999, 202-03; "Warners Plan Film About Seeing Eye Dog—One New," the *New York Times*, January 2, 1937, 15; "Bioff Ends Strike at Studio Which Lasted Only 30 Minutes," *Los Angeles Times*, April 6, 1940, A10.

196   **In 1953, Goldstein** "'Black Knights' in Joust; Hal Roach Jr. Expands; Warner Arguing for 3D," *Los Angeles Times*, March 23, 1953, A13.

196   **Six years later** "Dexter Will Star . . ."

196   **By 1930, when** 1930 federal census, Los Angeles, April 8, 1930, Sheet 5A, Ancestry.com, *1930 United States Federal Census*.

196   **By the mid-1930s** 1936 Los Angeles city directory, 694; 1938 Los Angeles city directory, 773.

196   **In 1950, when; She died in; She was eighty-four** Marjorie Gossett obituary, *Las Vegas-Review Journal*, January 8, 2003.

196   **Hamilton married, and** 1930 federal census, Los Angeles, April 9, 1930, Sheet 6A, Ancestry.com, *1930 United States Federal Census*; Rollin Hamilton obituary, *Los Angeles Times*, June 7, 1951.

196   **Hamilton died in** Rollin Hamilton obituary, *Los Angeles Times*, June 7, 1951.

196   **continued to live** 1928 Los Angeles city directory, 1033; 1929 Los Angeles city directory, 1035.

196   **work with Ham** 1929 Los Angeles city directory, 1035.

196   **Esther Hammond corresponded** Gabler, 62 (Esther Hammond letter to Disney, December 10, 1940).

197   **She eventually remarried; Esther lived in** Esther Ida Hammond Rush entry, March 9, 1950; Ancestry.com, *California Death Index, 1940–1997*.

197   **Fletcher Hammond moved** 1930 federal census, Webb City, Missouri, April 4, 1930, Sheet 4B.

197   **He died from a; Hammond was approximately** Death certificate of Fletcher Hammond, August 18, 1933, Missouri State Archives, www.sos.mo.gov, *Missouri Death Certificates, 1910–1957*; 1905 state census, Flora, Kansas, March 1, 1905.

197   **William F. Hammond; He hired his son** 1930 federal census, Webb City, Missouri, April 4, 1930, Sheet 4B.

197   **William moved to; Hammond died in Monterey** William Hammond entry, October 9, 1950, Ancestry.com, *California Death Index, 1940–1997*.

197   **high school student** 1930 federal census, Los Angeles, April 1920, Sheet 2A, Ancestry.com, *1930 United States Federal Census*.

197   **When she was** Email from Jim Hardwick to T. Susanin, May 27, 2009.

197   **"semi-skilled cement** Army Enlistment Record of Clarence Dodson, February 18, 1943, Ancestry.com, *U.S. World War II Army Enlistment Records, 1938–1946*.

197   **lived in Riverside** Lois Eleanor Dodson entry, November 30, 1978, Ancestry.com, *Social Security Death Index* and *California Death Index, 1940–1997*; Clarence

Dodson, entry, November 17, 1995, Ancestry.com, *Social Security Death Index* and *California Death Index, 1940–1997*.

197  **Lois died in** Lois Eleanor Dodson entry, November 30, 1978, Ancestry.com, *Social Security Death Index* and *California Death Index, 1940–1997*.

197  **Clarence died in** Clarence Dodson entry, November 17, 1995, Ancestry.com, *Social Security Death Index* and *California Death Index, 1940–1997*.

197  **Fred Harman returned** 1922 Kansas City city directory, 1292.

197  **Harman & McConnell** 1923 Kansas City city directory, 1233.

197  **Mac Advertising Company** 1924 Kansas City city directory, 1262.

197  **"[b]ut after a whirl** Harman, 11.

197  **He communicated with** Interview of Fred Harman, III, by T. Susanin, December 8, 2006; Barrier (2007 book), 30, note 81 (citing letter from Fred Harman to Walt, May 10, 1932; letter from Walt Disney to Fred Harman, May 23, 1932).

197  **After several years** Fred Harman obituary, *Variety*, January 6, 1982, *Variety Obituaries, Volume 9*.

198  *True West* Harman.

198  **He died in** Fred Harman obituary, *Variety Obituaries, Volume 9*.

198  **His son, Fred; The museum displays** Interview of Fred Harman, III, by T. Susanin, December 8, 2006.

198  **left Charlie Mintz** Maltin, 158.

198  **"liked [Charlie] very** Hugh Harman, Barrier interview of Harman and Ising, October 29, 1976, 55.

198  **"henchman[.]"** Barrier interview of Harman, December 3, 1973, 27.

198  **"George Winkler was** Hugh Harman, Barrier interview of Harman and Ising, October 29, 1976, 55.

198  **In 1929, Harman** "Harman, 79, Dies in California; Pioneer Animator With Rudy Ising," *Variety*, December 1, 1982.

198  *Bosko* **was distributed** Maltin, 220.

198  **In 1933, Harman** Maltin, 224.

198  **went to MGM** Maltin, 275.

198  **where they produced** "Harman, 79, Dies in California . . ."

198  **interlude around 1938** Maltin, 277–79.

198  **the early 1940s** Maltin, 285.

198  **Harman claimed that; "would have been** Barrier interview of Harman, December 3, 1973, 104.

198  **an Academy Award; dying in 1982** "Harman, 79, Dies in California . . ."

198  **writer for Hugh; He was also** Walker Harman obituary, March 16, 1938, *Variety Obituaries, Volume 2*; interview of Fred Harman, III, by T. Susanin, December 8, 2006.

198  **"Walker died, in** Hugh Harman, Barrier interview of Harman and Ising, October 31, 1976, 105.

198  **returned to work** Smith (1978 list), 1.

198–99  **Thurston later claimed** Letter from Thurston Harper to Dave Smith, October 20, 1973.

199  **for Harman-Ising** Letter from Thurston Harper to Dave Smith, October 20, 1973; 1938 Los Angeles city directory, 902.

199 **In the early; and joined the** Letter from Thurston Harper to Dave Smith, October 20, 1973.

199 **By the late** Letter from Thurston Harper to Dave Smith, October 20, 1973.

199 **His wife died; "in extremely good** Letter from Thurston Harper to Dave Smith, March 23, 1978.

199 **He died in; He was eighty-four** Carl Thurston Harper entry, March 25, 1987, Ancestry.com, *Florida Death Index, 1877–1998.*

199 **He made portraits** Kaufman interview of Ising, *Walt's People, Volume 1,* 53.

199 **had a mail-order** Barrier interview of Ising, June 2, 1971, 12.

199 **worked at MGM's** Kaufman interview of Ising, *Walt's People, Volume 1,* 53.

199 **"the nose job** Kaufman interview of Ising, *Walt's People, Volume 32,* 53.

199 **"still had the** Cynthia Ising made this comment to Michael Barrier during his Interview of Rudy Ising on June 2, 1971. See Barrier interview of Ising, June 2, 1971, 46.

199 **"an imitation of** Barrier interview of Ising, June 2, 1971, 46.

199 **own Harman-Ising studio** Merritt and Kaufman, 52.

199 **"Our pride in** Gabler, 272–73 (citing telegram from Harman-Ising Studios to Walt Disney, December 22, 1937).

199 **Two of Rudy's; One, Max Ising** Rudy Ising, Barrier interview of Harman and Ising, October 31, 1976, 106; 1923 Kansas City directory, 1331.

199 **Rudy and Hugh** Rudolf Ising obituary, *Variety,* July 27, 1992, reprinted in *Variety Obituaries, Volume 14: 1991–1992,* Garland Publishing, New York, 1994.

199 **which Rudy directed** Email from Michael Barrier to T. Susanin, June 27, 2010.

199 **During World War II; After the war** Rudolf Ising obituary, July 27, 1992, *Variety Obituaries, Volume 14.*

199 **He died in Los Angeles** Rudolph C. Ising entry, July 18, 1992, Ancestry.com, *Social Security Death Index* and *California Death Index, 1940–1997.*

199 **He was rewarded** Smith (1972 article), 34.

199 **fully animated *Plane*; leaving Walt to** Ub Iwerks obituary, July 14, 1971, *Variety Obituaries, Volume 7.*

200 **hurt Walt deeply** Miller, 120–21.

200 **Iwwerks was paid** Iwerks, 86.

200 **After a ten-year; In 1965 he; death in 1971** Iwerks obituary, *Variety Obituaries, Volume 7.*

200 **sons David and** Thomas (1998), 139.

200 **He was named** Smith (2006 ed.), 179.

200 **Louis Katsis was** Louis E. Katsis AKA Katsigianis death certificate, January 23, 1956, Missouri State Archives, www.sos.mo.gov, *Missouri Death Certificates, 1910–1957.*

200 **Kansas Court of Appeals; He was mayor** "William E. Kemp: Mayor, 1889–1968," Susan Jezak Ford, *Missouri Valley Special Collections: Biography,* The Kansas City Public Library.

200 **the Beyer Theater** It appears that the Beyer is listed on Kloepper's Proof of Debt as his current address as of December 1923. Kloepper Proof of Debt dated December 8, 1923 (attached to his Laugh-O-gram bankruptcy claim, January 3, 1924).

200 **Thompson Avenue and South** "Fire claims Beyer here," Van Buckley, the *Daily Standard,* July 2, 1983, 1.

200 **He claimed that; "My answer to** Tape-recorded communication to David R. Smith from Jack Kloepper, 4725 30th Avenue NE, Seattle, Washington, October 1970, from a private collection.

200 **In 1924, he** 1924 Kansas City city directory, 1452.

200 **By 1930, Kloepper** 1930 federal census, Minneapolis, April 19, 1930, Sheet 19B.

200 **He eventually worked** Adolph "Jack" Kloepper obituary, *Atchison Daily Globe*.

200 **That same year** Gabler, 65 (citing Kloepper Transcription of Tape, October 1970).

200 **He died in Kansas** Kloepper obituary.

200 **Alex Kurfiss worked; He lived with** 1924 Kansas City city directory, 1466; 1930 federal census, Kansas City, April 14, 1930, Sheet 18A.

200 **Kurfiss later studied** Alex W. Kurfiss obituary, *Sioux City Journal*.

200 **By the late 1940s** Marjorie Kurfiss obituary, *Sioux City Journal*, November 1993.

200 **his son died** Baby Boy Kurfiss birth information, November 9, 1948, Ancestry.com, *Minnesota Birth Index, 1935–2002*; Baby Boy entry, November 9, 1948, Ancestry.com, *Minnesota Death Index, 1908–2002*.

200 **By 1950, the** Death certificate of Addie Smith Kurfiss, November 15, 1950, Missouri State Archives, www.sos.mo.gov, *Missouri Death Certificates, 1910–1957*. (Addie Kurfiss was Alex Kurfiss' mother).

200–201 **Kurfiss worked as** Marjorie Kurfiss obituary.

201 **The couple retired; he died in** Alex Kurfiss obituary; Marjorie Kurfiss obituary.

201 **Kurfiss is listed in** *Who Was Who In American Art, 1564–1975: 400 Years of Artists in America, Vol. II: G-O*, Editor-in-Chief: Peter Hastings, Sound View Press, Madison, Connecticut, 1999, 1917.

201 **Hazelle A. Linston** 1927 Los Angeles city directory, 1273 (spelled "Hazel"); 1928 Los Angeles city directory, 1352; 1929 Los Angeles city directory, 1370 (spelled "Hazel").

201 **John Lott remained** Email from Dave Smith to T. Susanin, March 25, 2009.

201 **and probably into** 1930 federal census, Los Angeles, April 11, 1930, Sheet 5A, Ancestry. com, *1930 United States Federal Census* (Lott was a janitor in the "Moving Pictures" business).

201 **In the early** Hugh Harman, Barrier interview of Harman and Ising, October 29, 1976, 13.

201 **Lott married, and** 1936 Los Angeles city directory, 1129; 1938 Los Angeles city directory, 1272; 1939 Los Angeles city directory, 1289; 1942 Los Angeles city directory, 1481.

201 **until his death** John Lott entry, October, 1970, Ancestry.com, *Social Security Death Index*.

201 **remained at Film** 1923 Kansas City city directory, 1570; 1923 Kansas City city directory, 1482; 1924 Kansas City city directory, 1526.

201 **relocated to Los Angeles** Email from Dave Smith to T. Susanin, May 27, 2008.

201 **Lowerre died in** George E. Lowerre entry, January 30, 1962, Ancestry.com, *California Death Index, 1940–1997*.

201 **Red Lyon left** Death certificate of William McAtee Lyon, June 3, 1923, County of Los Angeles, State of California.

201 **Wilfred in Inglewood** Death certificate of William Lyon; "Three Men Swept Out Into Ocean," the *Redondo Reflex*, June 8, 1923, 1.

201 **On Sunday, June 3** "Three Men Swept Out . . . ," 1.

201 **near Clifton** "Three Bodies Recovered," the *Redondo Reflex*, June 22, 1923.

201  **The group included; After lunch, the; The girls became; Lyon and the; overcome with exhaustion; The three men; She, the Kleins; Lifeguards and policemen; Victor's body washed** "Three Men Swept Out . . . ," 1.

201  **Red's body was** "Three Bodies Recovered."

201  **Red Lyon was** Death certificate of William Lyon.

202  **remarried and moved** 1930 federal census, St. Louis, April 2, 1930, Sheet 1A.

202  **He later became** Death certificate of Leslie B. Mace, February 8, 1977, County of Orange, State of California.

202  **Mace died in Santa Ana** Leslie Mace entry, February 1977, Ancestry.com, *Social Security Death Index.*

202  **James MacLachlan appears; Marjorie MacLachlan remained** 1924 Kansas City city directory, 1537.

202  **He died between** 1930 federal census, Kansas City, April 12, 1930, Sheet 17A.

202  **filmed *Steamboat Willie*** Interview of Ub Iwerks by Bob Thomas, circa 1956, courtesy of Didier Ghez.

202  **on June 30, 1928** Smith (1978 list).

202  **Mount Holly Hotel resident** 1928 Los Angeles city directory, 1451, 1555; 1929 Los Angeles city directory, 1754.

202  **Paul Smith** 1928 Los Angeles city directory, 1941, 1555.

202  **Les Clark, who** 1928 Los Angeles city directory, 646, 1555.

202  **tried his hand; as a cameraman** 1928 Los Angeles city directory, 1451.

202  **In 1929, at; The following year; By then, Mike; Frances, like Irene; Ardis was a** 1930 federal census, Los Angeles, April 2, 1930, Sheet 1A, Ancestry.com, *1930 United States Federal Census.*

202  **By the late** A search of Los Angeles city directories for 1936 and 1938–39 shows no entries for Mike or Irene Marcus.

202  **"was in a** Thomas interview of Iwerks, circa 1956.

202  **He died in** Michael J. Marcus entry, January 20, 1957, Ancestry.com, *California Death Index, 1940–1997.*

202  **(although the warden** Email from Warden Terri L. Gonzales, California Men's Colony, to T. Susanin, June 1, 2010.

202  **Irene died in** Irene Marcus entry, July, 1975, Ancestry.com, *Social Security Death Index* and *California Death Index, 1940–1997.*

202  **worked with Hugh** Barrier (1999 book), 155–56.

202  **"The name 'Bosko** Rudy Ising, Barrier interview of Harman and Ising, October 29, 1976, 51. According to Michael Barrier, "Maxwell's nickname was 'Uncle Boscomb,' from which the name 'Bosko' was derived." Email from Michael Marrier to T. Susanin, June 27, 2010.

202  **He was later** Barrier (1999 book), 287.

202–3  **On May 23, 1972; The studio had** Harris.

203  **Max died in** Carman Griffin Maxwell entry, September 22, 1978, Ancestry.com, *Social Security Death Index* and *California Death Index, 1940–1997.*

203  **Thomas McCrum continued** 1923 Kansas City city directory, 1503.

203  **dentist with the** Death certificate of Thomas McCrum, January 30, 1948, Missouri State Archives, www.sos.mo.gov, *Missouri Death Certificates, 1910–1957.*

203  **McCrum died in** Death certificate of Thomas McCrum.

203  **approximately one year** 1924 Los Angeles city directory, 1526, 2651.

203 **seventy-seven years old** 1920 federal census, Los Angeles, January 16, 1920, Sheet 15A, Ancestry.com, *1920 United States Federal Census.*

203 **Charlie Mintz bumped; Walt remained in; Walt did not** Thomas (1994 ed.), 96–97.

203 **Mintz lost the** Barrier interview of Harman, December 3, 1973, 56–57.

203 **Mintz and his** 1930 federal census, New York, April 3, 1930, Sheet 1B, Ancestry.com, *1930 United States Federal Census.*

203 **By the middle** 1936 Los Angeles city directory, 2615.

203 **By 1938, Mintz** 1938 Los Angeles city directory, 1848; 1939 Los Angeles city directory, 1459.

203 **Among the cartoons; He died in; At the time; "pioneer cartoon producer** Charles Mintz obituary, January 10, 1940, *Variety Obituaries, Volume 3.*

203 **Baron Missakian opened** Abel, 60.

203 **He and Nadine Simpson** 1930 federal census, Kansas City, April 16, 1930, Sheet 33A.

203 **"internationally known portraitist** Abel, 60; see generally *The Baron Missakian Collection.*

203 **When Walt visited** Burnes, Butler and Viets, iv–v.

203 **he suffered a** Baron Missakian obituary, the *Kansas City Times*, July 8, 1964; Stollings.

203 **He kept in contact** Stollings.

203 **Missakian died in** Baron Missakian obituary.

203–4 **After his death** *The Baron Missakian Collection,* University of Missouri—Kansas City; Stollings.

204 **George Morrell continued** George Morrell obituary, May 4, 1955, *Variety Obituaries, Volume 4.*

204 **He was married; Morrell died in** 1930 federal census, Los Angeles, April 8, 1930, Sheet 5B, Ancestry.com, *1930 United States Federal Census.*

204 **He was eighty-three** George Morrell obituary, *Los Angeles Times*, May 1, 1955, A26.

204 **Frank L. Newman sold; He later moved; In 1932, Newman; He retired in 1954** Frank Newman obituary, *Variety*, July 11, 1962, *Variety Obituaries, Volume 5.*

204 **In 1929, Nolan** Maltin, 158.

204 **His last series; Nolan died on; He was sixty** William C. Nolan obituary, December 15, 1954, *Variety Obituaries, Volume 4.*

204 **Walter O'Donnell continued** 1926 Los Angeles city directory, 1553; 1930 federal census, Los Angeles, April 15, 1930, Sheet 23B, Ancestry.com, *1930 United States Federal Census*; 1942 Los Angeles city directory, 1804.

204 **"character actor, bit; He died at** Walter O'Donnell obituary, *Daily Variety*, October 16, 1986.

204–5 **eventually owned thirty; "the most colorful; "1929 crash hit; He sold his; "comeback . . . didn't go; "stable of race; His wife Lois; Pantages himself was; Pringle sued Pantages; Pantages reportedly spent; He won a; He later settled; Pantages died of; He was sixty-five** "Pantages, Vet Vaudeville Showman, Dies at 65; Had a Colorful Career," Joe Bigelow, February 19, 1936, *Variety Obituaries, Volume 2.*

205 **Lois also died** Lois Pantages obituary, *Variety Obituaries, Volume 3.*

205 **The Pantages' grandson** "Carmen Pantages Considine, 89, Gave Time And Money To Veterans," Carole Beers, the *Seattle Times*, September 18, 1998.

205 **through the 1920s** 1927 Los Angeles city directory, 1515.

205 **By 1930, her mother** 1930 federal census, Los Angeles, April 12, 1930, Sheet 13B, Ancestry.com, *1930 United States Federal Census.*

205 **Dawn changed her** "Anne Shirley; Actress Starred . . ."
205 **Dawn was known** 1936 Los Angeles city directory, 1656; 1938 Los Angeles city directory, 1881.
205 **and Mimi was** 1936 Los Angeles city directory, 1656.
205 **retirement in 1944; she was nominated; "breaking the ice; She was married** "Anne Shirley, Actress . . ."
205 **Fourth of July** Anne Lederer entry, July 4, 1993, Ancestry.com, *Social Security Death Index.*
205 **Rudolph Peiser continued; his death in 1927** 1923 Kansas City city directory, 1699; 1924 Kansas City city directory, 1761; death certificate of Rudolph Peiser, June 19, 1927, Missouri State Archives, www.sos.mo.gov, *Missouri Death Certificates, 1910–1957.*
205 **Lou Pesmen parted; By 1921, Pesmen** 1921 Kansas City city directory, 1879 (Pesmen worked at Pesmen & Haner in 1921).
205 **The Pesmen Studio** 1923 Kansas City city directory, 1706.
205 **in Chicago, where** 1930 federal census, Chicago, April 17, 1930, Sheet 20A.
205 **Kraft Foods** Email from Sonny Jaben to T. Susanin, April 9, 2008; email from Sandra Pesmen to T. Susanin, April 14, 2008.
205 **He visited Walt; Walt gave him** Email from Sonny Jaben to T. Susanin, April 9, 2008.
205 **"To Lou Pesmen** A copy of this photograph was provided to T. Susanin by Sandra Pesmen.
205 **Pesmen retired to** Email from Sonny Jaben to T. Susanin, April 9, 2008.
205–6 **In 1971, Pesmen** Pesmen.
206 **Pesmen died in** Louis Pesmen entry, February 21, 1987, Ancestry.com, *Social Security Death Index* and *California Death Index, 1940–1997.*
206 **John Pfeiffer served** 1930 federal census, Kansas City, April 7, 1930, Sheet 8B.
206 **He died in Los Angeles** John Pfeiffer entry, February 28, 1953, Ancestry.com, *Social Security Death Index* and *California Death Index, 1940–1997.*
206 **Studio in 1935** Smith (2006 ed.), 529.
206 **Pfeiffer was honored** Thomas (1998), 4.
206 **Pfeiffer retired from** Smith (2006 ed.), 529.
206 **He died in Los** Walter Pfeiffer entry, August 14, 1976, Ancestry.com, *Social Security Death Index* and *California Death Index, 1940–1997.*
206 **Fred Quimby became** Email from Michael Barrier to T. Susanin, June 27, 2010.
206 **By his retirement; He died in; At the time** "Rites Set for Film . . ."
206 **Jerry Raggos moved** Gabler, footnote at 352.
206 **He died sometime** Death certificate of Lillian (Mrs. Jerry) Raggos, January 17, 1944, Missouri State Archives, www.sos.mo.gov, *Missouri Death Certificates, 1910–1957* (indicating that Lillian Raggos was a widow when she died in 1944).
206 **convened in 1936; corrupt Democratic machine; Reeves retired** "Albert L. Reeves: Judge, 1873–1971," Nancy J. Hulston, *Missouri Valley Special Collections: Biography,* The Kansas City Public Library.
206 **Aletha Reynolds worked** 1930 federal census, Kansas City, April 9, 1930, Sheet 12A.
206 **She got married** Baxter J. Fisher and Aletha Pearl Reynolds Application for License to Marry, May 29, 1936, Ancestry.com, *Missouri Marriage Records, 1805–2002.* The application states that Aletha was thirty-one at the time of her marriage, but according to the 1920 federal census, she was born in 1902 which would make her

thirty-four at the time she married Fisher. 1920 federal census, Kansas City, January 1920, Sheet 7B.

206   **Bill Rubin left** 1920 Kansas City city directory, 1825; 1921 Kansas City city directory, 1999.

206–7   **He continued to work** 1922 Kansas City city directory, 1936; 1923 Kansas City city directory, 1807; 1924 Kansas City city directory, 1877.

207   **death in 1944; Rubin was survived** Death certificate of William Rubin, February 22, 1944, Missouri State Archives, www.sos.mo.gov, *Missouri Death Certificates, 1910–1957*; William Rubin obituary, the *Kansas City Times*, February 24, 1944, 14.

207   **Fred Schmeltz ran; His wife, Lizzie** 1930 federal census, Kansas City, April 17, 1930, Sheet 2A.

207   **The Schmeltzes died; He was eighty-eight** Elizabeth A. Wigge Schmeltz entry, April 1, 1955, Ancestry.com, *California Death Index, 1940–1997*; John Fredrick Schmeltz entry, August 7, 1955, Ancestry.com, *California Death Index, 1940–1997*.

207   **still lived in** 1942 Los Angeles city directory, 2132.

207   **Charles was seventy-eight; Nettie was seventy-seven** 1900 federal census, Plymouth, Iowa, June 11, 1900, Sheet 5B, Ancestry.com, *1900 United States Federal Census*.

207   **as a gardener** 1929 Los Angeles city directory, 1901; 1936 Los Angeles city directory, 1612.

207   **who lived with** 1926 Los Angeles city directory, 1782; 1927 Los Angeles city directory, 1743; 1928 Los Angeles city directory, 1857; 1930 federal census, Los Angeles, April 11, 1930, Sheet 23A, Ancestry.com, *1930 United States Federal Census*.

207   **an electrician** 1926 Los Angeles city directory, 1782; 1928 Los Angeles city directory, 1857; 1930 federal census, Los Angeles, April 11, 1930, Sheet 23A, Ancestry.com, *1930 United States Federal Census*.

207   **and a mechanic** 1930 federal census, Los Angeles, April 11, 1930, Sheet 23A.

207   **Lester still lived** March, 1961 Los Angeles street address directory, 434.

207   **He joined such** "Film Kiddies to Be Hosts," *Los Angeles Times*, November 30, 1927, A11.

207   **continued to live** 1926 Los Angeles city directory, 1800; 1927 Los Angeles city directory, 1764; 1929 Los Angeles city directory, 1922.

207   **In 1930, the; By then, twenty-four-year-old; Robert, nineteen, worked** 1930 federal census, San Rafael, Marin County, April 7, 1930, Sheet 3B, Ancestry.com, *1930 United States Federal Census*.

207   **By 1933 the; That year, Leon** "Death Takes One In Crash," *Los Angeles Times*, January 30, 1933, A1. See also 1936 Los Angeles city directory, 1631.

207   **a Sunday rainstorm** "Juvenile Actor in Crash Sues," *Los Angeles Times*, February 3, 1933, A8.

207   **hit a lamp; Darro was bruised** "Death Takes One . . ."

207   **Within days, Leon** "Juvenile Actor in . . ."

207   **Later, Leon's family** 1938 Los Angeles city directory, 1851.

207   **filed for divorce** The Greenes (2001), 37.

207–8   **moved in with** Barrier (2007 book), 192; Gabler, 163.

208   **Hazel started dating** Gabler, 193.

208   **a native of South Bend** Introduction to interview of Bill Cottrell by Richard Hubler, March 12, 1968, reprinted in *Walt's People: Talking Disney with the Artists who Knew Him, Volume 8*, edited by Didier Ghez, Xlibris Corporation, 2009, 177.

208  **Bill Cottrell had** Email from Michael Barrier to T. Susanin, June 27, 2010.

208  **went to work** Bill Cottrell Legend Bio, Disney Legends, http://legends.disney.go.com/legends/detail?key=Bill+Cottrell.

208  **He lived on; Cottrell was ten** 1930 federal census, Los Angeles, April 9, 1930, Sheet 18A, Ancestry.com, *1930 United States Federal Census.*

208  **and received degrees** Introduction to Hubler interview of Cottrell, *Walt's People, Volume 8*, 177.

208  **Hazel and Bill** Introduction to Hubler interview of Lillian Disney, *Walt's People, Volume 6*, 140; Barrier (2007 book), 173 (Hazel supervised the ink and paint department until her marriage to Bill Cottrell); Smith (1978 list), 1 (Hazel left the studio on May 28, 1938).

208  **Hazel left her** Smith (1978 list), 1.

208  **supervisor** Barrier (2007 book), 173.

208  **In her resignation** Gabler, 353 (citing letter from Hazel Sewell to Walt Disney, May 12, 1938).

208  **"greatly shocked by** Gabler, 353 (citing letter from Walt Disney to Hazel Sewell, May 13, 1938).

208  **Cottrell became a** Bill Cottrell Biography, Disney Legends website.

208  **Hazel died in** Hazel Cottrell entry, January, 1975, Ancestry.com, *Social Security Death Index.*

208  **her husband retired; Cottrell died in** Bill Cottrell Biography, Disney Legends website.

208  **moved in with; "very good to me** The Greenes (2001), 37.

208  **Marjorie married Marvin** Email from Diane Disney Miller to T. Susanin, May 17, 2009; Marvin Davis Biography, Disney Legends, http://legends.disney.go.com/legends/detail?key=Marvin+Davis.

208  **He later worked** "Marvin A. Davis, Master Planner for Disneyland," *Los Angeles Times*, March 13, 1998, B6.

208  **(he worked on; Davis retired from** Marvin Davis Biography, Disney Legends website.

208  **In 1994, he** Marvin Davis Biography, Disney Legends website.

208  **Marvin Davis died** "Marvin A. Davis . . . "

208  **Marjorie Sewell Davis** Diane Disney Miller email to T. Susanin, May 17, 2009; email from Dave Smith to T. Susanin, July 7, 2009 (citing Marjorie S. Davis, entry, December 22, 1999, Ancestry.com, *Social Security Death Index*).

209  **for Metro Pictures** 1924 Kansas City city directory, 1954; 1930 federal census, Kansas City, April 16, 1930, Sheet 33A.

209  **She married Baron; By 1930, they lived** 1930 federal census, Kansas City, April 16, 1930, Sheet 33A.

209  **After Walt's death** See photograph of Simpson with Roy Disney and Iwerks (and megaphone), *The Baron Missakian Collection.* This visit occurred between Walt Disney's death in 1966 (see Young, 1A, 5A), and Ub Iwerks' death in July of 1971.

209  **she provided an** Smith interview of Missakian, *Walt's People, Volume 5*, 22.

209  **In her later** Young, 5A; Nadine Missakian obituary, the *Kansas City Times*, December 14, 1988, E6.

209  **Nadine died in** Nadine Missakian obituary.

209  **Paul Smith continued** 1928 Los Angeles city directory, 1941, 1555.

209    **by George Winkler** 1929 Los Angeles city directory, 1990.

209    **Smith later worked; The veteran animator** Paul J. Smith obituary, November 1, 1980, *Variety Obituaries, Volume 9.*

209    **Carl Stalling, while; He also wrote; By the early; In 1936, Stalling joined; He retired from** Carl W. Stalling obituary, December 6, 1972, *Variety Obituaries, Volume 7.*

209    **Tague turned to** 1924 Kansas City city directory, 2044.

209    **By 1930, he** 1930 federal census, Dickinson, Kansas, April 28, 1930, Sheet 8A.

209    **radio electronics technician; He died in; His wife, Frances** Lorey Tague obituary, the *Manhattan Mercury.*

209    **"fun, excitement, adventure** Tague, 84.

209    **as a photographer** 1926 Los Angeles city directory, 1938; 1927 Los Angeles city directory, 1905.

209    **After his retirement; Tannura died in** Philip Tannura entry, December 7, 1973, Ancestry.com, *Social Security Death Index* and *California Death Index, 1940–1997.*

209    **and was survived** Philip Tannura funeral announcement, *Los Angeles Times,* December 8, 1973, B13.

210    **Mary Tebb left** Smith (1978 list), 1.

210    **went back to** Los Angeles City Precinct No. 1025, *Index to Register of Voters, Los Angeles County, California, 1930,* Ancestry.com.

210    **Within a year; Her father Thomas; Her mother Jane; Mary had a** 1930 federal census, Aberdeen, Washington, April 14, 1930, Sheet 10B, Ancestry.com, *1930 United States Federal Census.*

210    **By the 1940s** 1942 Los Angeles city directory, 2366.

210    **In 1945, she** Smith (1978 list), 1.

210    **working on** "Socializing with the Social Lion," Jeff Pepper, http://www.2719hyperion. com/2009/03/socializing-with-social-lion.html, March 3, 2009.

210    **became the head** Mary R. Tebb obituary, the *Review* (Bainbridge, Washington), March 24, 1993, A24.

210    **She retired from** Smith (1978 list), 1.

210    **seventy-two years old** Mary Tebb entry, March 16, 1993, Ancestry.com, *Social Security Death Index.*

210    **She died on** Mary Tebb obituary, the *Review.*

210    **acted in movies** 1930 federal census, April 14, 1930, Los Angeles, Sheet 19A.

210    **as Dorothy Wade; "went on to** Email from Ruthie Tompson to T. Susanin, November 29, 2009.

210    **After attending Hollywood; Walt offered her** Ruthie Tompson Biography, Disney Legends, http://legends.disney.go.com/legends/detail?key=Ruthie+Thompson.

210    **in 1935, at** Email from Dave Smith to T. Susanin, March 5, 2009.

210    **age of twenty-four** 1930 federal census, Los Angeles, April 8, 1930, Sheet 5B, Ancestry. com, *1930 United States Federal Census.*

210    **went to work** Ruthie Tompson Biography, Disney Legends website. See also 1939 Los Angeles city directory, 2089.

210    **Ruthie received numerous; She remained at; She retired in** Ruthie Tompson Biography, Disney Legends website.

210    **lives at the** Email from Dave Smith to T. Susanin, March 5, 2009.

210    **Otto Walliman went** 1924 Kansas City city directory, 2125.

210    **Otto died in** Death certificate of Otto Walliman, June 3, 1935, Missouri State Archives, www.sos.mo.gov, *Missouri Death Certificates, 1910–1957.*

210   **His wife Dorothy** Dorothy Walliman entry, May 2, 1936, Ancestry.com, *Minnesota Death Index, 1908–2002.*

210   **eventually married and** 1930 federal census, Los Angeles, April 18, 1930, Sheet 19A, Ancestry.com, *1930 United States Federal Census.*

210   **cartoonist and studio** 1929 Los Angeles city directory, 2278, 2340; 1930 federal census, Los Angeles, April 18, 1930, Sheet 19A; 1942 Los Angeles city directory, 2598.

210   **in the mid-1930s** 1936 Los Angeles city directory, 2615; 1938 Los Angeles city directory, 1848.

210   **Walt later wrote** Gabler, footnote at 352.

210–11 **Winkler left the; He lost his; Winkler's second wife; He died in** "From the *Film Daily Year Book* for 1927," Michael Barrier, September 20, 2009, www.MichaelBarrier .com.

211   **raised her children** Canemaker (1991), 82.

211   **Katherine and William** 1930 federal census, New York, April 3, 1930, Sheet 1B. Ancestry.com, *1930 United States Federal Census.*

211   **In 1989, seventy; Margaret had been** Canemaker (1991), 160–61.

211   **Margaret died on** Canemaker (1991), 166.

211   **Edmund J. Wolf** 1922 Kansas City city directory, 2274; 1923 Kansas City city directory, 2110; 1930 federal census, Kansas City, April 25, 1930, Sheet 19A.

211   **He died in Kansas** Edmund Wolf entry, Missouri State Archives, www.sos.mo.gov, *Missouri Death Certificates, 1910–1957* (indicating that Wolf died in June 1955); letter from Missouri State Archives to T. Susanin dated May 20, 2008 (stating that Wolf died in Kansas).

211   **Lillian Worth continued** 1938 Los Angeles city directory, 2251; 1939 Los Angeles city directory, 2277.

211   **died in 1981** Lillian Worth entry, August, 1981, Ancestry.com, *Social Security Death Index.*

211   **Newman Laugh-O-Grams made** Merritt and Kaufman, 125.

211   **Lafflets made by** Merritt and Kaufman, 126.

211   **The seven** Merritt and Kaufman, 125–26 (listing print sources for *Little Red Riding Hood*, *The Four Musicians of Bremen*, *Puss in Boots*, and *Cinderella*). *Jack and the Beanstalk* and *Jack, the Giant Killer* were identified by David Gerstein. *Goldie Locks and the Three Bears* was identified by Gerstein and Cole Johnson.

211   **were reissued shortly; the 1925 titles** Merritt and Kaufman, 82, 85.

211   **Forty of the fifty** Merritt and Kaufman, 127–50; www.youtube.com (*Alice's Little Parade*); "Home Again," Michael Barrier, www.MichaelBarrier.com, August 19, 2009 (*Alice's Spanish Guitar*).

211   **all twelve reels** Merritt and Kaufman, 127–28, 133–34, 136.

211   **all eighteen reels** Merritt and Kaufman, 136–41; www.youtube.com (*Alice's Little Parade*).

212   **nine of the twenty-six** Merritt and Kaufman, 142, 145–50; Barrier, "Home Again."

212   **Universal later gave; Oswald remained a** "Disney Loses a Voice, Pulls Rabbit Out of NBC's Hat," Kim Christensen, *Los Angeles Times*, February 10, 2006, A1.

212   **Thirteen of the** Merritt and Kaufman, 150, 152–54, 157–59.

212   **ESPN sports network; By then, ESPN; ESPN offered to** "Ebersol Hops to It to Land Michaels," Larry Stewart, *Los Angeles Times*, February 10, 2006, D3.

212   **NBC agreed, and** Christensen; Stewart.

212   **"When Bob was; "[a]s the forerunner** Christensen.

# Bibliography

In addition to the following articles, books, collections, correspondence and interviews, databases, and directories, other sources, as set forth in the endnotes, include: many issues of the *Kansas City Star* (and advertisements therein from 1919 through 1922 for such entities as Gray Advertising, the Isis Theatre, Kansas City Slide Company, Kaycee Studios, Laugh-O-gram Films, and various Newman Theatres); the *New York Times* (for 1928 Loews Theater advertisements); and various state death certificates.

The Laugh-O-gram Films Articles of Association, Statement of Increase of Capital Stock, Forfeiture of Charter and other corporate information are from the Missouri Secretary of State's file for Laugh O Gram Films, Inc., Charter No. 00039844.

All Laugh-O-gram Films bankruptcy documents come from the bankruptcy case file, *In the Matter of Laugh O Gram Films, Inc.*, U.S. District Court for the Western Division of the Western District of Missouri, Case No. 4457.

Unless otherwise noted, the Internet Movie Database website, www.imdb.com, was used for certain artists' pre- and post-Disney career histories. Uncited information about Academy Award nominees and winners comes from the Resources and Databases page of the Motion Picture Arts and Sciences' website, www.oscars.org.

Finally, although not included in this bibliography, numerous DVDs that include Walt Disney productions from 1921 to 1928 are cited throughout the endnotes.

## Articles

"A Condensed Program Of Legion Week," the *Kansas City Star*, October 30, 1921, 1.

Abel, Charles. "More About Some of the Speakers You Will See and Hear at Chicago," *The Professional Photographer*, August 5, 1937.

"Actors Mix With Cartoons," *Los Angeles Times*, July 6, 1924.

"Adolph 'Jack' Kloepper" obituary, *Atchison Daily Globe*, March 3, 1985.

"After First Shock of Disney's Demise Spotlight Shifts to Brother & Staff," *Variety*, December 21, 1966, reprinted in *Variety Obituaries, Volume 6*, New York, Garland Publishing, Inc., 1988.

"Alex W. Kurfiss" obituary, *Sioux City Journal*, December 1983.

Alexander, Jack. "The Amazing Story of Walt Disney," the *Saturday Evening Post*, October 31, 1953.

Alpert, Don. "The Man of the Land Disney," *Los Angeles Times*, "Calendar" Section, April 30, 1961.

"Animator Friz Freleng Dies at 89 in Hollywood," *Los Angeles Times*, May 27, 1995.

"Anne Shirley; Actress Starred in Childhood and as an Adult," *Los Angeles Times*, July 7, 1993.

"Baron Missakian" obituary, the *Kansas City Times*, July 8, 1964.

Barrier, Michael. "Commentary: *Walt Disney's* Errors and Ambiguities," www.michael
    barrier.com/Commentary/Gabler/GablerErrata.htm, posted December 19, 2006, and
    updated numerous times through May 31, 2010.
Barrier, Michael. "A Day in the Life: Disney, February 1927," www.MichaelBarrier.com,
    March 6, 2008.
———. "Home Again," www.MichaelBarrier.com, August 19, 2009.
———. "From the *Film Daily Year Book* for 1927," www.MichaelBarrier.com, September 20,
    2009.
Barrier, Mike. "The Careers of Hugh Harman and Rudolf Ising," *Millimeter*, February 1976, 46.
Barrier, Mike. "An Interview With Carl Stalling," *Funnyworld*, Spring 1971.
Beers, Carole. "Carmen Pantages Considine, 89, Gave Time And Money To Veterans," the
    *Seattle Times*, September 18, 1998.
"The Big Bad Wolf," *Fortune*, November 1934.
"Bioff Ends Strike at Studio Which Lasted Only 30 Minutes," *Los Angeles Times*, April 6,
    1940.
"'Black Knights' in Joust; Hal Roach Jr. Expands; Warner Arguing for 3D," *Los Angeles Times*,
    Mar 23, 1953.
Buckley, Van. "Fire claims Beyer here," the *Daily Standard*, July 25, 1983, 1.
Burnes, Brian. "Cartoon history stars KC artists," the *Kansas City Star*, February 22, 1990.
Butler, Robert W. "A groundbreaking for Walt: KC group rebuilding Disney's Laugh-O-
    Gram studio," the *Kansas City Star*, April 10, 2001, E1.
Byrnes, Garrett D. "Walt Disney's Success Laid to Ability to Think as Child Does," the
    *Evening Bulletin,* Providence, December 27, 1935.
Carr, Harry. "The Only Unpaid Movie Star," *The American Magazine*, March 1931.
"Child Marvel At Memory," *Los Angeles Times*, December 31, 1927.
Christensen, Kim. "Disney Loses a Voice, Pulls Rabbit Out of NBC's Hat," *Los Angeles
    Times*, February 10, 2006.
Churchill, Douglas W. "Now Mickey Mouse Enters Art's Temple," the *New York Times*, June
    3, 1934.
Clampett, Bob. "Hugh Harman" interview, *Cartoonist Profiles*, June 1983.
"Companies at a glance," *USA Today*, September 1, 2009.
"Company Overview," The Walt Disney Company, http://corporate.disney.go.com/
    corporate/overview.html.
"Dave Allen Loses His Mate," *Examiner*, October 20, 1936,
"Dave Allen Of Casting Bureau Is Accused," clipping from unidentified newspaper dated
    May 17, 1934, from the National Film Information Service, Margaret Herrick Library,
    Fairbanks Center for Motion Picture Study, Academy of Motion Picture Arts and
    Sciences.
"Dave Allen Once Hired 5000 Extras," Fred W. Fox, *Los Angeles Mirror*, March 20, 1954.
"Dave Allen's Costly Victory," *Variety*, December 4, 1935.
"Death Takes One In Crash," *Los Angeles Times*, January 30, 1933.
De Roos, Robert. "The Magic Worlds of Walt Disney," *National Geographic*, August 1963.
"Dexter Will Star in '12 to the Moon," *Los Angeles Times*, April 14, 1959.
Disney, Mrs. Walt, as told to Isabella Taves. "I Live with a Genius," *McCall's*, February 1953.
Disney, Roy. "Unforgettable Walt Disney," *Reader's Digest*, February 1969.
Disney, Walt. "Growing Pains," *Journal of the Society of Motion Picture Engineers*, January–
    June 1941.

"Disney Gets Clean Bill From Doctors," *Daily Variety*, November 23, 1966.

"Disney in Hospital for Checkup After Surgery," *Los Angeles Times*, December 7, 1966.

"Disney Undergoes Surgery on Lung," *Los Angeles Times*, November 23, 1966.

"Disneyland designer dies at 83," the *Burbank Leader*, October 17, 2001, electronic version.

Eddy, Don. "The Amazing Secret of Walt Disney," *American Magazine*, August 1955.

"Extends Winkler Contract for All Three Years," the *Film Daily*, February 16, 1928.

Farley, Ellen. "Disney Heirs' Stock May Be King," *Los Angeles Times*, April 1, 1984.

"Father Goose," *Time*, December 27, 1954, electronic version.

"Film Kiddies to Be Hosts," *Los Angeles Times*, November 30, 1927.

"Five Counties Freed Of Ban," *Los Angeles Times*, May 3, 1994.

"Flame Alight!" the *Kansas City Star*, November 1, 1921, 1.

"Fliers In The Air Today," the *Kansas City Star*, October 30, 1921, 8A.

"Frederick Clinton Quimby Funeral Announcement," *Los Angeles Times*, September 19, 1965.

Friedwald, Will, with Jerry Beck and Mark Kausler. "Hugh Harman (1902–1982)," *Graffiti*, Spring 1984.

"Gas Fumes Kill Disney's Mother," *Los Angeles Times*, November 27, 1938.

"Gen. Jacques, First Guest," the *Kansas City Star*, October 29, 1921, 1.

"George Morrell" obituary, *Los Angeles Times*, May 1, 1955.

Gray, Milton. "The Death of Walt Disney," *APAtoons*, May–June 2001.

"Growing Up Disney," *People*, December 21, 1998.

"Hail The Guests!" the *Kansas City Star*, October 30, 1921, 1.

Hall, Mordaunt. "The Blonde's Victory: Lorelei Lee Comes to the Screen," the *New York Times*, January 22, 1928.

———. "The Screen: Lorelei Lee and Dorothy," the *New York Times*, January 16, 1928.

Harman, Fred. "New Tracks in Old Trails," *True West*, October 1968.

"Harman, 79, Dies in California; Pioneer Animator With Rudy Ising," *Variety*, December 1, 1982.

Harris, Michael. "Original Disney cartoon gang remembers Laugh-O-Grams," the *Burbank Daily Review*, May 25, 1972.

Hartt, Reg. "Interview with Fritz Freleng," *Griffithiana*, December 1988.

Hollister, Paul. "Walt Disney," the *Atlantic Monthly*, December 1940.

"Honor Guests At Station," the *Kansas City Star*, October 28, 1921, 1.

"Hugh Harman (1903—1983)," *Graffiti*, Spring 1984.

Jamison, Jack. "He Gave Us Mickey Mouse," *Liberty*, January 14, 1933.

"John Alicoate Dead," the *New York Times*, June 22, 1960.

"John V. Cowles" obituary, the *Kansas City Times*, June 12, 1943, 54.

"Johnny Cannon" funeral announcement, *Los Angeles Times*, December 10, 1946.

"Juvenile Actor in Crash Sues," *Los Angeles Times*, February 3, 1933.

"Kansas City's Own 'Daddy' of Ad Films Is Honored by His Hollywood 'Alumni,' *Boxoffice*, February 3, 1945.

Kaufman, J. B. "Wonderland Revisited," *Griffithiana*, No. 65, 1999.

Kingsley, Grace. "Rehearsals of Gay Musical Show, 'No, No, Nanette,' Reflect Brilliant Array of Talent," *Los Angeles Times*, March 8, 1925.

"Laugh-O-Gram Cartoons Announced," *Motion Picture News*, June 17, 1922, 3257.

Lawrance, Lowell. "Mickey Mouse—Inspiration from Mouse in K.C. studio," *Kansas City Journal-Post*, September 8, 1935.

"Les Clark, Animator of Mickey Mouse, Snow White," *Los Angeles Times*, September 17, 1979.

Loew's theater ads, the *New York Times*, February 25 and 26, 1928.

"Lorey Tague" obituary, *Manhattan Mercury*, December 17, 1984, A2.

"M. Mouse a Local Boy," the *Kansas City Star*, February 13, 1942.

Mann, Arthur. "Mickey Mouse's Financial Career," *Harper's Magazine*, May 1934.

"Manufacturers Buy Old Disney Studios," *Los Angeles Times*, May 11, 1941.

"Marjorie Kurfiss" obituary, *Sioux City Journal*, November 1994.

"Marjorie T. Gossett" obituary, *Las Vegas Review Journal*, January 8, 2003.

"Marvin A. Davis, Master Planner for Disneyland," *Los Angeles Times*, March 13, 1998.

"Mary R. Tebb" obituary, the *Review* (Bainbridge, Washington), March 24, 1993.

"Mickey Mouse's Father," *McCall's*, August 1932.

"Morals Retrial of Dave Allen to Await High Court Decision," the *Citizen*, October 3, 1935.

"Mr. & Mrs. Disney," *Ladies' Home Journal*, March 1941.

"Music Play Has Opening Tomorrow," *Los Angeles Times*, March 8, 1925.

Nachman, Gerald. "Walt Disney: A Portrait of the Artist," *New York Post*, October 10, 1965.

"Nadine Missakian" obituary, the *Kansas City Times*, December 14, 1988, E6.

*Newman Theatres Magazine*, Volume One, Number Sixteen, 1920.

"'No, No, Nanette' to Leave Mason Saturday, July 4," *Los Angeles Times*, June 4, 1929.

"Norman Blackburn; Producer and Advertising Executive," *Los Angeles Times*, February 7, 1990.

Oliver, Myrna, and Diane Haithman. "Lillian Disney Dies at 98," *Los Angeles Times*, December 18, 1997.

"Oswald" ad, *Universal Weekly*, May 28, 1927.

"P. D. Cochrane, 81, Film Pioneer, Dies," the *New York Times*, August 10, 1958.

"Parade To Thousands," the *Kansas City Star*, November 1, 1921, 1.

Pepper, Jeff. "Socializing with the Social Lion," www.2719hyperion.com/2009/03/socializing-with-the-social-lion.html, March 3, 2009.

Pesmen, Louis A., untitled article, 1971.

"Philip Tannura" funeral announcement, *Los Angeles Times*, December 8, 1973.

"Plan Distribution of Laugh-O-Gram," *Motion Picture News*, August 26, 1922, 1055.

"Prize-Fight Film Inquiry," the *New York Times*, September 9, 1927.

Province, John. Interview of Virginia Davis McGhee, 1992, *Hogan's Alley*, www.cagle.com/hogan/interviews/davis/home.asp.

"R. H. Cochrane, Led Universal Pictures," the *New York Times*, June 2, 1973.

Rathburn, Morris. "Statistical Facts About Los Angeles," *Los Angeles City Directory*, The Los Angeles Directory Company, Los Angeles, 1923.

"Recording The Baby's Life In Films," the *Kansas City Star*, October 29, 1922, 3D.

Redelings, Lowell E. "The Hollywood Scene," *Hollywood Citizen News*, February 18, 1957.

"Rites Set for Film Cartoonist Fred Quimby," *Los Angeles Times*, September 20, 1965.

"Rollin Hamilton" obituary, *Los Angeles Times*, June 7, 1951.

Santora, Phil. "A Kid From Chicago, With Ham & Plenty of Mustard," *Daily News*, September 30, 1964.

"Scouts Rumor Of Deal For Universal Films," the *New York Times*, August 4, 1927.

Seldes, Gilbert. "Mickey Mouse Maker," the *New Yorker*, December 19, 1931.

"Services for Walt Disney Held as He Asked—for Family Only," *Los Angeles Times*, December 17, 1966.

Sewell, C. S., editor. "Timely Reviews of Short Subjects," *Moving Picture World*, August 13, 1927.

——, editor. "Timely Reviews of Short Subjects," *Moving Picture World*, September 10, 1927.

"Shake-Up In Police Jobs," the *Kansas City Star*, February 6, 1921, 1.

"Showman of the World Speaks," *Motion Picture Exhibitor*, October 19, 1966, 1.

Silas, Faye A. "Even at 50 Years of Age, A Mouse Named Mickey Hasn't Lost His Appeal," the *Kansas City Times*, November 11, 1978.

Skolsky, Sidney. "Mickey Mouse Meet Your Maker," *Hearst International-Cosmopolitan*, February 1934.

Smith, Chester J. "Opinion of Current Productions," *Moving Picture News*, August 19, 1927.

Smith, David R., "Walt Disney Productions: Chronological List of Personnel—October 1923–April, 1930," April 28, 1978. (Unpublished).

——. "Ub Iwerks, 1901–1971," *Funnyworld*, Spring 1972.

——. "Up to Date in Kansas City," *Funnyworld*, Fall 1978.

——. "Disney Before Burbank: The Kingswell and Hyperion Studios," *Funnyworld*, Summer 1979.

"Star Witness to Testify In Dave Allen Trial," *Los Angeles Evening Herald Express*, July 12, 1934.

"Starred in Cartoons," *Los Angeles Times*, February 3, 1924.

Stewart, Larry. "Ebersol Hops to It to Land Michaels," *Los Angeles Times*, February 10, 2006.

Stollings, Virginia. "Photographer's Table a Gift to College," undated newspaper article, The Baron Missakian Collection, Department of Special Collections, Miller Nichols Library, University of Missouri—Kansas City, circa 1976.

Storck, Dorothy. "Art Work of Walt Disney in School Here," *Chicago's American*, April 27, 1967.

Syring, Richard H. "One of the Great Geniuses!" *Silver Screen*, November 1932.

Thomas, Bob. "Disney's Brother Has Plans for Future," *Arkansas Democrat*, January 9, 1967.

"The Throng Fades Away," the *Kansas City Star*, November 3, 1921, 1.

"Three Bodies Recovered," the *Redondo Reflex*, June 22, 1923.

"Three Men Swept Out Into Ocean," the *Redondo Reflex*, June 8, 1923.

"'Times' Fund For Relief Of Flood Victims," *Los Angeles Times*, May 10, 1927, 3.

"Trial of Ex-Casting Bureau Head Dropped," *Daily News*, December 3, 1935.

Trimborn, Harry. "Death Comes in Hospital Near Burbank Studio," *Los Angeles Times*, December 16, 1966.

"'U' to Release 'Oswald,'" *Moving Picture World*, March 12, 1927.

"'U' Will Release Animated Cartoon Comedies," *Motion Picture News*, March 25, 1927.

"Voting Will Not Suffer By Quarantine," *Los Angeles Times*, May 3, 1924.

Wallace, Peter. "Mickey Mouse And How He Grew," *Collier's*, April 9, 1949.

The Walt Disney Company Annual Report 2008.

"Walt Disney: Images of Innocence," *Time*, December 23, 1966.

"Walt Disney, 65, Dies on Coast; Founded an Empire on a Mouse," the *New York Times*, December 16, 1966.

"Walt Disney Star Virginia Davis dies," Associated Press, the *Hollywood Reporter*, August 17, 2009.

"Warners Plan Film About Seeing Eye Dog—One New," the *New York Times*, January 2, 1937.

"The Wide World of Walt Disney," *Newsweek*, December 31, 1962.

"William Rubin" obituary, the *Kansas City Times*, February 24, 1944, 14.

Winter, Alice Ames. "Animated Cartoon Pictures Speak Universal Languages; Secrets of How These Fantastic Comedies of the Screen Are Produced," the *Motion Picture Monthly*, January 1931.

Wolfe, Roy. "An Oregonian in Disneyland," the *Sunday Oregonian Magazine*, July 8, 1951.

Woolf, S. J. "Walt Disney Tells Us What Makes Him Happy," the *New York Times*, July 10, 1938.

Young, Rosalind K. "She Liked Disney as Her Boss," the *Kansas City Times*, December 20, 1966.

# Books

Acker, Ally. *Reel Women: Pioneers of the Cinema, 1896 to the Present*, New York: Continuum, 1991.

Barbera, Joseph. *My Life in 'toons: From Flatbush to Bedrock in Under a Century*. Turner Publishing, Inc., 1994.

Barrier, Michael. *Hollywood Cartoons: American Animation in Its Golden Age*, New York: Oxford University Press, 1999.

———. *The Animated Man: A Life of Walt Disney*. Berkeley: University of California Press, Berkeley, 2007.

Burnes, Brian, Robert W. Butler, and Dan Viets. *Walt Disney's Missouri*. Kansas City: Kansas City Star Books, 2002.

Canemaker, John. *Felix: The Twisted Tale of the World's Most Famous Cat*. New York: Pantheon Books, 1991.

———. *Walt Disney's Nine Old Men & the Art of Animation*. New York: Disney Editions, 2001.

Crafton, Donald. *Before Mickey: The Animated Film, 1898–1928*. Chicago: The University of Chicago Press, 1993.

Culhane, Shamus. *Talking Animals and Other People*. New York: St. Martin's Press, 1986.

Finch, Christopher. *The Art of Walt Disney: from Mickey Mouse to the Magic Kingdom*. New York: Harry N. Abrams, Inc., 1995 edition.

Gabler, Neal. *Walt Disney: The Triumph of the American Imagination*. New York: Alfred A. Knopf, 2006.

Ghez, Didier, ed. *Walt's People: Talking Disney with the Artists who Knew Him, Volumes 1* (2005), 2 and 3 (2006), 4 and 5 (2007), 6 and 7 (2008), and 8 (2009). Xlibris Corporation.

Gifford, Denis. *American Animated Films: The Silent Era, 1897–1929*. Jefferson: McFarland & Company, Inc., 1990.

Green, Amy Boothe and Howard E. Green. *Remembering Walt: Favorite Memories of Walt Disney*. New York: Disney Editions, 1999.

Greene, Katherine and Richard. *The Man Behind the Magic: The Story of Walt Disney*. New York: Viking, 1998 edition.

———. *Inside the Dream: The Personal Story of Walt Disney*. New York: Disney Editions, 2001.

Hanna, Bill with Tom Ito. *A Cast of Friends*. Da Capo Press, 1996.

Hastings, Peter, ed.-in-chief, *Who Was Who In American Art, 1564–1975: 400 Years of Artists in America, Vol. II: G-O*. Madison, Connecticut: Sound View Press, 1999.

Hollis, Richard, and Brian Sibley. *The Disney Studio Story*. New York: Crown, 1988.

Iwerks, Leslie, and John Kenworthy. *The Hand Behind The Mouse*. New York: Disney Editions, 2001.

Jackson, Kathy Merlock. *Walt Disney: A Bio-Bibliography*. Westport: Greenwood Press, 1993.

Jackson, Kathy Merlock, ed. *Walt Disney Conversations*. Jackson: University Press of Mississippi, 2006.

Kinney, Jack. *Walt Disney and Assorted Other Characters: An Unauthorized Account of the Early Years at Disney's*. New York: Harmony Books, 1988.

Maas, Frederica Sagor. *The Shocking Miss Pilgrim: A Writer in Early Hollywood*. Lexington: The University Press of Kentucky, 1999.

Maltin, Leonard. *Of Mice and Magic*. New York: McGraw-Hill Book Co., 1980.

Merritt, Russell and J. B. Kaufman. *Walt in Wonderland: The Silent Films of Walt Disney*. Pordenone: Le Giornate del Cinema Muto. Baltimore: distributed by The Johns Hopkins University Press, 1993 edition.

Miller, Diane Disney, as told to Pete Martin. *The Story of Walt Disney*. New York: Henry Holt and Company, 1956.

*Muybridge's Complete Human and Animal Locomotion: All 781 Plates from the 1887 "Animal Locomotion" by Eadweard Muybridge, Volumes I—III*. New York: Dover Publications, Inc., 1979.

Peri, Don. *Working with Walt: Interviews with Disney Artists*. Jackson: University of Mississippi Press, 2008.

Smith, Dave, ed. *Walt Disney: Famous Quotes*. Lake Buena Vista: Walt Disney Theme Parks and Resorts, 1994.

Smith, Dave. *Disney A to Z: The Official Encyclopedia*. New York: Disney Editions, 2006 edition.

Smith, Dave and Steven Clark. *Disney: The First 100 Years*. New York: Disney Editions, 1999.

Tague, Lowry. *Divine Frequency*. New York, Exposition Press, 1962.

Thomas, Bob. *Disney's Art of Animation: From Mickey Mouse to Beauty and the Beast*. New York: Hyperion, 1991.

———. *Walt Disney: An American Original*. New York: Disney Editions, 1994 edition.

———. *Building A Company: Roy O. Disney And The Creation Of An Entertainment Empire*. New York: Hyperion, 1998.

Thomas, Frank, & Ollie Johnston. *Disney Animation: The Illusion of Life*. New York: Abbeville Press, 1981.

Tieman, Robert. *The Disney Treasures*. New York: Disney Editions, 2003.

Tytle, Harry. *One of "Walt's Boys."* Airtight Seals Allied Productions, Royal Oak, 1997.

*Variety Obituaries, Volumes 2–7, and 9*. New York, Garland Publishing, Inc., 1988.

*Variety Obituaries, Volume 14*. New York, Garland Publishing, Inc., 1994.

Watts, Steven. *The Magic Kingdom Walt Disney and the American Way of Life*. New York: Houghton Mifflin Company, 1997.

# Collections

*The Baron Missakian Collection*, Department of Special Collections, Miller Nichols Library, University of Missouri—Kansas City.

Barrier, Michael. *Interview with Rudolf Ising*, June 2, 1971.

———. *Interview with Rudolf Ising*, November 30, 1973.

———. *Interview with Hugh Harman*, December 3, 1973.

———. *Interview with Hugh Harman and Rudolf Ising*, October 29 and 31, 1976.

———. *Notes from the [Disney] Archives' folders of Disney correspondence with the Winklers and Charles Mintz*, June 1994. (Private collection).

———. *Notes from the [Disney Archives'] earning account book labeled on its cover General Expense Account 1925–1926–1927 By Roy O. Disney*, February 1997. (Private Collection).

———. *Notes from the [Disney] Archives' file of Walt Disney's 1928 correspondence from New York*, June 1994 and February 1997. (Private Collection).

———. *Additional notes from the [Disney] Archives' file of Walt Disney's 1928 correspondence from New York*, February 1997. (Private Collection).

Ghez, Didier. *Interview with Ruthie Tompson*, December 21, 2007.

———. *Interview of Ub Iwerks by Bob Thomas*, circa 1956.

Korkis, Jim and Didier Ghez. *Interview with Mickey "Royal" Clark*, August, 2008.

*Missouri Valley Special Collections: Biography*, The Kansas City Public Library.

## Correspondence/Interviews

Barrier, Michael, March 19, 2008; April 7, 2009; June 26, 2009; July 1, 2009; June 27 and 30, 2010.

Cauger, Ted, January 5, 2007; June 20, 2008.

Disney, Robert S., III, June 5, 2009; July 1, 2009.

Hardwick, Jim, May 27, 2009.

Harman, Fred, III, December 8 and 14, 2006.

Heinbaugh, Marie Cowles, May 29 and 30, 2008.

Jaben, Sonny, April 9, 2008.

Kaufman, J. B., March 5, 2009.

McGhee, Virginia Davis, March 7, 2009.

Miller, Diane Disney, May 16, 17, and 30, 2009; January 19, 2010.

Pesmen, Sandra, December 5 and 12, 2006; April 14, 2008; May 16, 2008.

Smith, David R., February 25, 2008; April 2, 2008; August 25, 2008; October 14, 2008; March 5 and 25, 2009; May 18 and 27, 2009; June 5 and 30, 2009; July 7 and 20, 2009; August 18 and 19, 2009; July 23, 2010.

Tompson, Ruthie, November 29, 2009; December 9, 2009.

## Databases

*California Birth Index, 1905–1995*, Ancestry.com.

*California Death Index, 1940–1997*, Ancestry.com.

*Florida Death Index, 1877–1998*, Ancestry.com.

*Index to Register of Voters, Los Angeles County, California, 1930*, Ancestry.com.

*Kansas State Census Collection, 1855–1925*, Ancestry.com.

*Minnesota Birth Index, 1935–2002*, Ancestry.com.

*Minnesota Death Index, 1908–2002*, Ancestry.com.

*Missouri Death Certificates, 1910–1957*, www.sos.mo.gov.

*Missouri Marriage Records, 1805–2002*, Ancestry.com.
*New York Passenger Lists, 1820–1957*, Ancestry.com.
*Social Security Death Index*, Ancestry.com.
*United States Federal Census, 1900*, Ancestry.com.
*United States Federal Census, 1910*, Ancestry.com.
*United States Federal Census, 1920*, Ancestry.com.
*United States Federal Census, 1930*, Ancestry.com.
*World War I Draft Registration Cards, 1917–1918*, Ancestry.com.
*World War II Army Enlistment Records, 1938–1946*, Ancestry.com.

# Directories

*Kansas City, Missouri City Directory*. Kansas City: Gate City Directory Company, 1919–1924.
*The Kansas City Telephone Book*, Kansas City, 1921.
*Los Angeles City Directory*. Los Angeles: The Los Angeles Directory Company, 1915; 1924–1929; 1936; 1938–1939; 1942.
*Los Angeles Street Address Directory*. Los Angeles: The Pacific Telephone And Telegraph Company, May 8, 1956; March 29, 1960.
*Manhattan and The Bronx Telephone Directory*. New York: New York Telephone Company, Winter, 1928–29.
*New York City City Directory*. New York: R. L. Polk & Company, Inc., 1925.
*1926 Los Angeles White Pages*. Los Angeles: Southern California Telephone Company, September 1926.

# Index